Joseph Stadtmiller

Copyright © 2019 by Joseph Stadtmiller

Copy Editor: Patricia J. Carlsen

Cover Design - Front Cover Image: [Kotoffeil] / [Eco-Friendly, green energy concept-Illustration City, Pollution, Planet Earth, Planet Space, Apartment- iStock]/Getty Images

ISBN-978-1-7340731-0-2 - Paperback book

Printed by Kindle Direct Publishing

Kirkus Reviews – Stadtmiller *(Those We Touch Along the Way*, 2017, etc.) considers consumption from a historical perspective, tracing the usage of Earth's resources from early humans through today. The first half of this illuminating work presents an abbreviated version of the salient points of human history, including the development of tools and weapons, the creation of clothing, the domestication of plants and animals, the exploration of the world, the use of various resources to generate power, the advent of the Industrial Revolution, and the rise of consumerism. The author summarizes key global occurrences of the millennia in largely readable prose, although some sections are dense and a bit too heavy on historical details.

The second half of the meticulously researched book concentrates more directly on consumption, broadly defined by the author to encompass the use of all of the planet's resources, including fossil fuels, water, and food. Stadtmiller writes: "Consumption levels of the world's wealthiest countries…are draining the remaining stockpiles of critical nonrenewable natural resources at untenable rates; the disparities of this consumption are glaring. Twenty percent of the population from the highest income countries consumes 86% of all private consumption."

Several chapters highlight some of humanity's most egregious environmental abuses. "The Promise of Polymers," for example, clearly discusses the relatively recent invention of plastics with particular attention to their toxicity. Stadtmiller knowledgeably writes about the shortcomings of the plastics recycling system and the bodily hazards of BPA. Another engaging chapter addresses the pros and cons of genetically modified organisms, particularly with respect to food production. One of the more eye-opening chapters delves into "Mount Waste-More," the author's clever name for the world's trash crisis: "Globally, garbage waste is accumulating at 2.12 billion tons per year, 555 pounds of garbage each year per each global citizen."

On the positive side, he wisely observes that some American communities are adopting a "completely new concept of a world without garbage" called "Zero-Waste." Also pertinent are the five profiles (Brazil, India, China, Russia, the United States) provided as examples of energy and environmental usage by individual countries. Stadtmiller's lucid discussion of a "Nature-Conscious Consumer" reflects a sensible depiction of human accountability. With a rather remarkable eye for detail, he takes a broad view of human consumption, neatly dividing the topic into understandable segments while relating them to the whole.

An impressive, impassioned call for fundamental change in the way humans interact with their world.

To Hannah Marie

Other books by Joseph Stadtmiller:

Electronics Project Management & Design - 2000: an applied handbook for the design and management of electronic product development and design projects.

Applied Electronic Design - 2002: an applied design handbook for key electronic functional electrical and electronic building blocks.

The Nature of Life & Humanity - 2016 : The story of humanity and nature; how culture, religion and technology have shaped modern society and precipitated most all of the difficult issues we face today. *Why we must ... how we can change the way we live*, Third Edition 2019. How Relevance, Respect and Simplicity can restore our sense of humanity and our future.

Those We Touch Along the Way - 2017: a historical novel, *an American story about love, baseball and the Korean War , an average man's pursuit of glory, the true meaning of magnificence.*

"Man is a Tool-using animal. Weak in himself, and of small stature, he stands on a basis, at most for the fattest soled, of some half-square foot, insecurely enough; has to straddle out his legs, lest the very wind supplant him. Feeblest of bipeds! Three quintals are a crushing load for him; the steer of the meadow tosses him aloft, like a waste rag. Nevertheless, he can use Tools, can devise Tools: with these the granite mountain melts into light dust before him; seas are his smooth highway, winds and fire his un-wearying steeds. Nowhere do you find him without Tools; without Tools he is nothing, with Tools he is all."

Carlyle, Thomas: *Sartor Resorts*, Chapter V.

Chapters

-Introduction-

Embracing Sufficiency is about the history of human consumption: what, why and how we consume; the acute issues caused by our over-indulgence and how to resolve them. Humanity has evolved from hunter-gatherers consuming wild resources, sharing food without creating a surplus to the complex web of humanity depleting Earth's resource stockpile that took billions of years to create. It's a story about life on Earth embracing the essence of nature to lead us to a better place.

The incredible variety of consumer items we purchase has increased as much as consumption itself: food, clothing, transportation, tools, weapons, fuel and building materials, manufactured and distributed across the globe and delivered to our doorsteps daily. The overabundance of consumables; the waste from their manufacture, transport and use are proving to be more than Earth's life-friendly environment can handle. The impact of such high consumption has caused sociologists, psychologists and ecologists to explore the drivers of human consumption, their influence on everyday life. Determining how and why we consume along with ways to minimize it are critical steps towards achieving a more viable long-term lifestyle.

The surging human population is the main driver of increasing human consumption, combined with the energy driven technology that's replaced the human-time and energy needed to perform many tasks. While we welcome how technology saves us time and effort—it comes with a heavy price: vast amounts of fuels and synthetic materials are consumed in the process, generating considerable amounts of toxic and unnatural wastes.

Food is a primary contributor to excess human consumption and waste. A majority of Americans maintain unhealthy eating habits; many are overweight, consuming unbalanced diets with heavy intake of meats, dairy and processed foods in lavish portions. Studies have shown that individuals—via their personal diet—can use sustainable food practices that are healthier for us and significantly decrease resource consumption, the generation of pollutants as well as heat trapping CO_2 and methane gases.

Utility consumption: issues regarding air and water pollution; energy, water, biodiversity and topsoil resources are discussed along with the status of global resource reserves. Plastics and GMOs are critically important to understanding the size and scope of the consumption and waste footprint: pesticides in our food; toxic plastic materials spoiling our air and freshwater supplies and reducing biodiversity.

Consumerism has impacted modern lifestyles: instant gratification and extravagant tastes; too many choices; single-use throwaway products; congested non-stop lifestyles pushing full speed ahead; addictive technologies and entertainment options that consume us; the lack of desire to wonder and learn about nature and the reason why for all things.

The book fosters an appreciation for the history of human creativity: the development of knowledge and tools; the influence of technology on humanity and the natural world; the comprehension of why current consumption levels can't continue — what each of us can do to decrease consumption and waste: at home, at work and around the world.

Benefits for the reader include a better understanding of the history of human production and consumption; the mistakes we've made along the way; how to correct them for the future — individually and collectively as one unified society of humankind.

Over the centuries the finest human minds have pondered how life on Earth began. Perhaps the most relevant question is: what is the purpose of life? I believe all lifeforms perform a unique function in Earth's biosphere; that the continuum of life throughout the cosmos fulfills critical functions in the life-cycle of the universe. Consumption and life are symbiotic — like the relationship between energy and matter. If the creation of life on Earth signified the beginning of consumption here…what happens when the species at the top of the food chain rescinds its support of life's sole purpose — the continuation of life on Earth?

1

The Essence of Life

Another day on infant planet Earth; sunlight splashes over the horizon, the air is still, the oceans unusually calm. A very special dawn has arrived...

Before there was life there was water. When astrophysicists probe the cosmos searching for signs of life—water is the ingredient they venture for most. Where there's water there's potential for life, without it—hard to imagine. Earth's water is believed to have been contained within the glowing mass of magma that became primordial Earth billions of years ago, a theory that's still being debated. Over time Earth's atmosphere began to cool, releasing liquid water from the magma and collecting in pools on Earth's surface. Ever since, water has been on the move, changing states in a continuing cycle: liquid to vapor, then ice and so on. Volcanic activity continues to release water from Earth's core into the atmosphere, increasing the quantity of surface and groundwater available on the planet.

Most of Earth's water is in the oceans. The sun heats ocean salt water and transforms it into water vapor, leaving the salt behind. As the vapor rises it cools and condenses. Air currents push the clouds upward and merge them together into storms, releasing precipitation falling from the sky back to Earth as rain, ice or snow. Most precipitation falls directly back into the oceans and remixes with the saltwater. In the coldest climates snow accumulates in the ice caps and glaciers that can remain frozen for thousands of years. Over land in warmer climates, ice and snow melt in the spring and flow back into the streams and rivers, eventually flowing back to the oceans. Runoff and groundwater seepage accumulate in freshwater lakes; the remaining runoff soaks into the ground where it's absorbed by plants; emerges as new freshwater springs; or replenishes existing underground aquifers. With no end in sight, water remains on the move never quite completing the Sisyphean task of supporting all life on Earth.[1]

Since the period known as the Enlightenment humans have explored the mystery of how life began here. Initially, it was believed that lifeforms arrived on Earth via debris from another planet. More recently, the discovery of fossils in Greenland made of stromatolites dated 3.7 billion years old tell a different story.[2] Stromatolites are constructed of layered mounds, columns and sheet-like sedimentary rocks originally formed by incremental layers of cyanobacteria—a single-celled photosynthesizing microbe. Today stromatolites can be found in a wide range of environments: along the continental shelf, in lakes, rivers and the soil. Cyanobacteria are considered the simplest form of modern carbon-based life because they lack a DNA-packaging nucleus. Bacteria and cyanobacteria are believed to have been the only life-forms on Earth for the first 2 billion years that life has existed here.[3]

Cyanobacteria evolved by consuming sunlight, water and CO_2 for energy, storing the carbon within its microbe, and releasing the oxygen into the atmosphere. The light captured by photosynthetic chlorophyll in all plants is converted into chemical energy and used to split two water molecules into high-energy electrons, releasing carbon from the CO_2 that is stored in the plant and giving off one molecule of oxygen, O_2.[4] The accrual of oxygen in the atmosphere filters the sun's rays and cools the planet. When the iron in the oceans cooled and solidified the seawaters turned blue. Some two billion years later, Earth's atmosphere attained the oxygen levels still maintained here today.

Algae and sophisticated plant life evolved; sea creatures and land animals consumed the plant life. Insects, reptiles, birds and mammals followed in succession, each creating a more intricate system of checks and balances, spinning an increasingly complex web of life, dependent on one another for their survival. Eventually a breed of mammals called primates evolved: apes, monkeys and lemurs characterized by enlargement of the cerebral hemispheres, advanced binocular vision and specialization of the arms or legs for grasping. Most primates evolved and survived in the tropical or subtropical regions of the Americas, Africa and Asia.

Certain species of primates evolved into hominids. Millions of years of changing climates converted the rain forests into grassy woodlands, forcing the early hominids out of their tree dwellings. The reduced nourishment available for tree dwelling apes drove them to scavenging for food on the ground. With arms more adept at climbing, four-legged travel between the barren woodlands became treacherous. Sometime between 6 and 2 million years ago, hominids began walking upright.[5]

Many years and evolutionary stages later the hominids became homo-sapiens. The evolving human foot was a key formative aspect of bipedalism: robust, adaptable and efficient; serving as lever-arm and landing pad during locomotion; increasing the efficiency and speed of bipedal motion. The broadening bipedal capabilities improved hominid travel efficiency. With each stage of their development, homo-sapiens became more adaptable and efficient at competing for and acquiring food resources; their brains increased in size and they began making simple stone tools.

Humans spread out across the planet, encountering new and differing climates, terrain, plants and wildlife. Their survival depended upon the ability to adapt to new landscapes by creating new lifestyles and tools. Humans are not unique in this regard. A wide range of animals—insects, fish, birds and mammals—use tools to acquire food, water, for grooming and to build shelters. Studies regarding common chimpanzees indicate they not only use sticks and grass to gather ants and other larvae, they also sharpen sticks to stab small mammals while hunting. Sea-otters use sharp stones to extricate food from rocks and to pry abalone from their shells. Crows, ravens and finch family birds are known to poke sticks into trees to snag larvae. Most amazingly, seagulls have been observed dropping shellfish onto roadways in front of cars to crack them open.

The first tools created by early hominids were stones used to crush seeds. Later, stones were used to fashion other types of stones, sharpening them for use as cutting tools. Flint, jasper, chalcedony and agate were some of the stone types frequently used to make tools. Fracturing these stones allowed toolmakers to break off razor-sharp flakes. By utilizing a variety of techniques, early craftsmen were able to work differing stone types to perform a wide range of functions: the finer-grained the stone— the flatter and thinner the fragments that could be chiseled away. Their size and shape depended upon the methods used to remove them. Early toolmakers would have required years of practice to develop their skills, collecting extensive knowledge about the characteristics and varieties of the stone materials available.

The range of animal bone and stone tools developed by the early hominids include: hammer stones, arrows and spear heads, razors, knives, axes, adzes, awls and anvils. Forming wood with these early stone tools was demanding and inefficient. The wood types hunter-gatherers selected to build their shelters were chosen from pieces of wood similar to the size and shape needed. Driftwood obtained from along waterways was often used as structural members for dwellings.

The wood used to fabricate bows, arrows and spears had to be cut from a tree, split and then formed with stone scraping tools into the proper shape with the properties capable of functioning for use in hunting, self-defense or making war. The development of hunting tools allowed humans to increase the raw meat in their diet; they also created stone tools to mill grain.

The first evidence of hominids using fire dates back 125,000 years. Fire had a profound impact on humankind, providing light to extend daily activities, warmth in colder climates, protection from animals and the ability to cook food. Cooking allowed their diets to expand greatly. Food was easier to chew, digest and could be kept for longer time periods without spoiling.

Humans learned how to use fire in small steps gradually over time. It's theorized that initially they transported burning wildfire materials into unburned areas to clear the land to provide access to desired food items. Next, they developed base-camp fires started with wildfire material and maintaining them for long periods of time. The ability to start fires came later with the creation of a device called a fire-drill: a hardwood rod rotated against a softwood fire-board, creating embers to ignite tinder bundles that could be used to start a fire. The archeological evidence suggests that this occurred somewhere between 1.7 and .20 million years ago.[6]

Before the advent of fire hominids had subsisted mostly on fruits and seeds comprised of carbohydrates and sugar. Fibrous, starchy leaves, the stems and roots of some plants were indigestible to them. Plants known to contain toxins were avoided. Cooking plants, grains and meat made them more palatable; they remained edible for longer time periods. Their reduced consumption of raw meat protected them from ingesting harmful bacteria. Fire provided hominids with a process for consuming meat safely and efficiently; meat became the staple of their diet. Consuming more meat maximized their food energy intake, almost doubling their caloric input from proteins and starches, increasing hominid subsistence and procreation.

The evolutionary response to the abrupt change in the hominid diet caused the molar teeth to gradually shrink. Throughout the jaw, teeth became smaller and varied; the entire hominid digestive system decreased in size. Over time these changes lessened the need for large canine and herbivorous teeth; hominids had used them to chew through raw meat and crush coarse vegetables. With the need for large teeth diminished, the human skull continued evolving toward a smaller jaw, providing room for an even larger brain.

The discovery of how to start a fire allowed hominids to

survive in a variety of environments, prompting their expansion from warmer climates to more temperate ones. Fire was used at night to provide warmth and to ward off predatory animals; it broadened their ability to fabricate tools and weapons: fire-hardened spears and arrow heads. Archeological digs have provided numerous examples of hominids using fire to heat-treat rocks that were tempered into cutting blades and hunting tools. Various types of stones and ivory were heated and formed to create statues as works of art; clay was formed and heat-treated to produce the first pottery.

As humans spread across the continents, they experienced a broader range of environments. Their success was largely determined by their use of fire and basic tools. Fire was also a factor affecting the structure of developing societies; those who could make and control fire possessed greater authority. Fire light at night lengthened the time for day-light activities. The time spent around a fire provided more opportunity for social exchange; it's believed to have prompted the creation of spoken language. The utilization of fire improved human health while expanding the range of environments where humans could survive, promoting the expansion of the human species across the globe.

Over the period from 2 to .8 million years ago differing groups of hominids spread out across Earth, discovering new continents, encountering changing climates and terrain. Their bodies and brains continued increasing in size to meet the challenges posed by the new environments. The claws on their hands disappeared; their hands became more pliable. Fossil records suggest that hominids lost their body fur during warmer climatic periods, while gaining the ability to sweat. The enhanced ability to cool down their bodies increased their stamina, allowing groups of hominids to run down large furry mammals that would eventually collapse in the heat.

The period from 800 to 200 thousand years ago was a time of dramatic climate change. Early humans continued to evolve; their brains progressed further increasing in size and complexity, capable of handling and storing more information. The human brain has almost tripled in size over the course of human evolution, providing significant advantages regarding human social interactions and encounters with unfamiliar habitats. The modern human brain is the most complex of any living primate.[7]

The human practice of wearing clothing is unique among animals. Scientists speculate that crude forms of clothing were adapted to provide hominids protection and warmth as far back as 100,000 to 500,000 years ago, predating the first exodus from Africa. Recent studies have linked the origin of clothing lice as an indicator of when humans began wearing clothing around 170,000 years ago.[8] Items appearing to be sewing needles have been found dated 40,000 years ago. The earliest samples of sewing needles originate from the Solutrean culture in France from 19,000 to 15,000 BCE. The earliest dyed flax fibers were discovered in a prehistoric cave in Georgia—near the Caucasus Mountains—dating back older than 34,000 years.[9] Later evidence shows artworks and figurines of humans wearing clothing. Early humans fabricated clothing from animal furs and wool, the fiber extracted from plants (flax) and the silk fiber produced by insect larvae to form their cocoons.

Before using animal furs as carriers or clothing they had to be tanned: a process that permanently alters the protein structure of the animal skin, making it durable and less susceptible to decomposition. Ancient tanners cleaned and softened the skin by washing it in water; the inner layer of flesh and fat was removed by pounding and scouring it away. Hair was removed from the outer skin by soaking it in urine and scraping it off with a knife. The skin was softened by pounding animal dung into the hide, or soaked in a solution of animal brains. Curing was accomplished in colder climates by preserving the hides and skins at very low temperatures.

Neolithic (New Stone Age) people fashioned needles out of small animal bones to sew leather and fur garments created from the tanned hides of the animals they raised to make their clothing. The oldest evidence of larger scale fur tanning comes from India where leather was used to make bags, armor, quivers, sandals and water carriers sometime after 7,000 BCE. Much later the Sumerians used leather attached with copper studs on chariot wheels.

The use of human urine and animal dung to tan decaying animal flesh was at the very least, odoriferous. Consequently, ancient tanners were always located in the poor sections near the outskirts of ancient towns and cities. Children were paid to gather pigeon and dog dung for use by the tanners; so-called *piss-pots* were located on ancient street corners to collect human urine for use by local tanneries. The purpose of tanning was to purify, clean, soften and strengthen the final leather product and prevent its decay. It's interesting to imagine the humans who initially developed the process for tanning furs. How and why did they develop their method? With few materials at their disposal, what prompted them to use urine and animal dung in the process?

The very first human textile products were fabricated out of felt. There are two basic types of natural fibers: animal and plant fibers. Animal fibers are made of proteins that possess *scales* that affix to each other; plant fibers consist of cellulose material without scales. Felt is a textile product made either of matted or compressed fibers or furs pressed together and then heated with moisture under pressure without interlocking threads to hold it together. Felt can only be made from natural animal fibers: wool or certain synthetic fibers, since it requires the scale features to hold the fibers together.

The oldest known textiles were created from felt fabric. Since the fabric is not woven—it's held together by heat, moisture, pressure and the scale features of the fiber—fabric made of felt can be cut to vary in width, length, color or thickness depending on its intended application without regard to size. The edges may be cut without fear of the threads becoming loose and unraveling. Because it can be made very thick, the resulting matted and dense material is particularly useful as padding or a lining. Two types of felt processing were used by early humans: wet felting applies hot water to layers of animal hair continuously mixed and condensed, promoting the fibers to connect into a single piece of fabric; needle felting is a process of jabbing wool with a special needle with irregular ends, as the wool is pushed and compressed it becomes harder.

Basket weaving is one of the oldest and widely used processes in human history. Yet few samples of ancient baskets have been found since the materials they were made of readily decay. The oldest baskets discovered are between 10,000 and 12,000 years old. Ancient humans created baskets to meet their unique needs: those living along the coastlines used baskets to carry fish; those living inland made baskets to carry plant life and game. Thousands of basket types have been created around the world varying in material, weave, patterns and colors. Weave type is highly dependent on the size and weight of the material it's designed to carry: an open weave is used for large objects, a thinner weave for smaller items. Some baskets can be woven so tightly that they hold water.

The earliest baskets were fashioned out of locally available, naturally occurring materials such as vines. Vines possess strength, pliability and grow fairly straight. Pliable materials like the kudzu vine and more rigid woody vines such as bittersweet, grapevine and honeysuckle are all good basket weaving materials. Even though vines can be inconsistent in size and form they can be modified to make them useable for most contemporary basketry. Vines are split and dried before use; they can be soaked or boiled in water before weaving to increase their flexibility.

The establishment of trade routes between east and west created a need for baskets designed specifically to handle the variety of items traded along the way. Weaving designs and methods were shared throughout the world and across cultures, and adopted for their practicality, design and craftsmanship. There are two basic types of basket weave: coil weaving with winding fibers in adjacent circles that are stitched together; splint weaving that uses flat materials.[10]

Rope was another critical tool developed by ancient humans to help them accomplish various tasks: pulling, carrying, lifting or securing. The use of rope for construction, seafaring, hunting, fishing, exploring and climbing dates back to pre-historic times. The ancient Egyptians were first to document the tools they used for making rope. The first ropes were actually naturally occurring lengths of plant fiber in vines. Impressions of cordage found in Europe on fired clay provide evidence of string and rope-making technology dating back some 28,000 years. Fossilized fragments of two-ply rope were found in a cave at Lascaux, France dating back to 15,000 BCE. There is evidence that string and netting were used for a variety of applications dating back to 10,000 BCE.

Ancient Egyptians were probably the first civilization to develop special tools for rope making. Egyptian rope dates back to 4000 to 3500 BCE and was generally made from water reed fibers. Other ancient ropes were made from the fibers of date palms, flax, grass, papyrus, leather and animal hair. Thousands of Egyptian workers used rope to move the heavy stones needed to build their monuments. Beginning around 2800 BCE China began using rope made of hemp fiber. Rope and the craft of rope-making spread throughout Asia, India and Europe over the course of the next several thousand years.

―――――――――――――――――――

One of the most recent samples of ancient clothing comes from Otzi the Iceman, the common name given to the natural mummy of a man who lived around 3300 BCE and died in the Italian Alps on the Austrian border with an arrowhead stuck in the back of his shoulder. Otzi the Iceman's clothing was made out of differing leather types and colors for a variety of purposes. The soles of his shoes were made of bear skin; the upper shoe covering was fashioned from deer skin. His shirt was created using strips of light and dark leather sewn together. He wore separate leggings, a loin cloth and a cap made of woven grass. The cause of Otzi's death has been a matter of intense speculation since his mummified body was discovered in a Tyrolean glacier in 1991. The man—who was between 40 and 45 years old—was warmly dressed and was well equipped for travelling high in the Alps. One of the latest theories is that he was shot in the back with an arrow some 5300 years ago. New images show a flint arrowhead stuck grievously in Otzi's left shoulder in a location where it would likely have severed one of a number of critical blood vessels. He most likely died from the loss of blood.[11]

―――――――――――――――――――

While bipedalism improved the flexibility, efficiency of human transport, it also applied increased wear and tear on the human foot. Our feet are well adapted to handle varieties of terrain and climate, yet they remain vulnerable to hazards. A variety of footwear types have been designed to protect our feet against sharp rocks, hot and cold, wet or uneven ground surfaces.

Spanish cave drawings older than 15,000 years show humans with animal skins or furs wrapped around their feet. The oldest leather shoe sample was located in Armenia and dated around 5500 BCE, but it's believed that humans began wearing shoes long before that. It is made from a single piece of cowhide laced with a leather cord along seams at the front and back. The earliest shoes were likely leather foot-bags wrapped around the feet to protect them from the rugged and colder terrain. Early natives in North America wore tight fitting soft soled moccasins made of leather or bison hides.[12]

As civilizations developed, thong sandals were worn by many people around the world for foot protection. The practice dates back to images of ancient Egyptian murals from 4,000 BCE. Thong sandals were worn by many cultures and made from a wide variety of materials. Ancient Egyptian sandals were made out of papyrus and palm leaves. The African Masai people crafted them out of rawhide while Asian Indians made them out of wood. In China and Japan straw from the rice plant was used to make sandals. South Americans used leaves from the sisal plant to make twine used to fabricate sandals and Mexican natives utilized the Yucca plant.

Not everyone in ancient times favored footwear: Egyptians, Hindus and Greeks saw little need for it preferring to go barefoot most of the time. Ancient Greeks viewed footwear as self-indulgent, unappealing and unwarranted. The Romans—who later conquered Greece and adopted much of their culture—disagreed with their opinion of footwear and clothing. The Romans viewed shoes and clothing as a sign of power, and life in a civilized world.[13]

———————

Years after humans developed stone tools and the process for making fire, new ways were needed to pass that information on to each other and future generations. The emergence of language occurred during the Middle Stone Age.

Hunter-gatherers living close to the sea in mixed habitats of sub-Saharan Africa enjoyed diets that included: seafood, eggs, nuts, fruits and meat. They used sharp hunting tools to supply the meat in their diet. As a group increased in size, they specialized in the types of game hunted. Local bands were politically autonomous and economically self-sufficient, comprised of ten to fifty individuals. As local groups increased in size and the land became barren, they moved on. Researchers suggest that the overwhelming success of the early hunter-gatherers brought about the extinction of many large species of animals from the continents.

Mobile hunter-gatherers constructed housing using temporary building materials or the naturally occurring shelter of the land. Violence within communities was rare. They believed the land belonged to all—that no one could claim its ownership. Warfare between communities seldom occurred. Fatalities were few but when the violence went too far tribes could readily move on to other areas.

Hunter-gatherers had few material possessions; they endured without maintaining a surplus of resources throughout their society. With few techniques to preserve or store their food, they consumed food quickly. The mutual exchange of food between groups was important for their survival. Hunter-gatherers are well known for their failure to produce an economic surplus; sociologists generally agree it was because they lacked any need to do so. Their success and affluence are attributed to having been satisfied with little in a material sense. It's generally believed they ate well, worked fewer hours and enjoyed more freedom than members of today's consumer society.

Earth experienced significant climatic changes nearing the end of the last ice age. While much of the world became warmer, other areas turned cooler prompting variations in the growth and distribution of wild grains. Large game migrated to northern pastures as the glaciers retreated; they were hunted to near extinction by the growing human population.

At this point hunter-gatherer lifestyles began to change. The evidence shows hunter-gatherers reluctantly modified their way of life over the span of 4,000 years. From 7,000 to 3,000 BCE increasing numbers of humans changed their habits, replacing hunting and gathering in favor of cultivating plants and animals. These more *advanced* groups became known as *hunter-cultivators*.[14]

In the Middle East and Africa, the nomadic hunters-gatherers were some of the first to settle down and construct more permanent housing. They cultivated crops and domesticated animals, developed new tools to support their new way of life. These fledgling farmers were quick to appreciate the need for ways to haul water to their crops and livestock. Transporting large amounts of water required a vessel made of a flexible, moldable material, readily available, inexpensive and light enough to carry. Clay was abundant in the region and met all those requirements. The very first pots were built by stacking rings of clay on a flat base. The rings were smoothed out and placed in the bottom of a pit underneath a bonfire, and *pit-fired* to solidify the clay. These pots were plain and usually disposable, produced as a method for transporting water.

As human communities scattered around the planet their lifestyles increasingly gravitated toward cultivating food. The changeover was protracted and occurred differently in various parts of the world. The choice to cultivate food instead of hunting and harvesting it from nature's garden was difficult. In retrospect I believe it was humanity's first *free-will* decision to step away from the natural world into a new, magical world fabricated by humankind. As ways of old turned to means of the new, I doubt they were able to grasp its significance.

When people realized that plants gathered by hunter-gatherers could be transplanted and mated to create new varieties that possessed more desirable qualities, some decided to cultivate more and hunt less. Others would hold onto their hunter-gatherer lifestyles for thousands of years. While need is often cited as the mother of invention, it's also the basis for driving cultural change. In some parts of the world the changeover to cultivation happened more quickly. Whereas the evolution of hominids to hunter-gatherers took hundreds of thousands of years, agriculture was being practiced on all continents except Australia in a mere 8,000 years.

The hominids that evolved into humans who abound across the planet today brought with them a unique set of characteristics: larger brains that possessed intellectual self-awareness; communication via speech; the efficiency of bipedal motion; a pair of dexterous hands for making tools and the ability to sweat. Humans had used these abilities to create methods for making fire, rope, tools, weapons, pottery, basketry, clothing, carriers and shoes. Yet, they lacked sharp teeth and claws, any physical means capable of protecting them from predators or catching and killing game. They were without fur to protect them from the sun, the wet and the cold. Humankind was different from all other mammals on the planet—*the human physical body had evolved into a species dependent on more than the natural world*. To make up for these short-comings humans require more resources than just food, water, sunlight and oxygen to survive.

Homo sapiens are a species whose survival depends on their ability to adapt to environmental changes more quickly than evolution, using their unique skill-set to create new methods and varieties of tools to support them. Consequently, humankind requires the consumption of more energy, material and natural resources than any species on the planet.

Early humans scavenged locally available materials to create shelter and tools to help them survive. The skin of those humans living in colder climates evolved to have a lighter pigment, more capable of creating nutrients from the sparse sunlight, less able to withstand direct sun. They grew more hair and were typically shorter, minimizing their body surface to hold in the warmth. They wore furs, hides and built more viable shelters to keep warm.

People who had evolved in warmer climates were taller, more able to dissipate the heat with darker hair and skin to protect them from the sun. They lived in lighter structures fashioned from thin animal skins and grasses; they wore clothing made from twine and animal skins.

Humans formed into tribes and groups, adapting to the landscape, learning to take advantage of the weather, terrain, animals and plant-life. They developed tools, art, language, culture and societies reflecting the natural world around them. Those living close to primary food sources built durable shelters out of stone and wood. Mountain dwellers fashioned homes out of caves; those on the move built simple temporary shelters.

As the changeover to cultivation began, hunting societies moved to more remote areas of the landscape, maintaining contact with the villages emerging in the agricultural areas. Hunters provided food when crops failed and controlled the wild animals harassing the villages. When the land was cultivated it attained value. Communities converted the hunters to become soldiers to protect the land; they were also used to acquire more land from one's neighbors. As the hunters became soldiers; aggression ensued and expanded; waring peoples organized and planned wars; technology increased war's capacity to achieve complete annihilation.

The great warriors, conquerors and military aristocracies were all founded on the ideology of the classical hunter. In this new world culture, the practice of blood sacrifices by the cultivators was a way to replicate the killing of game by the hunter. The hunters turned soldiers voluntarily took up arms, always with the belief that they were protecting their homeland. But the wars fought over the millennia of human existence would always be about the acquisition of land and the domination of people.

Hunter-cultivator villages were the first steps toward the development of larger cities which eventually led to the Agrarian Revolution. During the period from 8,000 to 3,000 BCE, the human population doubled to nearly 14 million. This vast increase in population led to the development of urban centers and eventually the great city-states. In the Middle-East this occurred in Mesopotamia—the land between the Tigris and Euphrates rivers—sometime during the fourth millennia BCE. Although very dry today this region was once rich in nutrients. The people there learned to use the rivers for irrigation and to enrich the soil.

The period known as the dawn of civilization extends from 5000 to 3000 BCE. In Mesopotamia (modern day Iraq) an ancient wheel was discovered believed to have been constructed by the Sumerians at about 3500 BCE. The development of the wheel extended land travel while seafaring vessels allowed the exploration of the seas and coastlines. With extended modes of travel, the trade of goods and technology increased the speed of human learning and development. Other signs of intellectual development included: the spoken word, myth-making, an awakening to the forces of the universe.

In Egypt, the Badarin culture cleared the jungles and swamps to grow crops. They utilized irrigation, pictographic writing and produced pottery. The existence of ivory spoons, shells from the Red Sea and turquoise beads from the Sinai suggest that early Egyptians had visitors from afar.

In modern day Iraq and Syria evidence of the wheel, plow and using cattle as beasts of burden have been found as early as 3500 BCE in the ancient city of Sumer along the Euphrates River. The early Sumerians irrigated their crops along the river resulting in richer harvests and the growth of towns. Their crops included barley, wheat, millet, beans, turnips, lettuce, cucumbers, cress and mustard. Years later the heavy irrigation and over planting led to soil infertility. The Sumerians also used sailboats and produced wheel-turned pottery. They created the duodecimal system of measurement, defining inches and feet, minutes and hours and the number of degrees in a circle. The clay tablets they left behind recorded their history back to 3300 BCE.

In Western Europe ancient agricultural settlements found in England, France and Belgium show evidence that small boats were used for coastal travel. Flint mines discovered in Belgium and England, dating back to 4300 BCE mark the development of flint and stone tools. A group of people thought to have originated from the European mainland settled in southwestern England near the Salisbury plain and the town of Avesbury. They built a number of living structures, the largest of which was atop what is now called

Windmill Hill. Dubbed as *the Windmill Hill People,* they were a farming community who maintained cattle, goats, sheep, pigs and dogs, cultivating wheat and gathering seafood to complete their diet.

———————

Flax and wool were commonly used to produce woven clothing several thousand years ago. As hunter-gatherers settled into life as hunter-cultivators they discovered the advantage of fabricating clothes from woven fibers over animal hides. The idea for lacing fibers together to make cloth fabrics came from basket-weaving. The methods for weaving thread into cloth fabric were critical for the development of humankind. It's hard to imagine how early humans developed the processes needed to convert certain plant fibers into thread and then into fabric to make clothing.

Textiles produced from plant fibers spun into yarn can be netted, looped, knitted or woven into fabric. As early as 50,000 BCE these types of fabrics began to emerge in the Middle East. Since then the methods for producing textiles have continued to evolve. The availability and variety of textile products have strongly influenced the types of clothing people wore, how they carried their possessions and their household décor.

Flax was likely the first plant fiber used to make fabric. The cultivated plant species known as flax was domesticated from the wild species called *pale flax.* Flax is a crop that produces both food and fiber; flax seed is used to produce linseed oil; the fiber is processed from the flax stem. Textile fabrics produced from flax fiber is called *linen.*

The flax seed grown by early humans required fertile well-drained, deeply plowed soil. One had to be careful sowing the tiny seed so as to evenly disperse it. One month later the plants are ready for harvest. To obtain the longest fibers, flax is pulled out by the roots rather than cut. It is bundled together, tied and stacked in the field for drying until completely dry. Over the years, humans learned that higher quality flax fiber turns white after drying; inferior quality fiber fades to brown.

Rippling is the process used to deseed the flax. The top ends of the dry flax bundles are pulled through a comb of wooden nails hammered into a board. The seeds are collected and used to make linseed oil. Flax is *retted* by submerging it in water. This prompts the bacterium in the plant to decompose the pectin binding the stalk to the outer fibers, allowing the fibers to be separated from the stalk without damage. The flax is rinsed off periodically during the four-day retting process; the fibers will rot if submerged in water for too long.

Once the fibers are loosened *breaking* is used to breakdown the inner woody stalk into small pieces to separate it from the flax. Handfuls of flax are placed into the wooden blades of a simple breaking machine; the flax is beaten with a stick from bottom to top. Most of the broken wood fragments fall through the fiber to the ground. The broken fragments that remain are removed by a process known as *scotching*. This is accomplished by swinging a wooden scotching knife down the flax to scrape and pull it away.

Hackling is the process that prepares flax for spinning. The flax is pulled through increasingly, tightly spaced wooden combs called *hackles*. The initial hackles with the teeth spaced farther apart removes the straw. The hackles with finer combs polish and split the fibers. The fibers falling off in the hackle are bundled for use on lower quality fabric; the finely hackled flax is cleaned to achieve a shimmer and softness which make it ideal for spinning.

Silk fibers come from the natural protein fibers produced by certain insect larvae to make cocoons. Silk has an iridescent look, the result of the prism-like nature of silk fiber. Silk is produced by many insects but the silk gathered from moth caterpillar cocoons — specifically the mulberry silkworm — is preferred for modern textile manufacturing. Silk is mainly produced by the larvae of insects that undergo all four stages of metamorphosis. So called wild-silk produced by caterpillars other than the mulberry silkworm have been identified and used since ancient times. However, the scale of production has always been small.

In China around 3000 BCE the bombyx mori silk moth was selected for domestication. The resulting domesticated silk moth cannot fly; its caterpillar is unable to find mulberry leaves for itself. It remains the only insect on the planet to have been fully domesticated—it cannot survive without the aid of humankind. Silk from bombyx mori was unearthed by archaeologists in China. The fragments date from between 2850 and 2650 BCE.

Any individual strand of plant or animal fiber that is woven into fabric has to connect to one or more strands of fiber to produce one long piece of thread. This one thread is then woven to make a fabric.

It is likely the first fibers ever spun were accomplished without any tools. The process is called *twisting-yarn* where the fibers are held in one hand while the other hand pinches off a portion of the fiber. The fibers are twisted together by hand between the fingers while concurrently being pulled out to make longer lengths of thread. A spindle is a device used to spin one or more strands of fiber together in a process called *spinning-yarn*. A hand-spindle is a manually rotated device that twists strands of fiber together to create yarn. A drop-spindle uses gravity to pull the spindle to the floor while threading the strands of fiber together. Spinning yarn with either kind of hand-spindle is truly a form of art. Try to imagine the time and patience it took for early humans to create enough yarn to make a piece of fabric that could be fashioned into an article of clothing. Most of the experts in this field believe that hand-spinning has existed for over 10,000 years. Spindles and hand-spinning have played a central part in the folklore and myths of many of the earliest cultures.

Once plant (either flax or cotton) or animal fiber (wool or silk) has been used to create thread or yarn it is ready for conversion into a cloth or knitted products. Early humans used a knitting technique to produce cloth or fabrics. Knitting has been a valuable technique for ancient nomadic and modern humans to produce fabric from one strand of yarn or wool.

Researchers are uncertain as to when, where and how the cotton plant evolved and was first domesticated. The earliest cotton samples of cotton were found in Mexican caves dated to be about 7,000 years old. Cotton is known to have been grown, spun and woven into cloth as early as 3,000 years BCE in Pakistan's Indus

River Valley. Around that time the natives of Egypt's Nile valley were busy fabricating and wearing cotton clothing.

Several species of wild cotton plants are known to have existed around the world: Australia, Africa, Arizona, Central America, Lower California, Brazil, Mexico and other tropical islands. These natural occurring plants have been domesticated into five cotton varieties that are cultivated around the world. All cotton varieties require at least 160 frost–free days to provide the optimum growing period needed—why they are cultivated between latitudes 45 degrees north and 30 degrees south. Around 800 CE Arab merchants introduced cotton cloth to much of Europe. In 1492 CE Columbus discovered cotton plants growing in the Bahama Islands. By 1500 CE cotton was generally recognized throughout the civilized world.

Three principal areas led the shift to hunter-cultivators: the Near East at Catal Huyuk and the city of Jericho; central Mexico; the Yantze River valley in China. In some cases, entire bands made the change over to cultivation. In others they separated into stationary cultivator and roving hunter groups that traded food with each other. The results were a growing and prospering human population that continued fostering plant cultivation and animal domestication in ways similar to the treadmill of production that all of humanity runs on today.

The Near East Natufian communities included sites in an area known to possess rich growths of wild wheat and barley; hundreds of edible fruits and seeds with wild game, including mountain gazelle, wild cattle, roe deer, wild boar and goats. It is speculated that certain bands of Natufian hunter-gatherers were stressed to the point of changing migration patterns or cultivating their own produce. This likely occurred first in the Near East where decreasing annual rainfall had diminished the yields of wild fruit and game.[15]

We may never know how life began on Earth; life's purpose might elude us forever. What we do know is that we are here now on this incredible planet, witnessing the impact left by humanity on this amazingly rich and diverse Earth ecosystem: the bountiful natural resources that remain—we can never take life on Earth for granted.

2

Domestication & Subjugation

Imagine you're a hunter-gatherer harvesting figs from a fig tree in a tropical forest. The figs are tiny and rough but still edible, one of many plants growing wild that comprise your diet. Over the years you notice that when the fruit falls to the ground animals eat the fruit and disperse the seed across the landscape. The following year a young tree of the same type takes root and eventually grows to fruition. Years later, you notice that the fruit of one tree is a little larger, more-tasty than the fruit from the other trees. You get the wild idea to gather up the seeds from the younger tree and plant them close to your shelter. And so, it was…the practice of plant and animal domestication was born.

The domestication of plants was humanity's first step toward taking more control of their future. The ability to plant, cultivate and harvest crops as needed must have seemed like such a sure thing compared to the chance of success hunting game or searching for fruit in the forest. Overall, the cultivation of crops has been pretty reliable; agriculture has supported human survival and expansion for all of recorded history, but the path of plant domestication has not been easy. The demands of a growing population, human conflict, the need for repetitive menial labor, weeds and pests, overplanting, soil erosion, climate change, water scarcity and evolving plant diseases have taken their toll on nature, planet Earth and humankind.

Domestication & Subjugation

Any native plant whose characteristics have been modified by humans—unable to survive in the wild and reproduce without human support—is considered to be domesticated. Plant domestication has transpired over thousands of years; it's been a cooperative relationship between people and plants that has prospered and matured. Humans and plants have coevolved in support of each other: humans harvest particular plants selectively dependent on desired traits; seeds from the best fruits as used for planting the following year. Having nurtured a plant and replanting its most successful seeds, humans were selecting which properties to be passed on, and those that would not.

The fig tree is one of the earliest domesticated plants in the world. Evidence for parthenocarpy fig trees—trees that don't require pollination to bear fruit—has been located in areas around the Mediterranean Sea dated between 11,700 and 10,500 years ago. Fig trees are native to the Mediterranean region; its fruit is a green globe with an opening at one end. Inside there are a cluster of hundreds of flowers that when pollinated produce tiny bubbles of fruit with a seed in the center. There are two variations within the species: those that produce only pollen (no seeds) and the female that delivers three crops of figs without any pollen. When any of the fig fruits are pollinated a seed is produced that will yield a new tree.

Native fig trees are symbiotic, meaning they can reproduce only with the assistance of an insect named the fig wasp. Without the fig wasp's pollination, a fig tree cannot produce a germinated seed for planting the next generation of fig trees. Likewise, the fig wasp cannot survive without the food and shelter of the fig tree.

Yet over the course of time a fig tree mutation occurred without the need for pollination to bear fruit: fig wasps are not required to enter the fruit and no embryos are among the fruit. This mutation is called parthenocarpy: a plant that produces fruit without pollination. Since these trees are infertile, parthenocarpic fig trees cannot reproduce without the aid of humans: all that's needed is to cut off a branch and root it in the soil. If humans hadn't intervened there would be no fig trees bearing fruit without the aid of wasp embryos—but what about the poor fig wasp? There is always another side to the story whenever humans intervene in the world of nature.[1]

Emmer wheat is one of eight traditional founder crops considered to be the foundation of agriculture; it's a small annual plant that's mostly self-pollinated with low yields of sizable oval grains, possessing rigid ears. The earliest samples of emmer wheat were collected from a region called Ohalo on the shore of the Sea of Galilee in current day Israel. The charred grains were dated at roughly 23,000 years ago; they had been processed into flour and baked. Emmer wheat is not of much use to today's farmers except for creating new hybrids.

Emmer wheat was at the center of the wheat domestication process. Hunter-cultivators began growing it around 11,000 BCE; within a couple of thousand years they had created many varieties of emmer wheat and an early wheat called *spelt wheat*: a hybrid of emmer wheat and goat grass. A few thousand years later both varieties had mutated to be more readily threshed (separating the seed from the plant). *Bread wheat* was created 8500 years ago from a cross between domesticated emmer wheat and durum wheat with a larger size seed, more nutrients and improved thresh-ability, all leading to better yield.

Emma wheat is considered the second domesticated plant to be created, developed along with some 60 other plant varieties domesticated around the world during the period from 9,000 to 1,000 BCE. The following list shows just a few of them: peas, potatoes, beans, maize, cotton, bananas, chili-peppers, olives, apples, squash, sunflower and rice.[2]

––––––––––––

Horses were the very first animals that humans attempted to domesticate. The history of horses begins in the tropical forests of ancient North America around 55 million years ago with an animal named *Eohippus* that looked like a horse but was the size of a dog. Over time certain horse species became extinct while others evolved to better compete with predators and the changing environment. Their legs grew longer and stronger and feet became hooves, all built for speed and endurance across flat open spaces and hard ground.

When the rain forests of North America had dried up the Rocky Mountains arose from the swamps to become grassy plains emerging alongside the peaks. Horses developed bigger teeth and stronger jaws to readily consume the rigid and plentiful prairie grass. Eventually horses crossed the Bering Land Bridge from America to Asia and spread out across Europe. Their bones have been located among the remains of early human meals; they're rendered in early cave drawings and paintings around the world. Some of the oldest fossil remains have been found in America. By the beginning of recorded human history wild horses of various sizes and types had spread across planet Earth.

Nearly 10,000 years ago horses vanished from the American continents due either to the changing climate or the arrival of humans from Asia who over-hunted much of the large game across the Americas. Horses were reintroduced to the Americas by European colonists in the 16th century CE.

The steppes of central Asia are the ideal horse habitat. The Asian steppes are a strip of exquisite meadowland stretching 5,000 miles from Eastern Europe to China with enough precipitation to support grass but not enough to grow trees. Naked mountain ranges divide the steppe into segments readily transcended by horses and the horsemen who became their masters. The people there have conversed and traded across this span of scenic, harsh terrain with the aid of horses and camels for much of recorded human history.

The Western Steppe—also known as the Eurasian Steppe—extends from the mouth of the Danube River to the Altai Mountains, a region spanning 2500 miles west to east, a few hundred miles north to south. East of the Altai Mountains the Eastern Steppe spans 1500 miles east to Mongolia, covering some 500 miles from north to south. The soil is lush with wildflowers and silvery-green beds of grass, leaning as they give way to the prevailing winds much of the year. The grasslands turn beige in the dry summer heat. The Eastern Steppe experiences a broader range of seasonal temperatures than anywhere else on Earth; only the fittest of beast or human can survive on the Eurasian Steppe.[3]

A hunting party departs their village in search of large game on the Western Steppe of Eurasia thousands of years ago. After hours of trekking through the sundry terrain they approach the ridge on a hill and come upon a small herd of wild horses gnawing on the parched fall grass. The horses abruptly raise their heads, staring at the humans gazing back; sizing up the other with equal wonder. The horses look coarse and worn, ragged standing at attention, their hides span from shades of tan, fading to white and gray manes, with bright white muzzles, dark gray nostrils.

A horse snorts a warning; muscles tighten, ready to bolt. The hunting party spreads out ready to surround them — the horses are having none of it. The leader whinnies; they turn and gallop away with a cloud of dust chasing them into the setting sun. The hunters watch on in awe. When the dust clears the horses have disappeared; all is quiet on the Western Steppe, as the sun slips below the horizon.

In the beginning hunter-gatherers in Europe and Asia had hunted horses for meat; it didn't take long for humans to realize the value of the horse for personal transportation. With the aid of the horse, humans could travel farther, quicker while transporting more goods by a factor ten-fold. Horse domestication marked the beginning of a new era of human interaction, transportation and communication. And for some strange reason there was a connection, a feeling of deep respect that humans experienced when looking a horse in the eye: a window into its soul.

Circa 3,000 BCE donkeys roamed wild in northeast Africa through the Fertile Crescent into Mesopotamia. While horses were being put to work on the Western Steppe donkeys were just beginning their domestication in Egypt. Due to their relatively small size, Egyptians used donkeys almost exclusively as a beast of burden, hauling materials and goods from place to place.[4]

The mammoth—the predecessor of current day elephants—

became extinct about 10,000 years ago due to changing environments and over hunting by humans. The Indus people of current day India were the first to capture and tame elephants in the year 4000 BCE. There are two current species of elephants: *Indian elephants* ranging throughout temperate Asia and the Middle East; *African elephants* living in the areas north and south of the Sahara Desert.

With their capacity to learn, understand and retain knowledge, elephants have supported humankind for thousands of years. Training begins when they are very young. Despite a willingness to be trained elephants are never completely tame, especially males when in musth; why only females are used for domestic purposes. Over the century's elephants have been domesticated to provide hard labor, entertainment and to wage war.

Elephants possess brains roughly four times the size of the human brain. One can't help wonder about the true intelligence they possess. You would think we could offer them a better fate than to end up in a trophy case; harvested for their ivory to make piano keys, billiard balls and other decorative objects of value. If elephants could talk—what wisdom might they pass on to us?

By the year 300 BCE elephants had become an important military resource in India, North Africa and eventually China. Only males were utilized for military purposes; females tend to run away from males on the battlefield. While elephants provided an obvious size advantage, they could also charge at high speeds, overwhelming an army inexperienced in opposing such a force. In Asia, fighting turrets were strapped on the backs of elephants, carrying infantry or archers, creating a height advantage for soldiers firing down on the enemy from above. Elephants were also used to haul heavy loads of equipment and supplies to provide support for prolonged campaigns.[5]

Camels were first domesticated in Arabia around the year 1500 BCE. Within 500 years they had become a vital transport animal utilized across the barren territories of North Africa and Asia. Two species were domesticated: the single-humped *Arabian* camel in North Africa, the Middle East and India; the double-humped

Bactrian camel in central Asia and Mongolia. Both breeds are hardy and capable of traveling long distances without water, using their ability to convert the fat stored in their humps into water. By 1000 BCE camels were hauling a variety of goods up the west coast of Arabia, connecting India with Europe and Mesopotamia. As beasts of burden and transport they occupy an important place alongside horses and donkeys in their service to humankind.[6]

Alpacas and llamas are both members of the camel family originating on the plains of North America around 10 million years ago. Both species were on the verge of extinction when they were domesticated by Native Americans; neither species exists in the wild today. The llama is the larger of the two animals and is primarily used as a beast of burden; the alpaca is prized for its wool. Neither have the strength to carry or pull heavy loads. Consequently, Native Americans were denied any means of transporting heavy loads over long distances, a capacity that aided the survival and distribution of human civilizations across Europe and Asia for over a century.[7]

Around the year 2000 BCE a red jungle fowl, a member of the pheasant family that's still thriving in the forests and jungles of India and Southeast Asia, was domesticated for their meat and eggs. All domestic poultry existing today are believed to be descendants of this particular species.[8]

In China, the bombyx mori silk moth was selected for domestication around 3000 BCE. The domesticated silk moth cannot fly; its caterpillar is unable to find mulberry leaves for itself. This particular silk moth is the only insect on the planet that's been fully domesticated: it cannot survive in the wild or reproduce without the aid of humankind. Silk from bombyx mori was unearthed by archaeologists in China. The fragments date from between 2850 and 2650 BCE. The silkworm caterpillar has been utilized to produce silk fiber since 3000 BCE. A native to China, the silkworm moth named Bombyx mori—commonly known as the *mulberry silk-worm*—was domesticated there from a cousin that still survives in the wild today. Many years later the domesticated mulberry silkworm was introduced around the world; it's been employed by humans to produce silk for thousands of years.

Varieties of native wild silkworms survive in countries around the world from the Americas to Europe, Africa and Asia, ranging from temperate to tropical climates. The native silkworm that preceded the domesticated species—Bombyx mandarina—is unique to China and feeds only on white mulberry trees. It produces a more circular, finer and smoother thread when compared to other silkworms.

Chinese legend tells the story of the Emperor ruling China around 3000 BCE whose wife is known as the Goddess of Silk. She is acclaimed for introducing the methods for raising silkworms and the invention of the loom. The Chinese experimented with numerous types of silkworms to develop sericulture over many centuries, eventually developing the mulberry silkworm to become the specialized silk producer that it is today. Over the period of its domestication the mulberry moth developed a smaller and weaker jaw with tiny wings. It emerges from the cocoon incapable of flight, barely able to eat, cable only of mating and producing eggs for the next generation of silk producers. The mulberry silkworm is more delicate and sensitive than wild varieties, unable to survive extreme temperature and humidity variations.

Silk was originally reserved for use by the ruling emperor, his highest dignitaries and relatives. As production increased the upper classes began wearing tunics made of silk. Eventually silk was used throughout China for clothing, decoration and industrial uses: musical instruments, fishing-lines, bowstrings and luxury paper. Even common people could wear silk clothing; near its peak silk was traded like gold. Civil servants were paid in lengths of silk; it was used as currency when trading with foreign countries. Silk had become a key component of the Chinese economy, so important that the Chinese limited the transfer of information regarding the technology. As silk was traded over the sea lanes, western empires became acutely interested in the magical fiber.

Around 200 BCE many silk industry workers emigrated from China to Korea; Koreans were the first foreigners to learn the intimate details of silk production. News regarding silk production began traveling westward during the period 100 to 300 CE. The Silk Road—actually a narrow caravan trail—originated in Sian, China extending 4000-miles along the western edge of the Great Wall, passing north of the Takla Makan Desert over the Pamirs Mountains through Afghanistan and onto the Mediterranean shores where merchandise was shipped across the sea. Goods were transported depot to depot, bartered or exchanged for other goods by middlemen along the way. As silk items moved west; wools, gold and silver traveled eastward. The Silk Road also provided the means for trading ideas and knowledge between western and eastern civilizations; religious ideologies including Christianity, Islam and Buddhism also made their way to China via the Silk Road.

By the year 300 CE enough information regarding sericulture had trickled into India enabling the cultivation and manufacture of silk products there. In 550 CE, two Nestorian monks smuggled silkworm eggs out of China hidden in the hollow of their bamboo canes; they presented the eggs to Justinian, the Emperor of Byzantine. Under the monks' supervision the eggs hatched into caterpillars and began spinning cocoons. Long last, the Byzantine Empire was able to partake in the lucrative silk market. The Byzantine state and the church developed sericulture workshops; together they monopolized silk production, keeping the details about critical processes secret.[9]

What do mulberry silkworms and people have in common? Mulberry silkworms are identical to their wild cousins except they emerge from the cocoon with smaller, weaker jaws that are difficult to process food — and they cannot fly. In their cycle of life, the silkworm moths only function after exiting the cocoon is to mate; the females lay their eggs and both male and female die. Without the ability to process food or to fly, there's little chance domesticated moths could ever connect with a mate—why they are unable to survive as a species in the wild.

Domestication & Subjugation

Domesticated silkworms require the assistance of people to survive. Humans utilize a separate egg production operation to generate fertilized eggs; a selected male and female silkworm pair progress through the moth stage and emerge from the cocoon to mate. The female lays her eggs and the parents die.

On the silk production side if moths are allowed to exit the cocoon they would tear through the fiber, breaking the single silk thread and making it harder to process the fiber as a single thread. After harvest the cocoons pass through a series of hot-cold immersions to soften the sericin — the natural glue produced by the silkworm to affix the fiber in the cocoon — killing the moth. Each cocoon produces a consistent silk fiber approximately one kilometer (.6 miles) in length. It takes about 2500 cocoons to produce one pound of raw silk. Since human interaction is required for the mulberry silkworm to survive it is the only insect truly domesticated by humankind — the mulberry silkworm depends on humans to survive.

On the other hand, humankind is a species free to consume, reproduce and roam the planet. From the time that humans once existed as hunter-gatherers to the fully evolved Homo sapiens of today, we are a species unable to survive unassisted. Without body fur, sharp canine teeth and claws, overwhelming strength, speed and the ability to climb trees, humans are unable to survive in the wild without the aid of the many tools and accessories we've created over the eons. Humans have flourished for as long as we have by relying on the ideas and creativity, the broad range of skills and intellect, the respect and compassion of our fellow humans — like the mulberry silkworm, humans depend on their fellow humans and all the species comprising Earth's ecological domain to survive.

Around 3500 BCE the Mesopotamian civilization of Sumer was first to enter the Bronze Age, the third phase of human development following the ancient cultures of the Old and New Stone Ages prevalent throughout the Middle East, Asia and Europe. The Bronze Age signifies the first human use of metals to create tools and weapons.

While gold was the first metal to catch the eye of early humans its availability in small nuggets and relative softness made it useful for decoration only. Copper was another metal found in nature in pure form; it's harder than gold but soft enough to be hammered into shape. Somewhere around 7000 BCE a few Stone Age communities began hammering copper into knives and sickles.

The copper, bronze and iron ages followed in succession in accordance with increasing melting temperatures as humans struggled to determine which types of rocks could be reasonably melted, and the temperatures where that occurred. Bronze is an alloy of copper and tin: copper melts at 1972 °F (1083 °C) while tin's melting point is 422°F (232 °C) and iron's melting temperature is 2795 °F (1535 °C). Of course, early humans had no practical method for measuring temperature and no way to describe it. It's most likely they initially discovered the size and type of fire that would melt tin and repeated the process for copper and iron.

Smelting is the process developed by early humans to separate a metal from its ore—a naturally occurring solid material from which a metal can be extracted. They used charcoal and reed pipes to provide more air flow, reaching smelting temperatures as high as 2000 °F.

During the New Stone Age humans exhibited incredible creativity in their ability to fashion tools out of stone. Stone was not only heavier than most metals, it was extremely difficult to form into shapes to produce a variety of sharp, light-weight, long-lasting weapons and tools. By 3500 BCE the Mesopotamians were capable of mining copper ore, processing and shaping it. Like gold, copper was used mostly to create decorative items and jewelry. Copper was impractical for use in producing tools and weapons.[10]

In the far-east section of Turkey sits its largest and most beautiful lake. Lake Van is one of the world's largest endorheic lakes—a lake without an outflow to external bodies of water. Long ago, a volcanic eruption blocked the lake's natural outlet. An old Armenian church sits atop a broad plateau on the eastern shore dwarfed by the surrounding hills. Its simple elegant Urartian design stands erect; its gaze facing west into snowcapped mountains.

31

Lake Van is classified as a saline soda lake, strongly alkaline and fed by many small streams descending from the surrounding mountains. Although Lake Van sits well above sea level in a region with severe winters, its high salinity keeps much of the lake from freezing year-round. Lake Van was the likely source for much of the copper ore used by the Mesopotamian metalsmiths who later created bronze and copper alloys to produce pots, trays, plates and drinking containers and tools that included chisels, razors, arrow and spear-heads.

After years of copper being the primary metal Mesopotamian civilizations began a metallurgical revolution by creating a process for combining copper and tin to produce the metal alloy known as bronze. Ancient bronze was made up of proportions of 5 to 10% tin with the balance copper (today bronze is 12% tin, 88% copper). Tin, with its relatively low melting point and increased hardness was the ideal metal to combine with copper. Bronze was much harder than copper and easier to cast in molds; it could also be hammered into the desired shape.

The Egyptians had also developed an extensive knowledge of metallurgy by 3400 BCE. Copper was the metal they used most often; they even preferred it over gold. The copper ore mined in the Sinai contained about 12% pure copper. Considering the lack of fuel available for smelting and the difficulty of its acquisition and transportation—it's amazing that the Egyptians were able to press on. The earliest copper artifacts recovered in Egypt contain high levels of impurities, but as their smelting process developed the quality of the metal improved. Since hardness wasn't required, metals like copper were preferred for casting statues and vessels; softer metals were easier to form and engrave. Copper tools became dull quickly and required frequent re-sharpening.[11]

The Egyptians initially used copper to fabricate mirrors, razors, weights and balances, pillars and other decorations in their temples. As their processes for producing bronze alloys improved, they produced more elaborate designs of needles, saws, scissors, axes, harpoons, arrow tips and knives. Samples of their work have been found within the grave sites of Egyptian leaders. From the earliest Dynasties onward Egypt developed a high degree of civilization and the exploitation of metals—copper, bronze, gold and silver—was an essential part of their culture. Initially, the Egyptians produced copper and bronze tools similar to their stone equivalents; later the malleability and hardness of the metals influenced their designs.

Copper and bronze were also being used throughout the Near East: current day Turkey, Iran, Greece and Azerbaijan. By 2000 BCE large quantities of bronze items were being produced in parts of China. Bronze castings found in and around the Henan and Shaanxi provinces are considered the inception of the Bronze Age in China. Literature from that era indicates the exact proportions of copper and tin yielding different alloy grades for casting various items including cauldrons and bells, axes, spears, swords, arrows and mirrors. It's important to note that in the regions where new metals were being developed, it was the rulers of these civilizations and their armies that utilized the superior metals of the day: copper, bronze or the use of iron and steel that would follow. As far as everyday people were concerned, the Stone Age continued on for many centuries.

The Iron Age denotes the beginning of an era around 1000 BCE: a period of prehistory where iron was the primary metal used by humans to make tools. Much earlier around 3200 BCE humans began using meteoric iron: metallic iron deposited on Earth by meteors. The Egyptians called meteoric iron *black copper*. Meteoric iron could be hammered into shape without smelting but it was seldom discovered in large deposits; it was usually found in small bits scattered across the countryside. As such, black copper was used to make ornaments and jewelry. Blacksmiths occasionally used meteoric iron to craft swords; these cherished weapons were given only to men of great power.

Raw terrestrial iron-ore is a nonchemical mixture of *iron-ore proper* and loose earth called *gangue*; the two can be separated by crushing the raw ore and washing away the lighter soil. Since iron-ore proper is actually a chemical compound possessing a variety of impurities, separating the iron is problematic.

Even though terrestrial iron is abundant in nature its melting point is relatively high 2,795 °F (1538, °C), beyond the capabilities of more customary uses until later in human history. There is evidence in the Middle East that blacksmiths were smelting iron below iron's melting point and hammering it into shape by the year 2500 BCE. This type of iron is not as hard as bronze, decreasing its value as a weapon, but as the latest and greatest technology of the day it did enjoy strong appeal.

Primitive furnaces were only capable of reaching 1300°C, adequate for copper but not nearly high enough for iron. There was an important breakthrough around 1100 BCE when a sample of iron was reheated with charcoal some of the carbon in the charcoal was transferred to the iron, increasing its hardness. Further experimentation showed that the resulting iron product was even harder when the metal was cooled more quickly; centuries later this technology was developed further.

The Chinese were the first civilization to build a furnace hot enough to melt iron and produce the world's first cast iron in the year 513 BCE. When cast iron was reheated with charcoal the carbon combined with the iron to form steel. Steel can be worked as easy as any softer iron but it keeps a finer edge and is capable of being honed to sharpness. Gradually, from the 11th century CE onward steel weapons replaced bronze in Europe and the Mideast to begin the Iron Age. From this point forward it became essential to possess a good steel blade heading into battle, rather than a soft, mediocre one.[12]

––––––––

During the Middle-Ages the ability to use a variety of metals, sailboats and domesticated animals to wage medieval war across Europe, changed the technological, cultural and social aspects of war, prompting a dramatic transformation in the character and tactics of warfare. The use of fortifications would take on a whole different look, moving away from using the natural fortifications of the terrain to man-made structures; the advent of the castle swept throughout Europe and spread into Asia.

Noblemen were duty bound to respond to incursions and defend the early Middle Age homeland with their own equipment, infantry and archers. However, the burgeoning decentralized feudal system often resulted in troops with inconsistent abilities, training and equipment. At their core, feudal armies were made up of capable knights and local troops and mercenaries hired for the length of a campaign, paid for by levies fulfilling feudal tax obligations. Towns and communities would often field their own militias. But as central governments grew stronger, they began to recruit native and mercenary soldiers; town and village leaders became their recruiting tools. In theory, all Englishmen were obliged to serve forty days as a soldier, not long enough for most campaigns especially those fought in Europe. The *scutage*— money paid from vassal to lord in lieu of military service—was introduced whereby Englishmen could pay to evade their service. The money was used to pay for a permanent army. Most high-level medieval armies in Europe were composed largely of paid troops; in Europe there was a large mercenary market for much of the early 12th century. The best infantrymen were reported to be the younger sons of land owners and farmers.

In Europe the breakdown of centralized power led a number of groups to begin the large-scale plunder of communities as a source of revenue. The Vikings, Arabs, Mongols, Huns and Magyars were among those groups who regularly raided portions of the European continent, Africa and England. These groups were relatively small, nimble and able to move quickly. Fortifications were the simplest way to provide a sanctuary and defend the populace and prosperity of the territory. Throughout the Middle-Ages the fortification types and methods favored evolved around the castle. Since their inception the castle served as protection for local elites, their families, soldiers and servants. A castle offered protection from the raiders, capable of harboring a cavalry that could drive the enemy from the area or disrupt the efforts of larger armies that would send out foraging parties, attempting to resupply themselves.

The weapons used were designed with only one goal: to be

versatile and functional; capable of maiming or killing as many of the enemy as possible. Ever since the days of early hunter-cultivators, humankind has spent an inordinate amount of resources protecting or acquiring more homeland. Once humans figured out that acquiring a surplus of goods provided us something close to eternal life, we kept increasing production, piling up the goods we desire and the weapons necessary to protect our wealth—and we've never looked back.

Medieval times were wrought with pestilence and warfare across Europe and Asia. Bands of warriors roamed at will with the latest weaponry, the result of improved processes for smelting iron and steel. Some of those new weapons included: the single-handed cruciform sword; straight broad swords with double-edged blades; falchions: a one-handed, single-edged versatile sword with the weight and power of an axe; the longsword with cruciform hilts; the stiletto (dagger) with a long slender blade.[13]

The longbow was a powerful medieval bow used by the English and Welsh as a weapon in medieval warfare. A longbow projects arrows using the elasticity of the bow. When the bow is drawn, kinetic energy is stored as potential energy in the bow that's transformed back to kinetic energy when the string is released; the string is the mechanism for transferring the energy to the arrow. A longbow is usually as tall as the archer. This allows the archer to have a fairly long draw. The average length of arrow-shafts was 75 cm. or 30 in. A longbow is not significantly curved. Traditional longbows are made from one piece of wood. They've been used for hunting and warfare for thousands of years. The average power for bows of all designs is about 50 pounds at 70 cm (28 inches) of draw, suitable for hunting. Longbows for warfare were more powerful; the most powerful approached the 200-pound mark.

Many men in the medieval period were capable of shooting longbows with 150–200 pounds of force. During the Middle-Ages, the English were famous for their powerful longbows used very effectively in the civil wars of the period and against the French in the Hundred Years' War.

A typical longbow archer would receive between 60 and 70

arrows per battle; most were unable to reach the maximum rate of launching six arrows per minute. Not only would the arm and shoulder muscles tire from exertion, the fingers would strain from holding the bowstring. Ranged high-arc volleys were used like artillery at the beginning of battles, shifting to closer targeted shots as the enemy neared. Archers rationed their arrows to make sure they didn't run out before the battle ended.[14]

Crossbows are longer range weapons with a horizontal bow assembly mounted on a frame, handheld like the stock of a gun to shoot arrow projectiles. The traditional bow and arrow were considered a specialized weapon, requiring considerable training, physical strength and expertise to utilize accurately and efficiently; bowmen were considered a superior class in many cultures. In contrast, the crossbow was the first simple projectile weapon, inexpensive and much less physically demanding to be used by large numbers of conscripted soldiers.[15]

The spear was a pole weapon with a shaft and sharpened head, either thrown or used in direct man-to-man combat. Spears used for thrusting were sturdier while those meant for throwing were lean and aerodynamic. A thrusting spear has the advantage of reach. The medieval spear was an economical weapon, requiring only a small amount of steel along the sharpened edges of the spear-tip. Quick to manufacture and requiring less skill than a sword the spear was the main weapon used by common infantry soldiers.

A pike is a very long thrusting weapon called a pole weapon used by infantry to attack enemy foot soldiers and defend against cavalry assaults. The pike is not intended to be thrown. Pikes were used by infantry deployed in tight formation from the early Middle-Ages until the 17th century CE. The long length of the pikes presented a concentration of extended spearheads to the enemy; if the lines broke down the pikes were clumsy in close combat. Pikemen needed to carry with them a sword for their defense should the fighting collapse into a free-for-all; they seldom were able to carry a shield. Pikemen avoided such combat since they were at a disadvantage.[16]

During the Middle Ages virtually all large cities had walls. The most important cities had citadels, forts or castles. Great effort was expended ensuring a good water supply inside the city in case of a siege. In some places, long tunnels were built to carry water into the city. The balance of power favored the defender until the invention of gunpowder-based weaponry, especially the canon.

Armies on the battlefield included heavy and light cavalry, infantry and archers. The heavy cavalry consisted of soldiers wearing full armor, usually a knight or someone connected with nobility. They could have come from the lower classes and could possibly have been a slave. The cost of armor, horses and weapons was great, serving to transform the knight into a distinct social class separate from other warriors. During the crusades, holy orders of Knights fought in the Holy Land.

Light cavalry consisted of lightly armed and armored men carrying lances, javelins, bows or crossbows. Light cavalry units were usually made up of wealthy commoners or sergeants: men who'd trained as knights but couldn't afford the equipment to become a knight. Light cavalry was used as scouts, messengers or to ambush the enemy. Differing countries developed various types of light cavalry: Hungarian archers; Spanish jennets and English currours—light horseman armed with javelin, sword and shield; Italian and German mounted crossbowmen. Across Europe infantry were recruited and trained in a variety of methods throughout the Middle-Ages; they were largest component of the medieval field army. In prolonged wars, most infantrymen were mercenaries; most armies contained large numbers of spearmen, archers and other unmounted soldiers.[17]

The smelting of iron was limited to producing weaponry until the 18th century. Smelting iron with charcoal supplies the carbon needed to strengthen the iron. Charcoal is produced by burning wood in a low oxygen environment, a process that can take days. The production of charcoal gives off a number of volatile compounds: water, hydrogen, methane and tar. The required charcoal and the noxious emissions required ironworks to be located away from the cities and close to forests.

In 1709 an ironmaster by the name of Abraham Darby from Coalbrookdale, England on the Severn River discovered that coke could replace the charcoal used for smelting pig-iron to produce cast-iron products. Coke can be manufactured by burning just the outer layer of coal in mounds, leaving the interior of the pile in a carbonized state. Using coke in the process of smelting pig-iron reduced the cost of cast-iron products so significantly that the Severn region became the center of iron production in Great Britain at the beginning of the Industrial Revolution. Coke was increasingly substituted for charcoal; the harvesting of forests to fuel charcoal production was unable to meet its demand. Later in the 18th century CE brick *bee-hive* ovens were designed for the production of coke allowing more control of the burning process.[18]

Seventy years later in 1781 the world's first iron bridge with a single span over 100 feet required just a few months of assembly. Casting the iron for the bridge components and the large curving ribs had taken significant time back at the mill, but little effort was needed to assemble the parts on the bridge site. The bridge was located just downstream from Abraham Darby's Coalbrookdale iron mill over the Severn River. It was reported that the seemingly light structure of the bridge amazed initial observers. It was the only bridge left standing over the Severn River after a major flood in 1795. Over the years there have been many repairs but the bridge remains as it was when installed some 237 years ago; it is still in use but for pedestrian traffic only.[19]

In 1775 a man by the name of Henry Cort purchased an iron-mill near Portsmith in Hampshire. Mr. Cort had just completed serving 10 years as a civilian official in the Royal Navy. In 1783-84 he applied for patents for two processes he had developed that would become critically important to future metallurgical processes. He named the first process *puddling*, a technique for shaking the molten iron in a special furnace and mixing it with air. The oxygen in the air combines with the carbon in the iron leaving almost pure iron behind. Pure iron is much more pliable than pig iron (cast iron); it can be readily hammered into shape, making it much more useful for industrial processes.

Henry Cort also patented a machine to draw out red-hot chunks of semi-molten pure metal out of a blast furnace, in between grooved rollers. As the rollers turned, the hot metal was formed into useable bars of the desired thickness without need for further processing. Both of these processes jump-started the development of steel mills producing uniform bars of rolled steel around the world. Unfortunately, Mr. Cort had spent all of his own money developing his inventions. He had to borrow money to develop his ideas further so as to make a profit. When it was later revealed that his partner had invested stolen funds, Cort was deprived of his patents and forced into bankruptcy. For all his hard work and creativity, he was eventually granted a modest pension.[20]

———————————————

Medieval Asia had far surpassed the West in the development of warfare, communication and science. Gunpowder was widely used by the Chinese as early as the 11th century; they were using moveable type printing five hundred years before Gutenberg created his press. Buddhism, Taoism, Confucianism were the dominant philosophies of the Far East during the Middle-Ages. Medieval Asia was the kingdom of the Khans. Never before had one person controlled as much land as Genghis Kahn. He built his power by unifying separate Mongol tribes before expanding his kingdom south and west. He and his grandson, Kublai Khan, controlled lands in China, Burma, Central Asia, Russia, Iran, the Middle East, and Eastern Europe. Estimates are that the Mongol armies reduced the population of China by nearly a third. Genghis Khan was a pagan who tolerated nearly every religion except Islam; their culture often suffered the harshest treatment from Mongol armies. The Khan armies pushed as far west as Jerusalem before being defeated in 1260.[21]

3

Painted Words

The wind streams unremitting across the parched Persian landscape; ancient windmills churn away like it was yesterday. A thousand years is a long stretch for any human-made machine made of stone, wood, clay and straw to continue working. The windmills feature a vertical shaft with six vertical blades fashioned out of wooden boards, attached with horizontal boards crossing every few feet; the structures stand nearly 65 feet high. Mohammad Etebari has cared for these ancient wonders in the northeast Iranian village named Nashtifan since he was a young boy. Etebari has dedicated his life to performing the daily maintenance on a few dozen of these infamous windmills. As he nears the end of his term he wonders if any of the younger generation will bother to take on the demanding maintenance needed to keep these windmills turning and churning.

"It's the pure, clean air that makes the windmills rotate—the life-giving air that everyone can breathe," Etebari said in a video made for this story.[1]

The Persians are believed to be the first to develop windmills between 500 and 900 CE, used mostly for the purpose of grinding grain. These early windmills stand vertical with sails spinning the shaft, connected directly to a grind-stone or pump. Windmills first appeared in Europe about the time of the Crusades (1096-1270 CE).

The application of the wind to do work was initially used by

41

humans to power sailing vessels in Mesopotamia over five thousand years ago. These primitive boats used a simple square sail made of cloth that seized the wind and ran with it. The sail's position was not adjustable so the wind was useable only when the wind and boat were headed the same way. Otherwise, the sail had to be taken down and the sailors would commence by rowing to remain underway.

Years later the Vikings had a better idea. They also used square sails but theirs were adjustable for *roundness* facing horizontally in either direction—catching the wind to go with it or flattened out when sailing against it—adjustable at an angle to minimize wind resistance. In addition, the Vikings added a keel—a flat surface running front-to- back on the boat's bottom—to keep from sliding sideways when sailing at an angle to the wind.

Arab sailors used a triangular device called a *lateen sail* to perfect their sailing vessels. The lateen sail hangs loosely, presenting a curved surface to the wind, creating a force that's proportional to the pressure difference between the convex and concave sides of the sail. In the 1800's the Viking hull and the lateen sail were brought together allowing for windward sailing, or sailing close-hauled to the wind (when sails are trimmed tightly to act like a semi-closed wing). The first sailboat of this kind was called a *lug-rig*.

The Chinese Junk is a type of ancient sailing ship still in use today. Junks were a type of *lug-rig* design used as seagoing vessels as early as the 2nd century CE. Throughout history the sailing technology of the Chinese was unmatched with superior ship designs and navigation skills. Sailing has been a key component promoting ongoing human progress around the world, affecting fishing, religion, trade, warfare, art, language, human migration and colonization.[2]

For over 1500 years humans have utilized wind-power on land. The Persians were the first to develop wind powered grain mills and water pumps in the period from 500-900 CE, followed by the Chinese in 1200 CE. Early windmill designs included four blades with a weathervane to point the windmill into the wind.

Embracing Sufficiency

Much later in 1854 American inventor, Daniel Halladay developed a windmill water pump design in his Connecticut machine shop. His design was very successful, providing a method for pumping water on ranches and farms across the expanding American west. The windmill water pump was also pivotal in supporting railroad expansion by supplying the water needed to operate early steam driven engines. Safety devices were added later, protecting the windmill from damage from excessive winds. Eventually, factories across the country began manufacturing water-pump windmills. Between the years 1850 to 1970, in excess of six million windmills were installed in the United States.

The first windmill designed to produce electricity was installed in Cleveland, Ohio in 1888. The turbine had a diameter of 50 ft. with 144 rotor blades constructed with cedar wood, with a generating capacity of 12 kilowatts (kW) of power. Early in the 20th century many rural areas were still without electrical service. Small wind turbines ranging from 5 kW to 25 kW were developed to meet the electrical needs of remote homes, farms and ranches. In 1935, midway through the Great Depression the U.S. Federal Rural Electrification Administration (REA) was formed to support extending electrical service to rural areas where the costs of installation would otherwise have prevented private electric companies from doing so.[3]

_____

For centuries Chinese alchemists had experimented with various chemical mixtures attempting to develop an elixir to bestow immortality on all those who ingested it. Eventually they experimented with a compound called potassium nitrate (better known today as saltpeter). In the fateful year of 850 an alchemist whose name is lost to history concocted a mixture of 75 parts saltpeter, 15 parts charcoal and 10 parts sulfur. When taken orally or applied to the body the mixture didn't produce any obvious life-lengthening properties; when exposed to a flame it erupted—with a flash and a bang.

Initially the Chinese used gunpowder primarily for fireworks. In 904 the Song Dynasty began using the elixir against its arch enemy: the Mongols. The weapon was called *flying fire*: arrows with a burning tube of gun powder attached to the shaft. They were like miniature rockets, terrorizing the men and horses of the Mongol ranks; one can only imagine the terror they felt. The Chinese used gunpowder to produce crude hand grenades, flame throwers, poisonous gas shells and land mines. China produced the first cannon in 1120, a century and a half before the Europeans. Near the end of the eleventh century the Song government became concerned that gun powder might become available to the rest of the world. In what must have been the first major effort to limit the proliferation of a potential military weapon—the Chinese banned the sale of saltpeter to foreigners. Notwithstanding, word of this incredible concoction would eventually pass down the Silk Road to India, the Middle East and onto Europe. By 1249 a complete recipe for gunpowder was found amongst published writings in Europe.

The very first guns were actually crude canons designed by the Chinese and then the Europeans, but the need for smaller hand carried devices was quickly realized. The first rifles consisted of long metal tubes fashioned out of brass or iron. The gunpowder and lead ball were loaded from the front; the tube's rear end was sealed, except for a small hole to light the charge. Aiming the gun and lighting the charge in the middle of a heated battle must have been a challenging task; the range of these early guns was only thirty-five yards[4].

All firearms work the same way: a mechanism detonates the gun powder which explodes to propel a projectile down the gun barrel. The first mechanical firing mechanism called the match-lock was designed in the year 1400. It featured a slow burning wick attached to a movable, S-shaped arm. Movement of the arm positioned the wick into a small pan of priming powder. During the Age of Discovery explorers wore little armor; they carried match-lock type guns on their ships to subdue the more numerous populations of indigenous peoples. Match-locks were used for many years due to their low cost and ease of manufacture, even after much improved firing mechanisms had been developed.[5]

The flintlock was the next significant innovation; it included a flint sparking mechanism to ignite the gun powder. Much later in 1807, a Scottish clergyman named Alexander Forsythe invented a percussion firing mechanism with a mercury fulminate compound that exploded on impact with a trigger mechanism. This design led directly to cartridges that combined gunpowder, mercury fulminate and bullet all in the same package for standard size gun barrel casings, a design similar to those in use today.[6]

———————

Late in the Middle Ages a steadily rising western economy prompted social and cultural development. The growing middle class and rising literacy rates boosted the demand for ideas and knowledge; people became more enriched by the information gained from reading books. A growing entrepreneurial spirit championed new designs and methods for production of almost everything. The period of the Enlightenment had only just begun. At the time, books were still being produced in Europe the old-fashioned way, hand copying one at a time.

In China, printing had evolved to mechanical wood-block printing on paper during the 8th century CE; it quickly spread to other East Asian countries. While the Chinese had first used clay and wood movable type, metal movable type was developed in Korea by the 13th century. Newer print era technologies had already been deployed in Europe: including the manufacture of paper and ink and the development of eyeglasses. The codex method of printing (using individual pages instead of a continuous scroll) had already been adopted, reducing costs while allowing printing on front and back.

Johannes Gutenberg was in the right place and time in the year 1439, possessing a unique background to design his printing press. The process he created greatly improved the efficiency of type setting and printing by treating them as separate operations. He created his *type-characters* from a lead-based alloy that's still in use today and developed a method to mass produce the characters with a special hand mold he called the *matrix*. Printing in Latin—with as few as two dozen different letters—provided a significant typesetting advantage. The movable type was sorted in a letter case and loaded in with a composing stick.

Gutenberg adopted the basic screw-press design used in the early wine presses, allowing direct pressure to be applied on a flat plane. He adapted the design to exert pressure evenly across the platen with the needed flexibility. He sped up the process by providing a transportable under-table with a flat surface allowing the sheets to be changed quickly. After much experimentation, Gutenberg surmounted issues regarding water-based inks that wet the paper by using an oil-based ink suitable for use with metal-types to produce high-quality printing.

The Gutenberg Bible was the first major book printed in Europe using mass-produced movable metal-type. It marked the beginning of what came to be known as *the Gutenberg Revolution* — the era of the printed book in Europe. Written in Latin the book became an icon. Since its initial publication only 49 copies have survived; they're considered among the most valuable books in the world.[7]

Humans began making hand-tools many thousands of years ago. By medieval times the relics of many common hand-tools had already been well developed and are still in use today. What's amazing about studying ancient tools: knives, hammers, axes, chisels and saws are how contemporary they seem. The concept of sawing, first used in the Early Stone Age, was to rub a piece of wood against another, creating sparks to fall into sawdust and ignite a fire, a technique commonly used around the world. Early samples of flint saws have been found in archaeological digs in Southern France from the Old Stone Age some 15,000 years ago. The length and shape of pre-metal saws produced during this period were determined by how the stone was formed. Craftsmen used their stone cutting and flaking skills to create crude saw blades — usually just a few inches long — that were most useable to them. Many such saws were still being used countless years later during the Bronze Age that had been copied into metal.

Saws dated at 7000 years old made from black obsidian have

been uncovered in excavations at Ur, the ancient Sumerian capital in Mesopotamia. These small blades were used by Sumerian craftsmen in the area between the Tigris and Euphrates rivers. Hunter-gatherers around the world have used a variety of materials to produce saws: obsidian, flint, shark's teeth, the snout of saw-fish and eventually copper, tin, bronze, iron and steel. The first metal saws developed in Egypt were made of copper or bronze; hardened copper was used to make the first copper saw blades. As time went on saw-teeth became wider as the saws became longer. During the 5th Dynasty Egyptians used four feet long open saws with large triangular teeth for stonecutting. When the bronze alloy was developed it replaced copper for most cutting tools, including saws. At that point saws were increasingly being used for woodworking; saws began looking like the standard crosscut handsaw of today.[8]

Ancient craftsmen were confronted with difficult issues regarding typical saw applications. Saws are most often used to cut larger pieces of material into smaller sections to form a particular shape. However, the copper and bronze saw blades of the time were labor intensive and inaccurate; at their best the rough-cut outputs of their saws required significant touchup with a rasp or an adze.

Bronze was superior to predecessor flint blades because they were thin; less likely to become wedged in the material while making a cut. Bronze was also proficient at making edge tools such as wedges: tools that could be used to split woods along the grain instead of saws. Forest timber could be split and hewn with wedges. Bronze saws would eventually be replaced with jeweled teeth for stone-cutting applications and in later years with iron saw-blades.

During the Iron Age—500 BCE to 50 CE—there were many developments that provided momentous improvements in saw performance. Most noteworthy was the *raking* of saw-teeth to cut more in one direction: on the down stroke or the pull stroke. To cut more on the down stroke the saw teeth were raked towards the saw handle, meaning the angle of the blade was steeper facing forward. To cut more on the pull stroke the saw teeth are raked away from the saw handle. (Rake is the angle along the front of the saw-tooth with the line perpendicular to the line drawn along the edge of the saw-teeth.) The purpose of rake is to vary the aggressiveness of the saw; saws cut more aggressively when the rake angle is decreased. Ancient toolmakers used the concept of raking to resolve a different problem: reducing the force on the push stroke so that earlier blades made of softer metals—copper, bronze and iron—wouldn't bend under the greater force. This was a significant advance over teeth with a constant rake angle, even though the pull strokes are usually weaker than the push strokes on most saws today. Saws designed to cut more on the push stroke were unsuccessful until a method was discovered to prevent saws made of weaker metals from bending. High quality steel would eventually overcome the problem but that didn't occur until many years later. In general, the goal of the rake angle is to make the saw easier to start, taking advantage of the momentum and powering the saw to the end of the stroke. Today's rip saws are designed to cut with the grain on the pull stroke; crosscut saws that cut perpendicular to the grain have an equal rake angle for cutting in both directions.[9]

The next Iron Age invention was the frame-saw, a clever way to prevent the bending and buckling of soft metal blades by setting the blade either centrally in the frame or at one side of a frame. Previously, saws were typically a blade with handles on one or both ends. During the Iron Age the frame-saw with a single handle-frame attached to a blade looked much like a modern hacksaw. On frame saws with the blade located in the middle of the frame, the sides provided two handles for manually powering the saw. The Romans used long two-handled saws to rip felled timber into boards similar to the saws Egyptians used to cut large stones.

Throughout the Medieval period saws were increasingly in use across Europe; both the axe and the saw would become the symbolic tools of the age. Many new varieties were created including: handsaws, two-man hand saws, frame saws, pit saws and later machine saws. Pit saws were used to cut felled timber into square beams or boards. This was accomplished by placing the timber flat over an open pit with supports sustaining the timber at ground level. With one man above, another in the pit below, the two-man saw was used to rip the timber into boards and beams. The work was strenuous and time consuming, yet it provided work for many people who were unemployed.

At this point the age of mechanization was merely a spark in the imagination of an inventor's minds-eye. We've briefly discussed the use of wind and water-power to mill grain. In order to convert wind or water-power to be functional for powering sawmills, the rotary motion of the wheel had to be converted to the linear push-pull motion needed to power a two-man saw. The end result was using the concept of a crude camshaft—a lever-arm attached to a u-shaped cam, connected to a rotating shaft—to push the saw upward in the first half of the stroke and pull back down during the second half. During the 17th century sawmills were adopted in much of Europe and later in the American colonies.

In 1490, blast-furnaces were introduced in Great Britain that provided cast iron saw-blades. But sawmills were adopted gradually; the pit-saw remained in use until the late 18th century. It wasn't until the development of the steam-engine that woodworking machinery would enjoy widespread use. A sawmill near Augsburg in Germany was one of the earliest known. In 1420, the Portuguese built mills in Madeira to exploit the island's timber resources. The first Norwegian sawmills to practice what contemporaries called—the latest methods for manufacturing timber—was opened in 1530 to meet the demands of the expanding export lumber trade. During the 15th and 16th centuries, sawmills were in operation in Germany, Norway, Holland and Sweden. The pit-saw method was so labor intensive and costly that there were few orders for boards made in England. It was cheaper to import them from Danzig, Germany where they were made more cheaply with the use of windmills; the thriving Baltic and Dutch ports all had sawmills.

England was late to embrace the new sawmill technology beginning in 1663. With rampant unemployment English woodworkers, fearing the loss of their jobs, were adamantly opposed to any form of automation. Yet thirteen years later in Southampton a mill was turning out ships' blocks for the Royal Navy using a new circular saw that was quite successful.

The first sawmill in America was built on the Piscataqua River near York, Maine in 1623. Since the colonies possessed an abundance of forests the mill was built primarily to supply England with lumber. The British Navy desperately needed trees to make masts for their largest warships. Since England did not possess suitable trees to make the ships, they had to look elsewhere. In 1634, the first shipment of white pine trees fashioned into masts were sent to England; the first water-powered sawmill was built near Berwick, Maine.

The new sawmills constructed in New England over the next 200 years were essentially the same—a waterwheel with a crank connected by a crankshaft to a wooden frame-saw. The reciprocating motion of the vertically mounted saw showed the characteristic straight push-and-pull saw marks on the boards and timbers cut by these types of saws. Subsequently, as the frontier moved westward across North America most towns acquired a new sawmill. Over the years, sawmills were built across New England, some 5500 of them by the year 1840.

In 1803 a new steam-powered sawmill in New Orleans was destroyed by hand sawyers upset about the automation provided by the mill. Two years later a mill in Natchez, higher up on the Mississippi River was smashed to pieces. The impact of powered sawmills on American productivity was immediate: two men by hand could cut 60 beams or trunks in 120 working days; wind or water powered mills required only 5 days. Yet the sawmill being used possessed only a single vertical, reciprocating blade, relatively slow when compared to the newer mills being built in Europe. Wind or river-water turned the mill-wheels; the saw blades were maintained in constant tension in tough wooden frames. Later models had several blades connected together called gang-saws.[10]

When the climate of North America became unstable some 10,000 years ago, Paleo-Indians began to spread out across both American continents. They survived much like the hunter-gathers of Europe and Asia had, hunting and gathering, moving from place to place as resources ran out. Inland, they subsisted mainly on large animals: the mastodon and ancient bison. They carried with them a variety of tools: arrowheads, knives, devices for butchering and processing hides. The vast North American continent, its assorted landscapes, ecology and climate prompted the creation of many distinct paleo-Indian cultures, languages and lifestyles. Over the course of a few thousand years Native American Indians had domesticated, bred and cultivated a number of plant species that now comprise more than 50% of all crops cultivated around the world.

Over the course of several thousand years advanced civilizations had emerged across North America. In the Lower Mississippi Valley, Native Americans built complex earthwork mounds, likely for religious purposes around 6500 BCE. Mound building continued at many sites in the Mississippi and Ohio River valleys including effigy, conical and ridge mounds, as well as other shapes.[11]

In the year 1540, a Spanish expedition led by Hernando de Soto wandered across the American southeast for a period lasting four years. During that time, he and his men encountered many of the Native Americans living there, with devastating results for both sides. When de Soto and his troops arrived in Mexico they were bedraggled, and just a fraction of their original size. However, the Native Americans he encountered fared much worse. They were susceptible to the contagious diseases carried by the Spanish; the Native American population was completely devastated. Nearly a century later, when European explorers returned to the area all the native Mississippi tribes had vanished; all signs of their communities, their vast stretches of land had disappeared.[12]

In today's tooled-up automated world drilling a hole might seem like a pretty simple endeavor, yet for much of human history it was difficult to achieve. Developing tools to drill accurate size holes in a desired location, in a variety of materials would take centuries to develop. The first drilling tool was simply a sharp stone with a bone point, or a pointed blade of flint or copper that could be attached to a wooden shaft. The awl was a device that was created more to punch holes in leather and other dense fabrics. It was also used to drill crude holes by rotating the blade: the wider the diameter of the awl, the larger the hole it could drill. Drilling a hole this way was labor intensive, especially in a dense material such as stone. A device known as a strap drill was used to ease the burden of using the hand drill. It consisted of an awl type drill bit attached to a longer wooden shaft. The shaft was rotated by wrapping a strap of flexible material (like rope) once around the wood shaft, then grabbing each end of the rope with a hand. To operate the strap drill, one would press the drill (awl) bit into the material, pull one end of the strap and then the other, back and forth, spinning the drill into the material until the hole was drilled all the way through. The top of the shaft revolved in a mouthpiece held by the user's teeth capable of applying more downward pressure. It's complicated; I wouldn't advise trying this at home. The tool could also be used to start a fire; it's also known as a fire drill.

The bow drill was an advanced drill design created in Egypt about 6000 years ago that had a strap wrapped around the drill shaft attached to a bow. While holding the drill upright and the bow flat, the user pushed and pulled the bow back and forth while the shaft revolved one way, and then the other.

The other historical aspect of drill technology has to do with the cutting tools that actually do the drilling. The first drill bits were actually tapered flint blades, bones or shells. Much later during the 13th century CE humans were using pieces of metal stuck onto tubular lengths of wood to gradually grind out an area of the material until the metal wore off and had to be replaced. It wasn't until steam and then electrical power became available that a vast array of drill bits and accessories would evolve along with rotary powered drills and saws around the world.[13]

In Monroe, Oregon the Hull-Oakes Lumber Company is an amazing story of adaptation and resilience in an age of automation that's fueled by electricity and computers in lieu of steam. While the lumber industry had initially settled in eastern North America, by 1880 roughly 75 steam-powered sawmills were busy sawing up lumber in the Pacific Northwest. One hundred and thirty years later the Hull-Oakes Lumber Company saw-mill is the last steam-driven mill remaining in the United States. The mill produces some 18 million board-feet annually; a pittance compared to today's modern mills. The Hull-Oakes mill has survived by focusing on cutting very long and thick beams—up to 80 feet long and 3 feet wide—used for bridge construction, spars or the masts of tall ships.

Ralph Hall is the man responsible for building the factory in 1938 on the site of a mill that had burned down. He was able to salvage the boilers and the planer; all the other needed machinery had to be trucked in. At the heart of the mill is the 1906 Ames Regal Steam engine, weighing a mere eight tons and capable of spinning at 150 rpms. The workers there are a tightknit family of millwrights, foresters, lumber-graders and timber-fallers; they are as resilient and steadfast as the timber products they produce. Many have worked at the mill their entire working life; many more are the offspring of current or past employees.

The steady flow of trucks hauling timber to the mill matches the rate of timber entering the input bay for processing. Where before milling scraps used to be burned in open pits and essentially wasted, today the mill's byproducts are either sold or used to fire their boilers. The blades on the main saw run 52 feet in circumference at a price of $2,000 each; the saw is capable of ripping a 40-foot log in a few seconds. Each blade is rotated off the machine and re-sharpened after two hours of operation. The blades start out at 14 inches wide and are retired when they're worn down to 11 inches. Since new parts for many of the machines at the plant are no longer manufactured, they have to purchase parts from saw-mills that are going out of the business. The Hull-Oakes plant is at the end of a line for operating steam powered sawmills in America; it's located at the end of an old railroad track that's no longer running.[14]

4
Wooden Ships

Before there were fossil fuels—there were no dinosaurs. The climate was much warmer. Earth was covered with marshes and wetlands. Life was rampant, and primordial plants and trees blanketed the planet, ancient creatures roamed the countryside and sea-life flourished in the oceans. When the plants and animals died, they decomposed. Over time their remains were buried by layers of mud, rock and sand. Year after year, layer upon layer of new organic material was piled onto the heap, creating a giant pressure cooker of carbon-based materials capable of storing energy in the form of coal, oil and natural gas. The process would take millions of years.[1]

Humans began using wood to make tools and provide shelter long before evolving to lifestyles of living off the land. They burned wood for warmth and to cook their food. As the population grew so did the utilization of wood: to construct elaborate buildings, wagons and ships, tools and an array of weapons for hunting and to make war.

In ancient times great woodlands still spanned the Middle East; by the year 3000 BCE cedar forests still covered the region. Regional empires began consuming staggering amounts of timber to display their power and wealth. Cedar was used to construct temples and palaces in kingdoms across the Fertile Crescent. The Phoenicians—one of the oldest global sea-trading nations—are believed to have consumed a large share of the timber to build their fleet of ships. Within a thousand years the cedar forests were gone; much of the Middle East lay barren by 2000 BCE.

The center of trade shifted to nearby regions with significant timber reserves during the Hellenic period; Middle East kingdoms began importing timber and bronze from the island of Crete. As the Minoan civilization grew the economy depended on wood to fuel their furnaces and produce bronze, their major export. The Minoans flourished for another six centuries until the massive eruption of the Thera Volcano buried Crete in ash; the Tsunami that followed is credited with having destroyed much of the coast line. What remained of their woodlands was lost. From then on, the Minoans had to import fuel and timber from the Greek mainland. The remaining forests of Asia Minor, the Greek peninsula and Macedonia became the main sources of power in the region. With an ample supply of wood for ship building and extensive coastlines for promoting trade, Greece became the new center of Mediterranean trade.

Wood remained a valued commodity during the Roman period that followed. A book written by Pliny the Elder—Roman author and naval commander—titled *Pliny's Natural History* discusses the importance of wood and the forests to support human existence: "*...the trees and forests were supposed to be the supreme gift bestowed by her on man. These first provided him with food, their foliage carpeted his cave and their bark served him for aliment...*"

Wood availability had transformed the civilizations in Greece and Asia Minor into formidable maritime trading powers much like the discovery of Middle-Eastern oil has impacted that area today. It's not surprising that when Rome conquered Macedonia in 167 BCE they prohibited the Macedonians from cutting their timber. The Romans were well aware of the role wood had played in their rise to power. Their ban on harvesting wood was a precautionary measure, preventing Macedonia from developing into a maritime power that might rival Rome. It also assured them that the remaining timber would be available to meet Roman needs.

During Pliny's time Italy's forests were nearly stripped of all tree cover. Rome was forced to import timber from across the empire; smelting operations requiring charcoal to produce tools and weapons had to move out of Italy. Those regions in Rome where mining and smelting operations had continued were the most ravaged landscapes in the empire.

Very early in human history Pliny realized that the activities of humankind risked the destruction of forests and eventually all the natural wonders on Earth. He wrote about the massive forests in Germany: *"In the northern region is the fast expanse of the Hercynian Oak Forest, untouched by the ages and coevolving with the world, which surpasses all marvels by its almost immortal destiny."*[2] Romans truly realized the importance of forests for their industries; increasingly they imported wood from northern Europe to meet their needs. Eventually Rome was forced to import timber from areas east of the Mediterranean. Roman expansion into Syria had a detrimental impact on the remaining cedar forests there.

In 118 CE Roman Emperor Hadrian developed a set of rules protecting the cedar forests in Lebanon to slow their destruction. Over the years a strong cultural link had developed between the people and the cedar forests there, a bond so majestic it has survived for centuries—the cedar forests had become their symbol of *eternity*. Throughout the remainder of the Middle East the cedar forests became just a lingering memory of an illustrious past.

When the Middle-Ages came to pass Europeans shifted away from virtual isolation. Western Europe possessed few navigable rivers; extensive wetlands, thick forests and poor roads hindered the transport of goods overland. The push to increase commerce and trade had to be achieved via the sea. Europeans began cashing in their forest preserves to build the ships needed to explore the unknown, expand trade and acquire colonies.[3]

Farther east the Chinese were well ahead of the Europeans on many fronts: technology, shipbuilding, navigation, gunpowder, paper-making and printing. By the 13th century brisk Chinese population growth had driven the construction of housing and factories creating shortages of forest timber. Nonetheless, the Chinese continued expanding their fleet of sea-going vessels. Chinese dealers worked alongside Muslim and Indian traders to create an exchange network extending beyond Southeast Asia to the Indian Ocean in search of unique spices, medicinal herbs and raw materials.

By the 11th century Chinese junks had traveled as far as the Persian Gulf and the Red Sea. Two centuries later China had established regular trade routes between India and East Africa. During the Yuan Dynasty (1271–1368) the Chinese began reaching out to trade with the world beyond, overland on the Silk Road and via ships across the oceans. They extended their global supremacy further by invading Japan and Java.

The Chinese had invented magnetic compasses for use in navigation, two centuries earlier than western societies. When the skies were clear Chinese sailors navigated via the stars using printed manuals with star charts and compass bearings available in China as early as the 13th century. With advances in navigation, ship building and sailing technology China became the preeminent maritime power in the region—the Chinese Navy was unmatched around the world. Scholars have often questioned why Chinese explorers never ventured further than the African coast. Many believe that Chinese rulers had no desire to convert the outside world to their religious beliefs; they thought western civilization had nothing to offer them.

When the Portuguese first arrived on China's southeast coast in 1513, they were viewed as, "*just another bunch of pirates—people with beards, large eyes, long noses. No real threat.*" A 17th century Chinese discourse on navigation declared: "*Coming into contact with barbarian peoples you have nothing more to fear than touching the left horn of a snail. The only things one should really be anxious about are the means of mastery of the waves of the sea—and, worst of all dangers, the minds of those avid for profit and greedy for gain.*" On the other hand, Spain and Portugal chartered expeditions searching for trade partners, the procurement of colonies and the spread of Christianity.

Zheng He was a Muslim eunuch—a man, castrated in his youth to guard women's living areas at an oriental court—who became the commander of the Chinese Navy and ascended through the ranks of the Chinese nobility. By 1402 Zheng He had conducted six exploratory voyages west around the Indian ocean to the coast of Africa. At the time Chinese naval technology was well advanced over that of the Europeans. Zheng He's westward expeditions had been costly but had not produced any significant wealth. The expeditions and China's system of taxation resulted in inflation as high as 1000%. Many of China's scholar-bureaucrats regarded Zheng He's voyages as wasteful, contending the money could be better spent on the construction of roads, canals and granaries. China didn't need to waste money abroad; China was already the all-perfect Center of the Universe. There was a battle within the Imperial court between the eunuchs and mandarins for political power. When the mandarins prevailed, all programs associated with eunuchs—including Zheng He's expeditions—were curtailed. China's age of discovery was followed by the Great Withdrawal.

In 1433 CE decrees were passed prohibiting Chinese from travel abroad; offenders were often punished with decapitation. The Chinese fleet was reduced significantly; it became a crime to build a junk with more than two masts. Espionage was redefined to include making sea voyages in vessels with multiple masts. Overtime the knowledge and skills required to build and navigate large ships dissipated and disappeared.[4]

Europe with its vast coastlines provided ease of navigation along its shores. In order to promote trade, the European powers needed seaworthy vessels capable of transporting goods over long distances and turbulent seas. Venice was the first western Mediterranean city-state to develop a modern fleet of sea vessels. They were able to build vast quantities of superior quality ships for many years to become Europe's preeminent maritime power. By the end of the 15th century Venetians began noticing the early signs of a timber shortage; by 1590 Venice was importing complete ship hulls from Northern Europe. Eventually, the center of maritime endeavors shifted to the North Sea and Atlantic coasts; Venice had lost its position as a preeminent maritime power.[5]

During the 15th and 16th centuries Spain had been developing a colonial empire, extending from the Far East to the Americas. By 1580 the construction of the great Spanish Armada had depleted their forests of trees. In 1490 Portuguese explorer Vasco da Gama sailed around the Cape of Good Hope to reach India by sea. He brought back a cargo of spices netting a huge profit that brought about the establishment of profitable trade routes between Western Europe and the Far East.

The English and Dutch followed the European example and began exploring the seas. Pirates of all stripes routinely raided Spanish trading vessels along Africa's coast; English seafarers traded openly in Spanish territories. Spain was prompted to retaliate. In 1588 Philip II of Spain ordered the Spanish Armada — a fleet of 130 ships — to invade England with the goal of overthrowing the Queen, reversing her decision to make Protestantism England's official religion; preventing English interference in the Spanish Netherlands and eliminating English and Dutch privateering. The invasion utterly failed, and the Armada was completely destroyed, marking the end of Spanish naval supremacy.

The virgin forests in Scandinavia, the Baltics and Germany provided enough timber for England, France and Holland to construct the large seagoing vessels needed to explore the expanding ancient world. Though short of wooden terrain, Great Britain's relatively late entry into the grand colonial competition allowed their meager supply of timber to suffice for a while. It wasn't until the 1620's — the Thirty-Year Wars against France — that symptoms of a wood shortage appeared. England was forced to import wood from Scandinavia, the Baltics and eventually the North American colonies to construct a strong naval fleet.[6]

Halfway through the 18th century all Europe began feeling the impact of a severe wood shortage. Humanity's first energy crisis was impacting the core of global society: the basic needs of cooking food and keeping warm competed with building the warships and trading vessels needed to promote the trade of lucrative goods and wage war.

From the beginning humans have used wood as a primary energy source. The only other viable heat source was coal, discovered in Scotland exposed along the seashore, called *sea-coal*. In select locations humans had mined sea-coal for thousands of years. Coal was first used domestically to produce heat in areas where wood wasn't readily available. The most commonly available coal was unsuitable for smelting iron. The demand for wood, capable of being transformed into charcoal for smelting continued to expand.

Iron was in short supply and expensive; production was dwindling as the wood needed to make charcoal dwindled. England began managing their woodlands using a rotation system of harvesting known as *coppicing*: cutting back the stem of certain broadleaf wood species near the ground and allowing the regrowth of stems from the stump. Yet over time the existing woodlands were unable to supply the charcoal needed to meet the growing demands, especially the iron industry.

At the end of the day, the increasing population in rapidly growing dense settlements caused a shift from using wood for cooking, heating homes and industrial processes to burning coal. This most likely occurred first in China around 1000 BCE, eventually moving westward to the Middle East, Mesopotamia, Europe, England and the Americas as local wood supplies in each area were unable to meet the growing demand: dominoes made of timber falling upon each other, one after the other across the continents and around the world.

———————

Coal is an organic rock containing an excess of carbon by weight. The differing types of coal (listed in order of highest to least carbon content) are: anthracite, bituminous, subbituminous and lignite. Coal with high carbon content is the best and cleanest coal to burn. Scientists estimate that roughly .1% of Earth's crust consists of carbon. Carbon is the primary component of all living cells; capable of forming strong chemical bonds with itself, oxygen, hydrogen and nitrogen. Carbon is lightweight and small in size, allowing enzymes to manipulate carbon molecules. All life-forms require carbon to survive, grow and reproduce. It's a finite resource passing through Earth's ecosystem in many forms, available to living organisms to maintain their balance with atmospheric reactions and in bodies of water. Carbon is an essential element for life on Earth; the principal energy source being consumed by humankind.

When the wood shortage first appeared in England it prompted the changeover to coal. The coal burned in domestic hearths in use at the time was unsuitable for smelting iron; sea-coal had been used mostly by artisans and some industrial processes.

In London increased coal burning raised air pollution levels, causing anxiety and discontent. In 1306 the king of England issued a royal proclamation prohibiting the burning of coal in furnaces; he directed the people to use wood or charcoal. Midway through the 14th century domestic hearths were redesigned to burn coal with lower emissions; domestic coal burning was restored in Britain's coal mining regions. The demand for coal increased gradually within mining districts and in the coastal towns where coal was being shipped to Europe.

In the year 1575 CE in Scotland, Sir George Bruce of Carnock opened the first coal mine capable of extracting coal from under the sea called a *moat pit*. He accomplished this feat by creating an artificial island to off-load the coal in which he bored a 40 ft. shaft, linking two additional drainage and ventilation shafts. Mining from under the sea had never been accomplished before; Sir George Bruce's concept is recognized as one of the industrial wonders of that age. During the 17th century a number of other advances in mining techniques were made: the use of test bores to locate potential coal deposits; using chain pumps driven by water wheels to drain water out of the collieries.

It wasn't until the early 18th century that a process for converting coal into coke was first developed by British ironmaster Abraham Darby I and sons after many years of experimentation. This process was important: it eliminated the need for charcoal (made from wood) to fuel the smelting industry; the coke fuel output was of better quality for smelting iron. As a result, smelting operations were able to move out of the forests; furnace capacities and production rates were increased significantly.

Darby also patented a new sand-casting method capable of casting iron flatware at a much lower cost than Dutch counterparts. In 1708 Darby founded the Bristol Iron Company in the town of Coalbrookdale on the Severn River in close proximity to supplies of low-sulfur coal. He produced iron in a coke-fired furnace, demonstrating coke's low cost and improved efficiency in furnaces much larger than those fueled by charcoal, capable of supporting a heavier batch of iron. Darby was capable of casting high quality iron, thin enough to produce castings for cookware.[7]

In 1712, Thomas Newcomen's invention of the steam engine brought about an entirely new market for iron castings. Later in 1758, Darby's eldest son Abraham Darby II had taken over the family business; he began manufacturing cylinders in production quantities at the Coalbrookdale plant for the new Newcomen engine.[8]

Abraham Darby III was born in Carbondale in 1750, the eldest son of Abraham Darby II by his second wife Abiah Maude. His father passed away when Darby III was just thirteen; he inherited his father's stake in the family iron manufacturing business and began managing operations in Coalbrookdale when he turned eighteen. Over the course of his tenure, young Darby III significantly improved the working conditions of his employees. He purchased farms to grow food for his workers during food shortages; he built them housing, offering higher wages than the local averages.

In 1779 CE, under Darby III's leadership the Bristol Iron Company completed one of the largest cast iron structures of his era: one of the first iron bridges in the world, built over the Severn near Coalbrookdale. The bridge is still intact today serving as a walking bridge, located in the current day community of Ironbridge near Carbondale, England that grew up around the site of the bridge.

In 1776 CE, Darby III married Rebecca Smith of Doncaster. They had seven children, of which only four survived to adulthood. Abraham Darby III died at the youthful age of 39; he was buried in the Quaker burial ground in Coalbrookdale. Both of their sons, Francis and Richard continued on with the family trade at the Coalbrookdale Company, which went on to complete the first high-pressure boiler for a railway locomotive for the English engineer and inventor Richard Trevithick in 1802 CE. The average human life expectancy during the 1750's in England was just 30 years. Of the number of babies born during this era, 150 of every 1000 would die before their first birthday; one out of five mothers would die too.[9]

As the expertise for making coke spread throughout England and Europe, iron production grew appreciably along with the consumption of coal needed to make the coke. With the design modifications to domestic hearths and furnaces, coal became the fuel of choice for the future. The increased coal output required the solution of logistical problems: mining, transport and combustion. In some places deposits of coal were visible at ground level; outcroppings of the black fuel were ready for the taking. When a seam of coal was depleted, miners dug deeper: to 50 meters by the late seventeenth century, and so on. Eventually, deeper pit mines required pumps to remove the water; ventilation shafts had to be provided to haul out the coal. Horses, donkeys, waterwheels and windmills supplied the power; humans labored to do the mining.

The Industrial Revolution began in Britain during the 18th century; it later spread to Europe, North America and Japan, driven by the availability of coal to fuel the steam engine. With coal-fed steam engines powering railways and steamships, international trade expanded over land and water as never before. For most steam engines coal was a cheaper and more efficient fuel than wood. Coal mining was predominant in central and northern England where coal deposits were abundant. The tedious methods of surface coal extraction could not keep up with the increasing demand. As the Industrial Revolution progressed, deep shaft mining became the predominant coal mining process.

In 1800 the innovation of using wooden beams to support mine ceilings was introduced. Other critical factors were providing air circulation for breathing and controlling concentration levels of explosive gases. In the past, fires were burned at the bottom of mines to create currents to circulate the air; the fires were replaced with steam engine driven fans. Miner safety was further improved with the invention of special lamps that burned methane and other dangerous gases harmlessly, yet their illumination was very poor.

It was common practice to use women and children to labor in the mines at a fraction of the cost of men; this practice was abolished in 1842 by English law. The need to procure a secure supply of coal was a major factor leading up to both world wars that would follow. Concerns about energy supplies, especially coal, became political issues regarding the difficult working conditions for miners and how they were treated by owners. At the time, coal was so abundant in Britain that the supply could be stepped up to meet increases in demand. During the period from 1700 to 1830, coal production in the U.K. rose tenfold from 3 to 30 million tons per year. Coal became the fuel of choice that would propel the Industrial Revolution around the world during the 19th and 20th centuries. Coal fueled the steam engines on railroads and steam boats; coal propelled steam turbines that generated electricity, powered lighting and heated buildings. Expanded and reinforced railways were capable of transporting coal across continents, promoting the production of iron in many locations.

The steam engine concept—an aeolipilea: a simple bladeless radial steam turbine that spins when the central water container is heated—was first recorded by Heron of Alexandria during Roman times in the 1st century BCE. Several steam-powered devices were developed later including: a steam turbine during the 16th-century Ottoman Empire in Egypt; Thomas Savery's steam pump in 17th-century England; Thomas Newcomen's atmospheric engine—the first commercial engine using a piston and cylinder—the basic steam engine used until the early 20th century.

Initially, the Newcomen engine was used mostly to pump water out of coal mines. Throughout the Industrial Revolution steam engines slowly replaced water-wheels and windmills. They became the primary power source by late 19th century, maintaining that position until internal combustion engine efficiencies and the steam turbine, ended the age of the steam engine in the 20th century.

Coal remains an important fossil fuel today: powering electric generators and producing coke for smelting metal alloys. Coke is essentially a fuel with high carbon content possessing few impurities. Coke is a solid carbonaceous material derived from the destructive distillation of low-ash, low-sulfur bituminous coal. Coke made from coal is gray, hard and porous.

Coal was the main source of energy powering homes, industry and transportation around the world from the 18th century to the 1950s; it maintains by far—the largest natural reserves of any fossil fuel. Due to its relative low cost and availability: coal continues to be an important power source generating electrical energy. Today most coal is mined in large open pit mines that scrape off the topsoil and mine the coal below. Oil—especially natural gas of late—are increasingly being used as coal alternatives due to issues regarding: the health of miners; strip-mining and mountain-top removal mines that destroy the natural landscape; air pollution; and most importantly—coal's heavy CO_2 contribution to global climate change.[10]

Today, steel and concrete are the predominant materials used to build towering buildings and lengthy bridges. The current global depletion of forests across sizable portions of both the developed and developing world is a new saga, repeated from an earlier time. Currently, the destruction of the world's forests is of major concern. According to the UN about 40% of Central America's forests were destroyed between 1950 and 1980; during the same period Africa lost about 23% of its forests. A range of environmental problems are linked with deforestation: flooding, soil erosion, desertification, declining soil productivity; declining carbon sequestration. While it may seem that these problems are unique to our time, vast areas of Earth were deprived of tree cover by human activity long before the modern ages.[11]

In 2008, global competition grew within the American coal mining industry as some of the mines reached the end of their useful lives. Other coal-producing countries stepped up production, taking a share of traditional U.S. exports. Coal has been the primary source of electrical generation for many years; the decline in price for natural gas due to fracking has made it the cleaner fossil fuel of choice for the future. By the late 20th century coal was being replaced by oil, natural gas, nuclear, wind, water or renewable energy sources. By 2010 coal produced only 40% of the world's energy.[12]

———————————

Thus far, we have explored the most significant historical developments promoting human survival and well-being: production and consumption. At this juncture we begin reviewing some two and a half centuries regarding some of humanity's most incredible ideas and inventions, illustrated by widespread lifestyle changes that are occurring faster each cycle.

I like to think of human production, consumption and waste as consisting of six steps: resource extraction, production, distribution, consumption, disposal and decomposition. Up to this point in history these steps have occurred in relatively close proximity, the exception being goods traded overland via the Silk Road and the seaways, as there was no need to distribute goods; they were usually consumed close to where they were produced. And since most goods consisted of only natural resources, they readily decomposed in the soil. Tools and utensils were built to last; most were capable of being sharpened, repaired or completely recycled.

The First Industrial Revolution was a period of significant and abrupt change, beginning in 1760 and lasting until roughly 1850. It's important because it denotes the initial shift from making handmade goods to products made almost entirely by machine. Other important factors include: increased use of steam power and chemicals in manufacturing processes; the use of machine tools: drills, saws, shears, grinders etc.; the development of the *factory system* — an organized structure of manufacturing.

As the Industrial Revolution began, textiles remained a significant percentage of all goods produced by human hands around the world. As discussed in Chapter 2 the production of textile products involved making thread by spinning raw fibers of wool, flax, cotton or hemp, which were used to produce fabric via processes of felting, knitting, crocheting or weaving. Since textile production required a significant investment in capital and people, it became the prime target for the application of automated machinery and modern production methods.

By the mid-18th century Great Britain was the leader of global commerce with a trading network extending from North America to Africa and India. The Industrial Revolution was the result of significant increases in trade and manufacturing activity around the world, centered in Great Britain, near the source of many of the technical innovations that became its driving force. Accordingly, we will review the changeover from mostly agricultural to manufacturing commerce from Great Britain's perspective because that's where it began.[13]

The Industrial Revolution was a defining moment in human history—affecting most all facets of everyday life. The global population level and average income for individuals experienced high rates of continuous growth. Historians generally agree that the Industrial Revolution is the most significant event in human history since the domestication of plants and animals.[14]

The precipitous mechanization began in Great Britain soon after key inventions were developed that spurred the efficiency of manufacturing. The Industrial Revolution was powered by the steam engine; after 1800 steam power expanded rapidly with increasing fuel efficiencies on the order of 90%. Newer steam engine designs were modified to have rotary instead of linear outputs, more applicable for meeting industrial needs. They also weighed less, providing ease of transport.

The use of coke to fuel iron production increased the size and performance of blast furnaces, lowering costs. Another important development was *hot blast*, a process for preheating the air blown into a blast furnace to increase fuel efficiency. *Rolling* is a metal forming process where metal-stock is passed through rollers, reducing its thickness and making it uniform. Rolling was 15 times faster than hammering wrought iron into shape to accomplish the same task. Machine tools were created to perform specific machining tasks: screw cutting lathes for cutting accurate screw threads into metal; milling machines with rotary cutters to remove material; cylinder boring machines to bore out cylinder walls to desired dimensions.[15]

Regarding textiles, the cotton gin is a machine that separates cotton fiber from its seed, increasing speed and efficiency compared to manual methods. Short cotton fibers are processed into long cotton fibers and used to make a variety of fabrics. The seeds gathered can be used for planting next year's harvest or processed into cottonseed oil.

Either steam or water-power was used to mechanize the spinning of cotton into thread, increasing worker output by a factor of 500. A power loom is a mechanized loom powered by a line shaft (a power-driven rotating shaft for power transmission throughout a production facility), a key development in the industrialization of the weaving process during the early Industrial Revolution. Edmund Cartwright designed the first power loom in 1784 and constructed it the following year. It was refined over the next 47 years until a design by Kenworthy and Bullough made the operation completely automatic, increasing worker output by an additional factor of 40. By1850 there were some 260,000 power looms in operation in England. Belgium followed England to become the second country to embrace increased industrialization; France, Germany, Sweden, Japan and the United States would eventually follow suit.[16]

Before the Industrial Revolution, spinning thread and weaving fabric was typically performed in the home as a cottage industry. The fabrics produced were intended for local domestic consumption. The system was called a *putting-out system* where home-based workers labored under contract to merchant sellers who often supplied their raw materials. Farm families typically produced the fabrics. Most often the women did the spinning and the men performed the weaving. Roughly 4 to 8 spinners were required to supply enough thread to meet the needs of one weaver. During the day wives and children took care of household chores and would spin thread as they were able; meanwhile the men worked the fields. In the evening women would spin more thread while the men weaved it into fabric.[17]

Amid all the technological developments, skilled laborers were being replaced with machines on a scale humankind had never experienced. For example, early in 18th century British cloth was noncompetitive with cloth made in India; Great Britain's equivalent labor rate was five times India's labor costs. In the early 1700s, the British government passed *the Calico Acts* enacting a tariff to protect their linen and wool industries from the growing imports of Indian fabric.[18]

James Watt was working as an instrument maker and repairman at the University of Glasgow in 1759 when he first learned about steam power. Watt was captivated by the concept; he set out to learn all he could about the current theories, the operation of existing designs. The university owned a small working model of the existing Newcomen engine that was nonfunctional. Watt inspected the machine and was able to repair it. He got the engine running again and stood back; he watched in dismay at the poor efficiency he was observing. After studying the device further, he concluded that nearly 80% of the steam created was being wasted by constantly reheating the main cylinder. In the Newcomen design each power stroke began with a cold-water spray that condensed the steam, cooling the cylinder walls. The cylinder had to be reheated in order to accept steam again, yet steam was the cylinder's only source of heat. When the steam valve opened again most of the steam condensed on the cylinder walls, requiring a considerable time before the cylinder warmed up and steam began refilling the cylinder. Watt improved the engine's performance by providing a separate cold-water cylinder alongside the power cylinder. When the induction stroke was complete a valve opened between the two cylinders; the steam entering the cylinder condensed inside the cold cylinder creating a vacuum pulling more steam into the cylinder until the steam had condensed. When the valve closed the cycle continued as it would have on a conventional Newcomen engine. Since the power cylinder maintained its operational temperature throughout, the engine was ready for the power stroke as soon as the piston returned to its starting position. An insulating jacket was placed around the cylinder to help maintain the cylinder temperature.

Six years later in 1765, Watt had produced a working model of his modified steam engine. He continued improving his engine working tirelessly to refine the engine components until releasing his design in 1774. Since portions of Watt's design could be retrofitted to existing Newcomen engines, they could be modified in the field to include any of the new features as desired.

James Watt never ceased refining his steam engine. He increased the speed of the operating cycle using governors and automatic valves; designed double-acting pistons to improve efficiency; provided a variety of rotary power takeoffs and many other improvements. Watt's steam engine technology enabled the widespread commercial use of stationary steam engines around the world.[19]

Material processes were another key area where creativity and new technologies worked together in concert to create the Industrial Revolution. Building methods were enhanced with the development of manufacturing chemicals including sulfuric acid and sodium carbonate. These chemicals were important because they prompted other inventions, replacing many small-scale operations with procedures more easily controlled and cost-effective. Sodium carbonate was used to produce glass, textiles, soap and paper. The early uses for sulfuric acid were rust removal from iron and steel, and to bleach fabrics.

In 1800 the development of bleaching powder (calcium hypochlorite) by Scottish chemist Charles Tennant revolutionized the use of bleaches in the textile industry by significantly reducing the time required—from months to days compared to the processes in use—requiring textiles soaked with alkali or sour milk to be exposed repeatedly to the sun in bleach fields. At the time, Tennant's factory at St. Rollox, North Glasgow was the largest chemical plant in the world. In 1860, the focus on chemical innovation shifted to dyestuffs where Germany had taken a leadership role by promoting a robust chemical industry. Aspiring young chemists flocked to German universities to discover the latest techniques.[20]

In the year 1843 the world's first underwater tunnel—the Thames Tunnel—was completed; an impossible feat without Joseph Aspdin, a British bricklayer turned builder who patented the process for making Portland cement in 1824. This was an important development supporting all types of construction during the Industrial Revolution and thereafter. Portland cement is manufactured by a process called sintering: producing a solid material using heat or pressure, without melting the material to liquefaction. A mixture of clay and limestone is sintered to about 2,552 °F (1,400°C) and then ground into a fine powder to make Portland cement. Portland cement can be mixed with water, sand and gravel to produce concrete.[21]

Gas-lighting was another major Industrial Revolution invention: the production of a gaseous fuel manufactured by a process of gasification of coal in furnaces; its purification, storage and distribution. The first gas lighting utilities were established in London between 1812 and 1820. Gas lighting allowed factories and stores to maintain longer hours; nightlife flourished in cities; streets and businesses were lit up on a larger scale than ever before.[22]

Early in the 19th century a new process for producing glass called *the cylinder process* was developed in Europe capable of manufacturing sheet glass. By 1832 the process was used by the *Chance Brothers* to produce the first sheets of glass; they became the leading producers of windows and plate glass. The capability to produce large glass panes without interruption prompted a Renaissance in building design.[23]

Nicolas-Louis Robert was born in Paris in 1761; he was frail and plagued by persistent health issues. Feeling he was a burden to his family he joined the French Army and ended up serving in the Caribbean during the American Revolutionary War. After the war he worked for a paper-mill owned by the Saint-Léger Didot family in France that supplied paper to the

Ministry of Finance to manufacture currency. Robert was driven to resolve numerous mechanical issues with the papermaking process. During his tenure there he developed a unique method for producing paper as one continuous sheet, utilizing a specially woven fabric mesh to contain the moving liquid pulp. In 1799 he was granted a patent for his design that resulted in a dispute with the Didot family over its ownership. He eventually accepted the 25,000 francs that the Didot family offered to buy the design. The Fourdrinier paper machine took the name of the eventual financiers of the project. While Nicholas-Louis Robert's design has undergone significant improvements and variations over the years, it remains the principal method for producing paper today. His design concept illustrated novel design techniques that resonated around the world, prompting new processes for continuously rolling iron, steel and many other continuous production operations.

Towards the end of the 19th century the Fourdrinier paper machine experienced continuous development in England, while Nicholas Louis Robert pursued a quiet life in France. In 1811 the first paper-making machine was installed in France; Robert was 50 years old and ready to leave the paper making business. He opened up a small school in Vernouillet near Paris where he worked for little pay as a teacher; he never enjoyed the acclaim or the financial benefit of his revolutionary idea. He died broken-down and penniless on August 8, 1828. In 1912 a monument was erected in Robert's memory.[24]

The revolution of British agriculture in the early 18th century is another key contributor to the Industrial Revolution. Significant improvements in agricultural productivity allowed workers to labor in other sectors of the economy. The Dutch plow and the seed drill were new devices that revolutionized agriculture; both used key components made of iron. Jethro Tull invented an improved seed drill in 1701, and a mechanical seeder which distributed seeds evenly across a plot of land and planted them at the desired depth. Tull's seed drill was expensive and not very dependable, but it was a step in the right direction. Lower priced, more reliable seed drills were available by the mid-18th century. The Rotherham plough of

1730—invented by Disney Stanyforth and Joseph Foljambewas— was the first commercially successful plough designed with iron components, a significant improvement over traditional ploughs. The basic frame was constructed of wood similar to standard ploughs, but the fittings and cutting blade were made of iron; the moldboard and ploughshare were covered with iron plates. It was lighter than traditional ploughs and easily worked by a pair of horses.[25]

In 1784 Andrew Meikle invented the first threshing machine to remove seeds from the stalks and husks of grain crops. Hand threshing was accomplished with a device called a flail, consisting of a longer stick of wood attached by a short chain to a shorter stick. The larger stick is held and swung, causing the shorter stick to smash into a pile of grain crops (wheat, barley, rye etc.) loosening the husks; threshing grain by hand consumed roughly a quarter of the total time spent on farm labor.

On the original threshing machines, grain was well separated from the straw but the straw, chaff and grain all ended up in a pile that still had to be sorted out. The addition of rakes to guide the straw and fanners to funnel and separate the seed, all driven by the same source—manually, horse or steam power—allowed the process of threshing, shaking and separating seed from the chaff to be performed together, leaving the grain separate and ready for market.[26]

The response to the progressive use of technology improving the efficiency of farm tasks came in the form of the Swing Riots of 1830 by agricultural workers in southern and eastern England. It all began with the destruction of threshing machines in the Elham Valley area. By early December the riot had spread throughout southern England and East Anglia. Farm workers were protesting agricultural mechanization and harsh working conditions. The protesters attacked the hated threshing machines which had displaced so many workers; they rioted over low wages and the required tithes (a tax) paid to the churches. They destroyed workhouses and barns; they burned hay stacks and maimed cows.[27]

Coal mining began in Britain well before the Industrial

Revolution, especially in South Wales. Coal was pit mined in shallow pits that followed a coal seam along the surface; the pits were abandoned when all the coal was extracted. Coal was also mined in *drift mines* driven into the side of a hill. Shaft mining below the surface was practiced in certain terrain; the main problem was removing water. The introduction of the steam engine and pump facilitated the removal of the water, enabling shafts to be dug deeper and more coal could be extracted. Shaft coal mining was very dangerous due to the presence of firedamp: the flammable gases found in coal mines. Firedamp flare-ups could set off coal dust explosions. Casualties from rock falls grew throughout the 19th century; working conditions for the miners were very poor.[28]

By 1750 the British had established over 1000 miles of navigable rivers throughout the country: removing obstructions, straightening curves, widening, deepening and building locks. These canals and waterways allowed goods to be transported far inland, inexpensively: a horse could pull a barge ten times heavier than the equivalent load overland. A national network of canals was completed by 1820.

The organization and techniques used to complete England's canal system provided an example for the construction of the railway system that would follow. The Manchester Ship Canal—the last canal constructed in Great Britain—opened in 1894 making Manchester a seaport. At the time it was the largest ship canal in the world. When the new railway system was complete a few years later, the canal system was supplanted as a profitable commercial enterprise. The Manchester Port never achieved the commercial success projected; the new railway system was quicker and cheaper; the canal system's time had already passed. The canal network, the surviving mills and buildings are the most enduring features of the early Industrial Revolution seen in Great Britain today.[29]

Up until the 19th century, chronic hunger and malnutrition was the reality for most of the world's population. Life expectancies ranged between 35 and 40 years in Europe, 45-50 years in the United States. While agricultural technologies and techniques had increased the available food supply, the population had expanded as well. Overall, the manufacturing efficiencies of the Industrial Revolution had little impact on basic food prices.

Population growth was strong in newer industrial and manufacturing centers. Housing quickly became an issue as unemployed agricultural workers moved into the towns and cities looking for work. There wasn't enough capital to build them adequate housing; the lower income newcomers crowded into the already overpopulated slums. Fresh water, sanitation and public health services were inadequate; death rates in the cities were high, especially among infants. Many young adults were afflicted with tuberculosis (*consumption*).

British consumers enjoyed the decreasing in prices for clothing and household articles, especially: cast iron cooking utensils, cooking stoves and space heaters. Watches and household clocks became affordable to the growing middle class as well as the most favored goods: coffee, tea, sugar, tobacco and chocolate. Tableware in the form of china and porcelain were more common features on dining tables.

Historical studies show that Great Britain's population experienced little growth during the first half of the 18th century; its population more than doubled between 1750 and 1850. Europe's population had increased from around 100 million in 1700 to 400 million by 1900.[30]

Great Britain experienced high levels of air pollution during the Industrial Revolution prompting the passage of the first environmental laws by mid-19th century. Britain's environmental movement was in response to the increasing smoke pollution in the atmosphere. The materialization of immense factories and the simultaneous growth in coal consumption promoted unprecedented pollution levels in manufacturing centers. In addition to the coal-smoke emissions, harmful chemicals in the form of gases were being emitted from those factories using sulfuric acid, sodium carbonate, bleaching powder and chemical dyes.

The large volume of industrial chemical discharges added to the increasing amounts of untreated human waste in streams and rivers. The first significant environmental laws were passed in Great Britain in 1863; the Alkali Acts specifically regulated the harmful pollution of gaseous hydrochloric acid given off by the Leblanc process used to produce soda ash. An Alkali inspector and four sub-inspectors were appointed to address the pollution.[31]

During the early 19th century the manufactured gas industry expanded in many British cities. These gas companies used processes that produced highly toxic effluents that were dumped directly into the sewers and rivers. Many lawsuits were filed against them which they usually lost; they modified their practices only for the worst offenses. The City of London repeatedly indicted gas companies for polluting the Thames River and poisoning the fish; eventually Parliament would write company charters to regulate toxicity.

Local environmental experts and organizers in dense manufacturing areas took up the task of measuring the levels of environmental degradation and pollution; they initiated grass-roots movements to demand reforms. The highest priorities were usually applied to water and air pollution. The Coal Smoke Abatement Society was formed in Great Britain in 1898, making it one of the oldest environmental non-governmental organizations in the world.[32]

5

Eternal Combustion

The Second Industrial Revolution was another period of rapid innovation—1870 to 1914—prompted by key developments that occurred earlier: the invention of the Bessemer process to produce steel; the use of interchangeable parts for manufacturing. The broad and speedy expansion of so many new technologies was predominant in Great Britain, Germany and the United States. We will review the Second Industrial Revolution mostly from the North American perspective.

Railroad lines crisscrossed convoluted terrain maps extending throughout England and Europe. Steam powered machinery had replaced manual labor in many industries; iron and steel production increased in volume and quality. As companies grew in size and scope new methods of organization and operation were created and continuously improved. Advanced manufacturing techniques provided larger metal pipe sizes resolving many flow-capacity issues in larger cities: water and sewer systems; natural gas supplies for home heating and cooking.

The progression of railways and telegraph lines—infant Internet—provided the transfer of knowledge and ideas within countries and across the seas. Designs for generating and transmitting electrical power throughout cities were tested in selected manufacturing sectors; the age of telecommunication via the telephone was born. And then suddenly the focus shifted drastically—people across the globe prepared for a world at war billed as *the Great War*—even before it started.[1]

After the American Civil War and reconstruction, the U.S. economy began picking up speed again. By 1848, America had fulfilled its manifest destiny with the acquisition of new territories: Louisiana (1803), Florida (1819), Texas (1845), Oregon (1846) and the Mexican Session (1848).[2] The fledgling country overflowed with natural resources, capital investment, an increasing labor supply—European immigrants and emancipated African Americans—to fill out the workforce with an expanding market for manufactured goods.

Economic activity across America and around the world was localized before the Second Industrial Revolution. Global trade was accomplished through a system of bartering without the exchange of money. Railways, canals and steamboats joined distant local communities to connect with larger regional markets to trade their goods. The revolution in transporting people, information and financing opened up new opportunities for agricultural and manufactured goods to be marketed globally on credit.[3]

In America steam powered railways were still in their infancy; the country's roadways were limited and difficult. Water was the primary method used to transport heavy goods over long distances. The Mississippi and Hudson rivers were the most prominent natural inland seaways connecting with seaports located in New Orleans and New York, respectively. Having heard about the successful canal building in Great Britain, it was natural for Americans to pursue ways of extending these natural waterways further inland.

Between 1817 and 1825 the Erie Canal was constructed, connecting Lake Erie to Oneida Lake in upstate New York, and onto the Hudson River and New York City. During the construction some 9,000 laborers toiled digging the 4-feet deep and 40-foot wide canal mostly by hand, with occasional support from draft animals and explosives.

Traffic along the canal supported farms and industries, providing a way to market their goods along the canal path and beyond, through the seaport of New York. Farm products produced in the American and Canadian west could connect via the Erie Canal and across the Great Lakes; consumer goods from overseas and local manufacturers flowed along the canal on the return trip from New York. Smaller towns including Rochester, Syracuse and Utica housed the canal workers and attracted new industries, promoting their growth to become larger cities. By 1850 Rochester had developed into a key flour milling region; later it also became a leading manufacturer of men's clothing. The canal brought together the people and their goods with those in the cities sprouting up along the canal way, as well as people from afar. Many incoming immigrants heading further inland traveled the canal via steamships from New York to Albany, by train and canal boats to Buffalo, across the Great Lakes to Chicago or Milwaukee. The 363-mile span of the Erie Canal was not only a technological achievement, it was also a commercial success. Ten years later the added traffic prompted new construction to widen the canal; by 1918 the canal had been widened again, twice.

In fact, the old Erie Canal path resides about 50 feet from my front window as I sit here banging away on my keyboard. The Barge Canal that replaced it still operates about a mile to the north of here. Sadly, little barge traffic remains; mostly pleasure boats of all sizes and shapes travel the widened Barge Canal today. Interstate railroads and the New York State Thruway run alongside much of the old canal path that connected with the Hudson River to the east; passing through Syracuse, Rochester and Buffalo to the west. Rows of tandem tractor trailers roar across the overhead bridges of the NYS Thruway, spewing out smoke as they barrel along the highway in both directions.[4]

In Middle America, the infamous Mississippi River is a natural water highway to the ocean via the port of New Orleans. France, Spain, and the U.S. had all once claimed New Orleans as theirs. Since its inception the people there have evolved a unique culture:

music, food, language and customs. Much like New York City, New Orleans exported mostly farm goods from the American Midwest; manufactured goods flowed in from Great Britain and Europe. Prior to the availability of steam-powered ships, keelboats were used for river transport that were capable of travel up or downstream via sails, hand-rowing, poles or hauled by tow-lines.

Over the period from 1820 to 1890 the port of New Orleans had developed as both seaport and river-port: a critical link between mid-America and Europe. By 1829: grain, cotton, pork and furs from the West and Midwest were being transported down the Mississippi to New Orleans for consumption in the American South or loaded onto Packet Ships for shipment overseas.

The rise of steam powered riverboats brought increased up-river trade, opening up the Midwest to settlers and goods. By 1850 New Orleans was the second busiest port in the U.S. —fourth largest in the world. The Ohio River provided a natural water extension from the Mississippi River to Cincinnati, Ohio. Cincinnati was a leading commercial and manufacturing city at the time—almost four times the size of Chicago.[5]

Pre-Civil War Cincinnati had supplied the south with flour, whiskey, manufactured goods and pork. The city's location also profited from goods shipped upriver by canal destined for Ohio. After the Civil War, the U.S. government promoted agricultural and industrial development by establishing high tariffs to protect fledgling enterprises.

The government offered the railroad companies land to encourage the construction of new railways. In 1830, the majority of the Chickasaw, Choctaw, Creek, Seminole and Cherokee tribes were living east of the Mississippi. President Andrew Jackson pressed for passage of the Indian Removal Act passed to implement the federal government's policy towards the Indian populations, which called for moving Native American tribes living east of the Mississippi River to lands west of the river to the area that would become Oklahoma. The U.S. Army was given the task of displacing Native Americans from their occupied homelands, often land that was most desirable to incoming ranchers, farmers and mining companies. Many thousand Native Americans died as they traveled on *the Trail of Tears*. The combination of manufacturing, mining and railroad construction that resulted prompted the precipitous growth of the American economy.[6]

The Second Industrial Revolution improved living standards and the purchasing power of people around the world; the new technologies created played an ever-increasing role in the daily lives of working and middle-class societies. Between 1870 and 1920, roughly 11 million Americans moved off their farms and into cities; more than twice that number had emigrated from overseas. By 1913, the U.S. was producing about a third of the world's industrial output, at the time more than the total production of Great Britain, France and Germany combined. For the first time in American history the census of 1920 showed that more Americans lived in cities than on farms.

The inventions made during the Second Industrial Revolution were interconnected: new rail lines prompted the spread of telegraph lines and later telephone service; Bessemer and open-hearth steel processes fostered high-rise building designs and elevators; the development of electric light, the typewriter, phonograph, motion pictures and the electric generator all led to the creation of home refrigerators and washing machines. The emerging technologies and the moving segments of society changed the pace of everyday life, the manner in which people worked and how they lived. When considering the rapid change of lifestyles and people's thoughts about their future, this period was perhaps as significant as any other era in human history.[7]

Ancient humans had utilized lamps as simple as sea shells filled with animal fat and a wick, to provide night lighting as far back as the Stone Age. Oil lamps found in Egypt, Greece and Rome were made of stone, terracotta, bronze, stone and alabaster in the form of an open dish with a wick to prolong burning. Olive oil was the primary fuel for oil lamps in addition to beeswax, sesame, fish or whale oil. The open dish design was eventually enclosed with a spout that housed a wick. This design was manufactured in production quantities on a pottery wheel.

During the 18th century a Swiss Chemist named Aime Argand invented the *Argand Lamp* with a container for oil and a cylindrical wick, providing a larger flame surface with a glass tube chimney around the flame to direct the draft; features that provided a stronger flame and safer lamps. The Argand Lamp was widely used until the middle 19th century when it was replaced with the kerosene lamp.[8]

Accompanying all the developments in conjunction with the steam engine, gears and mechanical devices had magnified the need for lubricants to reduce the friction between moving metal parts. Previous to the availability of crude oil, lubricants were extracted from animal fats (butter, fish oil, shark liver, whale blubber and seals) and vegetable seeds and oils (walnuts, almonds, sesame, olives, castor and flax).[9]

In 1859, George Bissell and Edwin Drake constructed a specialized rig to drill for oil at a site located along Oil Creek near Titusville, Pennsylvania. The Drake well is considered the first commercial well purposely designed and drilled to search for oil. Other wells that had struck oil earlier were drilling for salt brine or water when they accidently struck oil. The Drake partners were excited about their oil find; they hired a Yale chemistry professor named Benjamin Silliman to test a sample from the site. He concluded that the oil could be readily distilled into oil products, including lamp oil. The ultimate success of the Drake well and public awareness of the event attracted investors for the development of oil well drilling, refining and marketing systems. Kerosene was the main oil product in demand in the U.S. during the latter 19th century; it was increasingly being used to replace whale oil as the preferred fuel for oil lamps. The Drake well's success sponsored additional drilling to establish a petroleum supply sufficient to support future applications.[10]

As the Drake well was being drilled in Titusville, French engineer J. J. Etienne Lenoir was perfecting his design of the *first dependable internal combustion engine capable of being powered by gasoline.* By

1859, Lenoir had experimented with electricity to design a system that would create an electrical spark to ignite combustion in his new engine design. He used an induction coil: a transformer accepting a small DC voltage input that outputs a high voltage spike to create a spark and ignite the gaseous oxygen/fuel mixture in the cylinder. Etienne's first prototype was converted from an old steam engine to burn coal gas; the fuel was not compressed before ignition. When operating, the engine performed quietly with a power stroke in each direction. The engine suffered from poor efficiency due to the lack of compressing the fuel prior to ignition.[11] Nevertheless, in September of 1860 Scientific American advised that the Parisian newspaper *Cosmos* had pronounced that *the Steam Age was over*.[12]

Lenoir completed a second prototype engine later in 1863. He mounted it onto a three-wheeled carriage; it was essentially a horseless wagon mounted on a tricycle. The engine utilized a simple carburetor design and produced an output of 1.5 horsepower; it was fueled by igniting liquid hydro-carbon (petroleum). To demonstrate his design, Lenoir drove his *Hippo-mobile* the roughly seven miles from Paris to Joinville-le-Pont and back in roughly three hours, the natural walking speed for a human adult. By 1865, 143 of Lenoir's engines had been sold in Paris; production by Reading Gas Works for Lenoir Gas Engines in London had begun. Lenoir's engine was used mostly as a stationary prime-mover to power printing presses, water pumps and machine tools. After sustained use the engines became noisy and rough; they had a tendency to overheat and seize up if insufficient cold water was applied. Ultimately, Lenoir was unhappy with the performance of his machine; he sold the patent and focused on designing a similar engine for small boats.

Less than 500 Lenoir engines ranging from 6 to 20 horsepower were ever built. They represent the first step towards a culture where internal combustion engines ran the world. In 1870 Lenoir was granted French citizenship for his assistance during the Franco-Prussian War. In 1881 he was awarded the *Légion d'honneur* for developments he made regarding the telegraph. Despite his great success, Lenoir spent his later years impoverished. He died on August 4, 1900 near Paris in the town of La Varenne-Sainte-Hilaire.[13]

———————

Nicolaus Otto is the German design engineer of the prototype engine that became the modern internal combustion engine in use today. He was born on June 14, 1832. In the autumn of 1860 when Etienne Lenoir was finalizing his design, Otto and his brother were reading about the gas engine built by him in France. They built a copy of the Lenoir engine and applied for a patent of their design copy; it was rejected by the Prussian Ministry of Commerce. Then Otto and his brother pursued methods to improve the fuel efficiency of the Lenoir engine, its key deficiency. When they learned of the idea of compressing the fuel before ignition, they modified their Lenoir engine copy to include compression. The test unit operated for a few minutes before blowing up. Later in 1862 they learned about the concept of a four-stroke engine described by inventor Alphonse Beau; their prototype of this improved design concept failed as well.

Early in 1864, Otto was seeking investors when he met Eugen Langen, the son of a sugar industrialist. They formed a partnership to become the first company to focus completely on the design and manufacture of internal combustion engines. Later that year the first Otto/Langen engine was released; it possessed twice the fuel efficiency of previous similar designs. The new engine was classified as an atmospheric, free-piston design: the ignition of the fuel created a vacuum; atmospheric pressure returned the piston. The Otto/Langen engine was a commercial success, producing some 634 engines by 1875. However, the engine's power output was only 3 horsepower; it required 10 to 13 feet of headroom for normal operation.

Later in 1864, Otto revisited the four-stroke engine that had previously failed in 1862. Otto and his team, including Franz Rings and Herman Schumm were able to determine a method for layering the fuel mixture into the cylinder, allowing the fuel to burn successively instead of exploding. Otto called this concept a layered charge. This allowed for a more controlled combustion of the fuel while extending the push of the cylinder. In May of 1876, Otto and his team completed the first commercially successful compressed-charge internal combustion engine. The Rings-Schumm engine used four cycles to create power. It was released for sale and became an instant success. The development of what came to be known as the Otto Cycle engine took 14 years to develop; it occurred nearly 15 years after the discovery of oil in Titusville, Pa. While the development of the internal combustion engine would promote the use of gasoline fuel refined from crude oil, it would take many years before the mutual reliance of the oil and auto industries would be established.[14]

The period from 1869 to 1900 was marked by scientific and industrial innovations as automobile developers reduced engine size while increasing output power. Petroleum engineers worked at improving the drilling, refining, production and transportation of oil products. Samuel Kier was a native of southwestern Pennsylvania and the first American to refine crude oil. In the mid-1840's Kier owned a business that drilled for salt water brine that would sometimes inadvertently strike oil. At the time the drillers viewed the oil simply as a nuisance that had to be cleaned up. Yet Kier was a businessman; he believed he could find something useful about the oil that was popping up in his salt wells.

Kier's first idea was to burn the oil to light up his salt works operation at night. The burning crude oil gave off a terrible smell and lots of smoke, but it was cheaper than the alternatives: whale oil. Kier actually tried bottling crude oil and selling it as a medicinal product. Half pint bottles of Kier's Petroleum sold for 50 cents, for internal consumption or for use as a rubbing compound.

Next, Kier pursued ways to market oil as an inexpensive lamp oil. He had an oil sample analyzed by a chemist; he determined that the oil could be used as an illuminant if it could be refined further. Kier experimented with distillation and by 1851 he was producing a lamp oil product called Carbon Oil that when burned, gave off little odor or smoke with a selling price $1.50 per gallon.

Eternal Combustion

Samuel Kier joined forces with John T. Kirkpatrick to create the first American petroleum refinery in Pittsburgh, Pennsylvania. He started with a small one or two-barrel still; by 1854 he had a larger five-barrel still in operation. When the Drake Well struck oil near Titusville, oil inundated the market which prompted the startup of seven new oil refineries in Pittsburgh. By 1870, there were a total of 58 refineries operating in Pittsburg.[15]

The process of refining crude oil has changed a lot over the last century. Crude oil is a mixture of many hydrocarbons. The first step in refining oil is called fractional distillation: a process that separates the various oil components for further refinement. The oil enters a high-pressure steam boiler that vaporizes oil at 1112°F. The vapor enters a pipe at the bottom of a distillation column. The distillation column is an elevated tank containing trays to capture the various hydrocarbons. The vapors cool as they rise, condensing at their boiling points in the trays in the column. The liquid by-products flow through pipes and are collected in separate tanks. The by-products include: gases, naphtha, gasoline, kerosene, diesel fuel, lubricating oils, heavy oils, and other materials which are conveyed to other areas in the refinery for further processing.

Oil has ten uniquely different end products: asphalt; diesel fuel; fuel oil used for heating; gasoline for internal combustion engines; kerosene used as heating oil or jet fuel; liquefied petroleum gas—a mixture of gases used in heating appliances including aerosol propellants and refrigerants; lubricating oil; paraffin wax; bitumen; and assorted petrochemicals.[16]

Oil impacts all aspects of human life. Pipelines, railroads, tankers and trucks transport crude oil to refineries where it's transformed into the products, we use daily. Today, crude oil is refined all over the world. The world's largest oil refinery is currently the Jamnagar Refinery (Reliance Industries) in Jamnagar, India with daily production levels of 1,240,000 barrels per day. Most of the oil industry's largest refineries are located in Asia and South America. Yet, the practice of refining oil began in the United States; oil continues to be a vital part of the American economy.[17]

The Wright brothers were the inventors of the first airplane heavier than air and capable of sustained flight. They had spent years studying the primary concepts regarding airplane aeronautics prior to their first successful powered flight. Their story begins when the brothers started a print shop using a printing press Orville had built with Wilbur's help. From there they opened up a bicycle repair and sales shop and proceeded to manufacture their own bicycle brand in 1896. They used profits from the bicycle shop to fund their burgeoning interests in manned flight, driven by newspaper and magazine articles on the endeavors of glider pilots, most notably Germany's Otto Lilienthal's experimental flights.[18]

During 1896, three events occurred that left lasting impressions on the Wright brothers: Samuel Langley's successful flight of an unmanned steam powered fixed wing model aircraft; Octave Chanute's group-tests of several glider types along the shore of Lake Michigan; the death of Otto Lilienthal when he crashed his glider. They later cited Lilienthal's death as the event that had prompted their most solemn pursuit of manned flight.

The Wright brothers viewed the problem of manned flight as threefold: engine design, wing shape and pilot control of the flight. They felt sufficiently knowledgeable to proceed except for the issue of optimum pilot control of the flight. In October of 1899, British aeronaut Percy Pilcher was killed in another hang-gliding crash, emphasizing the need for reliable pilot control for safe and successful flight. Despite Lilienthal's fate, the brothers favored his strategy of practicing gliding to master the art of control before attempting motor-driven flight; they also had concluded that his method of shifting body weight to provide balance and control was inadequate.[19]

They experimented with new designs using trial runs on their glider, proving them out with data collected from their homemade wind tunnel. Their results inspired the design and construction of wings and propellers more efficient than all previous designs. While previous investigators believed pilots would be unable to respond quickly to abrupt air turbulent changes, they pursued airplane designs that possessed inherent stability—the Wright brothers favored a design that gave the pilot complete control. They viewed airplane stability from three points of view: vertical rotation (the airplane nose rotating up or down) called pitch; rotating left or right called yaw (the airplane body rotating right or left); airplane rolling over called roll (picture the airplane body spinning on its axis). The brothers proposed a concept they called three-axis control: pitch control with adjustable horizontal rear flaps; directing yaw with vertical rear flaps; regulating roll with a horizontal flap on each side of the airplane on the main wing.[20]

The first flight of the aircraft *Wright Flyer I* took place on December 17, 1903 on North Carolina's Outer bank, four miles south of the small town of Kitty Hawk. In the years that followed the brothers worked at perfecting the plane's basic design into a more practical flying machine. Over the period from 1904 to 1905, the Wright brothers completed the development of a fixed wing aircraft capable of pilot control to steer the aircraft to maintain its equilibrium. Their three-axis control method became the standard for all fixed wing aircraft.[21]

Economic growth was extraordinary and yet unstable during the Second Industrial Revolution. In 1873 the world economy experienced a harsh depression, followed by a deep recession in 1897. Businesses around the globe competed intensely with each other. The largest corporations battled to swallow up entire industries; only those enterprises capable of exploiting the latest technological innovations were able to generate high growth and profitability.

During the last quarter of the 19th century designs for horseless carriages were being pursued by inventors and entrepreneurs around the world. After the development of the Otto four-stroke engine back in 1876, a multitude of technologies were being proposed by prospective automobile producers across the globe. Steam, electric and gasoline powered automobiles all vied for position along with competing vehicle body and structure styles, production materials, methods of control and drive-transfer (chain or drive-shaft). With a variety of automobile concepts flooding the market, new development extended beyond these designs to include: oil exploration and drilling methods; refinery processes; the creation of heat tolerant mineral lubricants; the provision of good and sufficient roads to drive on so people could travel to the places they wished to go.[22]

In 1885 Karl Benz had developed a gasoline fueled automobile, powered by a single cylinder four-stroke engine, considered a *first production vehicle* since Benz had produced a number of identical copies.[23] Henry Ford began manufacturing and selling the Ford Motor Company's Model-A in 1903. Ford's Model-T became the first mass-produced automobile in 1908. The Model-T was designed and manufactured to be affordable for the average consumer; by 1927 Ford had produced over 15,000,000 Model-T automobiles.

Nearing the conclusion of the Second Industrial Revolution, most people's perspectives had shifted to the prospects of a world at war. New industries and technologies provided advanced weaponry and machinery capable of being produced quickly: transportable machine guns, chlorine gas, flame throwers, zeppelins, airplanes, torpedoes and tanks. Airplanes were used mostly to scout enemy positions but some were equipped with guns. The tank had been developed by the British late in the war; it was the first tank ever used on the Western Front to break through the fortified German trenches. Mass production provided a supply of weapons and war machines manufactured faster than any time before: trucks, planes and jeeps were all mass produced. The performance of existing weapons was greatly improved: rifles, pistols, grenades and submarines. The new weapons combined with older war tactics set the stage for a killing capacity that would shock the world.[24]

World War I began in August of 1914. It continued until the 11th hour of the 11th day of the 11th month of 1918. It is still ranked as one of the largest wars in human history, involving some 70 million armed forces. Some 9 million armed forces were killed along with 6 million civilians. The 19th century technology advancements had increased casualty rates of both the fighting forces and civilians. It was one of the deadliest wars in human history, triggering key geopolitical transformations and promoting revolution in many of the countries involved. Instead of being the war to end all wars, the peace treaty signed to end WWI had sown the seeds for all future wars. The Second World War would follow just 21 years later.[25]

Towards the end of WWI humans around the world experienced the dreaded pandemic called the Spanish Flu. An estimated 20 to 40 million people throughout the world died of the disease, including roughly 675,000 Americans. The average estimate of 30 million Spanish flu deaths plus the roughly 15 million people killed during the war, then 45 million extra fatalities occurred during a seven-year period out of an estimated global human population of 1.8 billion, roughly 2.5% of the global human population at the time.[26]

The U.S. stock market enjoyed unparalleled growth during the 1920s, peaking in August of 1929 during a period of irrational speculation. Stock prices had risen well beyond their true value; overall production was down and unemployment was rising. Wages were low and debt levels were high with a surplus of large bank loans awaiting liquidation.

Stock prices began declining in September of 1929. On October 18 stocks began a steep decline. By October 24—Black Thursday—investors began to panic; almost 13 million shares of stock were traded by end of day. The market rebounded slightly the next day as the big banks and investment companies tried to tamp down the crisis by purchasing large blocks of stocks. When the market opened the following Monday the stock prices went into a free-fall. Black Tuesday hit Wall Street like a speeding freight train; investors traded some 16,410,030 shares on the New York Stock Exchange in one day. Thousands of investors lost everything; billions of dollars were lost. At the end of the day, America and the rest of the industrialized world began a spiral downward into a deep and dark place called the Great Depression.[27]

After Black Tuesday, quarter by quarter the economy crept

lower as prices, profits and employment all fell. By 1932 unemployment had reached 23.6%; it peaked at 25% early in 1933. That year drought continued to spread across the Nation's bread-basket. Farmers and businesses defaulted on loans causing some 5,000 banks to close their doors. Hundreds of thousands of Americans lost their homes; across the nation the homeless gathered in shanty-towns referred to as Hoovervilles, a jab at the president whom they felt responsible for their plight.[28]

President Hoover asked businesses to maintain their workforce and wages; they had little choice: wages were cut, workers were laid off and investments put off.[29] In June 1930, Congress raised tariffs on thousands of imported items to encourage the purchase of American-made products at home. Trading nations followed suite by increasing tariffs on American-made goods. International trade declined further, worsening the Depression globally.[30]

In 1933 President Franklin Delano Roosevelt took office. A drought in the Midwest combined with soil erosion to create the *Dust Bowl*; hundreds of thousands of people were displaced from their farms. In excess of 3 million young men were moved from the cities to 2,600 work camps created by the Civilian Conservation Corporation (*the CCC*) to build roads and provide labor for badly needed construction and conservation projects.[31]

The Great Depression brought about a rapid rise in crime; many of the unemployed resorted to theft to put food on the table. Hopelessness was on the rise; family units were in distress. Some businesses failed while others emerged stronger. The mass migration of people reshaped America. Yet in the culture of despair, new forms of expression flourished. Suicides and alcoholism increased along with reported cases of malnutrition. Prostitution rose markedly as women became desperate looking for ways to pay their bills. Health care was not a priority for most Americans; doctor visits were excluded except for the worst cases.

Higher education was out of reach for most Americans; enrollment at most of the nation's universities had declined further. However, more young males attended high school during the

Depression because of the poor prospects for finding any kind of work elsewhere. Declining tax rolls around the country caused a reduction in education spending, requiring reductions in school staff; some schools closed altogether. Marriages were delayed as many young men waited until they could provide for a family before tying the knot. While the percentage of divorced married couples dropped steadily in the 1930s, the rates of abandonment increased as many husbands chose to simply desert their families. As more Americans learned about birth control, birth rates fell sharply to avoid the added expense of children. Mass migrations continued throughout the 1930s, especially people moving away from rural New England and upstate New York to seek work elsewhere. The Dust Bowl sent thousands of Midwesterners to the west coast for a better life. People traveled around the country hitching rides on trains.[32]

In 1939 the beginning of World War II caused the Great Depression to expire. Abrupt increases in military spending accelerated growth and decreased unemployment in the U.S. In Europe, the rearmament leading up to the war had stimulated the economies there. Following the outbreak of war, the mobilization of armed forces ended unemployment. By the time the U.S. entered the war in 1941, the remaining effects of the Depression were gone; unemployment fell below 10%. In the U.S., massive war spending doubled economic growth. Businesses disregarded the rising national debt and new taxes, refocusing their efforts to benefit from lucrative government contracts in support of the war effort.[33]

When the war ended, all of humanity took a collective breath before rebuilding. After nearly a century of industrial revolutions, driven by creative new technologies, economic booms and busts, and war, humankind had progressed through one too many types of combustion. Burning fossil fuels had transformed almost every aspect of human life. The last act of World War II took us to the peak of the combustion pyramid. The bombing of Hiroshima and Nagasaki are the only time in human history that atomic bombs were used in an act of war. They remain as scars on the face of humanity, the ignition of an eternal flame that will either destroy us…or provide us the wisdom to see the error of our ways.

6

The Golden Age of Advertising

Advertising has always been synonymous with human commerce. No matter which type of business you're in the goal is quite simple: make people aware of a product or service, grab their attention, have them consider and ultimately purchase it. Advertising has been used by plants, animals and humans dating back to the beginning of life. The first notable advertisements occurred during the Middle-Ages in the expanding cities and towns across Europe. The printing press was non-existent in Europe and most commoners couldn't read or write. When people were in need of a product or service, word-written signs would not have provided them the necessary information.

Three types of advertising were used during this period: trademark icons for specific businesses (often the family insignia of the owner); standard product symbols used by similar businesses; the utilization of town criers. The trades and artisans within a town for similar items or services got together; they conferred and agreed on the use of standard symbols for particular products or services that could be posted outside their place of business. For example, the image of a boot was used to indicate a cobbler; the outline of a suit was the symbol used by tailors; the figure of a horseshoe signified the service of a blacksmith. In city squares a variety of peddlers and farmers would sell their wares from wagons or carts. Town criers were hired to announce the place and time vendors of certain products would be available for purchase.[1]

Advertising would become a major force in many capitalist economies via newspapers and magazines by the 19th century. The first printed advertisements began appearing in some of the daily and weekly newspapers in America and England. These advertisements were used mainly to promote newspapers and books, which had become more affordable with the advent of the printing press, also new medications in demand by a growing number of people who were declining the use of old-fashioned remedies.

In America, the newspaper *the New York Sun* was one of the first to embark on a path that would define a new genre of news coverage: the unique approach of using advertising as a primary source of newspaper income. The Sun was the brainchild of 23-year-old Benjamin Day who had previously worked as a proprietor for a newspaper print shop. The Sun's first publication was a morning newspaper released on September 3, 1833 carrying the slogan — *It Shines for All.* The unique aspect of Day's approach was that he wasn't selling newspapers to his customers — *he was peddling awareness to his advertisers.* And the stories didn't necessarily have to be accurate or good stories; all they had to do was draw in enough people to buy and read the paper, and ultimately develop awareness for the advertisers and their products. Each edition of the *Sun* was priced at just one-penny, compared to the competition valued at five-cents. The *Sun* was small and easy to carry; it's reporting and illustrations were ground-breaking, mostly personal stories about crime, suicides and divorces that were popular among working-class readers. It inspired a new type of newspaper across America called the *penny press,* making news available to lower income readers.[2]

In 1840 a man by the name of Volney Palmer founded the first advertising agency in the United States. Located in Philadelphia,

Palmer decided to jump-start his struggling business by purchasing large amounts of space in Philadelphia's largest newspapers at discounted rates, including: *The Inquirer, The North American* and *The Public Ledger*. He then offered the space to potential advertisers at high enough rates to earn a profit but lower than the space could have been purchased individually. At this point Palmer wasn't developing the advertisements, but was simply brokering the advertising space. The strategy, layout, artwork and copy of the ads were still prepared by the company doing the advertising.

Later in the 19th century, the advertising agency *N.W. Ayer & Son* was founded in New York. This was the first American full-service advertising agency, fulfilling all of the advertising needs of their customers: strategic planning; the creation and execution of complete advertising campaigns. *N.W. Ayer & Son* created many notable slogans for firms such as *De Beers Diamonds, AT&T* and *the U.S. Army*. Previously, advertising agencies had started out as mere brokers for advertising space; by 1900 they had established themselves as a critical profession at the center of strategic planning, creative concept development and ad creation.[3]

During the early decades of the 20th century the advertising space available in American newspapers nearly tripled. Annually, over 100 American companies spent in excess of $50,000 each on national advertising. Many of these companies sold patented medicines, which declined when federal food and drug legislation was passed early in the 20th century. Later, companies including Quaker Oats, Armour Meats, American Tobacco Company, Remington Typewriters and Procter & Gamble soap products, emerged as big-time advertising innovators.

By 1914 two thirds of the top advertisers came from four industries: food producers; automobile and tire manufacturers; soap and cosmetic products; and tobacco companies. As often happens with startups in new areas of specialization, advertising agencies across the country were establishing and then splitting apart to reform and start anew. Advertising in the early 20th century was essentially a clean sheet of paper offering fresh opportunities for the creative promotion of products and services.[4]

Embracing Sufficiency

At about the same time, the production side of the production-consumption equation was about to take a giant leap. Fordism is the euphemism that defines Henry Ford's business strategy for introducing the Ford Model-T in 1914: *the foundation of a contemporary social and economic system with high levels of industrialization to achieve standardized mass production and consumption.*

Where before steam-powered conveyor lifts were used in manufacturing plants to load and unload materials and final products, the electrically driven conveyor greatly improved the ability to move assemblies on a production line. The meatpacking industry was the first in the U.S. to use such a concept in 1867. In this arrangement a carcass systematically moved down a processing line while workers performed just one operation: removing a portion of the carcass before proceeding to the next station.

William Klann introduced the assembly line concept to the Ford Motor Company, after his visit to Swift & Company's slaughterhouse in Chicago, where he viewed the disassembly of hanging carcasses being butchered as they moved along the production line. The increased efficiency achieved by having one operator perform the same operation repeatedly, seemed obvious to him. While others are said to have presented the idea to Henry Ford, Klann's recollection of the idea is documented at the Henry Ford Museum.[5]

On October 7, 1913 Ford Model-T's conveyor driven assembly line began running at Ford's Highland Park Plant, reducing the Model-T's production time to just 93 minutes. The assembly process had been condensed into 45 steps. Model-Ts were rolling of the production line every three minutes. Assembly rates were later increased by a factor of 8 to 1 and required less manpower. Assembly times were so rapid that painting the vehicles became the key issue. While Ford had planned on continuing to offer a variety of colors, testing revealed that only one color, named *Japan-Black* dried fast enough to meet the requirements of the line speed. So, the Model-T was available only in the color black until 1926, when faster drying paints in other colors became available.

The Model-T automobile was paramount to many future events occurring during the 20th century and beyond. The assembly line concept, combined with using standard parts fabricated on machines in large volumes by unskilled workers; using specialized tools to perform the assembly; paying workers a living wage are all key aspects of what was called *the Fordism ideology*. The Model-T was priced at roughly $825 when first introduced in 1908. By 1913 the price had decreased to $525, well within the reach of the average Ford plant worker, as well as the budget of the American middle class. As we look back on the 20th century, the Model-T stands out as an essential component in the dissemination of the automobile and the concept of mass industrialization into American society.[6]

The product assembly was viewed as a work in progress as it moved down the production line, prompting workers to perform at a prescribed pace to increase efficiency. The assembly line also brought about improved plant safety by having machinery remain stationery instead of moving about the plant. Other companies quickly followed suit. In the run up to World War II the demand for war materials fostered the utilization of the assembly line in the manufacture of ships, aircraft, jeeps, tanks, trucks and other military goods. Working conditions were also improved: no heavy lifting, stooping or bending over; special training was not required; the tasks were within the capabilities of most people.[7]

As always, there's another side to the story. The large increases in productivity provided the means to raise the pay for Ford's factory workers from $1.50 to $5.00 per day after three years of service. At the same time the Ford factory reduced the hourly factory work week. The increase in pay combined with fewer working hours was reportedly an attempt by the company to reduce the high employee turnover experienced after the new assembly line was installed in 1913. It turns out that whenever the plant management wished to increase their assembly staff by 100 workers, they had to actually hire in excess of 900 workers to compensate for their high turnover rate.[8]

One of Karl Marx's prime criticisms of capitalism professes that workers need to see the impact of their work in the eventual product output in order to experience true satisfaction. Marx viewed human labor as a means of conveying aspects of our character into our work. When work is broken down into simple repetitive tasks, workers are hard pressed to feel true ownership of the final product. The worker becomes disengaged from the repetitive tasks as well as the product output and its contribution to society. I believe it's also true that an assembly line worker is more readily replaced and therefore less valuable.[9]

Somewhere near the beginning of Claude C. Hopkin's long-time career in advertising, he took a position as advertising manager for Swift & Company, a processor of beef products located near the Chicago stock yards (the same company where William Klann had observed the assembly line process he suggested to Henry Ford). He was hired after competing with over 100 other bidders for the job by Mr. L. F. Smith, the new president and son of the company's founder. When he arrived for his first day of work, Mr. Hopkins was surprised to see just how unwelcome he was. Mr. G. F. Swift, the company's founder had built it without the aid of print advertising; he catered to nobody and asked no-one for their business. He considered advertising people as irrelevant. His concept of advertising was the use of signage painted *Swift & Company Beef Products* on railroad cars and simply handing out the company's annual calendar.

Swift & Company's only true advertising project for Claude Hopkins to consider was a product called *Cotosuet*, a compound-lard product used for cooking and baking as a lower cost substitute for butter and lard. N.K. Fairbanks Co.'s *Cottolene* was the original product and current market leader when *Cotosuet* was released. Both products offered similar quality and price, so there was not too much to crow about. *Cotosuet* had started to capture market share when the *Cottolene* product began making strides at taking it back. Six weeks into the campaign Mr. G. F. Swift began complaining about *Cotosuet's* advertising costs, while adding that there wasn't much of any sales to show for it.

Swift & Company had recently opened up a new sales office in

Boston and began a new advertising program across New England. Realizing how similar the two products were, Hopkins was perplexed about how to proceed. After pondering the problem for quite some time he realized that his previous successes had not resulted from asking the customer to buy brand Y instead of brand X—he had offered incentives which naturally led them to buy brand Y. When he learned that one of their distributor stores, Rothschild & Co. was opening a new store, Hopkins approached the store's advertising manager, Mr. Charles Jones with an attention grabber idea for their opening celebration. The store's grocery department was located on the 5th floor with a large bay window. Hopkins pitched the idea of baking the largest cake in the world using *Cotosuet* instead of butter, then placing it in the bay window and lighting it up to be visible from the busy streets below. He promised Mr. Jones that he would, "advertise the cake in the newspaper and make it the greatest feature in your opening." He instructed the baker to bake the cake with *Cotosuet* instead of butter, how to construct the special baking tins needed, and how to decorate the cake magnificently, making it as high as the room.

Hopkin's pitch for the sale was—*that a product better than butter was certainly better than lard*. He inserted a half-page ad in the newspapers announcing the largest cake in the world at Rothschild & Co.'s new store opening. The opening was planned for a Saturday evening. Hopkins arrived after dinner and found a sea of people awaiting access to the store. When he finally made it into the store, he saw policemen at each entrance. Because the crowd was so large, the authorities had temporarily closed access to the building. Over the course of the week that followed some 105,000 people climbed the four flights of stairs to witness and sample the cake. Hopkins had hired demonstrators to offer samples. Prizes were offered for guessing the cake's weight, but each guesser had to buy a pail of *Cotosuet*. When the store opening was complete *Cotosuet* had gained many thousands of customers.

After that, Claude Hopkins and his crew followed the route of the New York Central railroad. In each city they learned new and creative ideas for marketing *Cotosuet*. Hopkins described this in his book *My Life in Advertising*, "We went to the leading baker and showed him the newspaper clippings of what we had done elsewhere. We offered to let him build the cake, to advertise him as its creator on condition that he bought a carload of *Cotosuet*, sometimes two carloads. We went to the leading grocery with the proven results of our cake-show. Then we hired boys on Main Street to cry out with their papers, 'Evening News, All about the Big Cake.' Wherever we went we sold enough *Cotosuet* to insure us a profit in advance."

When they finally returned home to Chicago, Mr. L.F. Swift met with Claude C. Hopkins and said, "That is the greatest advertising stunt I have ever known. You have made good with both father and me."[10]

The rest of Hopkin's career is well told in his memoir and any book that covers the history of modern advertising. Later in 1927 he published his own advertising book entitled *Scientific Advertising*. Today, his book seems as not so much rocket science but as basic as apple pie. I guess common sense when spoken bluntly always seems that way. I have summarized Claude C. Hopkins theories about advertising into one paragraph below:

The goal of all advertisements is to make sales. The advertising person must find out what people want and advertise to meet that need. The purpose of the headline is to pick out those people you can interest. Any ad desiring attention must stand out in a pleasing way. If one headline doesn't work, then try another and another...Curiosity is one of the strongest human incentives. The ad should tell a story and introduce a personality without trying to be too amusing. The ad should create a becoming style and be uniquely different. Each ad should tell a complete story, including specific facts that when stated carry their full weight and effect. Remember that people judge a product largely by price. And once you get the reader hooked, present every important claim you have. Competition must be considered. Questions about ads can be answered by a test campaign.[11]

Claude C. Hopkins is still remembered as the father of Scientific Advertising, sometimes referred to as *reason why advertising*. He published his memoir entitled *My Life in Advertising* in 1927; six years later he died at age 66.

———————

When the War finally ended in the summer of 1945, the United States was again the only major combatant that hadn't experienced severe damage to the homeland: the agricultural and manufacturing infrastructure remained in place. Yet the costs of the war in blood and treasure, the unforgivable atrocities and civilian deaths, all weighed heavy on the human spirit. At the time my father was serving in the U.S. Navy aboard the *USS Prairie* near Eniwetok in the western Pacific while the ground fighting continued in the Marianas and Carolines islands off the coast of Japan.

My father was in the middle of his senior high school year when he abruptly enlisted in the Navy just a few weeks after the Pearl Harbor attack. At the time he was just 17 years old so he had to lie about his age to be accepted. He attended the Navy's Great Lakes Training Center and began active duty on the USS Prairie. The Prairie was what they call a *mother ship* for a squadron of destroyers, lightly armed with the main mission of performing quick repairs in the open seas for any damaged sea vessels. The Prairie reported to Ulithi Atoll on October 8, 1945 as part of the occupying American forces in Japan. On November 30 she steamed homeward bound for San Francisco, returning home like so many thousands of veterans who'd survived the horrors of the Second World War.

As the soldiers returned home, they came to be known as the fighting forces and citizens of the acclaimed *Greatest Generation*, celebrated for their grit as a society that had fought courageously to survive the Great Depression and World War II. While many were able to rebuild their lives, for some—their memories would haunt them forever. In my father's case he never did finish his high school degree; I never asked him about the War, I just seemed to know that he didn't want to talk about it.

Across much of Europe and Asia much of human civilization lay decimated: many cities were but piles of rubble; many factories, banks, colleges, schools and businesses had been completely destroyed. Currencies had no value, and with little access to news information people wandered around in a daze wondering what might happen next. The markets and shops still standing remained closed; they simply had nothing to sell. There were no police, no law and order; men armed with guns roamed the streets taking whatever they wanted.

In America much of the land and buildings remained in place, but life would never be the same. Nonetheless, conditions were quickly changing to a new and different kind of *normal*. Soldiers came home looking for peacetime jobs or perhaps to attend college on the new GI Bill. Manufacturers that had churned out war materials began producing consumer goods that offered to make life in this new and different world a little more pleasant. American businesses and manufacturers were poised to grow the American economy to reach new heights; the American production treadmill was primed and ready to roll.

Major changes were occurring within the American populace. Up to this point in human history people around the world had struggled to supply the basic needs of food and shelter to support the growing human population. People became dissatisfied with the old ways; they envisioned a better life in their future. They began moving out of the cities and small towns, buying or building new homes in the suburbs. Economies grew as new technologies were developed; they barely kept up with the increasing populace. Some 200 years earlier America began with an estimated four million people, with birth rates of eight to ten children per family. Back then many children died young and families needed lots of help on the farm, so they had lots of children. By 1900 the average birth rate for American women was three to four children; the population had risen to 63 million. The birthrate declined during the Great Depression to just two children per family. After the War, Americans were hopeful about the future; the birthrate increased markedly. By 1950 the U.S. population had climbed to more than 150 million; between 1950-60 the number of children between 5-15 years of age had increased by 10 million.[12]

In the years following the War, issues regarding the lack of human production had changed: the age-old human problem of not producing enough had transcended to creating more demand. The end of World War II signaled the end of *thrift-based consciousness*. Credit was readily available; purchases could be made over time. Advertisers relentlessly urged people to shop. For the first time, consumers believed the American Dream was within their grasp. Across the homeland strong employment and pent-up demand for consumer goods, pushed strong economic growth through the post-war period. Auto manufacturers had converted back to producing automobiles; new industries including plastics and electronics provided unique new arrays of products. Many couples had postponed their plans for marriage during the war. As the soldiers returned home, the number of newlyweds spiked, producing the infamous baby-boom generation, a group I'm proud to be part of. Affordable mortgages were available to military veterans, prompting a housing boom. By the close of the decade one third of Americans lived in suburban areas surrounding metropolitan centers, lured by affordable housing and increasing transportation options for the new middle class. The U.S. GNP increased by 50% from 1940 to 1950, another 67% during the decade that followed.

The survival lessons learned from the Great Depression motivated the U.S. government to realize its central role in managing the economy. Businesses consolidated into vast diversified corporations; the number of American workers providing services grew to equal those who manufactured the products. With all the improvements in farm productivity, small farmers found it difficult to compete. Many left their farms to look for work in the cities. During the last half of the 20th century the number of people employed by the farm sector had decreased by 50%. As peacetime and prosperity settled in, the pent-up demand for consumer goods: clothing, refrigerators, automobiles and appliances—in short supply during the war—skyrocketed. Businesses began realizing that where before they'd focused on increasing production to meet consumer demand—the problem would become prompting shoppers to buy more.[13]

Advertisers had been anxiously awaiting their return to the limelight, supplanting consumer awareness from their everyday worries to the fertile land of unbounded consumption. New media and advertising methods were pursued while salesmen followed up leads to fill in their order books. Manufacturers primed the treadmill of production to crank out new widgets; the race to become *the biggest and the best of all* had commenced.

During the Great Depression and the War, radio had become advertising's newest media darling. During the 1950's newspapers, magazines and radio would continue to function as essential marketing media. Yet, television was about to take center stage and would quickly become the foundation of many national media advertising programs. Television advertising's major drawback was cost: from $10,000 to $20,000 for 1-minute spots—more than 10 times the cost of radio ads; it's lure and the promise of prosperity would eventually offset the cost. Television broadcasters took in $41 million in advertising revenue in 1951 and $336 million in 1953.

Despite attempts to continue new products flowing to maintain consumer demand, shoppers began experiencing consumer anxiety during the latter 1950s. Advertisers counter attacked with new focused selling techniques: motivational research, demographic targeting and generational marketing. Advertising expenditures increased to unprecedented levels throughout the decade. U.S. advertising bookings grew nearly three-fold, approaching nearly $6 billion by 1960.[14]

The boom in new home construction increased the need for appliances and other goods to furnish the new households. Competing companies churned out a greater variety of products; others churned out completely new types of appliances and consumer electronics. Many new products—kitchen and laundry appliances, decorating accessories, prepared and frozen foods—were promoted as time-savers that increased productivity and leisure time at home.

Many technical innovations of the War were transformed into new labor-saving products. The aerosol spray can was a by-product of the bug-bomb developed for use in the Pacific theatre. Adding a spray top transformed the bug-bomb into a dispenser for everything from processed cheese; whipped cream to shaving cream hairspray and deodorant. Nylon— which had been developed to make parachutes—replaced the costly silk used to make stockings. Many new plastics and a new material trademarked *Styrofoam* were applied to applications including home insulation and furniture.

During the post-war period advertisers also suggested a thoughtful revisiting of old-fashioned family values. In just one generation the lingering memories of the Great Depression and the War were supplanted with the image of the modern nuclear family—father, mother, son and daughter—enjoying life along within the comfort of their homes; freedom to travel by car to unlimited destinations; the ability to buy new things to make life a little easier. Many ads portrayed the upward mobility and prosperity of American society, its technological superiority and renewed optimism. Even though only 59% of American families in 1950 owned one car, the necessity of having two cars was heavily promoted throughout the 1950s. Car owners began viewing their automobiles as extensions of themselves. New car designs possessing unique fin designs with lots of chrome were modified each year, prompting consumers to buy the newest styles annually, independent of improvements in performance or efficiency. Automobiles had surpassed packaged goods and cigarettes as the most heavily advertised products by the mid-1950s. Advertisers also began targeting teenagers with products including: phonographs, records, radios, magazines, clothing and soft drinks.[15]

TV programming was initially sponsored and produced by advertisers. Advertising agencies produced the shows; the networks provided advisement opportunities, facilities and the airtime. Program names typically included the name of the advertising sponsor: shows like *Hallmark Hall of Fame, Texaco Star Theater, Colgate Comedy Hour, Goodyear TV Playhouse* and *Kraft Television Theater* were some of the leading programs during the 1950s.

By 1954, TV had overtaken radio and print media to become the leading advertising medium. Most TV ads utilized a readily identifiable spokesperson with the products they demonstrated. Memorable ad campaigns of that period include Dinah Shore singing *See the USA in Your Chevrolet*; newsman John Cameron Swayze's delivery of *It takes a licking and keeps on ticking* for Timex watches; and Speedy Alka-Seltzer with the slogan *Plop, Plop, Fizz, Fizz ... Oh, What a Relief it is*. But one ad considered the best of the 20th century was produced for Anacin pain reliever. Through slogans, demonstrations and much repetition Anacin had positioned itself as the cure for the tension headache offering — *Fast, fast, fast relief* — while flashing the image of an imaginary headache with lightning bolts and hammers pounding away at a person's head. Even though the ad increased Anacin's sales substantially, the way in which it was continually repeated with only minor variations, drew stark reviews.[16]

The postwar abundance of the 1950s continued into the 1960s, providing a constant stream of mass-produced goods to consumers with more spare time, extra cash or credit than any preceding generation. Nearly all aspects of human life were influenced by the cultural and social changes of the '60s. Advertisers gradually absorbed the thinking of the widening youth culture reflecting: modernism, creativity and profound thinking, providing the information and the impetus to push consumption to new highs. On the other hand, 1960's advertising was often funny, brazen, poignant or evocative to the point of drawing criticism from those consumer advocates who protected consumers' rights.

The postwar baby-boom generation came of age in the 60s; by the middle of the decade nearly 50% of the U.S. population was under the age of 25. Beliefs regarding government, culture, race, gender, age and war were all contested; many youths rejected the values of their parents: religion, racism, capitalism and consumerism. Advertising was castigated for its tendency to promote materialism; the use of exaggerated and often deceitful methods.

One of the most dishonest and damaging practices was the utilization of doctors posing as actors discussing the healthful aspects of cigarette smoking. One of the last cigarette ads to make that claim appeared in Life Magazine in 1954. In the ad a letter written by a *Dr. Darkis was inset into the advertisement stating that L&M cigarettes used a highly purified alpha-cellulose filter that was entirely harmless and effectively filtered the smoke.* Dr. Darkis was not a physician, but a research chemist. Hollywood actor Frederic Marsh is pictured in the ad and quoted—*This is it; L&M Filters are just what the doctor ordered! When I read Dr. Darkis' letter I tried L&M Filters. I'm really enthusiastic about them. They're a wonderful smoke—with a filter that really does the job. I'm sure you will like them as much as I do.*[17]

As the 60s progressed, marketers attempted to embrace the emerging youth counterculture. Where before advertisers had considered the rebellious youth unfavorably, came the sudden realization—they represented the future consuming class. Pepsi Cola's *Think Young* and *Pepsi Generation* ads are prime examples of this approach.

The 1970s began in the midst of a minor recession, followed by the OPEC oil embargo imposed against the U.S. for helping to re-supply Israel during the 1973 Arab-Israeli War. The gasoline shortages that followed had a huge impact on the economy and the sense of American invincibility. There were also direct product challenges to the U.S. in electronics, especially radios, TVs and video cassettes as competing Japanese products overtook the market.

The ongoing Vietnam War, the release of the Pentagon Papers, the Watergate scandal followed by President Nixon's resignation in 1973 created a lack of confidence in the American government. The 1970s were also plagued by high inflation—averaging 6.85% over the decade and peaking at 12.2% in 1974—based on the Consumer Price Index (CPI).[18]

By the 1970s, television viewing had become a central experience in American society; TV became the preferred advertising medium throughout the decade. In 1976, in excess of 69 million U.S. homes owned at least one TV set; home viewing exceeded six hours per day. While the 1950s had focused on products, brand image was promoted in the 60s. Product positioning: placing the product in the consumer's mind and focusing on its features and benefits, compared to the competition was the main advertising strategy of the 70s.

Computer technology was increasingly being applied to implement research and fact-based marketing. The American Association of Advertising Agencies estimated that the average American consumer was exposed to 1600 ads per day, with fewer than 80 of those ads being noticed, and only 12 evoking some response. The American public had become increasingly skeptical and disillusioned regarding advertising industry practices; this brought about the threat of government regulation. When the issue of lack of diversity in television programing and advertising was raised, advertising agencies worked towards increasing diversity in their ads as well as the workplace.[19]

Comparative advertising thrived with ads like: *7UP the Un-Cola* campaign that doubled the sales of *7UP*; Coca-Cola fought back against Pepsi with their *It's the Real Thing* ad campaign. The federal government and advertising code review boards scrutinized advertising thoroughly, revoking exaggerated or false claims. Generally, advertisers were allowed to claim their product was better than a competitor's; unable to assert a competing product was worse than theirs.

Computer use spread throughout the industry providing advertising executives with itemized data and analysis of ad performance. Public concerns arose regarding advertising practices, especially those regarding children and the use of subliminal sexual embedding. Television advertisers were spending millions of dollars peddling products to children while research suggested that children under eight years old were unable to discriminate between television programs and commercials. A group known as *Action for Children's Television (ACT)*, founded by Peggy Charren and Judith Chalfen of Newton, Massachusetts in 1968, is a grassroots organization dedicated to improving the quality of children's television programming. ACT first petitioned the FCC in 1970 to ban advertising from children's programming. In subsequent years it sought to eliminate commercials for certain categories of products. In 1971, ACT challenged the advertising promotion of vitamins to children, arguing that one-third of the commercials were for vitamin pills, even though the bottles were labeled stating *Keep out of reach of children because an overdose could put them in a coma*. In their response to ACT's campaign, vitamin-makers voluntarily withdrew their advertising. ACT was also able to limit the amount of advertising aimed at children's programming by petitioning the FCC to accept guidelines that included: a minimum of 14 hours of children's programming be made available as a public service for children of different ages each week; no commercials were allowed on children's programs; hosts of children's shows are not allowed to promote products.

In 1976, a Gallup Poll asked Americans to rate the honesty and ethical standards of those engaged in 11 fields of work—advertising executives came in dead-last. Yet in the same year, the U.S. Supreme Court extended First Amendment protection to include commercial speech. While the First amendment had long been applied to issues regarding defamation, privacy and prior restraint, the Supreme Court gave advertising legal standing and protection.[20]

The television industry was essentially reshuffled by cable TV during the 1980s. Cable channels were increasingly able to draw viewers from traditional commercial broadcast networks: ABC, CBS and NBC. By the 1990s the viewership of the leading broadcast networks had dropped to less than 60%; the balance of the market was maintained by independent and cable TV. VCRs allowed viewers to manage and control their favorite programs, using remote controls to skip over TV commercials.

Direct home shopping services were developed in the '80s including the Home Shopping Network and QVC, selling discounted goods directly to viewers that called in their orders to telephone operators. Thirty-minute infomercials became another method of TV advertising as well as a shift to 15-second TV commercials, down from the previous 30-second standard. The *Energizer Bunny*, introduced in 1989, was one of the top ranked ads of the decade. American carmakers responded to the burgeoning foreign competition defensively with ads boasting their quality: *At Ford quality is job one* and *GM puts quality on the road*.

In politics, President Ronald Reagan's re-election campaign modified the relationship between politicians and the media. His staff demonstrated a unique understanding of the power of visual media by staging the President's news events for maximum media coverage; announcements were timed to coincide with the largest TV audiences. Other historic events include the recall of *Rely* tampons by Procter & Gamble Co.—four months after their introduction when their use was linked to toxic shock syndrome. Two years later, Tylenol capsules were removed from store shelves across America after product tampering in Chicago resulted in the poisoning deaths of seven people. [21]

In America the 1990s signaled the end of a period of relative calm. The first Persian Gulf War, the war in Bosnia, the mass shooting of teachers and students at Columbine high school and the bombing of the World Trade Center all pointed to troubled times ahead. The ever-expanding Internet, miniaturized laptop computers, smart cell phones and wireless device networks all added to the mix of technological innovations creating new markets. Members of the baby-boom generation were becoming *empty-nesters*. Their offspring were putting off marriage and having fewer children, causing family birth-rates to decline as well as the size of the average family unit. Population throughout the U.S. continued the long-term relocation to the Sun-belt while the number of immigrants and minorities increased.

Many of the new technologies created new products that expanded the market for mass media; the wide-ranging features of the Internet served to redistribute the audience. Consumers were given such a host of options including: a broader range of information sources—newspapers, magazines, books, radio, TV and the Internet—that the choices for mass media became more costly and complex. In the mid-1990s the marketing capabilities once promised by the Internet began to emerge. Products and services were offered to customers directly on web pages that became storefronts. Purchases could be made directly using credit cards without leaving home. Companies including Ebay and Amazon were leaders of the so-called dot.com revolution. While many sites initially focused on limited product lines, so-called brick and mortar stores including Walmart, Home Depot and Lowes soon joined the fray.

In 1994, *Yahoo* developed a way to search for sites on the Internet—the search engine. Internet advertising began when a company named *HotWired* began charging a fee for placing ads on their website—the first on-line magazine with advertisements on colorful billboards. HotWired's success led other online service companies to utilize Internet advertising to draw people to their websites. When viewers clicked on the ads they were magically transported to the sponsor's Website.

Throughout the 1990s the number of websites continued expanding until the year 2000 when the dot.com bubble burst, drying up the available venture capital. As a result, fears that traditional advertising mass media—TV, radio, magazines and newspapers—would falter against Internet competition seemed less likely. Nonetheless, technology was transforming just about every aspect of the business world. New computer software provided methods for advertisers: creating ads, developing and altering images.

A few years later Internet advertising was transformed again with improved software capable of tracking responses and targeting prospective customers, opening up broader opportunities. The greatest prospect was to increase product sales in almost any business environment by creating an operating model allowing seller and consumer to approach the sale with a similar mindset: viewing the product in the same positive way. On the Internet, the consumer can progress effortlessly from persuasion—to product familiarization—to consideration—to purchase.

The famous marketer John Wanamaker once claimed, *"Half the money I spend on advertising is wasted; the trouble is I don't know which half"*. Today the information captured by Internet advertising is capable of providing that information, as well as generating a customer profile for potential customers. Using available prospective customer profiles from having monitored their Internet activity, Internet marketers can readily target product ads for optimum success by targeting customers who are likely to be interested in the product being sold, and measuring the effectiveness of their ad campaign. What consumers give up to become part of this activity is the privacy of their Internet travels via cookies that record one's previous activities while visiting a particular website.[22]

Advertisements can be modified to better match the targeted

market and the viewer, while the results are readily measured from a variety of perspectives with great speed. Ad blocking is the growing menace to ad placement from consumers increasingly averse to being interrupted or slowed down by trashy attention grabbers, misleading headlines on a path to nowhere. Advertisers will have to improve their creativity and quality to overcome the consumer's ability to fast forward through ads or block them out completely. Captivating content pulls viewers in while an invasive blitz locks them out. In order to reach people on their personal device's, ads must be formatted appropriately for the wider range of available devices: smart phones, tablets, laptops, computers and television.

Currently in America, consumption is broadly driven by images of successful people of all stripes, utilizing hassle free products, representing the very latest and best technology has to offer. Price is seldom mentioned except in regard to special promotions. Television ads are shorter with more of them; many seem to be questionable when you realize that the advertiser is never clearly stated. Experts say this is all according to plan and that any truly interested consumer will be hooked on the ad to the point of researching the product and thereby the source of the ad. As you skip around to various websites, do you ever notice products you've recently searched for on the Internet suddenly scrolling across your screen on clickable ads for your viewing pleasure? These are all signs that big-brother advertisers are watching your every move. Just a few clicks and you can have your completely unnecessary thing-a-ma-bob shipped to your door via free shipping—*life in consumer heaven is such a wonderful thing.*

7

The Rise of Consumerism

What is capitalism—its relationship to consumerism? In many ways capitalism and consumerism are two parts of the same story. In capitalist societies people are compelled by self-interest to earn as much money as possible. Businesses in capitalistic economies strive to be competitive and innovative: developing novel products, marketed with creative new methods, manufactured at competitive prices with the goal of earning the maximum profit. A mass of novel technology driven products advertised to be the latest and greatest humankind has to offer are capable of creating need— where previously none existed. As the population continues to grow, many millions more humans are consuming a wider range of products than any period in our history. The central choice for many strategic planners is deciding whether to focus on short...or long-term profits.

On the other hand, consumer choices often include the short-term use of commodities or the longer-term utilization of more durable goods. Consumerism has evolved over time from bare necessities to an unimaginable assortment of uniquely different products available today with too many variations. They are mass produced in highly automated manufacturing plants with a minimum number of workers: laborers performing hand assembly operations at lower pay rates; their products are shipped to markets and customers across the globe.

The act of consumption or utilization (the long-term consumption of durable goods) requires a product or service for sale and a willing customer to buy it. Capitalism's goal is to develop a competitive business climate supporting the creation and manufacture of products and services: their promotion, distribution and sale. Capitalism drives all activities along the production and marketing chain to compete in the marketplace, selling the most at the maximum level of profit. On the other side, the customer competes to buy the best product at the lowest price. In earlier times, the production treadmill's speed was regulated by the technologies available. For many centuries humanity's main problem was producing enough goods to meet even the basic needs of all potential consumers. The production capacity problem was somewhat resolved in developed countries after the Second Industrial Revolution early in the 20th century. Ever since — give or take the Great Depression and a couple of world wars — achieving maximum profitability has depended more upon increasing human consumption.[1]

The rise of advertising on billboards, newspapers, radio and TV, personalized pop-up ads on webpages all promote demand for a range of existing and uniquely new devices. Often these products were developed to save the time and effort of consumers in exchange for the energy, material and labor used to produce and market them. For many years — government officials, politicians and businessmen alike — have voiced the mantra of continuous economic growth as a solution to all human societal issues. Modern society has embraced this notion to the point that many of us have come to believe that human happiness depends on how much and what we consume — how rich we are and how much we can buy — which could not be farther from the truth.

Capitalism is a socio-economic system that encourages businesses and consumers to perform economic activities with minimal government interference, guided by the concepts of private property, maximum profit and consumer sovereignty. Consumerism is an ideology that induces individuals to acquire and consume a maximum of quality goods and services at the lowest price, advocating the production of goods by manufacturers according to the free choice of consumers who ultimately direct the economic policies and programs of the state. While capitalism and consumerism are two distinct concepts—they are inherently linked.[2]

Other pieces of the consumption pie are the availability of consumer credit and achieving the *American Dream*. The *American Dream* has been defined as, *"a national ethos of the United States, the set of ideals in which freedom includes the opportunity for prosperity and success, as well as an upward social mobility for the family and children, achieved through hard work in a society with few barriers."* In addition, *"life should be better and richer and fuller for everyone, with opportunity for each according to ability or achievement, regardless of social class or circumstances of birth."*[3]

With the largest GDP of any country, the key question remains for a majority of Americans: has America fulfilled the promise of the American Dream or has it created a monster of overconsumption and waste that's compiling a natural resource debt that future citizens will be incapable of repaying over time?

The American story has been memorialized and transcended in many ways; a tale about a mixed group of courageous and persecuted colonists, who made a treacherous journey across the ocean to a place so mysterious it was like they had landed on the moon. A treaty with the Native American Pawtuxet tribe helped the New Plymouth colony get started. It was one of the earliest and most successful colonies founded by the English in North America; active from 1620 to 1691. New Plymouth served as the capital of the Plymouth Colony; over the years it developed into the modern town of Plymouth, Massachusetts. At its peak the Plymouth Colony covered much of southeastern Massachusetts. It was founded by a group of Puritan Separatists known as the Pilgrims; most of them had escaped religious persecution in search of a place to worship as they wished.

Other successful colonies were founded at Jamestown and settlements in Virginia, consisting mostly of entrepreneurs in search of a better life. The social and legal systems of the individual colonies reflected the English customs of its citizens: the freedom to strive for a better quality of life and to exercise their religious beliefs freely.

But there's more to the story. Before the Pilgrims, the Separatists within the Protestant Reformation that eventually journeyed to America—they first sailed to Holland in 1609 to escape persecution in search of religious freedom. In Holland the pilgrims were free to worship there for more than a decade; their subsistence there was dreadful. As immigrants the only work available was hard labor at very low pay. They struggled on for years in poverty growing old before their time while their children adapted to Dutch culture, forsaking the beliefs and values of their parents. While their lives in Holland provided the ability to worship freely, the Separatists believed their children faced an immoral and dishonest future there.

At that point the Pilgrims made the historic decision to immigrate to America for the benefit of their children and their children's children—to enjoy their culture anew in a world without pre-existing cultural limitations. There were many costly sacrifices; by the end of their first winter in the New World half of those who'd sailed on the Mayflower had perished. Yet the Pilgrims persevered; they remained faithful to their beliefs and their culture.[4]

The American Dream in its utopian form exemplifies a perfect human society. Nonetheless the American Dream has been reconstituted over time from providing all persons with equal treatment and the same opportunities to worship and pursue a better life, to affording the ability to consume as much, as often as we want without concern or regard for the future of humanity or planet Earth. In the last hundred years Americans have moved away from a world where human consumption was reasonable in size and scope, compared to the incomprehensible, insatiable disbursement of resources that exists today. While historians and economists point out that Americans have never truly been thrifty; over the years we most certainly have become increasingly extravagant. Even the Pilgrims who traveled to America had to finance their trip on an installment plan: London merchants financed the New World expedition by requiring the Pilgrims to work without a profit for a period of seven years.

Debt has always been a part of American life—not for the purchase of items on a whim but as a means for survival in times of extreme need, or a way for improving one's future livelihood. During the 19th century moralists considered getting a loan to buy something on impulse to be *consumptive debt*, while borrowing for future financial gain was thought of as *constructive debt*.

The habit of installment purchases of consumer products began as far back as the Civil War: sewing machine and parlor organ manufacturers realized their products were more affordable if Americans could make the payments over time. During the Second Industrial Revolution the production of larger ticket items including phonographs, refrigerators and washing machines were produced faster and cheaper; they were usually bought on installment plans.

Later in 1908 the Ford Model-T was released for sale at the modest price of $850. Even at that low price many Americans could not afford the Model-T without the ability to buy it on time. But Henry Ford was old fashioned—he didn't believe in buying on credit. While many Ford dealers did offer other payment schemes, the Ford Motor Company maintained their existing layaway plan called the *Weekly Payment Plan*. Customers would select the car model they wished to purchase, make a down payment with subsequent weekly payments until their account totaled the car's selling price before taking delivery. In 1919 General Motors began lending consumers the money on time to buy their automobiles. GM auto loans at the time required a 35% down payment with the balance payable monthly over the course of one year. The consumer credit system we have today is a direct result of GM's effort to keep pace with the Ford Model-T. The Model-T provided basic transportation and was available in one color (black) at a much lower price than the competition, but you had to pay cash up front or accumulate it in weekly installments before taking delivery. GM cars were colorful and more stylish but carried a price tag only wealthier customers could afford.

GM had studied the market and detected a change in the way American consumers viewed consumer credit when making larger long-term purchases. While Americans after the war had become more willing to spend, they generally avoided luxury, especially at the expense of debt. During the Second Industrial Revolution increases in production, with the creation of new and exciting products, prompted Americans to consider taking on debt to enjoy some of these new creations being made available for the first time—perhaps it wasn't such a bad thing to own a convenience item and incur a little debt.

GM developed the General Motors Acceptance Corporation (GMAC) as a means for providing credit to consumers to become more competitive with Ford. For the first time GM was able to gain on the Ford Model-T in the marketplace. It wasn't long before Americans had used up much of the available credit. By 1930 most durable goods were purchased on installment plans, including some 60% of all automobile purchases. This was much to the dismay of Henry Ford who heartily disagreed with the concept of consumer credit. Eventually, Ford was forced to offer auto loans as well. After World War II the level of consumer credit rose at astounding rates, and by the year 2000 GMAC had loaned out over a trillion dollars to American car buyers.

By the end of the *Roaring 20's* purchases of durable goods made on time had increased the average percentage of consumer debt for Americans to the highest levels ever. In a very short period, the once immoral practice of purchasing for sheer pleasure on credit had become the norm. Once consumers became comfortable using credit more frequently, entrepreneurs and advertisers alike set about to simplify the requirements for obtaining credit, while increasing credit limits. They also found ways to coerce people to buy products on a whim, something they didn't absolutely need, what we now call impulse buying.

The Rise of Consumerism

During the 1950s Americans enjoyed a 30% increase in purchasing power. President Eisenhower's program of balanced budgets, low taxes and public spending provided the impetus for steady and strong growth. Eisenhower pursued a more neutral course with the economy while maintaining some of FDR's social programs: extending Social Security to some 10 million people left out of the initial plan. Unemployment was low, hitting its lowest point of 4.5% in the middle of the decade.

The GI Bill provided military veterans with the money to attend college, adding a large group of well-educated employees to the American work force. Low cost oil produced from domestic wells fueled the treadmill of production to run at full speed. Increasing numbers of Americans gave up any pretense of being thrifty, buying on credit became the rule rather than the exception. Advertisers incessantly pitched consumers to desire the latest, most improved widgets and more of them, driving advertising expenditures to more than double during the 1950s, exceeding $13 billion by 1963. Overall, the U.S. economy grew by 37% over the course of the decade.[5]

The Diner's Club card was the very first credit card released in 1950 with the limitation of paying for meals at selected restaurants. Other cards soon followed with broader capabilities, touching off another round of rapid growth in financing. Private debt more than doubled during the 1950s, exceeding $250 billion. Loans were used to buy houses, cars, appliances and swimming pools.

Consumer spending was a key factor that propelled the relative wealth of the 1950s. Americans enjoyed a standard of living inconceivable with the rest of the world. Adults of the 1950s had matured during a period of deprivation. Unemployment was extreme during the 1930s and the economy in disarray. Most people couldn't afford much beyond the bare essentials. During the War most everything from sugar to gasoline, tires and nylon stockings were rationed. When consumer goods became available after the war, people were ready and willing to spend. Yet the prosperity of the Eisenhower years wasn't good to all: 25% of Americans lived in poverty—a family of four with income less than $3,000. They consisted mostly of African Americans living in urban neighbor-hoods and whites from depressed rural areas; out of sight and out of mind to much of America.[6]

The American continent was renowned for its abundance of natural resources compared to Europe and the Middle East, where many nature reserves had been devoured over the centuries. The United States possessed enough resources and manufacturing ca-pacity to indulge in the production of consumer items that bor-dered on frivolous. While Americans made up just 6% of the world's population, they were consuming a third of the world's goods and services. As the older generation of penny pinchers passed on, their progenies consumed without constraint and trashed all their leftovers. America was on its way to becoming a throw-away society. The distinction between societies focusing on meeting the basic needs of people to a consumptive culture that ful-fills all consumer desires—is the difference between survival and extinction.

The prosperity enjoyed by Americans was based upon im-portant developments that had occurred right after World War II: the Korean conflict and the onset of the Cold War prompted signif-icant increases in military spending, stimulating the design of weapons and systems needed to defend a superpower. Aerospace and electronics industries were well supported by government spending, employing thousands of highly paid technicians and en-gineers to maintain America a step ahead of all potential adver-saries. New technologies raised productivity in all sectors of the American economy: farm yields of corn, wheat and cotton more than doubled, American manufacturers invested some $10 billion annually on capital improvements to increase productivity. Rising foreign investments helped create jobs and profits at home. But the bigger story was the change in American lifestyles—the escalating consumption and buying on credit that persists even today.

Americans' pursuit of happiness was complemented by a growing demand for entertainment: television, movies, pro and college sports all became part of the routine. Annual family vaca-tions became a rite of passage. By 1960, Americans were spending some $85 billion each year on entertainment, double that of the previous decade. Increasing car ownership via the available credit and improved highways prompted a mass relocation. American affluence was moving out of the cities and into the suburbs. By 1960 roughly a third of all Americans lived in suburbs. The prosperity of the 1950s revised the image of the American landscape. The American Dream had adopted new expectations, yet some 50 million Americans still lived in poverty. In broader terms actual U.S. GNP growth averaged just 2 to 3% per year, while Europe and the Soviet Union were reporting record economic growth.[7]

The 1960s began like a continuation of 50s—that's not how they ended. The burgeoning lifestyles of the growing consumer society had convinced many Americans that prosperity was possible for all; economic growth would continue without a glitch—but such expectations were too much to ask for.

The 1960 presidential election was a close contest between Democrat John F. Kennedy who defeated incumbent Vice President Richard Nixon, the Republican nominee. For the first time all 50 American states participated in the election; presidential terms were limited to two per the 22nd Amendment to the Constitution.

President Kennedy began his presidency with an inaugural address during which he asked Americans to consider a novel idea, "ask not what your country can do for you … ask what you can do for your country." It was a pertinent question for American society to ponder, though inconsistent with the culture of excessive consumption being promoted at the time.

———————————————

Just a year into JFK's presidency the economic news was awful and getting worse; by the spring of 1962 the stock market had fallen; unemployment had risen to near 7%. That October, an event known as the Cuban Missile Crisis brought the United States of America face to face with the Union of Soviet Socialists Republic in a 13-day confrontation—concerning American ballistic missile deployments in Italy and Turkey—with a subsequent Soviet ballistic missile deployment in Cuba—the threat of full-scale nuclear war hanging in the balance. I was 13 years old at the time and I can still remember the fear and concern exuded by my parents, as we watched the events unfold on the evening news each night.

On October 22nd the U.S. established a naval blockade to prevent more missiles from reaching Cuba. That evening, President Kennedy addressed the nation to announce to the nation—that the U.S. would not allow any more offensive weapons to be delivered to Cuba—he demanded that those weapons already there be dismantled and returned to the Soviet Union. After tense negotiations an agreement was reached between the U.S. and the USSR where the Soviets would dismantle their offensive weapons in Cuba and return them to the Soviet Union in exchange for the U.S. declaring that it would not invade Cuba. Secretly, the United States also agreed that it would dismantle all American-built Jupiter Medium Range Ballistic Missiles (MRBMs) deployed in Turkey against the Soviet Union. When all offensive missiles had been withdrawn from Cuba, the blockade was formally ended on November 21, 1962.

Ironically, a year and a day after the Cuban Missile Crisis was resolved, John F. Kennedy was assassinated while riding in a presidential motorcade through the Dealey Plaza in Dallas, Texas. The motorcade rushed to Parkland Memorial Hospital where the President was pronounced dead. A tax cut Kennedy had proposed earlier in 1963 included investment tax credits, improved depreciation allowances, lower capital gains tax rates and a reduction of the top marginal tax rate. After his death the Kennedy tax cuts were finally passed into law stimulating strong economic growth for a few more years.[8]

In 1962 author Michael Harrington published a book titled *The Other America* articulating the other side of the consumerism tale: the struggle of migrant farm workers, unskilled laborers, minorities, the elderly, immigrants and those with disabilities; located in the rural South, Appalachia and the ghettos across America. The book brought about an awakening that seemed to signal an end to the obsessive consumption party. The story about poverty in America wasn't new. It was told in the light of the excesses and burgeoning wealth of the 1950s—the contrast was like a smack in the head. The public reaction to Harrington's book was one of revulsion at the degree of poverty it described, but it also offered a sense of hope. Memories of Franklin Roosevelt's intervention in the economy that had brought about the end of the Great Depression were resurrected — that perhaps poverty wasn't part of the natural order of things and could be eradicated.[9]

Shortly after the Kennedy Assassination, Vice President Lyndon Johnson was sworn in as President aboard Air Force One on its return flight to Washington D.C. Johnson's wife Lady Bird and Kennedy's widow Jacqueline were at his side. When the plane landed, he gave a short speech to the nation, "I will do my best — that is all I can do."

Johnson was born and raised in Texas. After college his most invigorating work was the time spent as a rural teacher, inspiring his commitment to alleviate the suffering of America's poor. As president he proposed a generous domestic program called *The Great Society*: to reduce poverty and expand education while increasing services for the unemployed, providing health care and financial aid to the elderly. The cost of these programs was staggering, especially with the growing commitment of American support for the South Vietnamese government in the evolving Vietnam War.

By the end of Johnson's term inflation was rising quickly. The growing American fatalities in Vietnam provoked a strong anti-war movement along with a host of other social issues: racial discrimination, gay rights and poverty. The rise of the hippie counterculture; the assassinations of Martin Luther King and Bobby Kennedy only added weight to an American society already demoralized. Overwhelmed by it all, President Johnson decided against a run for president so he could maintain focus on resolving the serious issues facing the country. Richard M. Nixon won the 1968 election for president of the United States in a three-way race against Democrat Hubert Humphrey and George Wallace of the American Independent Party.

In 1970, the U.S. population stood at just over 200 million people; the new decade abruptly thwarted any prospects for continued economic growth. The costs of the Vietnam War pushed the national debt higher. The Nixon Administration's plan was to bomb North Vietnam into submission so that American and South Vietnamese soldiers could rout out the Viet Cong from their Cambodian sanctuaries. The last major battle between U.S. forces and North Vietnam was a 23-day affair that ended in July of 1970. From there the American strategy was to shift the fighting over to the South Vietnamese, a program called *Vietnamization.*

In June of 1971, the New York Times printed the first installment of *the Pentagon Papers*—a classified history of U.S. involvement in the Vietnam War—revealing the true status of American efforts there. Increasingly the war was creating deep rifts within American society. At the same time the 26th Amendment to the U.S. constitution granted 18-year-old American citizens old enough to fight and die for their country—the right to vote.

By the spring of '72, college campuses across America erupted in protest against the Vietnam War. On May 4th National Guard troops shot and killed four of unarmed students while attempting to control an antiwar protest at Kent State University. Ten days later, two black students at Jackson State University in Mississippi were killed when police fired into a dormitory—it seemed like America was coming apart at the seams.

In 1973, Arab oil states imposed an embargo on oil shipments to retaliate against the countries supporting Israel during the Yom Kippur War. As available oil stockpiles were consumed the price of oil on the global market quadrupled—from $3 to $12 dollars a barrel—with an immediate impact at the pumps. A national gas rationing program was imposed, requiring that Americans wait in long lines at gas stations to fill up. To reduce the lines, rationing programs were modified to allow only odd-even gas purchases, dependent on the last number on the license plate. It was a time of great anxiety for American commuters and consumers, especially those who commuted long distances to work every day.

Economists have described the 1970s American economy as suffering from *stagflation*. Stagflation is when unemployment and inflation are both high and economic growth is low; this was the case throughout much of the '70s. In other words—the economy isn't growing but prices are. Stagflation began after Nixon imposed wage and price controls in 1971. Over the course of the decade unemployment jumped from 5.4% to near 8%; GDP growth was negative from 1974 through 1975 and inflation exceeded 10%.

As the '60s melted into the '70s Americans were spending more time watching television, and divorce rates amongst American families were on the rise. Some economists believed that a decline in the work ethic, the desire to work less and enjoy more leisure time had contributed to the stagflation of the '70s. The lack of leisure time and income inequality, were driving worker discontent. Walkouts by a number of large unions negatively impacted the economy: 200,000 postal workers walked off the job; a massive longshoreman strike closed seaports around the country. In Pennsylvania, 80,000 state workers went on strike in 1975; miners around the country conducted the longest strike in mining history. While the richest Americans were still spending at high levels, the average consumer was unable to fulfill their consumptive desires without taking on more credit.

Advertising designers changed their strategies again during the 70's—from a precisely directed message to a more expressive approach. One new tactic was the use of subliminal messaging in ads: sexually charged words and photos hidden in ads to coerce the audience to associate the brand with their innate desires—a practice consumers found most objectionable. Today, some people still fear that advertisements can subliminally change their behavior to purchase something they would not normally buy. This belief is confirmed by the fact that the Federal Trade Commission (FTC) banned this type of advertising in the 1970s. Even though subliminal advertising is illegal, advertisers can still use manipulative techniques to improve their sales legally.

Manipulative advertising exploits imprudent claims of preferred results, in an attempt to convince customers to buy the product. Advertisers attempt to persuade consumers that buying a particular product will make them appear smarter or more attractive. Such advertising can be considered unethical when using a skewed presentation of the facts. Examples of manipulative advertising include: using an expert opinion for a medication presented by an actor who once portrayed a physician in a television series; a political candidate who distorts the opposition's view on an issue to win votes.

Subliminal advertising utilizes veiled messages which can be retained in the subconscious memories of consumers. One of the first experiments regarding the use of such a technique occurred in the late 1950s when psychologist James Vicay performed an experiment with an image stating: *Hungry? Buy popcorn,* for 1/3000th of a second in front moviegoers. Vicay claimed that his technique had improved the sale of popcorn by over 50%. Later, his inability to produce any hard data, forced him to admit that his study was fraudulent. After researching the degree to which subliminal advertising is currently being utilized in advertisements, I have been unable to detect any reports of extensive use of it or data suggesting that it is effective.[10]

Manipulative advertising can also be utilized by interest groups using fear in their infomercials to make their point: e.g. cracking an egg in a skillet and comparing the egg to a human brain on drugs. Repetition is a simple yet effective way that advertisers can build brand awareness by mentioning the product or company repeatedly. In general, successful ads create: a desire in consumers; ways to fulfill that desire; how to feel good about doing so.

Advertising is most often used to describe a product and promote its specific features, or to make claims about what the product or service can do for potential customers. They provide successful results by informing, educating and developing expectations in the buyer. Associating a product or company with a famous person, a catchy jingle or a desirable state of mind can promote a powerful emotion that creates a strong psychological connection with the consumer. And then there is the *bandwagon technique* that attempts to sell a product by convincing consumers that so many others are using it—they should join the crowd. These ads often employ generalities that evoke instant approval e.g. *America loves...* links patriotism with a product to create a positive response.[11]

The Rise of Consumerism

The combination of popup ads on web pages, with television, radio and print media advertisements are overwhelming the human psyche with their sheer volume and frequency. But how are they impacting our quality of life; their effectiveness in regard to purchasing the product? The prevalence of advertising on consumer preferences has long been debated. A new area of study suggests that human response to advertising is based on cognitive efficiency, rather than the influence of the ad itself. A study entitled, *A Functional Explanation for the Effects of Visual Exposure on Preference,* directed by cognitive scientist Mark Changizi of Rensselaer Polytechnic Institute has provided some answers regarding the vague impacts of advertising on the human spirit. A study published by the Perception Institute discusses how the repeated exposure to advertisements increases consumer preference for those products—even though their impact is greatest when consumers are least aware of having seen the ads. The simple viewing of ads can unconsciously impact our feelings, perception and preferences regarding advertised products. But the impact of repetition has limits—over exposure can lead to displeasure and disgust, diminishing any partiality for the product.[12]

At the onset of 21st century, a new world order had evolved with one superpower remaining—the United States of America. One province after another had seceded from the USSR dissolving it from within leaving Russia to stand alone. Fifty years after John Kennedy had declared the war on poverty, and Lyndon Johnson had signed into legislation laws to minimize it, Americans must have wondered if it had all been a tragic mistake. Perhaps, the only miscalculation was the false belief—that it would be a simple task. Government policymakers had failed to acknowledge the facts: the eradication of poverty throughout America would require sacrifice from all its citizens. Yet even today Americans continue to maintain an impractical understanding of the affluence that surrounds them; the cost of providing the government services they've come to expect. Rather than asking what we can do for our country, many would prefer that government take the steps to boost demand for investments and consumer spending, thereby removing the shackles that constrain consumer spending and economic growth.

Continuous economic growth is the mantra echoed by politicians, because it's a requirement of the capitalist system: interest is needed to pay back the cost of borrowing; economic growth is needed to create that money. Inflation, interest rates, the money supply, unemployment levels, consumer confidence and consumer product price indices are all key factors that determine the consumption levels that drive economic growth. Economists don't typically factor in the need for natural resource materials or the energy needed to complete manufacturing, distribution and sales. It's assumed as a given—Earth is considered capable of providing these necessities long into the probable future, perhaps forever. However, Earth's actual ability to provide these materials is dependent upon having an available remaining stockpile of recoverable resources to manufacture the needed products, while absorbing all the wastes resulting from the process.[13]

The simplest way of achieving continuous economic growth is to promote the enduring growth of the human population. For much of human history our population has grown at rates of less than 1% per year. Beginning in the year 1800 the growth rate began increasing almost linearly from .4 to .6% until 1920. During the period from 1920 to 1962, the growth rate jumped from .6 to 2.1%— the highest growth rate increase Homo sapiens have ever experienced. From there the growth rate declined sharply, but the population continued growing from 3 billion in 1962 to 7.4 billion in 2015. As I write this the global human population is approaching 7.6 billion people with projections of 8 billion by the year 2024. It's estimated that roughly 108 billion people have ever lived on Earth—the current population represents roughly 6.5% of the entire sum of humanity that has ever lived on Earth.

Estimates of future population levels are calculated based upon the current population; projected fertility rates and death rates and a variable called population momentum. Fertility rates are roughly defined as the average number of children born to a woman during her lifetime, who survive past the mother's child bearing years. The replacement value—the number of off-spring that replaces the parents—for human's fertility rates equal two. Death rates are the actual or expected death-rates per a certain combination of demographics (e.g. age group, geographic area, ethnicity, education level, income etc.) calculated or estimated over a specific period of time.

Population momentum is the most commonly misunderstood concept used to estimate future population values. It is often assumed that once fertility rates equal the replacement value of two or lower—replacing both parents—that zero-population growth is magically achieved. However, true zero population growth is not achieved until maybe decades later, when both parents are deceased. For example, when a high-fertility and high-growth rate population experiences an immediate drop in fertility rate to two or less, the population continues growing for several decades, or for as long as the children's parents survive. Eventually the population will achieve equilibrium at some new lower level. Estimates for future population growth are determined by calculating the projected rate of growth for the existing population using projected fertility, death and population momentum estimates.

Another perspective for evaluating population growth considers the time required for Earth's human population to double. From the 9th to the 16th century the human population doubled from .25 to .5 billion people. From that point the population growth rate slowly increased until the 20th century. The shortest doubling-time occurred during the period 1950-1987 when the population increased from 2.5 to 5 billion people in just 37 years. Humanity experienced the largest population growth rate ever during this period—2.1% in 1962. Since then the growth rate has declined slowly while the time required to double the population has increased. Over the course of the 21st century the time needed to double the population is expected to be one century (2000-2100). The global population of 5.5 billion is expected to double to 11 billion by the year 2100, roughly the same rate of doubling experienced from 1800-1900 when it grew from .9 billion to 1.65 billion people.[14]

America followed world population trends experiencing its highest growth rate of 1.69% in 1960 with a population of 187 million. The U.S. population in 2018 is 326.8 million people, representing just 4.28% of Earth's human population. The U.N. projects that the world population will increase 41% by 2050 to 8.9 billion people with nearly all of this growth occurring in developing countries. While at least part of the rise in global consumption is the result of population growth, it's a mistake to blame consumption increases solely on growing population levels.

Consumption levels of the world's wealthiest countries — especially the U.S. — are draining the remaining stockpiles of critical nonrenewable natural resources at untenable rates; the disparities of this consumption are glaring. Twenty percent of the population from the highest income countries consume 86% of all private consumption. Those from the poorest 20% consume just 1.3%. The top 20% consume 58%; the poorest 20% use less than 4%. The top 20% consume 45% of all meat and fish; the poorest 20% expend just 5%.[15]

Consumption via *Consumerism* has increased resource consumption and waste that's damaging the natural environment in ways inconceivable and irrecoverable. As consumers and citizens of humanity on planet Earth — we have the responsibility, the capabilities and the means to significantly reduce what and how much we consume, and ultimately our waste.

So, what is all this talk we hear from politicians about the need for continuous economic growth. Economists and most government leaders alike cringe when the growth in business activity declines. The reasons for their concern lie in the realization of the obvious: that when the economy declines, people (voters) lose their jobs, their spending declines, commerce decreases further and so on. But in countries where the population is increasing, economic growth is needed just to support the added workers with jobs so that they can earn the money to pay for the products they will ultimately consume. Yet, Laissez-Faire capitalism allows for natural barriers to wealth to form within the populace that creates the disparity of wealth accumulation occurring around the world.

What if economic growth was held constant with no-growth?

No-growth economies might be able to exist in countries where the working population is constant or declining except for one detail: the need to pay for all the interest accrued on the money borrowed to buy the goods and services required to support all the people.

By the middle of the 20th Century, the development of efficient and inexpensive transportation increased the contact between nations. This pressured cultures around the world to adopt western modes of thinking regarding industrialization and continuous growth. It's a model that has worked well in Europe and North America for a couple of centuries; increasingly there are signs that continuous growth is nearing the end of its time. In a finite world the rate of growth must slow at some point, eventually stop and decline. If we were to transition to a no-growth economy the need for capital investment would be lessened, causing the banking sector to contract. Investors would have a limited number of places to put their money. Stock prices would increase slightly and investments would shift to government securities that would have to be financed in some way.

Assuming the average human society is 55% productive, a steady state economy would require tax collections of 45% to cover the so-called *non-producers*. These funds would be redistributed in various ways to those not otherwise receiving income (social security to retirees or those unable to work, schooling for students etc.). In the long term we need to develop a society with a mechanism to provide a basic lifestyle for everyone subject to the limitations of Earth's resources. With an economic model based on continual growth, we are consuming an inordinate amount of natural assets just to maintain current lifestyles. We desperately need to transition to an economic system where at least 45% of income is recycled to the non-productive sectors of society to restore balance to both: our financial accounts and with our planet. But what is everyone going to do if we stop acquiring so much stuff? Pre-industrial societies are a good example. In the South Sea Islands there was a stable society based upon local produce and fishing. Housing was made of local organic material. It was a society which had enough material abundance to provide a subsistence life; the population had time for leisure activities such as relaxation, rituals and socializing. Without the need to produce a surplus the amount of work was modest. Today, most families have both adults working full time and are barely able to support a modern family. Continuous growth in a finite world cannot be sustained. Yet, in the short term a no-growth economy will result in harsh living conditions around the world. We need to find a middle ground where humanity can continue to thrive.

In the short term we're consuming vast amounts of fossil fuels and natural resources to maintain the current level of economic livelihood. If we don't significantly curtail consumption in the long term—we'll be forced to as finite quantities of these materials become exhausted. What we need is a way to reduce population growth while throttling back consumption and economic activity gradually until a semi-steady state economy can be realized. At best we should begin stair stepping down the level of consumption and resource extraction, reducing it to lower levels gradually one step at a time. And we had better start soon. At the same time, we need to continue and accelerate the transition over to using cleaner energy sources. We will review much more about this in the upcoming chapters.

One way money is created is by loaning it into existence. This happens when commercial banks make loans and accept deposits, but not enough money is loaned into existence to pay back the interest. Economic growth creates the money to pay back the interest on loans. As consumption and economic activity is scaled back, the challenge will be paying back the interest on existing debt. Economic growth is essential to produce the wealth needed to pay back interest bearing debt. A steady state economy requires a financial system with almost no debt. The human civilization capable of surviving in our longer-term future will have a smaller population, utilizing steady state regionalized economies with lifestyles, infrastructures and technologies capable of sustenance with renewable resources. The transition to this type of society is what humanity must contemplate and act on now, or the path leading to our future will be riddled with the worst kind of despair.[16]

8

The Promise of Polymers

If you're part of the aging baby-boom generation you might recall how the world was—before there were plastics. In the late 1950s I recall going shopping with my parents to the market down the street. Most of the produce we bought was locally grown seasonal vegetables and fruits, dairy products, minimally processed cereals and freshly slaughtered meats. The items we purchased were carefully loaded into heavy brown paper bags and hauled out to our '57 Chevy for the trip home. Fresh milk—in heavy refillable tapered glass bottles—was delivered to our doorstep daily; the empty bottles were picked up, cleaned and refilled until unusable. Occasionally, we'd ride over to the local drive-through beverage store with our containers to pick up beer and soda in refillable bottles housed in wooden cases. And then, out of nowhere…there were plastics.

Almost a century earlier, inventor John Wesley Hyatt responded to a New York company's offer of $10,000 for anyone capable of developing an alternative for ivory—a material in short supply due to the increase in appeal for the game of billiards. Hyatt began investigating a material called *Parkesine*—a hardened form of nitro-cellulose considered the first true plastic—developed by Englishman Alexander Parkes in 1862. Hyatt developed a practical method for manufacturing solid, stable nitro-cellulose, treating it with camphor to form a material he called *celluloid* in his 1869 patent application. Celluloid could be readily molded into a variety of shapes, replicating materials including: ivory, horns, tortoise-shells and linen. The discovery of celluloid was revolutionary; human creativity was progressing beyond the limits of nature. At the time celluloid was credited with saving elephants and tortoises from extinction; plastics were being hailed as protectorates of nature from ruthless human consumption.

In 1907, a Belgian born industrial chemist named Leo Baekeland invented a material he called *Bakelite* produced completely from synthetic materials. At the time, Baekeland was pursuing the development of a synthetic substitute for shellac—an electrical insulator—to meet the needs of the expanding electrical equipment market. Since Bakelite doesn't soften when heated, it's considered the first thermoset-plastic ever developed. Bakelite was also inexpensive, durable, nonflammable, heat-resistant and readily molded into almost anything. It is still used to make insulation for electrical wire, radios, knobs, cameras, telephones and many other items. At the same time, improved industrial processes were developed by manufacturers that were applied to polymers—*synthetic organic materials*—increasing the production efficiencies of plastics significantly. Most notably, the process of *injection molding* was created: liquefied plastic is injected into a mold and cooled, before ejecting the finished product.[1]

The huge success of celluloid and *Bakelite* prompted a general search for new polymers without any requirement for a particular set of characteristics. Polymer research was performed on the principle: *if you make it ... people will want it*. The rapid success of polymers attracted the attention of budding corporations to get involved in polymer development. New polymers including *vinyl, ethylene* and *acrylic* were developed in the research laboratories of companies including Dow Chemical, Du Pont, Monsanto, Union Carbide and Standard Oil.

The Promise of Polymers

With the onset of World War II, the importance of synthetic materials became paramount as the natural resources needed to support the war effort became scarce. The importance of the capacity to produce war materials rivaled the military might needed to fight the battles. The U.S. government provided a billion dollars to construct plastic research and manufacturing plants throughout the country. Companies were compelled to share information and work together, creating standards to improve the materials and perfect the processes. Nylon, invented by Wallace Carothers in 1935 as a substitute for silk, was the first new polymer developed in support of the war effort. During the war, nylon was used to manufacture rope, parachutes, body-armor, and helmet liners. Acrylic resins discovered in 1931 were used as clear, protective industrial coatings. Later, the development of transparent acrylic sheets: light, tough and readily formed were used as a bullet resistant glazing on American warplanes. Another acrylic variation called *Plexiglas* was used to replace glass in aircraft windows. Plexiglas remains clear and free from yellowing due to its superior weather-resistance; it is still used to make airplane windows today. Dow Corporation released a new acrylic called *Saran Film* to protect military equipment from salt and sea spray damage during overseas shipment.

Over the course of the war the production of plastic materials increased three-fold; by wars end some of the companies that had prospered supporting the war effort were going out of business. This occurred in spite of the significant pent-up demand for consumer goods unavailable during the war years. While plastics provided the potential to meet consumer demand more quickly at lower costs, it was still viewed as a cheap and fragile replacement for more robust materials.

During the war, the U.S. government investment in plastics helped build the infrastructure for the plastics industry that exists today. The Society of Plastic Industries (SPI) was created to promote and lobby for the use of plastics to the federal government and consumers. The SPI instituted measures which kept member companies from paying wages considered too high, or charging product prices deemed too low. SPI also joined forces with the trade journal *Modern Plastics* to help showcase the industry.

Over time plastics would challenge traditional materials—steel in cars, paper and glass in packaging and wood in furniture—with a safe, sanitary and inexpensive material that was readily formed into custom shapes. Formica tables and fiberglass chairs, hula-hoops, disposable pens, silly putty and nylon pantyhose were just some of the innovative plastic products created. While these products were all successfully marketed through sophisticated advertising campaigns, consumers quickly learned their weaknesses: they melted when heated; when broken they were irreparable. Nonetheless, the successful application and marketing of polymers to the American consumer led to a postwar expansion of the plastic market that exceeded GNP growth, to become one of the largest industry segments in the country.[2]

Issues posed by the toxicity of plastic materials intensified as environmental concerns heightened during the 1960s. By 1970 the increasing amounts of toxic, non-biodegradable plastics were filling up landfills; people began questioning the plastic throw-away concept. The plastics industry counter attacked by going after new markets while claiming that plastics were safe; they continued promoting the advantages of plastics to consumers.

Benzene is an important by-product of the incomplete combustion of certain materials: petroleum and coal. Today, petroleum supplies most of the benzene needed to produce the intermediary chemicals which in turn yield a wide range of polymer products. More than half of all benzene production is processed into styrene which is used to make polymers and plastics: *Polystyrene* and *Expanded Polystyrene (EPS)*. *Polystyrene Foam* is used to manufacture common *foam* products: coolers, wine shippers, molded end caps, corners, box packaging, and cups for the office water cooler. *Styrofoam* brand foam is a registered trademark of the Dow Chemical Company covering a full range of extruded polystyrene building products—commonly referred to as *blue board* in the construction industry—used primarily in construction for wall insulation, floor insulation and roof insulation systems. Expanded Polystyrene

(EPS) is the generic name for the white rigid material made by expanding polystyrene beads, using steam and pressure to bond them together to form blocks or shape molds. EPS is also used in the construction industry for insulation and to fill voids.

In 1975 the first *polyethylene terephthalate* (PET or PETE) disposable soda bottles were introduced replacing returnable, refillable glass bottles in the bottled water and soda markets. PET is considered a plastic resin, a type of polyester. It is lightweight, strong, shatterproof, transparent and readily recycled, possessing a strong inherent barrier (oxygen and moisture barrier durability). PET containers show a code #1 in the center of the rotating triangle recycling symbol located on or near the bottom. Bottles and containers made out of PET are readily recycled in many areas. However, since PET is semi-porous, it can absorb some of the food or beverage molecules it contains during its use—this residue is difficult to remove. While sterilization can fully purify the plastic during recycling, the high temperature will melt it. As a result, most recycled PET bottles are used to make lower grade plastic products—those that cannot be used in applications for human consumption.

The plastic resins available today consist of two basic varieties: thermoset and thermoplastic; separate classes of polymers that respond differently to the application of heat. Thermoplastics have low melting points on the order of 160°C (320°F); they can be re-melted and reformed by applying heat. Thermoplastics soften when heated and become more pliable; the curing process is completely reversible. Therefore, thermoplastics can be remolded and recycled without affecting their physical properties. Thermoplastic resins offer a variety of performance benefits including: high strength, shrink-resistance and flexibility. Depending on the resin, thermoplastics can fulfill low-stress applications such as plastic bags or high-stress mechanical parts. Some thermoplastic examples include: polyethylene, PVC, and nylon.

Thermoset-plastics retain their shape once hardened; they are capable of withstanding high temperatures without losing their shape. Thermoset-plastics have melting points in excess of 200°C (392°F); they will char or burn as opposed to melting. Thermoset-plastics differ because they are irreversibly cured when heated to form an infusible, insoluble material. Once hardened a thermoset resin cannot be melted and reheated for reuse—they are not recyclable. Thermoset polymer examples include: polyurethane, unsaturated polyesters, phenolics and silicones. Polyurethane is extremely tough, hard and resistant to wear. Applications include wood coatings, shock absorbers, shoe heels and refrigerator insulation. Unsaturated polyesters are used in composite products with extremely high strengths such as boat hulls, automobile bodies and artificial limbs. Phenolics are rigid and strong when compressed, temperature resistant and inexpensive. They are used to make billiard balls, end panels for toaster ovens and automobile brake system components.[3]

In 1988 the Society of Plastics Industry (SPI) introduced a system to help identify the different types of plastics that can be recycled; a system now used in many countries. The numbers located in the center of the *rotating-triangle-symbol* indicate the grade of plastic by its resin ID code—#1 being the most readily recycled plastic down to #7 which is the least.

1 – PETE or PET – Polyethylene Terephthalate is the easiest plastic to recycle; its initial use is to make soda and water bottles and common food packages. The prime uses for recycled PET are as polyester fiber, for strapping or non-food containers.

2 – HDPE – High density Polyethylene or polyethylene high-density (PEHD) is a polyethylene thermoplastic made from petroleum, sometimes called *walkathon* or *polythene* when used to make pipes. It possesses a high strength-to-density ratio and is used to produce plastic bottles, corrosion-resistant piping. The global HDPE market exceeds 30 million tons. HDPE is readily recyclable, initially used for packaging detergents, bleach, milk containers, hair care products and motor oil.

3 – PVC – Polyvinyl Chloride is used to make a variety of items including: plastic pipe, toys, furniture and packaging. It is difficult to recycle and poses significant environmental and health threats.

4 – LDPE - Low-density Polyethylene is utilized to manufacture different kinds of wrapping, grocery bags and sandwich bags, recyclable into more of the same.

5 – PP – Polypropylene is used in the production of clothing, bottles, tubs and ropes. It is recyclable in synthetic fiber.

6 – PS – Polystyrene (Styrofoam, a trademark of the Dow Chemical Co.) is one of the most widely used plastics; the scale of its production being several million tons per year. It's used to make cups, foam food trays for meats etc. and packing peanuts. Due to its large size and light weight, polystyrene poses significant recycling problems; by weight, there's not much material to recycle especially when considering transport costs to the few recycling facilities that will process it. Polystyrene foam is often used in packaging to pad appliances. When released into the environment polystyrene takes a very long time to break down, during which animals can ingest it, blocking their digestive tracts and causing starvation. Manufactured from petroleum, polystyrene is highly flammable.

7 – Other – Polyurethane or a mixture of any of the above plastics which are generally not recyclable.[4]

Generally speaking, the advantages of using plastics are due to its lightweight and conformability as a molded part. Plastics are chemically and corrosion resistant, useable in any climate. They possess excellent thermal and electrical characteristics with low temperature coefficients of expansion, good adhesiveness with high resistance to moisture. Many types of thermoplastics are recyclable, dependent on the type of resin and the application. Yet in many instances theses plastics can only be recycled down to lower level applications: i.e. from packaging of food products to non-food products, limiting the effectiveness of recycling them.

On the other hand, plastics are produced from mostly non-replaceable materials, so they're inherently nonrenewable in the long term. When plastic components break, they usually are not repairable; they become brittle at very low temperatures, subject to deformation under high pressure. Plastics used as containers for foods and drinks can leach harmful chemicals, including Bisphenol A (BPA) and phthalates into the foods they contain causing human health issues. Plastics are also health hazards when used to make small items such as toys, grocery or trash bags, any item that presents a choking hazard.

Thermoplastic resins can be recycled; thermoset resins cannot, yet both are problematic. The disposal of all nonrecyclable plastics involves their long-term internment in landfills or incineration. Incineration usually results in the recovery of some of the energy used to produce the plastic; it also allows for the release of noxious and poisonous gases into the atmosphere. In landfills, plastics will bide their time degrading over a period of 500 to 1000 years dependent on the polymer type; releasing gases from the toxic pile during that time.

Certain recyclable thermoplastic resins might not be recycled to the same level of function (i.e. level 2 to level 2) dependent on their application. The plastics most typically recycled are plastic containers, jars, bottles, plastic bags, plastic packaging and large industrial plastics. Recycling involves the sorting of plastics by type and application. Specially designed machines sort the plastics according to resin content and color, or they're screened manually. This process ensures that all contaminates are eliminated.

Next, the recycling mill sorts the scrap plastic according to the recycling symbols located on the bottom of each item. The sorted plastics are cut into small pieces; plastic bottles and containers are ground up and cut into tiny pieces or flakes. The heavier and lighter flakes are separated using a special sorting machine. The flakes and chunks are washed with detergents to remove any remaining contamination. The clean flakes are passed through equipment that further separates resin types; the plastic flakes are heated to dry. The dry flakes are melted down and remolded into a new shape or processed into granules. The plastic pieces are compressed into tiny pellets and transported to plastic manufacturers to be made into new plastic products.

The standard recycling number system described earlier shows the most recyclable plastics with a #1 designation. The lesser recyclable materials follow in order. Keep in mind that all the plastics identified in this system are thermoplastic: most all of the currently available thermoset plastics are not recyclable.

The most commonly recycled plastic is polyethylene terephthalate (PET #1). PET is used to make water and soda bottles, peanut butter and salad dressing bottles, medicine and many other common containers. After normal processing at a recycling facility, PET can be used as fiberfill for winter coats, sleeping bags and life jackets, to make beanbags, rope, car bumpers, combs, boat sails, furniture, and plastic bottles not intended for human consumption.

In order to use recycled PET to make food grade plastic containers the plastic must be hydrolyzed down to a monomer by removing the water and other solvents, creating a molecule capable of re-polymerization, which is then purified and polymerized to make brand new PET plastic. Due to the high cost of this process PET is usually recycled into lower quality level plastics. Generally speaking, PET#1 can be recycled to produce plastics rated as LPDE #4 and Other Plastics #7.

High Density Polyethylene (HDPE #2) possesses characteristics that include excellent strength and stiffness, resistance to moisture, flexibility, ruggedness and reduced permeability to gas. It is used to make many kinds of bottles: milk, fruit juices, shampoo, motor oil, laundry detergents and bleaches as well as trash bags.

HDPE #2 plastics are widely accepted at recycling centers. The plastic is sorted and cleaned to remove any contaminants before undergoing homogenization. Processes called *Sink-float separation* or *Near Infrared Radiation (NIR)* are used to remove other plastic resins. If other polymers are present in the batch the recycled end-product can be ruined. Recycled HDPE #2 is usually made into: toys, plastic lumber and fencing, crates, rope, lawn and garden products, floor tiles, piping, truck bed liners, trash receptacles and a host of other durable plastic products most often considered as Other Plastics #7 that are seldom recyclable.[5]

Polyvinyl Chloride (V or PVC #3) can be mechanically recycled when enough quantities of clean, sorted and consistent material is available. Mechanical recycling simply involves melting down the PVC to be recycled as an equivalent; this can be performed only a limited number of times before the polymers break down and the quality of the plastic degrades.

Feedstock recycling is another alternative to recovering plastic materials. In this process the original polymers are broken down into their basic components to become a recyclable feedstock. The valuable polymers are decomposed at high temperatures to recover the most valuable chemical elements which are used to produce new polymers.[6]

Virgin low-density polyethylene (LDPE #4) is used to make squeeze-bottles, shopping bags, clothing, carpet, frozen food and bread bags as well as food wraps; this is one plastic that is considered safe regarding human and animal exposure. Locally, my community picks up LPDE #4 from roadside recycle containers, however many areas around the U.S. do not, yet more are beginning to accept it. Those facilities that process LPDE #4 typically melt it down to eliminate as many of the contaminants as possible. Since it's not practical to remove all the impurities the resulting material is considered as degraded LPDE #4, which is molded into thin plastic sheets and sold to various plastic component manufacturers.

The reprocessed material is used to make clothing, compost bins, paneling, trash can liners and cans, floor-tiles and shipping envelopes.[7]

Polypropylene (PP #5) is a recyclable polymer used for applications similar to both high and low-density polyethylene. It's more rigid and resistant to heat and chemical solvents, bases and acids. Some of the applications where you will find polypropylene used are automotive components, reusable containers, plastic parts, packaging and labeling, and many more. Polypropylene is recycled into brooms, battery cases for automobiles, bins, pallets, signal lights, ice scrapers, and bicycle racks.

Polypropylene possesses properties that make it the most commonly used plastic packaging in the U.S. and the U. K. Yet, PP #5 is one of the least recycled plastics in both countries. As a component used in packaging its useful life is very short. Without more opportunities for recycling, polypropylene will wither away in landfills for decades. The additives used in many plastics contain toxins including lead and cadmium. Recent studies suggest that the cadmium in plastics can percolate out of landfills and have a negative impact on many ecosystems. And incineration of polypropylene can give off dioxins and vinyl chloride resulting in severe environmental pollution.

The recycling process for polypropylene PP #5 and most polymers has five basic steps: gathering, separating by group, cleansing, melting and the reproduction of new plastic components. However, in most cases the recycled plastic polymer possesses lower level characteristics and capabilities than the original polymer, due to the inability thus far to remove critical impurities. Many companies are working hard to resolve this critical issue.[8]

An English company named Nextel Ltd. has developed a process to decontaminate food grade recycled PP #5 back to the same level of functionality when mixed with virgin PP #5 at a 50:50 ratio. Scientists and engineers are developing similar solutions for other polymers, most notably PET #1. The creation of improved recycling capabilities at reasonable costs for the most commonly used polymers can make them sustainable for as long as energy is available to support the process.

The initial phase of the Nextek process melts the PP #5 to 250°C (482°F) to remove contaminants. Next, any residual molecules are removed from the polymer by placing it in a vacuum and re-solidification at around 140°C (284°F). The output of this process is projected to be equivalent to food grade PP #5. While this process is intended to reduce the amount of PP#5 incinerated or sent to landfills—the program can only work if significantly more than the current level of 1% of PP #5 is collected for recycling.

Back in July of 2017, Proctor & Gamble and Pure Cycle Technologies announced their process for recycling polypropylene to original quality, and their plans to build a polypropylene plant in Lawrence County, Ohio that will utilize their new system. Proctor & Gamble invented the process and has licensed it to PureCycle Technologies.

The following is a summary of an interview conducted by Packaging Digest with John Layman, Proctor & Gamble's R & D Technology Manager and founding inventor behind the PureCycle Technology. The interview was conducted prior to the Sustainable Packaging Coalition (SPC) Impact conference held in San Francisco, CA, in April of 2018.

Polypropylene (PP) is a versatile polymer with global annual production of 60 million metric tons. Recycled PP is usually grey or black in color making it difficult to use in a variety of plastic applications. The PureCycle process purifies recycled polypropylene back to virgin-like polymer. It can remove colorants, odor and contaminants from recycled plastic, offering recyclers a cost-effective method of recycling PP without trade-offs in performance.

Demand for recycled PP in North America is estimated at 1 billion pounds, with 720 million pounds needed for high-quality recycled PP. The PureCycle process is a solvent-based physical separation and purification process; a non-chemical process differing from chemical processes where the polymer is depolymerized back to a monomer. The purification process is physical, using a solvent to remove impurities that can migrate and then non-soluble contaminants from the recycled PP. The removal of impurities, odors and colors is accomplished in steps, each with a specific role in removing differing types of contamination. Virtually all impurities are removed. Because the PureCycle process purifies recycled plastics at the molecular level, there is no chemical reaction within the polymer molecules; they remain intact as the impurities are removed. The process works with all formats of recycled material.

The new plant's feedstock evaluation unit (FEU) will come online fourth quarter 2018. The FEU will enable PureCycle to develop a product portfolio and provide samples to potential customers. At maximum capacity, the plant will accept up to 120 million pounds of plastic per year, producing 105 million pounds of recycled polypropylene. The yield loss will depend on the amount of contamination in the feedstock. If the feedstock contains 5% calcium carbonate, 3% polyethylene and 2% pigments, the yield of recycled PP will be 90%.

This technology demonstrates P&G's commitment to sustainability and helps achieve P&G's 2020 recycling goals of doubling the use of recycled resin in plastic packaging, ensuring 90% of product packaging is either recyclable or programs are in place to create the ability to recycle it. PureCycle technology supports P&G's vision of using 100% recycled or renewable materials with zero consumer waste going to landfills. P&G has a long-term vision to use 100% renewable or recycled materials for all products and packaging. This process helps P&G and PureCycle Technologies make progress toward this vision. They are starting with polypropylene, while considering a range of other opportunities.[9]

––––––––––––––––––

Polystyrene (PS #6)— also known as Styrofoam, a trademark of the Dow Chemical Co. is a thermoplastic polymer made from styrene monomers that's relatively cheap to manufacture and process. PS #6 is moldable, inexpensive and light weight. It has many initial uses, such as packaging material for all kinds of products ranging from laptop computers to coffee cups. However, its low weight and larger size make it impractical to ship to recycling centers. It is stable when disposed of in landfills but requires large volumes of space. Without UV rays or oxygen, it can take anywhere from 50-1,000 years to degrade. When incinerated it requires high temperatures—above 900 °C (1632°F)—otherwise dangerous compounds can be released, e.g. alkyl benzenes, carbon monoxide and Benzghiperylene. PS #6 can be recycled but most of it isn't—many communities with curb recycling pickup won't pick it up because they can't process it. So, what does one do with all those polystyrene shipping peanuts that are so hard to coral and dispose of?

With polystyrene's light polymer structure, regrinding and molding it into recycled components is difficult without degradation. The best bet is to initially mold PS #6 into standard reusable shapes for packaging applications that can be reused over and over. In food applications the polymer is commonly contaminated with food which is difficult to remove. Polystyrene's light weight and low cost combined with so many custom applications make it hard to incinerate, recycle or dispose of. Perhaps the best solution is to minimize its use.[10]

It's finally time to review the remaining class of plastics: Other #7. As you might imagine this group of mystery plastics is least defined, a catch-all for all plastics not fitting into any one category, including most newly developed plastics and bioplastics. There are three main plastic resins that comprise much of the Other #7 category: styrene acrylonitrile (AS/SAN), acrylonitrile butadiene styrene (ABS), polycarbonate, polylactic acid (PLA). Plastics in this category are usually made from more complex, multi-layered resins; many include plant-based materials called bioplastics. Some examples of #7 plastics are: ketchup and citrus juice bottles, reusable water bottles and containers, Melamine, oven baking bags, plastic plates and cups.

Styrene acrylonitrile (SAN) is also known as simply *acrylonitrile*. It is a copolymer plastic comprised of styrene (70% to 80%) and acrylonitrile (20% to 30%) identified as SAN. Because of its greater thermal resistance, it is often used instead of polystyrene (PS #6). SAN is used to make food containers, water bottles, kitchenware, computer products, packaging material, battery cases and plastic optical fibers. SAN degrades very slowly in landfills. It contains dangerous materials and hazardous additives, including colorants, stabilizers and plasticizers that may contain toxic elements, including lead and cadmium. In landfills these pollutants can leak into the water and soil.

Somewhere around 2.8 million tons of household equipment, 10 million vehicles and a host of other products containing mixed plastics are scrapped annually. Although metal is often recovered from these items, many plastics and other non-metallic items are disposed of in landfills. The variety of plastics has increased making it difficult to separate high-purity plastics including SAN from the plastic waste stream.

SAN may or may not be identified as another #7 plastic, making it difficult for recyclers to identify. However, if identified as SAN a froth floatation process can be used to separate the highly pure individual plastics from waste streams that have a mixture of plastics. SAN has a high energy content that make it ideal for combustion with energy recovery. However, the combustion temperatures need to be more than 900°C (1632°F) to eliminate the emission of dioxins completely. Health risks are possible with lower combustion temperatures. Any recovered resins should be compatible with new material and capable for use in the same applications as the original material.[11]

Acrylonitrile butadiene styrene (ABS) is a plastic polymer made by fusing styrene and acrylonitrile with polybutadiene, another plastic included in category Other #7. ABS is often used with 3-D printers to construct three-dimensional objects using programmed models and designs.

ABS is relatively strong, due mostly to the way the polymers are bound together. ABS produces finely shaped 3-D printed models with tough surfaces and some elasticity over a range of temperatures. ABS also possesses good resistance to pressure, with adequate heat resistance for use in a host of products. At high temperatures, ABS boils and reacts chemically. ABS is used to make prototypes and many products, including Lego bricks and other toys, plumbing components, automotive parts and kitchen appliances.

The utilization of ABS and other similar materials for 3-D

printing has provided designers with important alternatives for evaluating the performance of components in prototype designs before they're manufactured in large quantities. Previously, prototypes of plastic components to be used in an array of products were evaluated by machining prototypes out of wood or other materials capable of becoming a model to form a mold that was usable for making sample prototype parts. One weakness of this process was that the plastics used in these soft-tool molds usually possessed properties significantly different from the plastic polymer intended to mold the production plastic part. The other obvious advantage of 3-D printing and ABS type plastics is the ability to make unique parts in very small quantities, e.g. prosthetics of all kinds, at reasonable cost.

ABS is an opaque, thermoplastic polymer with a non-crystalline shape, most often polymerized using an emulsion process—dispersion of droplets from one liquid to another non-soluble liquid. ABS is impact resistant and impervious to corrosive chemicals, a natural fit for prototyping: readily machined, sanded, glued and painted; available with cosmetic finishes and colored with relative ease. ABS includes no known carcinogens and no adverse health effects related to its exposure. Its many applications include: computer keyboards, power-tool housings and plastic wall-socket covers.[12]

Bioplastics are made from polyactic acid (PLA) plastic. Because PLA plastics are often used to make bottles and other items usually fabricated from HDPE #2 or LDPE #4, they shouldn't be mixed with any other plastic category in recycling bins. Mixing different plastic categories can contaminate recycling batches making the entire batch unusable. Until new classes of plastic number designations are created, bio-based plastics should be sent directly to commercial composting facilities. It's important to note that bioplastics cannot be composted in backyard compost bins, since bioplastics will compost only at temperatures much higher than those attainable in your average compost bin. Recycling procedures vary significantly around the U.S., so check with your local waste management organization about specific recycling policies and rules.

Bioplastics are the third major type of Other #7 category of plastics: polymer resins based upon an organic biomass instead of the petroleum that provides the base material for most synthetic polymers. Bioplastics are classified as *bio-based*, a derivative of plant-based substances. Cellulose and starch—derived from corn and sugarcane—are the common bio-feedstocks used to manufacture bioplastics.

The term biodegradable generally means that a material can be broken down by microbes in the soil under the right conditions. Practically speaking, only those materials that biodegrade in a reasonable time period—usually weeks or months—are considered biodegradable. Therefore, using this refined definition, some bioplastics are biodegradable, along with some petroleum-based plastics. In fact, some petroleum-based plastics biodegrade more quickly than some bioplastics. So, it's important to be aware of the meaning of the word *biodegradable*. Plastics that don't degrade within a period of weeks or months are referred to as *durable*.[13]

Another major concern about all plastics is: are they compostable? In this case *ATMS International* has provided a specific definition of what it means to be compostable: "*capable of undergoing biological decomposition in a compost site as part of an available program, such that the plastic is not visually distinguishable and breaks down to carbon dioxide, water, inorganic compounds, and biomass, at a rate consistent with known compostable materials (e.g. cellulose), and leaves no toxic residue.*" While some materials can be composted in home garden-type composters, others must be composted at commercial facilities capable of generating much higher compost temperatures. It is important to know which plastics are home-compostable and those that require commercial composting. The elevated temperatures provided by commercial digesters are capable of faster composting times for all compostable materials.

While bioplastics have existed for more than a century, petroleum-based plastics have been favored due to their relative cost and availability. However, as concerns grow regarding increasing oil consumption, the composting and waste of non-biodegradable plastics, bioplastics are increasingly considered as viable alternatives. Thus far bioplastics have been utilized to generate the normal assortment of plastic products: grocery bags, food packaging and food containers, biodegradable utensils. Bioplastics are also capable for applications as components in electrical and electronic housings and enclosures. And the Bioplastics developed thus far don't include bisphenol A (BPA). While the BPA issue overall remains undecided the European Union has banned the use of BPA in baby bottles. Whether broader restrictions will be forthcoming on BPA is unknown. The advantages offered by bioplastics are primarily that less pollution and energy consumption result due to their production, use, recyclability and disposal when compared to petroleum-based plastics.

Polylactic acid (PLA) is a popular bioplastic capable of being processed and molded using existing plastic molding equipment. PLA has the second largest production volume of any bioplastic, producing plastic films, bottles, and biodegradable medical devices, with characteristics similar to polypropylene (PP), polyethylene (PE) or polystyrene (PS). PLA can be used as the feedstock material in 3D printers, useable to print solids encased in plaster-like molds that can be fired in a furnace and used to mold melted metals. PLA contracts when heated making it usable as shrink wrap material, yet its low transition temperature makes many types of PLA unable to contain hot liquids.

The primary disadvantage of all bioplastics—as it is for all Other #7 plastics—is that they are unrecognizable for their unique polymer characteristics, recyclability issues, biodegradability, compost temperature requirements to determine proper recycling, compost processing or land fill issues.

Cups made from polylactic acid (PLA) have the appearance and texture of a regular PET plastic cup. Without any type of designation to identify Other #7 polymers, it is near impossible for conscientious home recyclers or recycling facilities alike to discriminate between these polymer types. When this occurs, either readily recyclable plastics are sent to the landfill or perhaps a batch of PET cups are recycled with enough PLA cups to ruin the entire batch, rendering it useless.[14]

The end result of all this confusion is that many Other #7 plastics, especially bioplastics, are not disposed of properly. Too many local trash haulers are without the capacity to sort, compost, or recycle Other #7 plastics so that it all ends up in a landfill; consumers are unable to determine which bioplastics are biodegradable or home compostable. What is needed is an expanded plastic resin ID code to cover many of the new and differing types of plastic polymers available, and perhaps a way of categorizing them into a simpler code that consumers can use to properly recycle all plastic components.

BPA is an acronym for the chemical bisphenol A, an industrial chemical that's been used to manufacture plastics and resins for the past 50 years. BPA is commonly used to produce transparent and rigid: polycarbonate plastics often utilized in food, beverage containers and many other consumer goods; and epoxy resins that coat the inside of metal food cans, bottle tops and water supply lines to isolate the contents from metal contact. The primary issue regarding BPA is its capacity to leak; over time BPA can migrate in small amounts into food and beverages stored in materials containing the substance. The health risks posed by BPA contact include disrupting normal hormone levels, brain and behavioral problems, increased risk of cancer and heart issues, with greater levels of risk for infants and young children.[15]

It has been known for many years that BPA mimics estrogens; it's capable of binding to the same receptors as natural female hormones throughout the human body. BPA testing has shown it can promote human breast cancer cell growth as well as decreasing the sperm count in rats. These tendencies have caused concern regarding the possible health risks of BPA. Other studies show that BPA leaches from plastics and resins when exposed to tough use or high temperatures in microwaves or dishwashers. The U.S. Centers for Disease Control (CDC) found BPA traces in most all the urine samples collected in 2004 to measure the occurrence of a variety of chemicals found in the human body. Some studies indicate that even those plastics that don't contain BPA can release estrogenic-like chemicals.[16]

Scientists predict that roughly 90% of humans today have BPA in their bodies, obtained from eating foods from BPA containers, or picked up from the air, dust or water. BPA plastics were very functional when made into baby bottles, sippy cups and the lining of cans used as containers for baby formula, as well as many other products suited for infants and young children. When the controversy regarding BPA leakage was first publicized early in 2009, six major suppliers of baby bottles and sippy cups—Avant America, Inc., Disney First Years, Dr. Brown, Evenflo Co., Gerber, Playtex Products Inc.—began using plastics without BPA to make their products. Many baby formula vendors changed their can-liners to use non-BPA materials.[17]

In May of 2011 the European Union was the first global governing agency to respond to the possible BPA threat by restricting the sale of baby bottles across the European Union. Baby bottles containing BPA had to be removed from the shelves in stores across the EU by June 1, 2011; the import of such products into the EU is forbidden. The ban was preceded by EU directive (2011/8/EU) adopted in late January, 2011. The EU then banned the manufacture of baby bottles containing BPA in the EU on March 1, 2011.[18]

Later, on September 5, 2017 the European Commission (EC) notified the World Trade Organization (WTO) of its intention to further restrict the use of BPA in specific food-contact products. The new restriction proposed a specific migration limit (SML) of .05 mg/kg for BPA compared to the previous .6 mg/kg and essentially expands the ban on the use of BPA in the manufacture of polycarbonate infant feeding bottles to sippy cups.[19]

The U.S. Food & Drug Administration was slower to take action. The FDA responded to a request for the FDA's current position on BPA use in a statement issued from the FDA's Office of Food Additive Safety issued by biologist Julie N. Mayer M.F.S. on July 31, 2007. The statement concluded that the dietary exposure of BPA from all food contact materials is thousands of times lower than levels producing no adverse effects in animals. The FDA also determined that the use of polycarbonate-based baby bottles and BPA-based epoxy coated cans used to hold infant formula are safe, and therefore no reason to ban or otherwise restrict the currently authorized food contact applications of polycarbonate polymers and BPA-based coatings. In 2010 the FDA altered its findings to warn that based on the findings of animal studies, the FDA expressed concern about the potential effects of BPA on the brain, behavior and prostate glands in fetuses, infants, and young children.[20]

On March 30, 2012 the FDA again stated a similar BPA position in their *Summary of FDA's Current Perspective on BPA in Food Contact Applications*: "FDA's current perspective, based on its most recent safety assessment is that BPA is safe at the current levels occurring in foods". Based on FDA's ongoing safety review of scientific evidence, the available information continues to support the safety of BPA for the currently approved uses in food containers and packaging. Four months later in July of 2012 the FDA reversed that decision, eliminating the use of BPA-based polycarbonate resins in baby bottles and sippy cups and disallowing BPA coatings on packaging for infant formula.[21]

While the promise of polymers has promoted the development of many unique products and provided capabilities unachievable before there were plastics, the down-side of their use includes: the extra fuel needed to produce them; the added pollution of the air, water, soil and biodiversity loss from their manufacture and disposal; health issues resulting from the migration of plastics into the food supply for all lifeforms; biodegradability and landfill issues.

As nature conscious consumers we can choose to use less plastic. When selecting plastics place a strong preference on bioplastics, especially those that are biodegradable or recyclable without significant chemical migration into foods via their production, use and disposal. It is important to support efforts by politicians and environmental organizations to establish improved systems to create new categories of materials that can be recycled together; to promote the broader recyclability of various sizes of plastics, metals and other appropriate components will help to increase recycling rates. Also, the promotion of recycling plastic components *in all products* (e.g. computers, printers, cell phones and automobiles) with proper labeling and adding value to their recovery (e.g. a deposit paid by customers redeemable at product dismantling centers for disassembly and sorting any recyclable components for sale to recyclers). As a first step we should eliminate the use of plastics from those applications most damaging to human health and the environment: BPA, plastic grocery bags and Styrofoam.

The impact of plastics on human health is still unproven. BPA is the plastic material drawing the most concern now, but there are many other plastic resins that have not been studied sufficiently to determine any health issues. The potential concerns regarding human consumption of plastics in contact with food include: the ability to act as a hormone to disrupt hormone levels and ultimately the development of fetuses, babies and young children; brain and behavior issues in young children; an increased risk of cancer; a higher incidence of heart problems; general issues such as obesity, diabetes and ADHD.

In the 1980s, the health and environmental hazards of plastics became the target of environmental activists concerned with the unrestrained application of Polystyrene (Styrofoam). This occurred at the same time that headlines regarding chlorofluorocarbons (CFCs) used to make Styrofoam were destroying the ozone layer. Proponents claimed that Styrofoam was benign when deposited in landfills. In the end, most fast food companies stopped using Styrofoam while manufacturers found alternatives to CFCs to use for its production.

By the 1990s most refillable bottles had been replaced with plastic throwaways of the PET #1 or HDPE #2 recyclable levels. It didn't take long for the growing piles of plastic trash in land-fills around America to cause concern among local residents. There was increasing pressure for states in the U.S. to pass so called *bottle-bill* legislation—a first step in mandating the handling of bottle trash—requiring deposits at the time of purchase for plastic bottles of soda and water as well as aluminum cans. The beverage container industry in America—bottlers of water, soda and beer and the corporate owners of grocery stores and convenience stores— spent huge sums of money lobbying against laws requiring new or amended beverage container deposit legislation. As a result—no new bottle-bill laws have been passed in the U.S. since 2005.

Currently only ten states: California, Connecticut, Hawaii, Iowa, Maine, Massachusetts, Michigan, New York, Oregon and Vermont have bottle-bill legislation in place requiring a deposit fee at the time of purchase on applicable bottles and cans. Around the world the following countries have bottle-bill laws in place: Australia, Belgium, Canada, Croatia, Czech Republic, Denmark, Estonia, Fiji, Finland, Germany, Hungary, Iceland, Israel, Lithuania, Netherlands, New Zealand, Norway, Sweden, Switzerland, the United Kingdom and the United States.

While bottle bills have been effective in those countries that have them, the plastic litter problem continues to expand around the world. The primary issue is the fact that synthetic plastics are generally not biodegradable; they will remain in landfills for a very long time without any appreciable degradation. More importantly, the plastic refuse that never finds its way to landfills ends up littering the land and seas in increasing volumes for millennia.

As we consider the future of polymers—how they fit into a viable future for life on Earth—we should examine the key issues regarding each polymer type: the amount and types of energy required to produce them; environmental issues regarding their manufacture; their recyclability and biodegradability; the amount of garbage they produce and their ultimate functionality for humankind, compared to the alternatives.

Petroleum and natural gas are generally used to make the ingredients most synthetic polymers are made of. Estimates for the energy consumed to produce plastics in the U.S. range from 2.5% to 4% of U.S. consumption. Plastics are currently produced using petroleum products including: carcinogenic chlorine, vinyl chloride, endocrine disrupting phthalates and bisphenol A (BPA). These chemicals release large amounts of pollutants into the air, water and soil during their production; some release toxins as they are used. For the most part the end products made of plastic can be recycled—but usually only to descending degrees of functionality.

This means that generally speaking, #1 PET soda bottles can be recycled down to #2 HDPE applications and then recycled again down to #4 LDPE grocery bags etc. From there they are largely recyclable to the same level #4 to produce more grocery bags—assuming people recycle them instead of throwing them in the trash. In the end, all synthetic polymers will end up as non-biodegradable trash contained in landfills or scattered across planet Earth. And there's lots of it—the U.S. alone produces roughly 270 million tons of new plastic trash each year— only 10 percent is recycled.[22]

For many years recycling has been offered as a primary solution for plastic waste issues. Recycling continues to be the solution emphasized for problems posed by plastic waste along with hopes for what I call loop recycling—recycling processes back the same level of function—as well as the development of new bioplastic, biodegradable polymers. Nevertheless, according to the EPA the total municipal solid waste (MSW) generation was increasing slightly each year, while overall recycling rates had leveled off by 2014 in the U.S. Since then, and especially in the past year plastic recycling rates in the U.S. have dropped markedly as plastic waste generation continues to grow. The volume of plastic waste grew dramatically in the 50-year period from 1960-2010 totaling 33.3 million tons with just 3.17 million tons recycled.

With the generation of plastic waste increasing, the recycling rate is dropping for many reasons: the Chinese ban on accepting plastic waste to recycle; increasing recycling costs due to the number of trucks needed to collect the various types of waste; as plastic production increases further the cost of new plastic material remains relatively low; increasing speculation that other southeast Asian countries that have previously accepted plastic materials for recycling from the U.S. will decline in the future, due to their own environmental concerns. Future projections are that the rate of plastic recycling in the U.S. could fall as low as 4.4% by year end 2019.[23]

Sadly, there are few alternatives for replacing our consumption of synthetic plastics without major inconvenience for human societies. We can go back to using the glass, wood, cloth, paper and metal alternatives we used before there were plastics; change our habits to minimize our use of plastics—especially single-use items such plastic shopping bags, plastic soda bottles, straws, eating utensils, packing materials etc.—or replace synthetic plastics with either *loop-recyclable* plastics or bio-plastics. A few bio-plastics have already been developed using bio-degradable natural polymers such as celluloid for their production. But so far, most bio-plastics cost more for most common applications, they are not yet capable of filling the shoes of the varieties of plastic applications in use today.

9

Synthetic Sustenance

Humans have been domesticating plants and animals for the past 14,000 years, using selective breeding techniques to produce offspring with preferred characteristics to benefit humankind. At the same time, most of these species eventually lost their ability to self-survive in the natural world — they're completely dependent on humans for their survival. Selective breeding was the precursor for what's come to be known as the manual selection of genes: the creation of genetically modified organisms (GMOs).

Generally speaking, GMOs are lifeforms where genetic engineering processes are used to manipulate genes by adding new genetic material from similar species. GMOs are used as tools to perform science and research, to develop food and medicine and to alter the characteristics of certain lifeforms for the benefit of humanity. GMOs have been in the works for many decades in laboratories around the world. *Transgenic* organisms are a group of GMOs altered by adding genetic material from unrelated species — an important distinction. *Cisgenic* GMOs are created using genetic material from related lifeforms. Until recently, the creation of transgenic organisms has been somewhat of an exception. The first GM-mouse was created in 1973; the first GM-plant was introduced in 1983.[1]

Well before the discovery of the genome in 1921, Frederick Banting and Charles Best extracted insulin—the hormone that controls blood sugar levels—from the pancreas of dogs. The following year, the hormone was administered to a 14-year-old boy suffering from type I diabetes mellitus. The insulin saved the boy's life, proving that insulin extracted from an animal could be used to treat human diabetes. When their discovery was made known virtually all of the insulin harvested for human use was collected from slaughterhouse animals, usually pigs or cows.

Some 25 years later the FDA approved *Humulin*, a recombinant-DNA (r-DNA) proven to be indistinguishable from pancreatic human insulin. FDA regulatory scientists worked alongside Eli Lilly researchers to solve the unique challenges regarding the production of human insulin from bacteria, playing a critical role to ensure that the first FDA approved medical product using gene-splicing technology would be safe and effective for use in humans. Since its release Humulin has been lifesaving for millions of patients.[2]

Recombinant-DNA (r-DNA) is when DNA molecules are formed by laboratory methods using genetic recombination, bringing together genetic material from multiple sources to create DNA sequences that otherwise wouldn't be found in the genome. The r-DNA process is possible only because: *DNA molecules from all organisms share the same chemical structure*. The r-DNA process began a new area of research and applied biology, a key component of biotechnology that's been expanding in size and scope.[3] The r-DNA method is only one of the many incredible scientific advances made possible by James Watson and Francis Crick with their discovery of the double-helix configuration of human DNA in 1953. Scientists had previously used breeding programs to alter the nucleotides in a genome; today there are a number of *mutagenic agents available—agents that can alter an organism's DNA by increasing the frequency of its mutations*.[4]

Synthetic Sustenance

Genetic engineering is the formal name for the process of gene cloning: *a gene copied from DNA extracted from one organism is incorporated in an unnatural host organism capable of continued propagation.* The genome can be viewed as a set of program instructions for building an organism: its growth, development and function. Changing an organism's genome can modify its characteristics.

A genotype is the name given to a complete heritable genetic identity for a species, e.g. Homo sapiens. A phenotype is a set of observable characteristics or traits of a particular genotype: shape, development, biochemical and physiological properties, behavior, and interaction with the environment. The term polymorphic is used when two or more clearly different phenotypes exist within the same species population. Cisgenic plants contain genes that have been isolated either directly from the host species or from a sexually compatible species.[5]

A gene identified as performing a certain function can be separated from its normal location using biochemical methods outside the living species: a procedure called in-vitro. Genes can also be synthesized with a gene machine: an automated instrument that can produce a predetermined DNA sequence. A *vector* or passageway is a DNA molecule used to transfer genetic material to another cell. Isolated genes can be transferred into microbial cells with the appropriate vector, where it can be expressed and/or replicated. When performed successfully the transferred gene will replicate normally and ensue in the next generation.

The first GMO was created in 1973 by Stanley N. Cohen and Herbert Boyer by demonstrating their process for combining genetic information; showing how the new combination could be duplicated in offspring. Soon afterward scientists established a voluntary moratorium on certain types of DNA-recombinant experiments. This resulted in a global scientific conference to develop guidelines for such experimentation that concluded: *recombinant-DNA research should proceed—only under strict guidelines.* These standards were eventually created and propagated by the National Institutes of Health in the U.S., and by equivalent agencies around the world. They provide the basis for the general regulation of

GMO research today.[6]

Rudolf Jaensch produced the first transgenic mouse in 1974 by successfully inserting foreign DNA into early-stage mouse embryos, all of which carried the modified gene in their tissues. In subsequent experiments leukemia genes were injected into mouse embryos to verify that the genes had integrated not only to the embryos, but were also passed on to their offspring. In 1983, Michael W. Bevan, Richard B. Flavell and Mary-Dell Chilton created the first GM-plant when they infected tobacco with *Agrobacterium*: bacteria with the unique ability to transfer its DNA to plants that was transformed with an antibiotic resistant gene. They used tissue culture techniques to grow a new plant containing the resistant gene.[7]

The primary uses of GMOs are for biological and medical research, experimental medicine, producing pharmaceutical drugs, agriculture and conservation. Bacteria were the first laboratory modified organisms; they continue to be important models used for experimentation in the field of genetic engineering, and to produce quantities of the pure human proteins needed for medicines. GM-bacteria are also used to produce insulin, biofuels, clotting factors and human growth hormone. GM-viruses have been used to make plants immune to a variety of diseases as well as providing the enzymes used to manufacture a variety of processed foods.

GMOs have been applied to alter plant life and to create new and uniquely different varieties. As consumers, GM-crops are of most interest as they account for much of what we eat, directly as a food source or fed to animals raised for human consumption. Examples of GM-crops include: those tailored to be resistant to diseases, pests or commonly used pesticides; to flourish in certain weather and environmental conditions; to provide improved nutrient levels and or shelf-life. GM-plants have also been developed to support the conservation of plant species threatened by other plants or diseases.[8]

Genetically modified animals are another important category of GMOs. In the early 1980s Ralph L. Brinster and Richard Palmiter developed the processes for producing transgenic mice, rats, rabbits, sheep and pigs. They also established many of the first transgenic models of human disease. The GM-animals under development include: those used for the research of human diseases, the production of industrial or consumer products, products intended for therapeutic use in humans and the enhancement of food production and quality traits.[9]

Before there were herbicides, weeds were controlled by selectively altering soil pH, salinity or the application of fertilizers; mechanical methods included plowing and cultivating. Later, petroleum oils were used to control weeds along irrigation ditches before herbicides were developed to control the unwanted plants. Initially, herbicides controlled broad categories of plants. As the science improved, seeds for food crops were made more resistant to particular herbicides with the aid on GM-technology.

Scientists began researching chemical herbicides early in the 20th century. The research was completed near the end of World War II in Great Britain and the U.S., regarding the potential for using herbicides in war. In 1940, W. G. Templeman at Imperial Chemical Industries in London, England developed the strategy of applying excessive growth substances to many broadleaf weeds to kill them, without harming most cereal crops. The organic herbicide named 2,4-d was created by Templeman in 1941. It was released commercially later in 1946, providing enhanced weed control for wheat, corn, rice and other cereal and grass crops, while killing most broadleaf plants with little effect on most common grasses. The release of 2,4-d brought about a revolution in global agricultural output, making it the first successful plant selective herbicide. The low cost of 2,4-d has provided for its continued use today; it remains one of the most commonly used herbicides in the world.[10]

Dicamba is another herbicide that was first developed and registered in 1967. This chemical is a chlorinated derivative of o-Anisic acid (a class of antiseptic compounds used as an insect repellent and in dyes, pharmaceuticals, perfumes and agrochemicals).[13] Dicamba selectively kills broad-leafed weeds with a lesser impact on grass family plants. It is commonly used together with other herbicides. Dicamba's various brand names include Banvel, Diablo, Oracle, Vanquish, XtendiMax (a newer formulation made by

Monsanto) and Engenia (a newer formulation made by BASF). According to the National Pesticide Information Center more than 1,100 herbicide products contain dicamba. Dicamba controls annual and perennial rose weeds in grain crops and highlands; it is also used to control brush and bracken in pastures as well as legumes and cacti. In combination with a phenoxy herbicide or with other herbicides, dicamba is used in pastures, range land and non-crop areas (fence rows, roadways, and wastage) to control weeds.[11]

So-called *phenoxy-based-herbicides* are all similar to the popular 2,4-d type, comprising a family of chemicals that mimic the growth hormone indoleacetic acid (IAA): the naturally occurring plant chemical that normally controls plant growth. Phenoxy herbicides essentially provide an excess of an IAA like chemical, prompting broadleaf plants to grow uncontrollably until they run out of fuel and die. On the other hand, the primary component in *glyphosate-based herbicides*—like Monsanto's Roundup and Ranger brands—inhibit the synthesis of amino-acids: specifically, the EPSP synthase enzyme used by many plants to promote new growth. *Phenoxy herbicides flood targeted plants with too much growth hormone—glyphosate-based herbicides inhibit its production.*[12]

Glyphosate was discovered by Monsanto chemist John E. Franz in 1970 and marketed in 1974 under the brand name *Roundup* as a broad-spectrum herbicide and crop drying agent used to kill weeds: annual broadleaf weeds and grasses that interfere with food crops, those plants affected by weeds early in their development. Roundup's initial release enjoyed only limited success because its active ingredient focused on killing weeds after they had emerged; its success would expand later when Monsanto improved Roundup's plant selectivity by developing GM-seeds with glyphosate resistance. Monsanto's patents on the Roundup herbicide expired in 2000.[13]

Herbicides are also rated according to their effectiveness into three distinct groups: pre-plant herbicides are applied before planting the crop; pre-emergent herbicides are dispersed before weed seedlings emerge through the soil; post-emergent herbicides can be applied after the crop is planted or when the weed seedlings have emerged through the soil surface. Herbicides are also classified according to their selectivity: some are designed to control a broad range of weeds; others regulate certain types of weeds.[14]

Most broadleaved plants minimally absorb glyphosate via the roots and readily through their foliage, transporting it to their growing points. There it inhibits the synthesis of the three important amino acids essential for the biological functions in many plant types. Glyphosates inhibit the creation of these amino acids, making them toxic to those plants. Glyphosate is an effective weed killer for actively growing plants (post-emergent) and ineffective as a pre-emergent plant herbicide.[15]

Monsanto's development of Round Up–Ready GM-seeds is another segment of the GMO story regarding the food crops that can have a serious impact on the foods we consume directly. Yet, the progress made to approve GMOs in the U.S. as legitimate food sources has progressed quickly, in spite of significant resistance and debate by opponents. At this point you could say *the cows have already been let out of the barn*. Let's review two stories regarding *GMO plant research and development that are—as different as night and day*.

Dr. Robert Fraley grew up on a farm in Hoopeston, Illinois. At age 27 he joined Monsanto armed with PhDs in microbiology and biochemistry. Shortly after his arrival, Fraley attended a meeting with veterans of Monsanto's pesticide division. During the meeting, they discussed news about the recent discovery of a bacteria that had developed resistance to the glyphosate herbicide. They suggested that Fraley and his team locate the bacteria, isolate the glyphosate resistant gene and then splice it into the genome of some popular seed crops to provide farmers with Roundup tolerant crops. At the time Dr. Fraley is reported to have replied: "if all we can do with biotechnology is sell more damned herbicide, we shouldn't be in this business". During the years that followed Dr. Fraley's opinion would change drastically—he would spend much of his career managing the development of Roundup resistant GM-crops, creating a 17-billion-dollar global industry and a new era of agricultural efficiency.

During the 1980s, Mansanto worked with a company named Calgene (which they later acquired) trying to create Roundup resistant crops. By 1985, Monsanto had developed a petunia plant somewhat tolerant of Roundup; neither company was able to develop a GM-seed worth commercialization. The Monsanto team plodded along making slow progress when they caught a lucky break from an unexpected source. At the Monsanto Roundup manufacturing plant in Luling, Louisiana, glyphosate residues were routinely released into waste ponds to break them down. Over time, the bacteria in these ponds had developed glyphosate resistance. When Monsanto's waste cleanup division discovered the bacteria, they reported their findings (this was the glyphosate resistant bacteria reported earlier in the meeting with Dr. Fraley). When Monsanto's GMO researchers tested the bacteria's resistance, they determined its glyphosate tolerance as better than any genetic material they'd previously tested for use in developing Roundup tolerant plants.

The main stumbling block for further advancement was a method for splicing genes into the genome of the most valuable farm commodities on the market: corn and soybeans. In 1989 Monsanto struck a deal with two companies: Agracetus had developed a gene-gun to perform the gene-splicing and Asgrow was a major soybean seed supplier. The companies worked together using Monsanto's Roundup resistant gene to develop a commercial GM-crop product.[16]

By 1992, Monsanto's executives had lost patience with their struggling biotechnology project. Dr. Fraley and his team were given an ultimatum—to implement their theories with commercial ventures or shut down much of their program. Their search came to fruition late in 1992 in a deal with Pioneer, a leading supplier of corn and soybean seeds. After much haggling, Pioneer made a one-time $500,000 payment to Monsanto for the right to use Monsanto's glyphosate resistant gene in its soybeans forever—Monsanto's only profits would result from the additional sales of their Roundup herbicide. In 1996, Monsanto and their seed company partners, Asgrow and Pioneer, introduced their own lines of genetically engineered-herbicide tolerant (GE-HT) soybean seeds. Later, Monsanto and other seed companies began marketing Roundup resistant seed with *versions for cotton, corn and soybeans. Monsanto's Roundup Ready GE-HT brand of GM-seeds became highly successful in the marketplace as the company rolled out new versions of seed for most food crops; which further increased sales of all glyphosate-based herbicides.[17]*

In the beginning Roundup Ready soybeans were being sown only on American soil—neither the European Union nor Japan had approved their import or cultivation. With U.S. soybean exports comprising nearly half of the global soybean harvest, American farmers had taken a huge risk by planting the GM-seeds. Fortunately, the EU decided to permit the import of GM-soybeans in April of 1996. Over the years spanning from 1997-2005, GM-soybeans would be followed by genetically modified: cotton, canola, corn, sugar-beets and alfalfa.

Today, the utilization of GMOs for food production across America is already fairly extensive. Currently, food companies aren't required to indicate the presence of GMOs on food labels or report any GM-seeds used for food production. However, some suppliers do claim *No GMOs* on their label seeking an advantage with GMO conscious consumers. More than 90% of all corn and soybeans currently produced in the U.S. are genetically modified. The FDA has approved many other GMOs for use in food products: alfalfa, apples, canola, papaya, potatoes, sugar beets and summer squash. Biotech corporations wanting to produce commercial crops have to apply for deregulated status, giving them the ability to cultivate and distribute without constraint.[20]

There are many potential attributes possible with the application of GMOs. They can be fortified with vitamins and nutrients or modified to have longer shelf-lives. Genetically modified tomatoes have shelf-lives up to 45 days. Food production efficiencies can be improved for a variety of inputs: water, nutrients and energy.[21]

However, GMOs were first developed commercially in the U.S. to develop crop varieties resistant to the herbicides in use, allowing for increased herbicide applications without fear of damaging the crops. Roundup—the Monsanto brand-name for the herbicide glyphosate—is a common weed killer that's been used by farmers and landowners since its release in 1976. Glyphosate inhibits plants from producing the proteins they need to survive; it's classified as a broad-spectrum herbicide because it impacts most broadleaf plants. The gene that provides glyphosate resistance was taken from the bacteria known as Agrobacteria. Since most plants make their essential proteins the same way, glyphosate has some impact on most plants. Roundup is not only a powerful weed killer, it also impedes the development of the crops it was developed to protect, limiting the dosage applied.

When farmers apply Roundup to Roundup-Ready crops resistant to glyphosate at recommended rates, using suggested farming practices the projected environmental impact should be less, due to the reduced pesticide use and the replacement of more harmful herbicides with Roundup. With Roundup-Ready crops farmers should be able to use no-till farming methods, eliminating the possibility of wind and water soil erosion in fields containing high concentrations of pesticides and fertilizers. However, when Roundup-Ready crops are working effectively their net environmental impact can be negative. One key negative outcome is the possibility of glyphosate resistant crops crossbreeding with weeds, producing: *glyphosate resistant weeds*. The manufacturers claim this is unlikely since most sexually compatible weeds don't thrive where Roundup-Ready crops are grown. Another problem is that lifeless Roundup-Ready plant matter might combine with other plants to create new toxic organisms.

While herbicide resistant GM-crops can minimize the damage from herbicides and provide better weed management, nature seldom sits idly by. Even if weeds don't crossbreed with Roundup-Ready plants directly, they have a tendency to evolve on their own, creating super-weeds resistant to glyphosate that effectively eliminate the benefit of applying the herbicide. The resulting weeds pose the biggest problem. Over time, so called super-weeds have already developed; they have spread over 60 million acres of American farmland, requiring more herbicide use, damaging the crops as well as the environment.

Synthetic Sustenance

A Union of Concerned Scientists briefing paper *The Rise of Superweeds...and What Do We Do About It?* published in 2013 explains how this occurred. When first released, Roundup-Ready seeds were very costly, yet widely accepted due to the time and energy saved while providing better weed control. Since glyphosate is less toxic than other popular herbicides, it's viewed as more environmentally friendly. As Roundup-Ready seeds were planted extensively, the genes for glyphosate resistance were able to spread to weed populations. Glyphosate resistant weeds evolved more rapidly as farmers ignored basic weed control practices. This allowed the weeds to adapt and flourish more quickly. Farmers could no longer rely on reduced glyphosate applications for weed control; overall herbicide use in the U.S. has been increasing instead of declining.[22]

The modern biotech companies responded quickly with the normal *bigger-and-more-of-them* response, developing a new generation of herbicide resistant crops impervious to: *two of the most popular herbicides: dicamba and glyphosate*. Monsanto's new *Roundup Ready-2* GM-seeds are resistant to glyphosate as well as dicamba — a herbicide in a chemical class with increased rates of disease in humans, including non-Hodgkins lymphoma. Dicamba is lethal to most broadleaf crops including common fruit and vegetables and more easily dispersed into the air than glyphosate, making it more apt to harm neighboring farms and uncultivated areas.[23]

The bigger problem is that weeds will eventually respond and develop resistance to dicamba and Roundup with increased herbicide immunity. At this point there are few other herbicides available to add to the mix; herbicides are like antibiotics and many key natural resources—there's a limited supply of them. The best nature friendly weed control solutions include: crop rotation; growing off season cover crops; using controlled tilling; utilizing manure and compost as fertilizer; taking advantage of the natural weed suppressing chemicals produced by some crops and natural insect control. Granted, these are all older practices that take more time, fuel, labor and land to produce the desired crop output—*the right way is not always the easiest or the cheapest. At some point very soon, we have to consider the long-term impact of our decisions on nature and all lifeforms on this planet, against the short-term decisions measured by in-flated—nature-worthless—dollars and cents.*

While Roundup Ready GM-seeds were actively being developed in America, another GMO story was progressing on the other side of the planet. Golden Rice is a GM-rice variety infused with more Vitamin-A. The Golden Rice Saga is about millions of people living throughout Asia and Africa subsisting on rice diets lacking in Vitamin-A, a deficiency that causes vision impairment and blindness in children, in some cases premature death. Vitamin A exists in three forms: retinols, beta-carotenes and carotenoids.

During the 1950s and 60s much research and development was progressing to develop solutions for agricultural problems occurring around the world, especially those issues hampering food production in developing countries. The implementation of these programs was called *the Green Revolution,* a program that was able to increase agricultural production worldwide substantially, beginning in the late 1960s. This initiative resulted in new farming technologies including: high yielding varieties (HYV) of cereal crops such as dwarf rice and wheat; chemical fertilizers; ago-chemicals; methods of irrigation and mechanical cultivation. Altogether these were presented as a package of modern methods to be applied together, replacing old practices with the new. An American by the name of Norman Borlaug has been called *the Father of the Green Revolution.* In 1970 he received the Nobel Peace Prize for his work and is credited with saving over a billion people from starvation.

Some 44 years ago researchers began discussing methods for creating an improved GM-rice. Twenty years later the Swiss biotech company Syngenta had completed the development of a GM-rice fortified with Vitamin-A that was not yet ready to market. As a humanitarian gesture, the intellectual rights for Golden Rice were transferred to the International Rice Research Institute (IRRI) for further refinement.[24]

The Golden Rice story begins in 1984 when a group of emerging biotech scientists gathered together for the first time to discuss methods for identifying and transferring genes to other organisms. The science was still in its early stages; genetically engineered crops didn't exist. One year later a second meeting took place in the Philippines to continue their discussion while reviewing the latest bio-tech developments. Many of the participants—those most comfortable with traditional crop breeding—voiced their concerns about GMOs in general. When the conference had concluded, a few of the scientists gathered at their guesthouse for a drink. After hashing over some of the key GMO pros and cons, the program leader asked each to name at least one gene—that they most wished to add to the rice genome. The group responded with a varied list of proposals including the addition of genes resistant to a variety of common plant diseases, and the ability to withstand drought.

Legendary plant breeder Peter Jennings was the last to answer: "Yellow endosperm," he replied, taking nearly everyone by surprise. Jennings had created the infamous rice variety named IR-8; he is credited with initiating the Green Revolution in the rice growing regions of Asia during the 1960s.

The program leader followed up by asking him, "why yellow endosperm?" Jennings went on to explain that the color yellow indicates the presence of beta-carotene—the source of vitamin-A in plants—and that natural white rice doesn't provide any. He described his extended search for natural varieties of yellow rice, noting that he had found none. Months later, a number of research institutes had begun studying the possibilities for the development of yellow rice.[25]

Vitamin-A deficiency is a huge problem in areas where people are reliant on rice. When their babies are weaned, they're fed a watered-down rice gruel. If denied the essential Vitamin-A during that period infants can be harmed for the rest of their lives. Vitamin-A deficiency causes vision impairment and blindness in about 250,000–500,000 children from developing countries each year, with the highest prevalence in Southeast Asia and Africa. Vitamin-A deficiency also undermines the human immune system, causing an estimated two million additional deaths; the younger the patient, the more severe the effects of Vitamin-A deficiency. Growth retardation and infections are common among children. Mortality rates can exceed 50% in children with a severe vitamin-A deficiency.

The actual inventors of Golden Rice were Ingo Potrykus, Professor emeritus of the Institute for Plant Sciences of the Swiss Federal Institute of Technology (ETH, Zurich) and Professor Peter Beyer of the Centre for Applied Biosciences, University of Freiburg, Germany (Ye et al 2002). The search for Golden Rice began in 1982 as a Rockefeller Foundation initiative. After years of study by a number of research groups another meeting of experts was held in New York City in 1992 to review the latest developments. It was at this meeting that Ingo Potrykus and Peter Beyer first met. They decided to begin a project that eventually led to the development of Golden Rice in 1999. Through their concentrated efforts they were able to show how to modify the intricate biosynthetic pathway to enhance the health-promoting virtues of the crop. The real breakthrough insight was that much of the needed pathway was already in place—only two genes were needed to create the proper process. Later, an improved version called Golden Rice-2 was completed using the same genetic strategy, capable of supplying some 60% of a child's vitamin-A needs, reducing the amount of Golden Rice needed to meet minimum dietary needs. Since then it's been a longer and more difficult struggle to further develop, test and get approval for Golden Rice.[26]

Generally speaking, the global scientific community has supported the Golden Rice initiative. Thus far, those countries standing to benefit most from Golden Rice have withheld their acceptance due mostly to cultural uncertainty and fear. A prime concern is that interbreeding and contamination will occur in the fields when cultivating GM-rice alongside standard rice varieties. And many developing countries have been influenced by the European Union's unified tough stance against GMOs, as well as global anti-GMO organizations.

At its beginning, headlines had praised the Golden Rice Project as a great humanitarian effort to save nearly half a million youngsters from blindness or premature death each year. According to a study published by Washington University in 2016, Golden Rice is still years away from field introduction; it may well fall short of the expectations and hopes of so many who have worked so hard and long on the project. The report noted that many advocates for using GMO technology to solve difficult human problems have backed this project from the start, as a simple way of providing poor farmers in remote areas with a subsistence crop capable of adding the Vitamin A missing from customary diets throughout Africa and Southeast Asia. Yet, the development portion of the project has dragged on.

At the same time, the project has attracted many opponents, including some of the more militant global GMO sceptics, as well as some local groups in the areas most affected by Vitamin-A deficiency who ethically or otherwise oppose the creation of any type of GMOs. Some anti-GMO groups portray Golden Rice as a project that biotech companies are using to pave the way, easing future acceptance and approval of future GM-crops to produce a variety of GMO foods.

The Washington University report concludes that after 24 years of painstaking research, *"Golden Rice remains years away from field introduction and it may not be able to meet the goals set at the onset of the project."* Golden Rice has not been able to achieve the yields provided by the non-GMO strains of rice currently being cultivated by farmers. The other key issue is whether the added beta carotene in Golden Rice can be stored between harvest seasons or cooked using traditional methods and ultimately be converted into Vitamin-A in the bodies of poorly nourished children. In the meantime, the Philippines has been able to reduce the incidence of Vitamin-A deficiency using non-GMO crops. Nonetheless, if genetic modification is capable of creating a strain of Golden Rice with yields where poor farmers can be successful, its impact on children's health is now questionable.[27]

It has been widely reported that 400 angry farmers attacked and destroyed a field trial of GM-rice in the Philippines on August 8, 2013. Yet, according to a Slate Group article written by Mark Lymas, "the crop was actually destroyed by a small number of activists, while farmers who had been bussed in to attend the event looked on in dismay." The article shows pictures of the event showing about 40 young people that appear to be "average teenagers, not farmers destroying the crops."[28]

Above and beyond the debate I think the crux of the Washington University report was presented sincerely by knowledgeable people, who've worked alongside this project for a long while. Perhaps Golden Rice doesn't yet meet the goals of its inception, maybe it never will. Yet, it has come a long way down the path of development having been supported along the way by good people for the right reasons; doing things the right way takes a lot more time. While I think this project still deserves a chance to prove its value or not, at this point that might not be in the cards.

Early in 2017, the Philippine Rice Research Institute (PhilRice) and IRRI submitted applications to the Philippine Department of Agriculture for permits allowing Golden Rice to be used for food, feed, or food processing. Food and feed safety applications were submitted to the U.S. FDA, Food Standards Australia New Zealand (FSANZ) and to Health Canada, stating that no health or safety issues had been identified. In the Philippines, PhilRice proposed that Golden Rice be approved for direct use as food, feed or processing marking the beginning of a 60-day public comment period. The developers are hopeful that once the Philippines, Australia and New Zealand have approved Golden Rice, that other countries will follow suit.[29]

The Roundup-Ready and Golden Rice stories exemplify the range in scope of the reasons for developing GM-crops: the benefits, risks and results thus far. The Golden Rice story is all about creating improved rice varieties for the consumption of humankind; it wasn't developed to improve profit margins. The main benefit of Golden Rice is to provide the needed Vitamin-A to humans who've survived for millennia on a staple rice diet; the risks are similar to those taken whenever humans tamper with nature. Is the end product safe for human consumption? What is its impact on the evolution and health of all species? Will it crossbreed or come in contact with other GM-crops? When we add something to an organism's DNA, what are we unknowingly changing or taking away? More generally we must ask: are GMOs the only viable way to feed our growing human population? What are the benefits and risks over the short term and most importantly the long term? And how do we mitigate any potential issues?

GM-crops can improve food quality with better appearance, increase nutrient content and elimination of seeds, provide longer shelf lives and tolerance to climate change with a goal of providing more fresh food for global distribution. They can be designed to grow in specific and challenging environments with greater resistance to pests, diseases and greater tolerance of herbicides. GM-crops are easier for farmers to grow, with less tilling and soil erosion, while increasing crop yields until the weeds adapt to resist the herbicide. The U.S. FDA requires that any GMO food must meet the same requirements as all other foods. Currently, the U.S. and Canada have not imposed restrictions or special labeling on GMO foods.[30]

Five companies: BASF, Bayer-Monsanto, Dow-Agrosciences, Dupont and Sangenta control most of the GM-seed market and a majority of the global pesticide market. To protect company profits, patents have been sought on certain seeds, resulting in patent infringement issues and penalties for farmers when GM-seeds cross-pollinate other crops.[31]

While food allergies are a growing problem in the U.S.—rising from 3.4% to 5.1% over the period from 1997 to 2011—a study from Harvard University concludes: there is no evidence that GMO foods are the cause of the increase. Other concerns are the transfer of allergies from one plant to another through genetic modification. The transfer of proteins from Brazil-nuts to GM-soybeans caused people allergic to Brazil-nuts to experience allergic reactions when consuming GM-soybeans. While those soybeans never entered the market, rules have been established by the UN Food and Agriculture Organization and the World Health Organization requiring GMO foods to be tested for their ability to cause allergic reactions.

When this is determined, any proteins transferred from the potentially allergic food item to the GMO must be listed as an ingredient and undergo testing to determine its ability to cause allergic reactions.

Antibiotic resistant bacteria are difficult to kill. The CDC reports that some two million people are infected by antibiotic-resistant germs, killing some 23,000 people each year. Antibiotic-resistant genes are often used to genetically engineer new organisms. There are concerns that the increasing numbers of antibiotic resistant germs are due to the growing use of antibiotic-resistant genes to make GMOs. As yet, there is no conclusive evidence, so more research is needed.

Other GM-food issues include: concerns they are increasing food allergies in the U.S.; the expanding resistance of bacteria to antibiotics; laboratory evidence that Roundup and Roundup-tolerant GM-corn can cause cancer and premature death in rats.

At this point some 33 corn and 20 soybean GMOs are being cultivated in the U.S., over 80% of the varieties being planted. Their harvests are used to create a variety of ingredients: corn-starch and high-fructose corn syrup used to produce processed foods and drinks. Some of the GM-corn is used to produce biofuels; most of it is used to feed livestock.[32]

By 2007, glyphosate was the top herbicide used by American farmers; second best in government, industry, commerce and home & garden; organic based 2,4-d was best. Glyphosate enjoyed a 100-fold increase in use between the late 1970s and 2016, somewhat in response to the spread of glyphosate-resistant weeds around the globe.[33]

Over the last three decades, GM-crops have been created using increasingly accurate genetic engineering processes, introducing new traits in plants that hadn't developed naturally. Some of these desirable characteristics include: pest and disease resistance; flexibility for environmental conditions; reduced spoilage; resistance to chemical treatments (e.g. certain herbicides); improved nutrient profiles.

Many farmers around the world have adopted GMO

technology: between 1996 and 2016 the total land area of GM-crop cultivation increased by a factor of 100, from 4.2 million to 432 million acres. In 2010 some 10% of global croplands were planted with GM-crops. In the U.S., by 2016 some 94% of planted soybeans, 96% of cotton and 93% of corn were genetically modified varieties. GM-crops have also expanded rapidly in developing countries. In 2016, roughly 18 million farmers grew 54% of worldwide GM-crops in developing countries.[34]

As of 2016 some 26 nations* have allowed growing GM-crops; nearly twice as many have banned their cultivation. Many of those nations that prohibit the planting of GM-crops allow their import, especially for animal feed. Other nations like Canada, Japan and China restrict the import of GM-foods until they pass normal regulatory standards. Data shows that some 460 million acres of GM-crops—half of them herbicide resistant—were planted by 18 million farmers in 2016, across the 26 countries allowing their cultivation, 19 of which are developing countries. Globally, half of all GM-crops planted are soybeans. The U.S. planted the highest acreage of GM-crops followed by Brazil, Argentina, Canada and India, their total comprising roughly 90% of the global GM-crop area.

Of those nations banning GM-crop cultivation there is a mixed bag depending on the source of the data: ranging from complete bans to significant and partial bans. The most populous country banning both the cultivation and import of GM-crops is Russia, with exceptions allowed for scientific research. In the EU individual countries can ban their farmers from growing GM-crops. In 2015, nineteen EU members, including Germany and France, voted to prohibit the cultivation of eight new GM-crops being reviewed for approval by EU regulators. Yet EU countries are one of the world's largest consumers of GM-crops, some 30 million tons of corn and soybeans are imported to feed livestock.[35]

---

*Countries growing GMO crops 2016: Brazil, U.S., Canada, South Africa, Australia, Bolivia, Philippines, Spain, Vietnam, Bangladesh, Colombia, Honduras, Chile, Sudan, Slovakia, Costa Rica, China, India, Argentina, Paraguay, Uruguay, Mexico, Portugal, Czech Republic, Pakistan and Myanmar.

I believe that creating GMOs to be resistant to herbicides is a turn down a path to no-where, except to promote obscene increases in herbicide sales. Monsanto's Roundup-Ready crops were first developed with the goal of creating crop varieties resistant to their popular Roundup herbicide used to control weeds. The result is highly proprietary—the profit motives are substantial. From a financial point of view, Round-up Ready seeds are high priced while also promoting increased consumption of Monsanto's Roundup herbicide.

Most Roundup Ready seeds also include what's known as a *Terminator Feature,* meaning these GM-plants produce infertile seeds. This precludes interbreeding with other species yet also prevents the farmer from utilizing seeds harvested for future planting. Many cite the terminator technology as restricting farmers from saving money on seeds and reusing their best seed (seed that has evolved to produce improved yields in local conditions). Instead farmers are forced to purchase the newest strain of Roundup Ready seeds each year for all their planting. Monsanto contends that the terminator technology was added to prevent the spread of glyphosate resistance to other species.

The possible benefits of Monsanto's Roundup Ready herbicide resistant crops include the use of increased herbicide applications without damaging crops and allowing no-till farming methods that reduce the possibility of soil erosion. For farmers the benefits touted are: improved yields due to better weed control; the time and energy savings realized from using no-till farming methods.

The main concern regarding herbicide resistant GMOs is the fear of passing on their herbicide immunity to other organisms. Since their release, the cultivation of Roundup Ready crops has become almost universal in the U.S. As a result, giant rag-weeds—super-weeds—resistant to Roundup have been created. Seed contamination is the other issue resulting from GMOs. Roundup Ready genes have been introduced into the food supply—their impact on the environment is unknown. Other concerns suggest that modifying one gene to affect a specific function may impact other functions as well. In other words, a variety of unexpected changes can result from modifying one gene.

It's extremely difficult to predict the impact of releasing artificially created organisms into the environment. Careful testing and analysis are needed to evaluate the hazards. The Environmental Protection Agency (EPA) is the lead agency responsible for the safe release of GMOs into the environment and establishing whether crops are safe to cultivate and consume. When it comes to the food supply, Monsanto claims to be addressing the needs of the world. Yet, there is little evidence Roundup Ready crops increase the yield or the profits of farmers. For the most part, the majority of GMOs being used have been developed to be herbicide resistant as opposed to increasing crop yields directly. Concerns about the effects of GMO foods on health are two-fold: the impact of the crops themselves and the toxicity of the herbicides. The EPA currently regulates the concentration of glyphosate in drinking water to levels safe for human consumption. With the added use of Roundup on crops, consumers may be ingesting more of the chemical than they realize.

Humans appear incapable of grasping the full ramifications of tinkering with nature's evolutionary process. Humanity faces a future of climate change, the depletion of underground water aquifers and shortages of clean water, biodiversity loss, top-soil erosion and increased energy consumption to produce fertilizer and to cultivate crops. Many GM-crops are simply short-term techno-fixes for problems resulting from previous solutions which have caused more problems than they solved.

We need to change our diets to be more reasonable and healthier, increasing the consumption of foods produced without chemicals. GMOs should be utilized if needed to increase crop yields or to improve key nutritional values of the most essential crops consumed by humanity, if accomplished without an increase in energy input. Such GMOs should be adequately tested to determine their toxicity, allergy potentials and their general impact on all lifeforms and the environment overall. The expected outcomes should be thoroughly explored and the proposed benefits should be strictly identified and evaluated.[36]

At the end of the day, no overwhelming evidence exists that indicate GM-foods completely tested and evaluated before their release, providing marginal improvements in quality, consistency and yield will cause human health hazards. Yet, as we pursue lifestyles of excessive consumption and waste, I don't think we can expect GMOs or any technology to take up all of the slack caused by our excesses and lead us to the promised-land, or the American dream.

However, GM-plants resistant to herbicides that promote increased herbicide use are a completely different question. In this case, many of the key GM-crops were developed for all the wrong reasons — they fulfill maximum profit requirements to a tee. It's important to realize *that the glyphosate-based herbicide called Roundup is not a GMO*. However, glyphosate tolerant GM-plants are GMOs; their unique properties make them resistant to both glyphosate (Roundup) and dicamba herbicides. The combination of the most popular herbicides and GM-seeds for crops tolerant to them — *is a hazardous combination for our food supply, and all of humanity*. While this chapter has been mostly about GMOs, the development of GMOs immune to herbicides has linked these two issues together — GMOs can increase the risks of herbicide exposure in general and it's showing up increasingly in our food.

Dewayne Johnson was a grounds-keeper for the Benicia Unified School District in California. He had worked there for three years (2012-2015) taking care of the various school grounds, including the application of Monsanto's Ranger-Pro herbicide to control weeds. He applied the weed-killer a maximum of 30 times each year. Healthy when starting his employment there, two years later he was diagnosed with non-Hodgkin lymphoma (NHL), a cancer that affects white blood cells. Four years later, the disease had progressed covering roughly 80% of his body with lesions; he couldn't speak and was unable to get out of bed. At that point his doctors thought he might have just a few months to live.

The trial began on July 9, 2018 with the plaintiff's lawyer making the case that Monsanto had ignored the health risks of its top-selling glyphosate Roundup weed-killer under the brand name Ranger-Pro. He claimed Monsanto had minimized the suspected link between the chemical herbicide and cancer; that they had bullied scientists and denied researchers when confronted with their claims. He concluded his opening statement suggesting that Monsanto had known about tests indicating that glyphosate—the principal chemical ingredient in their weed-killer—can cause cancer in lab animals.[37]

Judge Curtis Karnow had previously ordered that jurors in the trial could consider the scientific evidence regarding Johnson's cancer, as well as allegations that Monsanto had knowingly suppressed findings regarding glyphosate's potential cancer-causing dangers. Internal correspondence obtained by the plaintiff and provided to the jury supported the fact that for decades Monsanto had been aware that glyphosate-based herbicides are carcinogenic; that Monsanto had continuously sought to influence the scientific literature to prevent internal concerns from reaching the public, and to support its defense in product liability actions.[38]

The defense argued that even though Mr. Johnson's cancer was a horrible disease, the overwhelming scientific evidence had concluded that glyphosate-based products do not cause cancer, and therefor they did not cause his cancer.

Over the course of the 19-day trial, lawyers for the plaintiff and defense jockeyed back and forth. The plaintiff's lawyer claimed that Dewayne Johnson had little warning about the risks of Roundup. That he was told it was completely non-toxic and that you could drink the stuff. There were episodes on the job when a hose came loose and Johnson was drenched in the herbicide. The defense countered with the fact that Roundup had been in use for many years; it was approved by the U.S. Environmental Protection Agency under various presidential administrations and through generations of scientists there.

Both sides called on experts to testify supporting their positions and criticized errors in the studies cited by the other side. The defense concluded that Mr. Johnson's cancer began years earlier, before he started working for the school district as a groundskeeper.

After 19 days of testimony the case was sent to the jury on August 8,

2018. At San Francisco's Superior Court of California, the jury deliberated for three days before reaching a decision: Monsanto had failed to warn Johnson and other consumers of the potential cancer risks of exposure to its weed-killers. The plaintiff was awarded $39 million in compensatory and $250 million in punitive damages.[39]

Later that August, Judge Suzanne Bolanos lowered the punitive damages from $250 million to $39 million, the same amount awarded for compensatory damages, reducing the total financial award to $78 million. Dewayne Johnson has agreed to accept the $78 million settlement; the company said that it will appeal.[40]

———————————————————

10

Mount Waste-More to Recovery & Salvation

Following the rise of the hunter-cultivators and the creation of ancient communities, a new era began to emerge, the beginning stages of humanity's virtual wasteland—the accumulation of trash on Mount Waste-More. The Crete city named Knossos is where the first garbage landfill was created around 3000 BCE. Ever since, people around the world have burned or buried their waste, fed it to animals or simply tossed it over their shoulder. Over time, as some cities and towns became submerged in trash, others discovered novel ways to deal with it. As the types of garbage materials increased; the solutions became more complex. Recycling is one of many other trash alternatives. Nevertheless, Mount Waste-More has continued to climb high, currently at the rate of 2.12 billion additional tons per year, fueled by growing consumerism around the world, especially in the United States.[1]

In the year 1350 CE, the Black Plague emerged as one the most terrifying communicative diseases to assault humanity, 25 million people, estimated at 30-50% of Europe's population at the time were killed in just five years. The Black Plague was the result of a deadly infection caused by the bacterial strain: *Yersinia pestis* found in animals throughout the world, mainly rodents, particularly rats and the fleas that feed on them, who then transmit the bacteria to humans. The risk of the plague is highest in areas with poor sanitation and overcrowding with large rodent populations.

Life in Europe was uncivilized at the time, warfare was common, trash and filth were rampant; the common people reused everything they could. During this period Great Britain and a few European countries were the first to pass laws preventing garbage from being cast into city streets and piling up around homes. As the years passed, there weren't many other options for most people living in smaller towns and villages; they could bury their garbage, burn it or let it pile up.[2]

It wasn't until the population boom driven by the Industrial Revolution that increasing amounts of trash were viewed as a threat to human livelihood. Burning coal, for heat and as an industrial fuel, was the main driver for the Industrial Revolution. Increasing quantities of manufactured products brought with them more raw materials, expanded trade and new waste products. In the cities, scavengers evolved collecting anything from dog feces to cure leather, using ashes to mix with mortar.

In America, New York City was the first to develop a comprehensive garbage management system. The system included a new incinerator built on Governors Island, New York in 1885. By the early 1900s smaller municipalities were dumping their waste wherever it was easiest. In those days it was a fairly common practice to dump it in the ocean, in local wetlands or any other convenient waste areas.[3]

By the end of the Great Depression a majority of America's largest cities had put in place formal methods defining their waste collection process. Most small cities and towns used what they called small *piggeries*: small pig farms that were setup to have pigs consume raw and uncooked food waste. The remaining waste was typically pushed together into a pile and burned.

In 1904, the first aluminum recycling plants began operation in Chicago and Cleveland. About the same time a large number of old incinerators built to burn waste in some of the larger American cities were closed down, due to complaints of excessive smoke. Ten years later incinerator designs had improved enough that roughly three hundred across the U.S. and Canada were back in operation.[4]

When researching solid waste issues, the term *vector* is often used by scientists to describe a living organism that can transmit infectious diseases between humans, or from animals to humans. Most vectors are bloodsucking insects that ingest disease-producing micro-organisms from an infected host, injecting it into a new host. Mosquitoes are the most common vectors followed by ticks, flies, sandflies and fleas.

Landfills were a popular waste disposal option, or dumping waste in wetland areas and covering it with soil. In 1934, the Supreme Court ruled in favor of a federal ban on dumping municipal waste in the ocean. After World War II, the poor air quality caused by open-burning dumps was the main reason driving public complaints to put out the fires in communities and around the country. During the 1950s urban communities had tolerated open-burning in dumps because they reduced the volume of solid waste that remained, extending the dump's life and reducing costs. The smoking garbage dump would become the smoking gun that highlighted the looming solid waste problem. The smoking backyard trash barrel and the burning of commercial-industrial refuse also became targets for improved air quality that led to their prohibition.[5]

The push to prohibit open burning at landfills was the first significant national effort to modify refuse management in the United States. While the elimination of open-burning dumps decreased air pollution; it magnified the prospects for vector growth because solid waste was not being *cooked* in the dumps. The increased possibility of vector growth increased the threat to human health, creating new problems for waste management.

The driving force behind the national movement to improve solid waste management was based primarily on public health concerns. During the 1950s, the options for processing solid waste included incineration, composting, recycling, salvaging, sanitary landfills, burying and covering it with a layer of soil. Cost and flexibility across a wide variety of landscapes pushed the sanitary landfill concept as the disposal option of choice; they not only curtailed burning and the smoke, they could also eliminate mosquitoes, flies and rats as potential vectors for transmitting disease.

The ban on burning industrial and commercial waste and backyard burning caused a huge increase in the refuse collected and managed. Initially, sanitary landfills used direct burial of solid waste without compacting it; compaction was added later to squeeze more trash into less space. In order for adoption as a preferred solid waste management system sanitary landfills had to be constructed per a prescribed method along with criteria, standards and best practices.

After World War II, America stood alone as the only leading power where most of the homeland had been spared the massive damage that occurred around the world. With a solid agricultural and manufacturing base intact and a united country ready to get back to work, America was primed and ready to lead the rest of the world into the consumer era. The pent-up demand for goods combined with the ease of use and availability of exciting new materials developed during the war—primarily plastics—the production treadmill was ready to roll, and roll it did. After a few years, the consumption and disposal of goods—combined with the amount of packaging produced to market them—had increased by some 67%. Mount Waste-More enjoyed a growth spurt, *while America became the first country to embrace the concept of the throwaway society.*[6]

In 1961 the U.S. Public Health Service (USPHS) developed the first recommended standards for sanitary landfills. Two years later, the Clean Air Act was the first federal legislation passed to control air pollution. The program was administered by the USPHS to research techniques for monitoring and controlling air pollution. The Solid Waste Disposal Act was ratified in 1965, prompting the U.S. to speed up efforts to introduce the sanitary landfill as the preferred method for solid waste management.

Training programs were conducted specifying the design and operation of sanitary landfills; the proper methods for closing open dumps per the 1961 guidelines. Publications were crafted to clarify the function of the sanitary landfill for regulators, engineers, operators and the public. State governments established their own regulations while increasing funding to support solid waste management.

In 1967 the Air Quality Act was enacted to further expand federal activities supporting the control of air pollution levels. At this point most household heating systems had changed over from coal to natural gas, fuel oil or electricity. With no easy way to burn paper and cardboard packaging waste, most people put it out for collection as solid waste, adding more stuff to the growing waste-stream headed to open dumps, sanitary landfills and incinerators.

Nonetheless, sanitary landfills were still a concept in the process of further development. Gas migration in sanitary landfills created the possibility of explosion; this was resolved by venting off the gases or capturing it for use as an energy source, which caused concerns about the levels of greenhouse gasses given off by *Waste-to-Energy plants*. Groundwater contamination is another sanitary landfill problem, requiring groundwater leak monitoring systems to detect and fix landfill leaks, yet many still go undetected.

Initially, sanitary landfills lacked definition and description details, especially compaction requirements regarding cover densities, the frequency and depth of cover material. These were included in *a new sanitary landfill construction and process description*.

The *transfer station* concept was also introduced during this period as a way to allow larger cities to manage more waste. Transfer stations are large warehouses designed to package waste before transporting it to incinerators or larger landfills. They assist waste haulers by reducing travel times to distant landfills.[7]

Up until the 1970s the USPHS had used extensive research and development, demonstrations of new industrial approaches, training and technical assistance to convince states, local governments and private landfill owners to change over to sanitary landfills. When the Environmental Protection Agency (EPA) was created in 1970 the solid waste program was moved under its jurisdiction. The EPA was setup as an enforcement agency, contrary to the USPHS approach of promoting change via research, training and technical assistance. However, Congress had not given the EPA any specific enforcement authority over solid-waste. Consequently, the EPA took only minor interest and invested little money in sanitary land-fill programs; the progress made during the 50s and 60s came to a halt.

The Resource Conservation and Recovery Act (RCRA) passed in 1984 finally specified the EPA as the regulatory agency over landfills. The EPA then completed a set of rules called *Subtitle D* for adoption by the states, reflecting on fifty years of efforts by re-searchers, organizations, committees, solid waste managers, state and local governments to reduce air pollution and smoke from open burning and to eliminate mosquitos, flies, pigs and rats as vec-tor-paths for disease, providing a means of disposing waste in san-itary landfills. Since its release, the record shows that EPA's interest in implementing Subtitle D has been minimal, but many state and local governments and landfill managers decided to take up the slack.

Over the course of the 80s and 90s, the EPA monitored all waste content and recycling rates to determine which items makeup the bulk of garbage-waste to determine how to reduce it. By the year 2000 more than 5,000 Americans were using pay-as-you-throw programs with municipalities charging residents based only on the amount of garbage they throw away.[8]

Recycling is a process that converts waste products into materials that can be used for other purposes that can save energy and mate-rial. Of course, that depends on the true need for the item that's made from the recycled material and the potential for repeated re-cycling at the same functional level. *Reduce, Reuse and Recycle* is the process favored by most modern waste reduction programs. Recy-cling is an attempt to replace raw materials with recycled material, compared to the costs and energy associated with acquiring new material. Recyclable materials include: glass, paper, cardboard, metal, plastic, tires, textiles and electronics. The composting of other refuse or bio-degradable waste, food or garden waste is also considered recycling.

Materials to be recycled are brought to a collection center or picked up curbside; they're sorted, cleaned and reprocessed into new material to be remanufactured into useful items. In a perfect world the recycled material would be exactly the same and provide all the same functions as the original raw material; this is seldom true. Many items, especially certain plastics, can only be recycled down to lower levels of functionality. Which means they will eventually end up burned or buried somewhere until they fully decompose. Another type of recycling occurs when certain valuable materials are extracted from products such as lead from car batteries; the removal of mercury from mercury-filled thermostats and temperature sensors, for reuse in similar or other applications.

People have been recycling materials for a long time. After World War I manufacturers increased recycling as a means of providing the resources still in short supply. Metals were in demand then and they still are; most metals can be recycled by a simple cleaning, re-melting and re-molding, far cheaper than acquiring virgin ore. Today in most smaller cities and towns, all you have to do to get rid of a reasonable amount of metal—discarded machinery, pots, pans and other pieces of metal—is set it out by the road; by the end of day it will be gone, picked up by an enterprising metal recycler for cash.

New chemicals created in the late 19th century, materials including *Bakelite* added to the amount of materials that can be recycled into useful products. During the 1970s, rising energy costs stimulated further recycling investments. Recycling aluminum requires only 5% of the energy needed to process virgin material; glass, paper and other metals require less dramatic but significant energy savings when recycled feedstock is used. Throughout the Second World War recycling was a major issue for governments around the world. Material and financial shortages caused by the war effort prompted the need to reuse and recycle a number of goods and materials. The war and other global changes emphasized the importance of recycling. Governments promoted recycling via campaigns like *The Salvage for Victory* campaign in the U.S. and the *National Salvage Campaign* in Great Britain that urged citizens to donate metal, paper, rags, and rubber to support the war effort. Most homes during that period recycled much of their waste.[9]

Extracting and processing raw natural resources such as wood, oil and metal ores to process into usable materials: paper, plastic and metal products, requires a lot of energy. Recycling saves energy because the material being recycled usually requires less processing than raw material to convert into a usable form. The amount of energy saved depends on the material. Glass is created by heating a mixture of sand and other materials at very high temperatures, the most energy intensive part of the process. The molten mixture is cooled to form glass. Recycled glass must also be re-melted to make new glass products; the overall energy savings from recycling glass are relatively small but still worthwhile, between 20-30%. One ton of recycled glass can save 42 kilowatt-hours of energy. Recycling one ton of office paper can save 3000 to 4000 kilowatt-hours of energy; newsprint recycled yields energy savings of 601 kilowatt-hours of energy. One ton of recycled plastic avoids the consumption of 5,774 kilowatt-hours of energy.

Aluminum is made from aluminum ore called bauxite that requires extensive processing to extract aluminum metal, consuming large amounts of heat and electricity. Recycled aluminum requires only cleaning and re-melting, saving 95% of the energy needed to process aluminum from ore. One ton of recycled aluminum cans can save 14,000 kilowatt-hours of energy, equivalent to 40 barrels of oil.

Although the amount of energy saved depends on the material being recycled, almost all recycling operations result in energy savings. The greatest savings occur with metals that are more readily recycled, produced by energy-intensive mining and ore processing; energy savings can range from 50 to 95%.[10]

In 2015, over 92 million tons of municipal solid waste (food, plants, glass, boxes, cans, batteries, electronics, plastics, etc.) were recycled or composted in the United States, saving over 325,000

Giga-Watt-hours of energy—enough to provide electricity for 30 million homes.[11]

The Recycling Era began with a student competition held nearly 50 years ago to celebrate the first Earth Day on April 22, 1970. The Container Corporation of America, a large producer of recycled paper, created a contest to raise environmental awareness by sponsoring a nationwide design contest for high school and college students to develop a recycling symbol. The winning entry was designed and submitted by Gary Anderson, an architecture student at the University of Southern California. The familiar recycling symbol he created is recognized worldwide. Each symbol component is symbolic, three rotating arrows each trailing the other in a triangular closed loop that endures forever. Each arrow stands for one stage in the recycling process. Arrow one symbolizes collection: separating, cleaning and preparing items for transfer to recycling centers; arrow two represents the recycling process: reprocessing, sorting, cleaning and final processing at a recycling center; arrow three involves the sale and transfer of the recycled materials to manufacturing facilities. The system is most successful when the entire cycle is completed for the same materials, again and again.

If an item includes the word *Recycled* in the recycling symbol, that means the product or its packaging is made at least partly of recycled materials. If a number, e.g. 20% accompanies the symbol, this represents the percentage of recycled materials used in the manufacturing of the item. If an item includes a symbol with the word *Recyclable*, then the product is potentially recyclable—if identified as a material collected for recycling in your area. Plastics are often embossed with a simplified version of this symbol, including a number 1-7 in the center indicating the type of plastic resin used in the product.

Gary Anderson created the symbol inspired by the Bauhaus design school and M.C. Escher's graphic representations of the Mobius strip: a surface that possesses only one side when embedded in three-dimensional space, and just one boundary. The Mobius strip has the mathematical property of being unorientable; its discovery is attributed to the German mathematicians August

Ferdinand Mobius and Johann Benedict Listing in 1858. Anderson received a mere $2500 for his winning design which he used to pay for a year of study at the University of Stockholm Sweden. He went on to enjoy a variety of careers as a planner and architect, college teacher, researcher and manager that took him to a number of companies and colleges around the world.[12]

In 1974, Missouri was one of the first states to begin curbside recycling with a collection bin named *the Tree Saver* for the collection of paper. Two years later the EPA approved a $20,000 recycling grant for the state of Massachusetts to implement weekly curbside collection programs in two cities with a specially designed residential recycling truck. By 1980, nearly 220 curbside collection programs were in place in the U.S., 60 of which were multi-material collectors. Beginning in 2000, curbside organic waste collection began on the west coast in San Francisco. Goals for the most ambitious west coast cities achieved 80% recycling participation in some areas, prompting California law makers to set recycling goals for the entire state at 75% by 2020. McDonalds was the first of the large fast food companies to replace Styrofoam cups with recyclable paper cups.[13]

The notorious Long Island Garbage Barge named Mobro 4000 was put out to sea over three decades ago in search of a home for 3100 tons of garbage: a gift from the town of Islip and New York City. With the limited landfill space piling up, officials at Long Island's dump searched for new ways to handle the onslaught of incoming trash. Their master plan was to hire a private hauler to cart the obnoxious waste on a barge to North Carolina to be part of a pilot program to process it into methane at a fraction of the cost of disposing it locally.

The tugboat named "Break of Dawn" chugged along with the Mobro 4000— media called it the Gar-barge—in tow under the Verrazano-Narrows Bridge and headed south. The story caught most of the national headlines, after a few jokes landed by Johnny Carson on the Tonight Show in his monologue regarding a foul New York City Gar-barge headed south to dump its trash in North Carolina. The news spread quickly. By the time

Gar-barge arrived and docked at Morehead City, North Carolina, a news crew had been sent out to investigate. When the story hit the local news, residents complained. Some local irate officials investigated—the Gar-Barge was spurned and turned away.

For the next two months the tugboat, barge and crew wandered aimlessly from place to place, to Louisiana, Texas, Florida and then Belize. Authorities in Cuba and Mexico had threatened to fire their artillery at Gar-barge if it dared dock in their country. Eventually, officials from Islip and New York State negotiated a deal to burn the garbage in a Brooklyn incinerator, and bury the ash in the Islip Town landfill.

The Gar-barge story would change the way people think about garbage, landfills and incinerators around the world; it's credited with awakening Americans to the growing Mount Waste-More problem and the importance of recycling. That year New Jersey passed the first mandatory recycling law requiring all residents to separate recyclables from their trash.[14]

In 1993, Wisconsin issued the first statewide ban against placing recyclable materials within garbage intended for landfills. The ban prohibited yard waste in landfills. Later in 1995 Wisconsin issued a landfill ban on certain items: tires, aluminum containers, corrugated paper, foam polystyrene, plastic containers and newspapers. At the time America had attained 20% nationwide recycling participation, double what it had been 10 years earlier; three years later it topped 30%.

For a number of years, the recycling rate in America remained stuck at 34%, about where it is today. There are many reasons for this including the lack of federal direction on this issue, and the fact that the recycling programs developed over the years are all different—adding up to some 9800 different municipal recycling plans operating around the country. But most importantly, it's the apathy by citizens who think recycling doesn't make sense, and others who don't believe in it or simply don't want to make the effort, that stand in the way of further recycling rate improvements.

Most recycling legislation originates from city and state

governments. Landfill bans are decrees that make it illegal to dispose of certain waste items that usually include yard waste, oil and specified recyclables (e.g. plastic bottles) in a land fill. All states in the American union have landfill bans on certain items with the exception of Montana; they range from simply car batteries to the most extensive, including ten or more banned items. The states with the most extensive list of banned items are California and Connecticut. The items most commonly included in landfill bans include those causing the most environmental damage: car batteries, motor oil, tires, liquid waste (e.g., non-dried paint, household cleaners), untreated medical waste, cathode ray tubes (CRTs), screens (tube monitors and TVs), products containing mercury, yard waste, computers, nickel-cadmium, NiCad or rechargeable batteries.[15]

Mandatory recycling requires that citizens recycle specific items or face fines for throwing them away when exceeding a certain percentage of recyclable materials within their garbage waste. Other states like California and Illinois promote recycling by setting goals. Another method is to pass a bottle bill. The following states currently have bottle bills: California, Connecticut, Hawaii, Iowa, Maine, Massachusetts, Michigan, New York, Oregon and Vermont. These laws establish deposits paid by the customer at purchase that are refunded when the item is turned in for recycling. The deposit is simply an incentive to return the item. Deposits are usually set at five cents per can or bottle; Michigan and Oregon have a 10-cent deposit for bottles and cans.[16]

Bottle bills have been one of the most significant programs that have increased the rate of recycling. Bottle bills cover glass, aluminum and plastic cans and bottles; they are successful because a deposit is paid up front; the cans/bottles are processed at local stores by type on special machines that compress aluminum cans and plastic bottles, or break glass bottles while providing a receipt for return of the deposit fee to the customer. Nearly fifty years after the first Earth day, where are we? How much waste do we create and how much of it is recycled?

Globally, garbage waste is accumulating at 2.12 billion tons per year, 555 pounds of garbage each year per each global citizen; 99% of which is disposed of within 6 months of purchase. Recycling rates around the world show the U.S. holding at around 32%, ranking ninth behind the world's recycling leaders: Germany (65%), South Korea (59%), Slovenia (58%), Austria (58%), Belgium (55%), United Kingdom (43%), Italy and Australia (41%).[17]

In the U.S. 262.4 million tons of municipal waste was generated in 2015 having increased at a rate of about .5% per year during the period 2000-2015 67.8 million tons were recovered for recycling[18], increasing at a rate of 1.9% per year over the same period.[19] The gross percentage of bottles recycled across the U.S. began at a rate of 23% in the year 2000, peaking at 31% in 2014 and falling back to 27% in 2016.[20]

The current rate of annual garbage waste generation in the U.S. is roughly 267 million tons or 1638 lbs. per capita. However, most developing countries are not included in the global numbers since their level of participation is difficult to measure. While most lack formal recycling programs, many operate on a basis of allowing residents to retrieve items from landfills for potential reuse or recycling.[21]

Globally the World Bank categorizes waste generation and recycling in seven sections: Sub-Saharan Africa (AFR), East Asia Pacific (EAP), East Central Asia (ECA), Latin America & Caribbean (LCR), Middle East & North Africa (MENA), the Organization of Economic Coordination & Development (OECD) consisting of 34 developed countries.* By 2025 urban residents will produce over 6 million tons of solid waste per day, nearly twice as much as the rest of the world, while possessing only 25% of global population.

---

*The Organization of Economic Cooperation & Development (OECD) includes an international economic organization of 34 countries, founded in 30 September 1961 to stimulate economic progress and world trade. OECD countries are Australia, Austria, Belgium, Canada, Chile, Czech Republic, Denmark, Estonia, Finland, France, Germany, Greece, Hungary,

Iceland, Ireland, Israel, Italy, Japan, South Korea, Luxembourg, Mexico, Netherlands, New Zealand, Norway, Poland, Portugal, Slovak Republic, Slovenia, Spain, Sweden, Switzerland, Turkey, United Kingdom and United States.

As we look around the world, global population levels continue climbing along with the per capita generation of solid waste. Then why isn't the recycling level increasing as well...why should we care? Overall, recycling rates are abysmal with only 10 countries globally posting recycling rates equal to or above 24%. It's safe to say in a world that's increasingly human dominated, Mount-Waste-More will continue to climb, but only as a metaphor. Landfills are getting broader and deeper, containing a growing number of man-made materials that will survive intact for too many human lifetimes; many of them present long-term toxicological hazards. Plastic bags are among the most common sources of marine debris where they are mistaken as food by birds and fish. Plastic bags don't biodegrade; it will take many centuries for them to decompose.[22]

Plastics include three dangerous types of chemicals: manufacturing by-products, chemicals contained in the plastic and those capable of being absorbed by the environment. Toxicological responses can occur with any combination of the three. Some of these chemicals are considered priority pollutants regulated by governmental agencies due to their toxicity, or their survival in food or living organisms. They can include pesticides, heavy metals, polycyclic aromatic hydrocarbons (PAHs) and polychlorinated biphenyls (PCBs), which are capable of upsetting critical physiological processes in animals to cause disease and reproductive problems. At least 78% of the priority pollutants listed by the U.S. Environmental Protection Agency (EPA), 61% of those listed by the European Union are associated with plastic garbage, manufacturing by-products or the environment.[23]

Plastic garbage is all too common along California's once pristine coastline and plentiful beaches; one of many reasons that California has become the epicenter of the American movement against the use of plastic bags. San Francisco was the first American city to regulate the use plastic shopping bags with a goal of attaining *zero-waste* by the year 2020. San Francisco is one of a number of Californian cities that banned the use of polystyrene (Styrofoam) food containers in June of 2016. Plastic bag bans in California cover one-third of the state population; plastic bag purchases there by retailers reportedly fell from 107 million pounds in 2008 to 62 million pounds in 2012.

Plastics are persistent in landfills and waterways, lasting for hundreds of years, breaking down into smaller pieces while seeping out chemical components over time. Wildlife often mistake plastic bags for food; after consuming the plastic they are unable to digest it and eventually die. Studies show that plastic from discarded bags absorb additional pollutants such as pesticides and industrial waste in the ocean and deliver them to sea-life in large doses. The harmful substances eventually move up the food chain to humans. Plastics and their additives have been tied to a number of human health concerns including the disruption of the endocrine and reproductive systems, infertility and possible links to some cancers.[24]

To those who say that recycling isn't cost effective, that's only true if you completely ignore the nature-costs of polluting ecosystem after ecosystem, causing biodiversity loss across the oceans and the landscape. We should all realize the degree to which humans have invaded all ecosystems across the planet. The number of disappearing species that once performed critical functions supporting life and ultimately us, have created too many holes in the fabric of life, for life to continue, especially human life that's dependent upon the hard work of so many species we've probably never heard of.

Let's review some important reasons for improving waste management systems: to reuse materials that can be efficiently recycled (nature-costs included); to remove items from landfills with long decay periods or toxic residues; to eliminate compostable items from landfills, including most plant materials and food waste.

In excess of 20 million out of a total 328 million Americans (roughly 6%) live in communities with plastic bag bans or fees. Currently some 100 billion plastic bags pass through the hands of U.S. consumers each year, about one bag per person each day. *How can we do better and why should we?*

The first step is either an outright ban on single-use, high volume plastic shopping bags or for the general public to simply stop using them. In most cases we can readily do without them, replacing them with reusable cloth bags, or single use paper bags that can be recycled and are readily biodegradable in landfills. Plastic shopping bags are not typically recyclable through normal recycling centers; they can be returned to many participating stores that accept plastic shopping bags and provide for their return to those recycling centers that can process them.

The majority of the thinner, single-use plastic bags are produced with low-density polyethylene (#4 plastic); the thicker variety use higher density polyethylene (#2 plastic). Many stores that accept them collect them in special containers. To recycle plastic shopping bags, check for the #2 or #4 symbol on each bag and remove anything inside the bag; collect a number of bags and turn them in at a store that accepts them. Recycling one ton of plastic bags (about 450,000 bags) can save 11 barrels of oil. After recycled bags are processed into plastic pellets, they can be used to make new bags; they most likely will be reprocessed into products like plastic lumber or a host of other similar applications.

Over the years a number of states have considered enacting legislation related to labeling, recycling and reusing plastic bags. Maine was the first state to enact legislation requiring retail stores to promote recycling efforts. The law prevents retailers from supplying plastic bags without providing a convenient storefront receptacle to ensure that plastic bags are collected and recycled. Since then California, Delaware, New York, Rhode Island and the District of Columbia have enacted similar legislation.

In lieu of federal or state action to limit the use of plastic shopping bags, many cities around the U.S. have taken that step. Currently some 132 American cities have plastic bag bans and or bag fees in place, most notably Austin, Texas; Boston, Mass.; Chicago, Illinois; Los Angeles, Calif.; San Francisco, Calif; and Seattle, Washington.

At the state level, California forbids retailers from providing free plastic bags, customers must pay a 10-cent fee for them. Hawaii has a statewide plastic bag ban. New York, North Carolina and Maine promote the recycling of plastic shopping bags by requiring stores to accept them for recycling, and they must promote the use of reusable or paper bags.[25]

To fend off the growing number of city-wide bans around the country, nine states have enacted preemption bans forbidding the creation of plastic bag bans by cities and counties within their state. With the encouragement of the American Legislative Exchange Council (ALEC) eleven states thus far including: Arizona, Florida, Idaho, Iowa, Indiana, Michigan, Minnesota, Mississippi, Missouri, Texas and Wisconsin have enacted legislation using model legislative language often provided by ALEC, preempting all local attempts from forbidding or inhibiting the use of plastic shopping bags.[26]

Another plastic material, Styrofoam is one of the worst waste items dumped into landfills. Anyone interested in preserving the environment should refrain from using Styrofoam if at all possible. Without a government decree there's not much anyone can do except to forgo purchasing items that include Styrofoam in the product, or used to protect the product during shipping. In either case, be sure to make your concerns aware to the manufacturer. Styrofoam is most often used as light-weight, moldable, packaging for shipping a wide variety of items, or as single-use fast-food meal or drink containers. These single-use containers are the most prolific items that often end up as litter, similar to the way plastic shopping bags do. Perhaps, it is best to simply stop using them by refraining from doing business with the establishments that continue supplying them.

Styrofoam is the Dow Chemical trade name for expanded polystyrene (EPS) invented in 1941 by Dow Chemical scientist Otis Ray McIntire. Styrofoam is such an accepted everyday product that few of us realize that it's made from polystyrene, a petroleum-based plastic. A 2015 BBC report explains that polystyrene beads are processed using chemicals that are steamed and expand, creating the substance EPS that's 95% air, popular because of its light weight and good insulation properties, maintaining heat or cold and protecting products during shipment with little weight added. Even though Styrofoam has insulation properties that make it attractive for containing hot or cold drinks, using Styrofoam as insulation is dangerous and illegal; it's extremely flammable, making it unsuitable for use as insulation in a home, trailer or other similar environment.

Health concerns regarding Styrofoam begin with styrene, its main ingredient, listed as a possible human carcinogen in 2002, and a 2014 National Toxicological Program report on carcinogens that classifies styrene as a human carcinogen that's being linked to occurrence of leukemia and lymphoma cancer. The EPA report on styrene does not classify it as carcinogenic but lists the occupational hazards for those who are regularly exposed to it. Some of the acute health effects include irritation of the skin, eyes, the upper respiratory tract and gastrointestinal effects. The EPA report says chronic exposure to styrene can lead to further complications, including adverse effects on the nervous and respiratory systems and possibly the kidney and liver as well as other issues.

When Styrofoam is exposed to heat it gives off fumes that release neurotoxins. Styrofoam's petroleum base causes problems during manufacture and after disposal. During manufacturing, hydrocarbons and known carcinogens are released, putting human lives at risk. After disposal, polystyrene fills up landfills or breaks off in tiny pieces that can cause animals to choke or develop potentially fatal intestinal blockages.

Styrofoam contaminated with food is not recyclable. When heated, Styrofoam photodegrades and emits neurotoxins that can be harmful to human health. In the oceans these neurotoxins are absorbed by the water, plant and animal life and passed on up the food chain. Disposed of as litter it either ends up in the waterways or the topsoil exuding neurotoxins when heated to decompose.

When you're dining out and take-home leftovers many food establishments still offer Styrofoam carryout containers. The problem arises when you reheat the food in the container, the Styrofoam gives off neurotoxins that are absorbed by the food and taken into your body. A simple short-term solution is to reheat the food in a non-Styrofoam container in the microwave. The best action is not to buy the product in the first place. If you go to a restaurant and ask for a takeout container, ask for an eco-friendly container—not Styrofoam. You can also write to manufacturers and ask them to stop making Styrofoam products. At this point many of the larger national food and restaurant businesses have already stopped using Styrofoam products. It is the smaller local businesses that need to be addressed. It's more likely that smaller businesses will take note when a customer offers an opinion. If the businesses that manufacture Styrofoam are informed about the issues people have with it, they may try to develop an alternative that is less problematic and environmentally biodegradable.

Things to remember: Styrofoam gives off fumes containing a neurotoxin whenever exposed to heat; it photodegrades and adds to the overall pollution problem; since it is made from crude oil it wastes oil and other natural resources unsustainably; it is not accepted as recyclable in most municipalities.[27]

Beginning in the year 2012 a number of cities around the U.S. began initiating Styrofoam bans. In 2015 New York City had issued a ban on polystyrene foam products that was ultimately delayed by a lawsuit by the Dart Group, the world's largest manufacturer of foam cups and containers. On June 13, 2018 Mayor de Blasio announced that the lawsuit had been dismissed and New York City's Styrofoam ban would go into effect on January 1, 2019. As a result, stores and manufacturers cannot sell or offer single use foam items: cups, plates, trays, or clamshell containers in New York City; and so-called packing peanuts are also banned.[28]

Thus far we have reviewed the accumulation of waste in America and around the world, the problems generated and the potential cures. For the most part garbage can still be sent to open dumps, sanitary landfills, incinerators or recycled. Compostable food waste is still being sent to landfills instead of composting it at home, or separating it for transfer to regional or local composting facilities if available. We've also covered the issues regarding recycling as a potential solution. Thus far materials including aluminum and other metals, paper, glass and some plastics have been successfully recycled. Many other items including tires and auto batteries are being turned in and processed for recycling in a number of states across the U.S.

Recycling programs have not been embraced by many states in the U.S. and governments around the world. The percentage of waste recycled in the U.S. remains at about 34%. Yet, many city and county governments have taken steps to institute rules and programs to minimize garbage waste, either by outright bans on certain materials or mandatory deposits on beverage bottle purchases (bottle bills) to promote recycling. But these local efforts have prompted some state governments to enact preemptive legislation against local bottle bills or bans.

The good news is that a number of large American communities have embraced a completely new concept of a world without garbage. The name of this game is called Zero-Waste and it goes like this—communities across America and around the world are working towards eliminating waste altogether. One of the first cities to create a Zero-Waste plan was the City of Fort Collins, Colorado, entitled *Road to Zero Waste Plan* first published in December of 2013. The entire plan is available as a PDF file on line, the detailed planning and the ideas proposed are truly incredible. It's a prime example of how people can work together to accurately define a problem, develop a solution plan and take action to resolve it.

The U.S. Conference of Mayors adopted a resolution in 2015: *In Support of Municipal Zero Waste Principles and a Hierarchy of Materials Management.* Below are some excerpts from the EPA website:

WHEREAS, the concept of zero waste goes beyond recycling and composting at the end of a product's life cycle, to encompass the entire life cycle of a product, beginning with product design, and envisioning the use and management of materials in ways that preserve value, minimize environmental impacts, and conserve natural resources; and

WHEREAS, materials management through zero waste can begin to shift the fiscal burden of waste and empower industry to embrace resource responsibility by rewarding stewardship through purchasing and economic development incentives; and

WHEREAS, while industry and the federal government have variously defined and categorized zero waste strategies, it behooves the nation's cities, with primary responsibility for waste management, to devise a definition that encourages shared fiscal responsibility and legislative innovations.

NOW, THEREFORE BE IT RESOLVED, that The United States Conference of Mayors adopts a definition of Zero Waste, and set of Zero Waste principles, that recognizes a Hierarchy of Material Management as follows: Extended Producer Responsibility and Product Redesign, Reduce Waste, Toxicity, Consumption, and Packaging; Repair, Reuse and Donate; Recycle; Compost; Down Cycle and Beneficial Reuse; Waste-Based Energy as disposal; Landfill Waste as disposal.[29]

Many other localities and organizations have also expressed definitions of the concept of Zero-Waste: Seattle Public Utilities in Washington; the Solid Waste Association of North America (SWANA); The State of Connecticut; Middletown, Connecticut; San Francisco, Alameda, San Jose, Los Angeles, Fresno, Oakland and Pasadena California; Guam; King County Washington; Austin, Texas; the Santa Ynez Band of Chumash Mission Indians; the County of Hawaii; Ashville, North Carolina; the Central Vermont Solid Waste Management District.[30]

———————

Over the years, living and working in central New York State I've become increasingly aware of the high-quality products and services offered by the Oneida-Herkimer Solid Waste Authority (the

Authority), the area where I grew up and still call home.

Today, the Authority's Administrative Offices are centrally located in Utica, NY, with a Western Transfer Station, Eco-Drop area and stump remediation in Rome, NY; a regional sanitary landfill located in Booneville, NY. The Utica Recycling Center houses the Eco-Drop Utica area; Eastern Transfer area; a Compost site; Household hazardous waste disposition; Food2Energy processing and biogas generation.

In July of 2019 I had the opportunity to meet with the Authority's Executive Director, Bill Rabbia. I was able to see for myself their operation, the difficulties they deal with daily, how they have persevered to become a model for solid waste management and recycling.

While visiting their recycling facility, I witnessed first-hand recycling trucks being unloaded and recyclables being dumped into a huge pile. The mixed material pile is fed into a drum feeder and onto a conveyor, heading to the pre-sort area where workers pick out plastic bags filled with shredded paper (per the Authority's instructions), trash, plastic film and plastic bags that can jam up the sorting machines that follow. Coming out of pre-sort the conveyor drops down and the mixed-material passes through a cardboard sorter, where rotating screens force the larger corrugated cardboard pieces over the top. All other materials fall through and proceed to the post-sorter where any remaining cardboard or trash is manually picked off the conveyor. What's left after the post-sorter is paper, mixed (plastic and metal) containers and glass.

The material now passes through the glass-breaker where screens of various sizes—spaced varying distances apart—break the glass which falls below; the remaining paper is pushed overhead; all the other containers fall through below.

At this point all of the paper that's been separated from the line is heading to a separate sorting area where any trash and unacceptable paper material is manually stripped off the line. Any paper items remaining are sent to bins, awaiting the accumulation of enough material to be passed onto the balers. The balers compile large bales of the various recyclable types that are made available for sale to manufacturers with a need for that material.

Meanwhile, the mixed metal and plastic containers are moving down the line where magnets strip off the ferrous (iron) based metals off the conveyor; aluminum metal and all plastic containers pass by unaffected. Next, optical sensors individually detect either PET or HDPE plastic containers; the sensors activate an air stream that blows the item off the line into the appropriate recycling bin.

The remaining material includes a mix of category 3-7 plastic containers: milk and juice cartons, and aluminum (non-ferrous) containers. Eddy current sensors are used to push the aluminum cans off the line while a variety of sensors capable of sensing specific 3-7 plastic variations strip off any plastic types appropriate for separate packaging options. What remains on the line is considered garbage which is transferred to the Authority's landfill located in Booneville, NY.

As time goes on and new plastic variations are developed, the Authority's team is continually developing ways of detecting and sorting any significant new types of plastics or any other material for recycling, a challenge that gets more difficult as technological development continues to speed up.[31]

As we watched the recycling line in full operation, Bill talked about many of the problems they face during difficult central New York winters. He explained how the workers on the manufacturing floor had suggested beveling off the corners of the presort cardboard separators and installing metal studs to break off the snow and ice build-up on the recyclables. Process technicians listened to their idea and implemented the changes, resulting in a much smoother operation of the line during the winter months. This is the example of working together as a team, that brings about true progress, something we seldom witness these days.

At the end of my plant tour, Bill and I inspected some of the bales that had just come off the line. They were impressive, not anything like those you see in news-stories showing scraggly bales of recyclables being sent over to China, before China's ban on recyclables with less than 99.5% of nearly pure material was in place. The bale of PET bottles appeared to be near perfect except for a couple of scraps of paper here and there that were readily pulled out of the bale.

Bill explained that customers periodically come in and inspect the output bales of certain materials, tearing down the entire bale, counting each item as acceptable or not, and then calculating the acceptable product percentage. While the price paid for recyclables has declined due to the China ban, the Authority still has willing buyers. Despite the lost income due to low market prices for recyclables, the Authority is in a good position, with the infrastructure in place to continue delivering a quality product into the future. Many from the recycling community believe that the China ban can be a plus for recycling around the world, forcing all nations to remedy their own recycling issues or face the pollution issues that will eventually overtake them. The following is a reprint of an announcement on the Authority's website—it speaks for itself regarding the stewardship, principles and quality of the Authority's performance since its inception:

July 17, 2019 - The Oneida-Herkimer Solid Waste Authority (Authority) is proud to announce that since the opening of the Oneida-Herkimer Recycling Center in 1991, over 1 million tons of recyclables have been received, diverted from landfills and recovered for recycling. This is equivalent to the weight of over 3100 Statues of Liberty and has extended the life of the landfill by over 20 years.

The Authority takes its mission to manage the region's solid waste and recyclables in an environmentally sound, cost-effective, efficient and safe manner seriously. Since its inception in 1988, the Authority has served as a national model for comprehensive solid waste management. In 2018, Oneida and Herkimer Counties' recycling rate was over 54% compared to the national average of 35%. Oneida and Herkimer Counties' residents and businesses have made it possible for the Authority to set an example of responsible recycling practices and advanced solid waste solutions. The Authority's recycling program is just one critical part of the region's total solid waste management system.

The Authority's integrated system of facilities serves all the residents, businesses, industries and institutions of the two Counties and promotes the reduction of waste, maximizes recycling, and provides safe, economical disposal for non-recyclable waste. This year marks the 28th consecutive year of accepting recyclables at no charge. The Authority's revenue structure is primarily a fee for service system. A system tip fee is charged for all non-recyclable waste delivered to the Authority. These fees cover the majority of expenses in the Authority budget. The Authority receives no funding from the Counties.

Currently, the Authority accepts hundreds of items through its curbside recycling program, RecycleOne–One and Done. The RecycleOne program allows for all curbside recyclable items to be mixed together loosely in one container for collection. Recyclables cannot be placed in plastic bags for collection. No string, trash or green waste is allowed. Shredded paper is the only exception to the "no bag" rule and should be placed in a clear bag for collection. Curbside recyclables include, but are not limited to:

Corrugated & Lightweight Cardboard

Paper (newspaper, junk mail, office paper, magazines)

Plastic Bottles, Cups & Containers (excluding Styrofoam, prescription medicine bottles & motor oil bottles)

Metal & Aluminum Cans/Foil (including empty, non-hazardous aerosol cans)

Glass Bottles & Jars

"The fact that we have achieved over 1 million tons recycled is a testament that our system works. Residents and businesses in the two Counties do a great job recycling and the volume of recyclables delivered to the Oneida-Herkimer Recycling Center each year makes it clear that this community truly sees the value of the Authority's regional recycling program," stated Authority Executive Director Bill Rabbia. "Despite the plummets in global commodity markets, our comprehensive system allows us to continue to recover material for recycling, thus conserving landfill space, natural resources and energy," he continued.

"Every ton of material that is marketed through the Authority's recycling program is one ton of material that we are able to divert from the Regional Landfill and recover to produce brand new things. Without the participation from the two Counties' residents and businesses, these

successes would not be possible," stated Rabbia.[32]

Oneida and Herkimer counties have also been very supportive of immigration, which has ultimately helped fill in for those people who have moved away for more lucrative job opportunities, warmer weather or both. These newcomers are purchasing older fixer-upper homes, rejuvenating them and entire neighborhoods; filling in the workforce for construction jobs requiring hard-labor that would otherwise go unfilled. During my teaching days at a local community college I had the opportunity to teach a number of young immigrant students from many countries; most all of them were very hard workers, many would become some of my best students.

In central New York we have a broad range of immigrants from Central and South America, the Middle East, Eastern Europe, Asia, Southeast Asia and Africa that are helping rebuild the area into a newer more relevant economy. The Authority's website offers their Garage and Recycling Brochure in the following additional languages: Arabic, Bosnian, Burmese, Karen, Nepalese, Russian, Spanish and Vietnamese.

In this chapter we have previously discussed the need to capture both green and food waste to minimize the amount of material filling up land-fills, providing usable compost and energy production in the process. This year the Authority has just opened their new *Food2Energy* operation adjacent to their recycling center. In the past the Authority has promoted the composting of food and green-waste at homes and businesses. They have expanded their operation to include a product separator and an anaerobic aerator. The anaerobic aerator also serves the local wastewater treatment plant located nearby. The *Food2Energy* program is setup to accept food and green-waste material from businesses and individuals. With *Food2Energy*, businesses and residents will be able to divert food waste, which currently comprises roughly 22% of the solid-waste stream, from the Regional Landfill.

Food2Energy is simple and cost effective, saving as much as $22/ton on waste disposal. The cost for disposing of waste (the tipping fee) in Oneida and Herkimer Counties is currently $62/ton. The tipping fee for Food2Energy is $40/ton. Food scraps may be delivered in bags and there is no requirement to remove packaging. The Authority will be able to separate the packaging from the food scraps. The recovered food waste is sent to the Oneida County Waste Water Treatment Plant where they will be turned into energy through a process called Anaerobic Digestion.

While visiting their facility, I was able to witness the product separator in action. A local business had dropped off a couple of skids of bottled water that was no longer available for sale, alongside a skid filled with cans of soup past their allowable sale date stood waiting. The separator is designed to remove the contents of the package, sending the food products to a tank connected to the anaerobic aerator for processing. The spent containers are sent over to the recycling center to be recycled. The separator is designed to accept a variety of different package and food product variations. All the food waste is processed by the anaerobic aerator to produce biogas (methane and CO_2). The addition of the Food2Waste program fulfills all the key facets of the complete solid waste and recycling facility—what more could the businesses and residents of Oneida and Herkimer counties ask for?

Note: You can view the video for the recycling operation described in this chapter at:
https://www.ohswa.org/recycle/our-facilities/recycling-center/
along with some 96 other videos and questions regarding almost every aspect of the Authority's operations.

As part of the baby-boom generation who came of age during the tumultuous 1960s, I have witnessed a lot of change in the last fifty years, including: improved voting rights; civil rights for all races, ethnicities, gender, sexuality and the disabled; attempts to improve the plights of the poor; a woman's right to have an abortion; environmental regulations to protect nature and society. Over time, these topics have all been discussed and addressed with improvements, dependent on your point of view, made in one form or another, only to be watered down and rescinded later by opposing politicians, or the rulings of federal judges.

The political football we call a democracy has flipped back and forth over the issues of the day, like the daily computer-driven trades on the stock market. When one minority is awarded their rights, the other side figures out ways to disallow them. As Americans, most importantly Global Citizens, we have to work together to set a course for the future that considers the rights of all life on this planet, while favoring the natural world—the essence of life.

We must quickly evolve into a nature-friendly society, deciding to reduce our global population, consuming less energy and material while producing zero waste. There's no room for the massive military budgets that governments across the globe have been expending to protect certain groups of human beings from one another. The imaginary battle being waged amongst us is about changing the way we live; we need to embrace each other and the natural world and figure out a way to work together and coexist with all life on Earth.

Looking ahead, the mass accumulation of garbage is a big challenge, but it isn't the biggest problem—*what the garbage is made of, its impact on nature, the energy and nature-costs consumed to make it, compared to complete reusability—are!*

11

Utilities of Consumption

Other than the air we breathe, the food we eat and the climate we enjoy nothing is more important than the sun, water, topsoil and biodiversity, the natural resources that provide the energy and nourishment supporting all life. The sun is the ultimate powerhouse that creates the climate and food, the temperature variations driving wind and water, the solar energy stored in the fossil fuels we're consuming so rapidly. The nuclear materials on Earth were produced by stars like our sun; over time they were deposited here. Someday, the sun will irrevocably become the only energy source for life here, practically speaking—it always has been.

Physicists theorize that energy cannot be created nor destroyed, that energy and matter coexist as two forms of the same thing. As long as Earth maintains the atmosphere and climate that we enjoy the sun will provide the force propelling life on Earth for millions of years. It's quite a different story for the fossil and nuclear fuels we rely on to power our gadgets. Just how long the reserves of coal, natural gas, oil and nuclear fuels will last is simply a matter of how much remains and how fast we consume them.

Chances are the conditions that created fossil fuels on Earth won't exist here again; even if they did—it would take many thousands of years to recreate the fossil fuel energy humanity has guzzled down in just a few centuries. That's what we're faced with, what our children, grandchildren and however many generations that follow will have to contend with: the lack of nature-resources; the inability to burn the fossil fuels that have fueled the expansion of human society to where it is today. We should consider fossil fuels a gift of nature, spurring human creativity, giving us enough time to observe and learn about the nature of life and the energy that drives it. Yet, we're squandering all our resources as fast as we can. Our time is running out, we must learn to subsist on the only power source we can truly count on, our sun.

Before there was water, Earth's atmosphere was a work in progress, evolving to become the air we enjoy today. Earth's innermost atmosphere is the troposphere—extending 4-to-12 miles above sea-level—consisting of 76% nitrogen, 21% oxygen, 2% water vapor, .94% argon, .03% carbon dioxide. These ratios developed alongside Earth's plant and animal life; they've been maintained in delicate balance for millions of years—until now.

After the sun and air there is water, another of Earth's life-source partners. Together the sun, air and water comprise the sacred pact of life. In today's world, water is a utility we purchase and consume from municipal water sources or directly from wells or springs. As consumers we control how much water we consume, not its availability or quality.

Over the last two decades we've witnessed a number of leaks from coal mine processing plants of the chemical MCHM—a chemical used to separate coal from rocks—as well as other pollutants including oil rig, pipeline and fracking leaks across America. Excessive amounts of lead have been detected in city water systems in Detroit, Michigan and other cities around the country.

How much water is there on Earth? Earth's total water supply is estimated at 333 million cubic miles, mostly ocean saltwater. Freshwater is any naturally occurring water other than saltwater; it includes the water in ice sheets, ice caps, glaciers, icebergs, bogs, ponds, lakes, rivers, streams and groundwater. All freshwater isn't necessarily potable water (drinking water). Freshwater can be and is readily polluted by human activities or naturally occurring processes such as erosion. Without treatment, a sizeable portion of Earth's freshwater is unsuitable for drinking. Water is critical to the survival of all living organisms. Some species can thrive on saltwater, but the great majority of plants and land animals require freshwater to survive.

Over 96% of the world's water supply is saline. Of the remaining 4% that's freshwater, 68% is locked up in ice and glaciers, 30% is in the ground. The rivers and lakes that supply surface water for human use constitute roughly 2% of freshwater—roughly 22,300 cubic miles—0.007% of Earth's water. Rivers are the main source of the water people use.[1]

In 2018, the current estimated global consumption of freshwater was approximately 2.64 billion gallons. Overall, agriculture consumes 70% of annual global freshwater withdrawals, 20% goes to industry and 10% is used domestically. However, in most developed countries industry consumes more than half of all freshwater. Over the last 50 years, global freshwater consumption has tripled. The demand for freshwater is growing by 64 billion cubic meters each year; the world's population increases on average at the rate of 80 million humans per year.[2]

Throughout the world and America, groundwater—freshwater contained beneath the Earth's surface—is a critical water resource. In countries where lakes and rivers are few and far-flung, groundwater is used to fulfill the water needs of people everywhere. In the U.S., groundwater supplies the drinking water for about half the population—most all of rural inhabitants—while providing in excess of 50 billion gallons of water per day for agricultural needs. The term *groundwater depletion* is used to define the long-term decline of groundwater levels due to the excessive and continuous over-pumping of groundwater. Groundwater depletion is occurring in several areas throughout the U.S. and around the world.

From the beginning, groundwater has served as a critical water reserve for humankind. Today—as population and water consumption rates per capita continue growing—it is being pumped out exceeding recoverable limits, expanding beyond the available freshwater sources around the world. We are overdrawing Earth's available groundwater account similar to the way we buy goods excessively on credit. Groundwater and glaciers are nature's water savings account; we must be able to count on them for future freshwater deficits. As glaciers retreat, wells are drying up and groundwater is being depleted. With increased land subsidence, water tables are falling; water levels in lakes and streams are dropping and overall water quality is declining.

When water tables fall below the suction pipes on existing wells owners must drill new wells or extend the current ones. As water levels decline, pumping rates decline and costs increase. When water tables fall, seepage and saltwater contamination increase and groundwater quality declines. Groundwater is not necessarily made up of all freshwater, many of the deepest groundwater wells are partially saline.

We never really reduce our net water supply—we don't consume water in the same way we consume oil. When we burn fossil fuels they are chemically broken down into heat and some basic chemicals that are released into the biosphere. As the average temperatures on Earth continue to rise, glaciers are melting; rising sea levels are increasing the amount of saltwater vs. freshwater on Earth. We also lose freshwater when it is temporarily removed from the water cycle due to fracking, mining or manufacturing operations that bury waste-water deep in sanctuaries, where it will stay for a very long time before eventually working its way back to the surface. Approximately, the same water volume exists on Earth since its inception here.

The most critical water issues humanity must contend with include the growth in annual freshwater consumption, pollution and the changing rainfall patterns caused by climate change. When Earth's available freshwater is consumed over a year's time and the glaciers and aquifers have run dry—life on Earth is in a dreadful predicament. Those areas where humanity has traditionally gathered and set down roots have been left behind by changing weather patterns; they're already feeling some of the worst water scarcity effects.

The global nature of the ensuing water crisis is playing out across the globe. In Southeast Asia, groundwater aquifer reserves have declined significantly due to over-pumping in an area where 600 million people inhabit 800 sq. miles, in a land that's irrigated more heavily than anywhere else in the world, stretching from Bangladesh to India, across the sweltering parched plains into East Pakistan. Farmers there are throttling up pumping rates to water their crops, even as groundwater supplies are waning. Climate change is causing many regions of the world to experience varying precipitation cycles in quantity and type. Worldwide, glaciers are subsiding, causing water scarcity to those living downstream. The percent of global population that will experience water scarcity is expected to rise throughout the 21st century.[3]

Throughout human history, people, communities and nations have competed for Earth's basic resources: water, climate, energy, minerals and land. Information and technology have broadened the contested areas to include wealth, religion, military might, education, governance, energy sources and efficiency, space exploration, manufacturing efficiency, cyber warfare, immigration and sports to name a few. With less freshwater available, the competition for resources will result in more serious conflicts. Even in higher latitudes—regions on Earth where rainfall is expected to intensify—declining water quality will pose risks: due to rising temperatures; increasing sediment, nutrients and pollutants caused by heavy rainfall; the disruption of sewage treatment facilities during floods. The water crises the world will experience will have a severe impact on all earthly life.

For many years, groundwater depletion has been a key concern in the American Southwest and the High Plains. Across the U.S. increased groundwater pumping has overstressed aquifers in many parts of the country. Groundwater depletion is occurring at rates ranging from a few wells to complete aquifer systems located beneath several states. The severity of the problem depends on many factors: pumping rates compared to natural discharge capacities; the physical properties of the aquifer; existing natural discharge rates compared to those induced by humans.[4]

Along the Atlantic Coastal Plain in Long Island, New York, Nassau and Suffolk Counties, pumping water for domestic use has lowered the water table, reducing or in some cases eliminating base-flow levels of streams, causing saline groundwater to move further inland. Heavy development in the Ipswich River basin in Massachusetts has increased groundwater pumping, causing a significant reduction in surface-water flows there.

Heading south along the coastal counties in New Jersey to South Carolina's Hilton Head Island, Brunswick and Savannah in Georgia and much of the state of Florida, saltwater intrusion is occurring at alarming rates. Mean water-levels for a critical well in Cook County Georgia have declined by 7% from 1964 to 2003, due to long-term excessive pumping. This particular well serves most all irrigation and public-supply needs of the area.

In west-central Florida, groundwater development in the Tampa-St. Petersburg area has led to saltwater intrusion and subsidence in the form of sinkhole development and surface-water depletion from lakes in the area. Tampa has constructed a desalination plant to treat seawater for its municipal water supply to reduce its dependence on groundwater.

The Gulf Coastal Plain is another area feeling the impact of groundwater depletion. In Baton Rouge, Louisiana the pumping rate of groundwater expanded by a factor of ten from 1930 to 1970, causing groundwater levels to decrease as much as 200 ft. Excessive groundwater pumping in Houston, Texas has caused groundwater levels to drop some 400 ft., while area land surfaces have subsided by as much as 10 ft.

The states of Arkansas, Louisiana, Mississippi and Tennessee all draw water from the Sparta aquifer lying below. Beginning in the 1920s, continued pumping by industrial and municipal users has resulted in significant declines in groundwater levels. Memphis, Tennessee is one of the largest metropolitan areas in the world; the people living there rely solely on groundwater for their municipal supply and have experienced declines in excess of 70 ft.

The Ogallala aquifer underlies portions of eight states in the Great Plains area that have been intensively developed for irrigation. Water levels there have declined more than 100 feet in some areas; in other areas the saturated thickness of the aquifer has declined by more than one-half.

In the Pacific Northwest groundwater development—for irrigation, public and industrial uses—in the Columbia River Basalt aquifer of Washington and Oregon has caused water level declines in several areas exceeding 100 feet. In the Desert Southwest, groundwater pumping supports population growth in south-central Arizona, causing water level declines ranging from 300 to 500 feet. The Great Lakes watershed near Chicago and Milwaukee is the home for approximately 8.2 million people who depend upon groundwater as the sole source of their drinking water. Long term, increased pumping rates there have diminished groundwater levels by nearly 900 ft.[5]

The term *water-footprint* is a concept increasingly being used to report and analyze freshwater consumption by human activity. Freshwater has three components: green-water (equals rainwater); blue water (signifies ground and surface water); and gray water (denotes polluted freshwater). Globally, the term water-footprint is used to estimate water consumption for countries, considering their direct consumption of water as well as water consumed to produce goods. Virtual water flow patterns occur when water that's used to produce goods in one country is exported to others. For example, when farmers withdraw water from the Ogallala aquifer to grow corn or soybeans for export to the global market, the water consumed by those crops as well as any water used to process them is effectively exported to the importing country. While the water-footprint concept is an important measure for developing well-informed national policies, it can also help us as individuals to realize that the water we consume is more than just water we use in our homes, but also the water needed to produce all the energy, goods and services we consume.

The total water-footprint for global consumers during the period 1996–2005 was 9,087 billion cubic meters per year. Agricultural

217

production consumed 92% of that water; roughly 20% was related to items produced for export. The total volume of international virtual water flows related to trade of agricultural and industrial products was 2,320 billion cubic meters per year. The water footprint of the average global consumer was 1,385 cubic meters per year. The average consumer in the United States has a water footprint of 2,842 cubic meters per year, whereas average citizens in China and India have water footprints of 1,071 cubic meters per year and 1,089 cubic meters per year, respectively.[6]

A UN report in 2015 warned that the world could incur a 40% deficit of freshwater by the year 2030, unless nations and people markedly curtail freshwater consumption. As rainfall patterns become more unpredictable, global underground water reserves are already running low. By 2050, Earth's population will exceed nine billion. Unless water consumption rates per capita change, groundwater consumption will exceed what's needed to support personal consumption, farming and industry. As early as 2030, Earth will possess just 60% of the water needed to support humanity. At some point drought will overtake crops forcing them to fail, industries will be unable to function, ecosystems will disintegrate and water will become just another natural resource for humanity to fight over.

The World Water Development report of 2015 stated, "*Unless the balance between demand and finite supplies is restored, the world will face an increasingly severe global water deficit,*" while further noting that more efficient water use could guarantee enough water to supply humanity in the future. The report goes on to suggest that policy makers and communities reconsider water strategies to promote water conservation and the recycling of wastewater, increasing water prices while promoting the highest water-intensive sectors to become more efficient and less polluting.[7]

There are places, people and governments that have taken the lead in freshwater conservation. Israel has led the development of extremely efficient methods to preserve freshwater. From its very inception Israel established a national awareness of the critical nature of their water supply. From birth, each Israeli child is taught that every drop of water is precious—water is not to be wasted. In Israel, water is most respected throughout the land, shared equally with the entire population. Early on, the state of Israel initiated programs to fix leaks within their entire water infrastructure as well as methods for locating deep freshwater aquifers. They developed forecasts for aquifer pumping rates that matched their renewal, designed advanced drip irrigation systems and wastewater treatment plants, and created more efficient desalination processes.[8]

Australia is another country that developed water conservation methods that allowed them to survive the Millennium Drought experienced there from 1997 to 2009. They implemented measures that cut commercial and residential water consumption by 50%. Australia's severe drought engulfed the entire country, but mostly the densely populated southeast where its four largest cities reside: Sidney, Melbourne, Brisbane and Adelaide. The cities and towns there were forced to impose severe water restrictions; in some cases, outdoor watering was banned completely. With no irrigation or rainfall, farming was near nonexistent in the prime farmland of the Murray-Darling river basin that provides on average a third of Australia's food. Stream flows were reduced to almost nothing; 70% of the forests in floodplains were devastated and several animal species were threatened to near extinction.

Fortunately, Australians had developed plans early on to diversify their water supplies, improve water efficiency and conservation levels. During the drought the Sydney Water Company (SWC) was mandated by the state to reduce per-capita water consumption by 35%—the equivalent of 86 gallons per person per day. SWC's *Water fix* program was similar to Israeli programs that promoted fixing leaks, replacing toilet/shower fixtures and flow control devices with improved models to increase water use efficiency. Rebates encouraged residents to purchase water-efficient washing machines and rain-collection water-tank installations.[9]

The drought hastened the construction of water recycling facilities in Sydney and in other smaller communities built by private enterprises with public incentives. In 2010, Australia's Millennium drought came to a scriptural finale with a momentous rainfall and flooding of the Murray-Darling Basin—its largest yearly rainfall ever. In 2010, Sydney also endured an unusually soggy year, it's wettest in 150 years. Nearing the end of the drought the state utility built a $1.7 billion seawater desalination facility capable of supplying 15% of Sydney's daily needs. While desalination plants can create a reliable supply of quality drinking water, they are costly to build and operate due to the high material and energy content of their operation, not to mention the disposal costs of the salty brine they produce. By the time the drought ended the dams were full. When the desalination plant was complete it was tested and shut down, raising the price of water significantly to SWC customers for the next 50 years, a sizable water insurance policy against another dreaded Millennium drought. Australia, with a million more citizens, now uses less water that it did 30 years ago.[10]

A typical large-scale desalination plant produces 100,000 cubic meters of water per day. Assuming a per capita consumption of 300 liters per day, this equates to 300,000 people. The installed cost of desalination plants is approximately $1 million for every 1,000 cubic meters per day of installed capacity. Therefore, a large-scale desalination plant serving 300,000 people typically costs in the region of $100 million.

The cost of desalinated water, the majority of which is accounted for by plant capital costs and energy costs, is typically in the range of $0.5 to $3 per cubic meter of water (5-30 cents per liter of water). The lower end of the scale corresponds to regions where electricity costs are low (e.g. the Middle East) and higher end to regions where electricity costs are high (e.g. Australia, where electricity is sometimes mandated to be from renewable energy); the cost of the necessary infrastructure to distribute the water must be added to these estimates.[11]

The mass of forests around the world have provided us with the energy and materials that have warmed and housed us, recorded and communicated our thoughts and memories for millennia; offered us solace and peace, an open door to the world of nature. In return, we have clear-cut the forests for timber, eradicated them from mountain tops for mining, removed them for development and littered the landscape with their remains. While forest products are considered sustainable—trees can be replaced in a reasonable period of time—the extensive processes used to transport and manufacture their end products, are not. Over the lifespan of each piece of manufactured lumber, paper, cardboard or any other forest product, carbon emissions are exuded at each stage of its harvest, transport, processing, manufacture, distribution, sale and disposal. When we use forest products wastefully and excessively for single use applications: junk mail, inefficient office communication or virgin tissue paper, we shorten its life and increase its carbon footprint. A paper published by the European EPN in 2013 suggests that methods for producing and utilizing paper provide the creation of more greenhouse gases than the total emissions from global air travel annually.

The average American uses roughly 400 lbs. (200 kg) of paper per year, amounting to a couple of tons of carbon emissions, not to mention the energy consumed along with the other dangerous pollutants caused by its manufacture, and the chemicals added to it. We can significantly reduce the contributors to environmental damage by changing the ways we use forest products. Again, it is single use items that rise to the fore of most consumption and waste issues: pointless, short-term uses; junk mail; unwanted advertising and excess packaging.

Whenever a tree is cut down in the forest, carbon is released from the tree and the soil around it. This is especially true when logging occurs in natural forests that have never been cut before. Natural forests are still being cut to produce paper and other wood products. Some of the worst cases occur in Indonesia or Russia where deep peat-soils—that store large amounts of carbon—are damaged by logging and draining, emitting vast amounts of carbon dioxide. These results are amplified when the remaining vegetation is burned to clear the land completely.

Pulping is the process of mashing timber mechanically, and or chemically into a thick pulp biomass used to produce a variety of paper products. Pulping operations require large machinery, consuming vast amounts of energy and other materials, producing unique pollutants and waste products. While some pulp mills are powered by renewable energy sources, many use fossil fuels or wood which give off additional contaminants and carbon emissions. The production of paper products consumes significant amounts of energy and other unsustainable resources.

Increasing applications for wood-based biomass are projected as a major driver of forest reduction over the decades to come. The annual wood demand for energy is projected to reach 6-8 billion cubic meters—twice the wood harvest being removed today. This will cause severe problems for achieving sustainable land use: carbon sequestration; topsoil erosion; biodiversity; air and water quality. After timber is removed, it's transported, processed, sent to distributors and the marketplace. Each mile of transport adds to the energy footprint of the final forest product, most all of it in the form of carbon emitting fossil fuels. Raw paper from the mills is sent to a number of different types of final processors called *converters* that specialize in the final products they produce: cardboard boxes, paper bags, food packaging, sanitary materials, general office products and envelopes. When most paper products arrive at their final destination—the end user, glancing at a report, opening a package, scanning a piece of junk mail before tossing it in the waste bin.

In America and across Europe, paper and cardboard products are the largest component of domestic waste-streams. The wealthiest countries maintain the highest proportions of paper relative to overall waste. The garbage trucks that pick up all the paper product wastes are fueled by fossil fuels. Paper recycling rates have increased only slightly in recent years—roughly a quarter of all paper consumed is sent to landfills. When paper decomposes it turns into carbon dioxide or a more damaging greenhouse gas—methane.[12]

Salvaging our tropical forests is critical to diminishing the impact of climate change and many other ecological factors. Recent data from the Global Forest Climate Watch has released data showing CO_2 emissions created—those not being absorbed—by tropical forest cover-loss for 2017, amount to a net generation of CO_2

ranking third, behind the CO_2 created by emitters #1 China and #2 the United States. If the rate of tropical tree loss continues, there is virtually no way to meet the pledge of a two degree C (3.6 degrees F) limit of climate warming per the current Paris Agreement.

Between 2015 and 2017 an estimated 4.8 gigatons of CO_2 was allowed to collect in the atmosphere due to tropical forest losses each year. This amount exceeds the total amount of CO_2 generated by 85 million cars over their entire lifetime. The numbers are trailing upwards, average annual emissions in the past 3 years have been 60% higher than the previous 14 years (4.8 gigatons compared to 3.0 gigatons). Under the Paris Agreement forests account for nearly 25% of planned CO_2 emissions by 2030. Rain forests are important—not just for biodiversity and carbon sequestration—because forests possess critical, local cooling capacity measuring roughly 2 air conditioning units (approximately 70 kilowatt-hours of electricity) per tree per day by shading the ground and transpiring water. Otherwise, deforestation in the tropics or temperate zones can increase air temperatures by one degree C (1.8 degrees F) as well as raising daily temperature variations 2.85 degrees C (5.13 degrees F).[13]

Fossil fuels and nuclear material are the other key natural utilities consumed critical to human survival. In 2017, global consumption of oil equaled 99.7 million barrels/day or 36,390 million barrels/year, with expectations that consumption will continue to rise.[14] Global Coal consumption totaled 1,500 million tons with projections that coal consumption will remain steady throughout the decade.[15] Coal is also used to produce the coke used in steel and metallurgy. Coke is coal that's been processed to possess high carbon content with few impurities, the result of burning coal in the absence of air. Nearly 74% of all steel production requires coke for its manufacture; iron and steel are completely recyclable.

Globally, natural gas consumption grew to 3,738 billion cubic meters as fracking expanded around the world. Natural gas is the cleaner fuel of choice replacing coal to meet increasing electrical power demands; its continued growth is expected.[16]

The process called hydraulic fracturing (fracking) has improved the recovery rate of natural gas and oil. Fracking is the process of drilling and injecting fluid under high pressure into the ground for the purpose of fracturing shale rocks to release natural gas. The concept of fracking has been around for a long while; the technology has only recently been perfected and made cost effective. A similar process is being used to expand drilling for oil. Although fracking increases the amount of oil and gas recoverable from new and existing drilling fields, it comes with a number of environmental issues. There is considerable concern that fracking can lead to the contamination of groundwater due to spills, faulty well construction or water disposal into underground injection wells. Fracking can also cause the emission of methane, volatile organic compounds, hazardous air pollutants and other greenhouse gases into the air.

A large volume of freshwater is consumed to support the fracking process, placing a strain on available water resources. The fresh water consumed in the fracking process is turned into wastewater, which can contain high levels of dissolved solids, fracturing fluid additives, metals and naturally occurring radioactive materials. Most municipal water treatment plants are not well suited to remove all of these contaminants. Various drilling companies often use proprietary drilling liquids; they are often unwilling to disclose the chemicals they use. Only a few states require that drillers disclose the chemicals used in their fracking processes. Methods for the disposal of fracking wastewater include deep well injection; surface impoundment for storage or disposal; recycling methods and discharge to a properly licensed treatment facility.

Ever since fracking for natural gas has commenced across the U.S., there have been concerns that the fracking process could also affect seismic activity. In Oklahoma and Texas, significant increases in seismic activity have followed after fracking for oil or natural gas has proceeded. In the town of Jones, Oklahoma, some 2500 earthquakes have been recorded over the last 5 years. After studying the seismic data, scientists now believe that the disposal of fracking wastewater in underground wells is as much the cause of the added seismic activity as the fracking process itself. Jones is located near four high-rate injection wells that dispose of approximately 4 million barrels of wastewater underground each month.

Deep sea offshore oil well drilling is another example of the lengths to which oil companies must go to continue the flow of oil to our gas tanks. As new shallow offshore drill sites have become few and far between, oil companies have been forced to look for oil deeper and farther offshore. As they drill further downward and more distant from shore, there is an increasing risk of explosion, oil spills and fires, requiring more costly and complex processes, and equipment to do the drilling. Deep sea drilling involves an intricate arrangement of instruments and steel, located in severe climates, strung out over surface supports far offshore, extending some 18,000 feet below the surface. It's an environment where it's just a matter of time before a tragic accident happens.

Severe storms have an inherent capability to locate and test all the weak spots in the system. The Exxon Valdez and the Deep-Water Horizon spills are good examples. They represent the two most spectacular oil spills occurring in the American hemisphere with staggering environmental and economic losses. When the Deepwater Horizon drill rig exploded and sank, the well had been drilled to a depth exceeding 35,000 feet—over six miles deep—at the time the deepest of any oil well ever drilled.

Shell Oil is one of the major oil companies still searching and pursuing deep water drilling in the Gulf of Mexico. Shell's Mars oil field was the largest discovery in the Gulf of Mexico in over 25 years. Its daily production average is about 21,000 barrels of oil and 25 million square feet of natural gas with the potential to produce roughly a billion barrels of oil over the life of the well, approximately just 14% of the oil the U.S. burns through annually. In 2015 the United States consumed roughly 7 billion barrels of petroleum products, an average of about 19.4 million barrels per day.[17]

There are two accepted theories for how Earth's supply of uranium was first created, the explosion of one or more supernovas or the merger of two neutron stars. It's believed that Earth's uranium was produced through one or more of these high energy explosions capable of producing large amounts of heavy elements including gold, platinum and uranium, distributed throughout our solar system with some of it ending up landing here on Earth.[18]

As scientists have come to understand the laws of physics, engineers have applied them to make our lives easier in some ways, more complex and wasteful in others. When you think about energy sources, electricity is not really an energy source at all; it's essentially the result of PV-solar panels, wind or water turbines, the combustion of fossil fuels or nuclear fusion reactors, converted into electrical energy.

Presently, our rate of consuming natural resources has quickly gobbled up much of the energy stored as oil, natural gas, coal and uranium in the earth's crust, recoverable at reasonable cost. No one knows just how much fossil or nuclear fuel energy remains, but rest assured—it's not limitless. The time remaining to react is closing fast. Most of the remaining fossil fuels will require increased energy and higher pollution risks to extract and process; when depleted the only energy source remaining will be the sun. As a global society, we are passing on to our children and theirs, not only an overwhelming financial debt but an overheated planet devoid of fossil fuels, and key natural resources absent its once extensive biodiversity.

In order to present a more precise and better picture regarding various nations in the global realm, I'm including nation profiles regarding the energy, environmental and human issues—the unique problems driving them—for five important and uniquely different countries across the globe: Brazil, India, China, Russia and the United States.

—Brazil Profile—

Brazil, the land of the mighty Amazon has been rising out of the shadows as a global economic power, as voices from the past call out to her: Native Americans: her Portuguese colonizers; the African slaves uprooted from their homes by the thousands to labor in Brazilian sugarcane plantations. Brazil is the fifth largest nation in the world geographically, covering near half the continent, sharing borders with each South American country except Chile and Ecuador, with a formidable population of 190 million.

Powdery-white sandy beaches, crusty weatherworn rocks line the shores of Rio Di Janeiro; rhythmic melodies play throughout the cities comprising much of Brazilian heritage. Brazil is the only South American country that derives much of its culture, language, agriculture and religion from Portugal, mixed with significant influences from Africa, indigenous natives (mostly nomadic Tupí-Guaraní Indians) and other European cultures and traditions.

In 1500 CE, Admiral Pedro Alvares Cabral claimed the territory for Portugal. After three centuries of Portuguese rule, Brazil gained its independence peaceably in 1822. When slavery was abolished, Brazil became a republic of the military in 1888; the powerful coffee exporters dominated Brazilian rule until populist leader Getulio Vargas came to power in 1930. It wasn't until 1985 that the military ceded all power to civilian rulers. Today, Brazil continues pursuing industrial and agricultural growth and the development of its interior. Every day, Brazilian leaders face the choice of exploiting its vast natural resources and large labor force to continue development, painfully aware of the environmental issues at stake, the vast poverty and social inequity prevalent across the country.

Brazil's unparalleled natural treasures include the dense tropical rainforests of the Amazon—with the most biodiversity on the planet—covering almost half the country. In the west is Pantanal, the world's largest wetlands. Northeastern Brazil is desert, with patches of tropical moist forest along the coastline. Southeastern Brazil hosts the Atlantic rain forests, less well known than the Amazon, but 20 million years older.

The great Serra do Mar mountain range follows the southeastern coast before turning north to Rio de Janeiro. Near the border of Argentina and Paraguay is Iguacu Falls, one of the best-known waterfalls in the world, containing some 300 waterfalls. While the

Amazon is Brazil's most infamous biodiversity treasure, it's also home to incredibly unique wildlife and numerous indigenous cultures that maintain little or no contact with the outside world. The Amazon plays a key role in regional and global carbon cycles and climate variation. The Amazon River Basin shelters nearly one-third of the world's species, containing nearly a quarter of Earth's freshwater. In addition to its wealth of discovered and undiscovered flora and fauna, the Amazon is home to many diverse traditional and indigenous human populations.[19]

In addition to its breathtaking landscape, swarming with biodiversity, Brazil also possesses significant quantities of energy resources: coal, oil, natural gas and uranium.[20] In February of 2019 Brazil was ranked as the 6th largest energy consumer and producer.[21] In 2018 Brazil was listed as possessing the 13th largest oil reserves globally.[22] Many of the newly discovered reserves contain very heavy oil, not as readily refined as the preferred sweeter and lighter oils. Significant natural gas reserves have also been discovered around the country. Inland gas pipelines have been constructed throughout much of the territory linking key population centers. Brazil has coal reserves estimated anywhere from 10 to 30 billion tons, but the deposits vary in quality and quantity, along with significant deposits of shale oil. Uranium deposits have been found in eight of Brazil's states, together totaling the sixth largest uranium reserves in the world.

The Itapúa Dam in Brazil possesses the world's largest hydroelectric generating capacity; Brazil's overall hydroelectric generation capacities ranks 3rd after China and Canada. Nuclear energy accounts for roughly 4% of Brazil's electricity consumption. Brazil's total installed photovoltaic capacity is listed as 1.6 Giga-Watts. Wind power is yet another non-fossil-based power source estimated to have a potential of 140 Giga-Watts, with only 13.1 Giga-Watts of operating capacity. And lastly, Brazil's sugar cane crop—the largest in the world—has allowed Brazil to become the top exporter of sugar cane. Back in 1973, faced with the Gulf Oil Crisis, Brazil's government created a nationwide program to phase out gas guzzlers in favor of ethanol burners, replacing some 10 million gasoline fueled vehicles with those powered by ethanol. Many vehicles there still run on ethanol today.[23]

While maintaining a large stockpile of valuable natural resources, the dire environmental issues facing most industrialized countries are some of Brazil's major concerns as well. Brazil possesses more freshwater than any other country, but São Paulo—its largest city with a population of 9 million—was running dry after three years of continuous drought.[24] Deforestation is at the top of the list. Every minute of each day vast sections of the Amazon rainforest are being demolished for its raw timber, or for the land to be used for agriculture or economic development. Each time a tree is cut down more carbon dioxide is released into the atmosphere; the cleared land is subject to topsoil erosion. The over hunting of wild game, the reduction of forestland and the introduction of competitive species all serve to reduce the biodiversity of this rich rainforest ecosystem.

The rapid industrialization and urbanization occurring in Brazil has rapidly worsened the air pollution experienced in and around the burgeoning cities. As cities expanded in response to the shifting population, new infrastructure was built without consideration for more sustainable concepts and designs and little regard for environmental concerns.

Acid Rain occurs mostly when sulphur dioxide or nitrogen oxide result from the combustion of fossil fuels. The rain that falls in these areas possesses high concentrations of these gases which are harmful to plants and animals, especially those sensitive to acidic conditions. One of the major natural causes for acid rain is emissions from volcanic eruptions.[25]

With a growing economy and industrialization, Brazil has also realized a large increase in the accumulation of solid waste. Roughly 240,000 tons of waste is picked up and hauled from the cities each day. Landfills are the preferred choice as opposed to incineration; nearly 60% of Brazilian municipalities use landfills for waste disposal. Recycling is almost nonexistent due to a lack of waste management infrastructure; just 62% of Brazil's population has regular garbage collection. The pickup of recyclables is rare with little effort to communicate the importance of recycling to the general population.[26]

—China Profile—

China the country is a myth, mysterious, beyond imagination, with a culture so vastly different it appears to have sprouted from another dimension. The terraced landscapes, a border wall twisting along jagged mountain tops, megacity skyscrapers hemmed in by bulging freeways and the repugnant smog, all tell another story about a land that's as hard as it is beautiful, complex and yet simple, as tranquil as it is moving.

China is blessed with a diverse topography spanning 3.7 million square miles. Throughout the eastern plains and along the southern coastline, the foothills and fertile lowlands bestow most of China's agricultural output. South of the Yangtze River the landscape is mountainous and hilly. The west and north highlight a myriad of hollowed out basins named the Gobi and Taklimakan deserts, surrounded by rolling plateaus and majestic mountain ranges. The majority of the Chinese population has gathered in the central plains.[27]

While Russia boasts the largest land footprint, China has the most people; 1.42 billion of them—18.5% of global population—according to United Nation projections.[28] China began limiting child births to two per family during the 1970s, attempting to suppress the rapid rise in population. Later in 1979, the limit was reduced to one child per family, before gradually stepping back to a two-child policy in 2016. China's population growth rate (births per 1000 population) in 1950 was roughly 10% per year,[29] by 2017 that rate had dropped to around .5%, on par with many western countries including the U.S., Great Britain, Canada, France and Australia.[30]

As China's population grew, people increasingly relocated from rural to urban living to find work, representing some 55% of China's population. By the year 2030 China's urban population alone is projected to reach 1 billion, an increase of 350 million urban dwellers, roughly equal to the total population of the United States. China has at least 160 cities with population levels exceeding one million; seven megacities that surpass 10 million. As more of China's cities expand into megacities the quick growth across the country is sure to challenge funding for social services, applying pressure to the management of land, energy, water and the environment.[31] China's environmental problems run the full gamut of challenges: increasing air and water pollution; declining freshwater supplies; topsoil depletion; overfishing; overgrazing and desertification, excessive waste buildup; the rise in excessive natural disasters, not to mention the impact on China's ecosystems, biodiversity and ultimately the impact on human health. In some ways, China is the proverbial canary in the coal mine — the sign of things to come for the rest of the world.

China's sudden economic rise, averaging 10% per year for over a decade has severely affected the environment and ultimately public health. As one of the world's largest carbon emitters, the poor air quality of many major Chinese cities exceeds international health standards. Life expectancy varies throughout the country, largely dependent on air and water quality.

It's interesting to know that initially China's communist rulers believed that humans were capable enough and should be able to conquer nature — that only capitalist countries would be susceptible to environmental crises. Their thinking began to change after Chinese leaders attended a UN conference on *the Human Environment* held in 1972. Afterward, China began developing environmental regulations and institutions. Yet, economic reforms designed to encourage the development of rural industries stymied the enforcement of the new environmental regulations. While China's rapid growth has exacerbated the ruination of its environment, the ecological destruction began centuries ago from the culture, knowledge and technology that had developed over the centuries, in many ways similar as it had in the west. It seems that even though east and west pursued very different paths of cultural evolution — they ultimately ended up at the same place.

China is the largest producer and consumer of coal in the world, the largest consumer of coal-derived electricity — coal is China's primary energy source. China is also the world's largest emitter of greenhouse gases. The latest data shows China with 28% of global emissions in 2016, exceeding those of the United States, the second largest emitter at 16%.[32] China's second most populace city, Beijing has experienced numerous prolonged bouts of severe smog with concentrations of hazardous particles measured at forty times levels deemed safe by the World Health Organization (WHO).

As the world's largest coal producer, China accounts for nearly half of global consumption—burning coal is the largest contributor to China's poor air quality. However, the addition of some 17 million new cars hitting Chinese roads in 2014 has caused additional environmental distress. The increased pace of urbanization being encouraged by the government—to have 60% of the population living in cities by 2020—is increasing the energy forecasts needed to support the industrial and commercial activity necessary to accompany that much growth.

Supporting 20% of the global population with just 7% of the available freshwater has pushed water pollution and scarcity to the top of China's environmental concerns. Agriculture consumes roughly 70% of China's freshwater while 20% supplies the coal industry, leaving just 10% for public consumption. Excess consumption and pollution have caused severe water shortages with near 60% of China's cities experiencing water scarcities. When adding industrial pollution to the mix, groundwater supplies—for more than 60% of Chinese cities—were categorized as *"bad to very bad"*; some 25% of China's rivers were classified as *"unfit for human contact"*. In the cities the lack of adequate waste removal has added to the water pollution problem.

The ever-changing climate, overgrazing and generally poor farming practices have caused a scarcity of water that's transforming China's arable land into desert. Almost a million square miles of China's landscape is undergoing the process of desertification. All combined: over population; poor water quality and scarcity; the loss of arable land; are all significant challenges to China's ability to maintain its industrial and agricultural output with enough water to support the largest population on the planet. Recent studies have reported that emissions from China's industries are worsening air pollution as far west as the United States. China's neighbors, including Japan and South Korea, have also expressed concern over acid rain and smog affecting their populations. Environmental ministers from the three northeast Asian countries agreed to boost cooperative efforts to curb air pollution and to protect water quality and the maritime environment in 2014.[33]

China is expanding the use of nuclear, natural gas, solar and hydroelectric sources of electrical generation while reducing coal consumption in an attempt to meet the growing electrical demand with cleaner fuels. China operates 44 nuclear reactors with a total capacity of 40.6 Giga-Watts, with 13 new reactors being constructed to provide an additional 14 Giga-Watts, and plans to add another 36 Giga-Watts to meet the goal of 58 Giga-Watts of electrical generation capacity by the year 2020. In 2018, China's installed nuclear generation capacity ranks fourth amongst all countries.[34]

Since 2013, China has been aggressively installing photo-voltaic and solar thermal systems across the country. By the end of 2016, China's photo-voltaic capacity of 77 Giga-Watts rivaled Germany's. China plans on increasing their solar generation capacity to 1,300 Giga-Watts by the year 2050.[35]

Hydroelectricity is China's largest renewable energy source and second overall behind coal. In 2015 China's installed capacity of hydro-electric power stood at 319 Giga-Watts. China's lack of large fossil fuel reserves combined with the government's desire for energy independence has made hydroelectric power a key component of the country's energy policy, with the goal of achieving 350 Giga-Watts capacity by the year 2020. Yet, even with the lower greenhouse gas emissions of hydroelectric power generation, the environmental and cultural damage that comes with it—the forced relocation of masses of people, the extensive destruction of forests, land and ecosystems—is formidable.[36]

Looking ahead China has many daunting tasks: maintaining the world's largest population with increasing energy and commodity consumption; managing the population gap caused by the one-child limit per family; growing the economy enough to support the population without overwhelming the environment; reducing the consumption of coal to reduce greenhouse gas emissions; increasing wind, solar, hydroelectric and nuclear power generation; accommodating the expansion of the Chinese middle class and the retirement of a large portion of their workforce.[37]

—India Profile—

India is a wondrous country, stretching from the weathered Afghan frontier to Myanmar's misty jungles, including a diverse population with many dialects and cultures. The land is home to the Indus people— one of humanity's most ancient civilizations. To the north the Himalayas stand stiff, their jutting dark peaks a stark contrast to the vibrant green of the lower hillsides. Seven other mountain ranges meander across the south Asian continent; the great plains are made up of heavy forests with rocky areas running parallel to the Himalayas. The Thar Desert—also known as the Great Indian Desert—is seventh largest in the world, located in the northwest quadrant of the Indian subcontinent, forming a natural boundary between India and Pakistan. With a population density of 83 people per square kilometer, the Thar Desert is the most populated desert in the world. It's amazing to think that these people have figured out a way to live there, working together, combining animal husbandry and agriculture to survive in this harsh land.[38]

With a rapidly growing population, India has become the largest democratic government in the world. India's growing population and manufacturing capabilities have spurred economic growth, providing access to the global economy. In just a few decades, India has emerged as a nuclear-armed economic power to become a strong regional player in the east.[39] India, excluding Kashmir, covers 1.15 million square miles with a total population of 1.35 billion people—17.7% of global population—a population density of 1,180 people per square mile. India's urban population equals 33.2% of the total populace. If India's numbers continue growing at rates of 1.13% per year, in a few decades it will become the country with world's largest human population.[40]

India's urban living is most at risk as a steady migration of illiterate or unskilled people move to the cities looking for work. Even though college institutions have been producing more graduates, most are being trained in Liberal Arts without any applied training directly applicable to finding work. In segments of Indian society, having children is seen as an investment in the future. As parents age their children are expected to provide security by increasingly supporting them.[41]

With combined population and economic growth, India's environmental problems may be worse than anywhere else in the world. The categories are all familiar: deforestation; soil erosion; desertification; air and water pollution; agricultural pesticides; and heavy greenhouse gas emissions; are all prevalent there. While India is subject to the normal hazards such as cyclones and seasonal monsoon floods, the existing poverty, the fragile infrastructure throughout the country, the maldistribution of resources are symptomatic of a much bigger problem. In addition, the growing economy and industrialization are spurring more human consumption of goods by affluent segments of the Indian population.

Roughly 60% of cultivated land is subject to soil erosion, waterlogging and salinity. Between 4.7 to 12 billion tons of topsoil are lost each year. From 1947 to 2002, average annual per capita water availability declined by almost 70%. The overexploitation of ground water is worst in the provinces of Haryana, Punjab and Uttar Pradesh. Deforestation is predominant in the state of Madhya Pradesh and the seven states located in the northeast. The rich forest cover is showing significant decline due to harvesting wood for fuel and clearing more land for agriculture. The impact of increased motor vehicle traffic and industrial activity on the environment is creating unstable weather patterns, precipitation and drought across the land.

In a survey conducted of Indian expatriates living in Asia, the dirtiest countries were listed as India, China, Vietnam, the Philippines, Indonesia and Hong Kong. Singapore, Japan and Malaysia were said to be the cleanest. Thailand, South Korea and Taiwan were in the middle. And while India emits higher greenhouse gas levels than all other developed countries—except for China—India produces a net 4.2% of the world's total greenhouse gases, compared to 22% by the United States. The average American produces 20 times the greenhouse gases as one of India's average residents. A World Health Organization report has stated that New Delhi has the highest overall pollution levels in the world, followed in order by three of India's other major cities.

Each day the Ganges River is the recipient of some 345 million gallons of the foulest sewage, along with 70 million gallons of industrial sludge. Dead animals and sometimes people have been seen floating along in the froth. The people there characterize Ganges River water as having so many toxins that—even bacteria won't grow in it. Practicing Hindus believe that the Ganges cannot be contaminated. India's people drink the water, bathe in it and irrigate their crops with it. They say it's simply a question of mind over matter. Environmentalists there are careful not to describe the river as heavily polluted—they simply say that the sacred river is *suffering*.

Much of the developed world—including the U.S., Britain and Germany—send trash including plastics, car batteries, lead and cadmium as well as radioactive waste to India, Pakistan and Bangladesh, despite their import bans on toxic waste. Within India, cities are unable to collect all the trash as corrupt contractors rip off the local governments that pay them, collecting only a small percentage of the trash. The accumulation of garbage in Indian cities is nearing a national emergency.[42]

As India's economy and population continue growing, another large global consumer market will emerge there. More energy sources will be needed to meet the needs of that market, the increased business activity and consumption. In order to meet those needs without further environmental damage, India will have to curtail its reliance on coal and switch to cleaner alternatives. In 2017, India was the third largest energy consumer in the world, representing just 5.6% of the global share with China at 23.2%, the U.S. is 16.5%. India's total energy consumption that year consisted of mostly coal at 56%, crude oil 30%, natural gas 6%, hydroelectricity

4%, renewable power 3% and nuclear energy 1%. India imported 47% of the fossil fuels consumed that year. The numbers show that India is largely dependent on fossil fuel imports to meet its energy needs today and into the future. By 2030, India's dependence on energy imports is expected to exceed 53% of the country's total energy consumption.[43]

With growing energy demands and limited domestic fossil fuel reserves, India is banking on nuclear power generation and renewable energy to pick up the slack. India has a large potential for wind power and also plans on adding as much as 100,000 Mega-Watts of solar power capacity by 2020. India also envisions increasing the contribution of nuclear power to its overall electric generation capacity from 4.2% to 9% within 25 years.[44]

The most problematic issue facing India today is the shortage of clean water to support the world's second largest population. Past improvements made to address this water crisis have been negated by population growth, the over privatization of the solutions, and the trend toward urban living. A large part of the population living in rural areas has been left out. Many water sources remain polluted with biological and chemical pollutants; water contamination is listed as the cause of over 21% of disease. India's aquifers are increasingly being used to irrigate the expanding acreage of tillable land to fulfill India's growing need for grain. The added stress applied to these critical reserve water stocks could exceed their short-term refill rates. Rural communities situated close to the growing cities have been forced to dig new wells to access groundwater sources, drawing water away from other aquifers and wells.[45]

India's current rate of population growth is unsustainable: economically, environmentally and ethically. The land has limited food resources, capital is scarce and government solutions are inefficient. More humans armed with modern technology alone cannot create a viable human society there. Only by living more relevant, respectful and simpler lifestyles can all of humanity create a society consistent with the natural world, comprised of Nature, Sun and Earth.

Embracing Sufficiency

—*Russia Profile*—

Of all nations on Earth, Russia is largest in sheer size, covering more than 6.5 million square miles and 11 time zones, nearly twice the size of the United States. It has taken Russia many years to emerge from the shattered remnants, the economic and political mayhem of the failing Soviet Union, to reaffirm itself as a perennial world power.

Russia is one of the world's most northernmost countries, extending from Finland in the west to borders with Georgia, Azerbaijan, Kazakhstan, Mongolia and China in the south, the Arctic Ocean in the north. European Russia is the most densely populated and industrialized region with 78% of the population. Two large industrial cities, Murmansk and Norilsk are located above the Arctic Circle. The great plains are divided ecologically from frigid marshy tundra, transitioning to mixed coniferous/deciduous forests, mixed prairie and forest in the central areas, to Russia's minimal black-earth *breadbasket*, and lastly the grasslands and deserts reaching out to central Asia.

The Russian climate is mostly continental in the east, with cold, long winters and hot, short summers. Farther north, wintery days are mostly twilight; summer nights bask in dim daylight. Except for its breadbasket, Russia has fairly poor soil, below average precipitation, a short growing season with arid swaths of land unfit for agriculture without widespread irrigation and fertilization. Historically, these issues have led to massive crop failures and limited agricultural output, even in the best of years.

Russia possesses huge forests that provide foraging, hunting and logging. Several large rivers cut across the countryside linked by secondary waterways. Russian authorities have tried to curtail the excessive illegal logging there; limited funding has impeded the enforcement of new regulations. Inefficient logging practices and clear cutting have resulted in many harvested trees going to waste.

Russia's varied environment has shaped cultural, social and political norms, the development of infrastructure and commercial enterprises, local politics, agricultural methods and military strategies. Historically, the natural limits of the terrain have been ignored by the country's leaders on projects like the construction of St. Petersburg in the middle of a swamp in 1703, and more recently projects reversing the northerly flow of rivers to provide easy transport of natural resources to the south.

Russia's extensive natural resources—reserves of coal, oil and natural gas—have provided the economic impetus to transcend its near economic collapse in1998. The long run of prosperity that followed ended in 2014 with falling oil prices. Meanwhile Gazprom, Russia's state-run gas monopoly has maintained its position as primary supplier for a large share of the European energy market. Since the year 2000, Russia's dominant political figure, Vladimir Putin has enhanced his control over all state institutions and the media by promoting intense patriotism and competition with the west.[45]

Russia's population estimates totaled 144 million in 2018, 1.89% of global population. Population growth has been unstable there for the past 25 years, climbing in the 1990s, leveling off and declining in 2005 until stabilizing again. In the next decade the overall population decline is expected to worsen, largely as a result of economic and social upheavals of the post-socialist period which have impoverished the population and caused a decay of social services. Growing unemployment, long-term nonpayment of wages and pensions, wages that are below the poverty line, unsafe working and road conditions, the spread of infectious diseases, and the impoverishment of public health care systems have caused stress, depression, family breakdown, and rising rates of alcoholism, suicide, homicide, and domestic violence. Circulatory diseases, accidents, and suicides attributable to alcohol abuse are the leading causes of death among men. Malnutrition, disease, industrial pollution, poor health care and reliance on abortion for birth control, have reduced fertility rates and increased maternal and infant mortality.[46]

Russia is bursting with energy resources, self-sufficient and ranked #6 in the world with 323 million tons of coal production in 2009, two-thirds of which is consumed domestically. Russia's coal reserves total 160,364 million tons.[47] However, coal production has been declining as power generation is increasingly powered by natural gas, nuclear and hydroelectric energy sources. Massive gas reserves total 1,688 trillion ft^3 (Tcf), about a fourth of the world's proven gas reserves located in Siberia.[48] Oil reserves stand at 80,000 billion barrels (#8 worldwide). Russia can still boost its oil and gas reserves by beginning exploration beneath its holdings under arctic ice and seawater.[49]

Some 19% of the world's forest reserves are located in Russia; deforestation in Russia accounts for 300 to 600 million tons of the 1.5 billion tons of carbon dioxide sequestered each year by global forests. The clear cutting of large portions of this forest reserve is having a severe impact on CO_2 sequestration.[50]

Nuclear contamination is another major environmental concern. Russia is currently operating a number of first-generation nuclear power plants nearing the end of their intended life span. Their continued operation is a risk to workers and those living in close proximity to any of these plants. Waste from the former Soviet Union's nuclear weapons development and disarmament programs have resulted in permanent damage to areas in southern Siberia and Chelyabinsk in the Ural Mountains.

In addition to fossil fuels, Russia is also blessed with a vast supply of freshwater. With some 2 million lakes, 210,000 rivers and nearly 25% of Earth's freshwater reserves, Russia should be a haven for freshwater use. Yet much of this freshwater is polluted due to poor control of waste disposal. Dams for producing hydroelectric power have decreased water levels, increasing the relative volume of pollution in the water. In Moscow, high mercury and manganese levels have been found in local freshwater supplies.[51]

— USA Profile —

Conceived as the *Manifest Destiny* the United States is home to such a collection of nature displays, bringing to mind scenes of better times and magnificent nature landscapes. From New England's once pristine coastlines to the beauty still present there after four centuries of *civilized* human domination: wandering mountain ranges, autumn forests and craggy coastlines are an amazing spectacle, albeit showing some wear and tear from humanity and the ages.

The Florida Keys form a barrier between the Atlantic Ocean and the Gulf of Mexico; bleached white sands surround these tiny islands sitting atop coral reefs that are vanishing before our eyes. While corals around the world are in serious decline, the skeletal growth of corals in the Keys has remained stable; though skeletal densities are experiencing significant decay due mostly to ocean acidification.

Further along the southerly coastline the Bayou is home to a uniquely exquisite lifeform panorama. The Louisiana wetlands makeup a fragile ecosystem covering some 10,000 square miles, extending 30 miles inland from the mouth of the Mississippi River, totaling more than 10% of all wetlands in the U.S. Mammals including the coyote, muskrat and red fox survive there along with larger mammals: the black bear, bobcat and eastern cougar. The American alligator has bounced back from near extinction. Snake species including corn snakes, the venomous western cottonmouth, pit vipers and speckled king snakes all make their home in the Louisiana wetlands. The great blue heron and great egret love the fishing in the wetlands. Endangered brown pelicans have rallied back after nearly being wiped out by DDT. Osprey, black vultures and barred owl live further to the south in the marshes. Migratory waterfowl and songbirds seek solace as they overwinter there. A variety of very special plants survive in these wetlands called *hydrophytic* plant species that have evolved to survive in an oxygen deficient environment. The Cyprus tree, reeds and water lilies are the most prominent examples. Natural disasters and manmade hazards, pollution, dredging, soil erosion and levees pose a serious threat to the vitality of this bountiful marshland ecosystem.

There's a place in Colorado called *Garden of the Gods* where crimson-red-rock clusters appear as out-growths from the snow-capped alpine forests below, said to be one the most beautiful places on Earth. Along the Pacific Coast, tufts of granite mounds stand firm against the slashing waves of the Pacific as Monterey pines look on from their perches high above. Further north at the Badlands National Park in South Dakota, there is a place where a few buffalo still roam in one of the most unique landscapes of the wild-west, after their near extinction in the late 1800s.

Alaska, America's 49th state is a subarctic wonderland, from icy shores to mountain glaciers with wildlife ranging from killer whales to seals, penguins and grizzly bears. With a land area nearly twice the size of Texas, Alaska may yet contain more oil than Texas. Yet, Alaska's entire state population equals just one tenth of the residents of New York City. Leaving Alaska's subpolar cold, the last leg of our journey takes us to the tropics of the Kalalau Valley in Hawaii, an island kingdom, its fiery volcanoes and sunny beaches provide near perfect weather year-round.[52]

The United States government is considered a federation: a political entity made up of a union of partially self-governing states or regions under one central government. The federal republic is a representative democracy where majority rule is balanced with minority rights protected by law.[53] The U.S. is the oldest surviving federation in the world, encompassing an area of 3.8 million square miles with a population of 327.5 million, just 4.28% of global population, but possessing 33% of all the wealth in the world, the largest share of global wealth of any country.

The United States of America is a founding member of the United Nations, the World Bank and International Monetary Fund, the Organization of American States and other international organizations. The U.S. possesses the world's largest GDP economy, considered post-industrial, with a majority of knowledge-based or service activities. The manufacturing sector ranked second in the world in 2016; projected to surpass China and move into first place by 2020.[54] In 2017 the U.S. was the largest importer with imports totaling $2.35 billion[55]; second largest exporter at $1.47 billion[56]; ranked 17th in the quality of life category.[57] The U.S. is a foremost global military power, spending 37% of global military spending,[58] a leading political, cultural and scientific influence internationally.[59]

While many of these accolades still ring true, the compassion-ate, honest, fair-minded and righteous America has succumbed to the mother of all human weaknesses—the almighty American dollar. According to the latest happiness study America scored its lowest rating ever—19th in comparison to all nations. I guess the old saying rings true—*you can't buy love and you can't buy happiness.*[60]

Total energy consumption in the U.S. overall totaled 2234.9 million metric tons of oil equivalent in 2017, [61] remaining relatively flat since 2013. Over the same period, coal consumption declined 3 to 4% each year totaling 717 million tons in 2017; [62] consumption of coal's replacement natural gas has been steadily increasing to 27 trillion cubic feet from 2010 to 2017.[63] Total U.S. oil consumption has been rising steadily from 2012 to 2017 by about 1.8% per year to 913.3 million metric tons [64] while consumption of electricity was almost flat at 3,820 billion kilowatt hours.[65]

U.S. total water consumption of freshwater and saline-water for 2015 is estimated to be 322 billion gallons per day. Freshwater withdrawals represent 87% of the total and saline-water makeup the remaining 13%. Most saline-water withdrawals were seawater and brackish coastal water used to generate thermoelectric power. In 2015 there were significant drops in withdrawals due to a decrease in demand from thermoelectric power of roughly 28.8 billion gallons per day, while irrigation withdrawals increased just 2%. The drop in thermoelectric consumption was a result of increased efficiency in water use as well as the practice of recapturing and reusing water.[66]

Due primarily to the Clean Air and Clean Water Acts and legislation mandating increased gas mileage for vehicles passed during the 1970s, Americans enjoy cleaner water and air than many of the world's industrialized countries. Yet, many Americans still must contend with dirty air and polluted water. The Clean Air and Clean Water Acts provide the basis for the EPA to maintain clean water and fresh air for all Americans. Over the years, air quality has improved significantly, but roughly half of Americans are exposed to polluted air that can cause health problems, according to the American Lung Association report. Fine particulates are tiny (2.5

microns or smaller) and can penetrate deep into the lungs, precipitating health problems. The areas of the country exhibiting the highest levels of fine particulates based on their annual averages, are discussed in the paragraphs that follow.

The state of California has the most problematic air quality, which is why the state government there has been so proactive in addressing this issue. There are four areas within California with the lowest quality air: the San Joaquin Valley, Los Angeles, the San Francisco-San Jose area and the southern border. The people living in and around the cities and towns of Bakersfield, Visalia, Porterville and Hanford, areas located in the San Joaquin valley are all subjected to dust, pesticides and fertilizers, while the surrounding mountains create inversion layers that trap pollution with a lack of any wind to blow it away. Fine particles emitted from coal-fired power plants, wood burning, and diesel-powered vehicles penetrate deep into the lungs while automobile exhaust, heat and sunlight contribute to high ozone levels.

In and around Los Angeles, an area that's supports some 18 million people, the large population, automobiles, businesses, factories and shipping ports, the sun-filled consistent weather and sunken topography all promote local air pollution. South along the border in El Centro, California traffic bustles back and forth across two international border crossings with steady streams of traffic from both sides. Long lines of powered vehicles combine with the dry heat to increase risks for people with asthma and COPD. In the San Jose-San Francisco area roughly 8.6 million people struggle with poor air quality from automobile traffic, wood stoves and fireplaces in the summer.

Across the country near Pittsburgh, PA, and toward the Ohio and West Virginia borders, the processing of coal into coke and steel production combine with truck and car traffic to create small particle and ozone pollution. Further east near Harrisburg, York and Lebanon, Pennsylvania air pollution has increased drastically over the past few years due to strong wind patterns and heavy commuter traffic in Baltimore, MD and Washington, DC. Further south, Louisville, KY sits in a bowl surrounded by hills; the residents there suffer from air with excessive small particle pollution.[67]

Looking to the future, both clean air and water are at risk under the current administration's approach to *environmental non-protection*. The EPA has lost some 10% of its criminal investigators, while also working to mitigate previous legislation protecting the environment.[68] The current president continues his use of executive orders to reduce enforcement of environmental issues across the board, measuring economic gains against environmental losses.

Under the Obama administration gas mileage improvements for automobiles called for having vehicles average 55 miles per gallon by 2025. On April 2, 2018 the current administration indicated it will abandon that goal and replace it with weaker fuel economy standards that the administration will settle on at a later date. Automakers support the move, complaining the costs of achieving the Obama administration goals would increase vehicle prices. Yet, even without meeting the standards on all vehicles, industry analysts predict that automakers will have to meet the higher mileage standards anyway, so as to comply with stricter mileage and pollution requirements in California, Europe and China.[69]

Back in May of 2015, the U.S. Army Corp of Engineers, working in conjunction with the EPA, created the Clean Water Rule to eliminate confusion regarding which bodies of water are protected by the 1972 Clean Water Act. More specifically—it defines which type of water bodies are protected and which are exempt. The water resources at the center of the Clean Water Rule serve critical functions; nearly a third of all Americans get their drinking water from public sources that come from seasonal, headwater or rain dependent sources. On June 27, 2017 the current administration released a rulemaking change for the Clean Water Rule with the intention of invalidating it almost completely.

Wetlands include some 110 million acres of the continental U.S. These wetlands filter pollution from unsanitary runoff; they also serve to renew groundwater. Wetlands are capable of storing large quantities of flood water as well, and they provide habitat for fish and wildlife. Prior to the creation of the Clean Water Rule, confusion over the enforcement authority of the Clean Water Act prevented many investigations from proceeding to prosecution. When a body of water is protected under the Clean Water Act, a number of programs including pollution prevention, control and cleanup can be implemented including: the discharge of waste and sewage plants cannot be dumped into protected waters without pollution-limiting permits; storage facilities for large amounts of oil close to protected waters must have plans for preventing and responding to spills; plans must be in place for cleaning up protected waters when they fail to meet state water standards; industrial and commercial developers must obtain approval before discharging material into protected waters; any discharge of radiological, chemical, or biological warfare agent, any high-level radioactive waste, or any medical waste into covered waters is forbidden; entities disposing sewage that could pollute protected waters must abide by pollution control standards.

The Clean Water Rules were created after requests from a wide range of stakeholders ranging from regulated dischargers to environmentalists. The EPA and the Corp of Engineers completed a report after a review of 1200 peer reviewed scientific publications to confirm that streams and wetlands are connected to downstream waters in significant ways, and therefore can be protected. In other words, whenever a body of water is under the protection of the Clean Water Rule it can be protected under the Clean Water Act. After its inception, polling showed that numerous stakeholders supported the Clean Water Rules including 80% of small business owners, 83% of hunters and anglers and 80% of voters nationwide.

The current administration via executive order effectively tells the various agencies to consider interpreting the Clean Water Act as the late justice Antonin Scalia had in a 2006 opinion. Doing so would effectively disable federal protection for streams unless they are considered "relatively permanent" while excluding wetlands that do not have a "continuous surface connection to other covered waters." The administration's clean water rollback plan ignores the scientific evidence that demonstrates how various bodies of water affect downstream water quality and water flow, with no consideration for the costs associated with treating drinking water, increased water pollution and flood damage. And by the way, a majority of Supreme Court justices rejected Justice Scalia's opinion as the lone standard for Clean Water Act coverage, as did the Bush administration and every federal court of appeals to consider the question.

Currently, the administration plans to roll back the Clean Water Act in two steps: repeal the Clean Water Rule and then create a new rule that would roll back clean water safeguards for wetlands and streams as the executive order urges. Step one has already been taken with the announcement of the EPA's repeal rule. The EPA is in the process of getting input from selected interested parties to create a new rule with plans to complete the process for repealing and replacing the Clean Water Rule. Ultimately, if the two-step plan succeeds fewer streams, wetlands and other water bodies will be protected under the Clean Water Act's oil spill prevention program. More pollution will be allowed to access the lakes and streams we rely on for drinking water and the destruction of wetlands that provide protection from severe flooding will continue.[70]

———————

Let's review the global energy picture in 2017. Global energy production recovered some, increasing 2.4% above the historical trend. China contributed the most with an increase in coal output after three years of reduction. Higher global energy prices spurred oil and gas production in the U.S.—*none of this is good news for decreasing CO_2 emissions.*

In the European Union energy production continued to decline due to: moderate energy consumption growth; lower electricity production, especially nuclear and hydropower; the depletion of oil and gas resources; climate change policies driving reductions in burning coal.

Large oil and gas exporting countries: Russia, Iran, Canada and Nigeria, as well as fast-developing countries: India, Indonesia, Turkey and Brazil were the main contributors to energy production increases in 2017. Saudi Arabia decreased its oil production going along with the agreement to cut OPEC oil output.

Global electric power consumption accelerated again in 2017 (33+2.6%). Electricity consumption globally increased at a faster pace than other energy sources, due to electrification of many energy uses; most of the increase occurred in Asia. Electricity consumption growth in China amid an industrial recovery—despite strong energy efficiency improvements—contributed to more than half the global electricity consumption rebound. Power demand also grew in Japan for the first time since 2013, and in India, Indonesia and South Korea. Electric consumption in the U.S.—which had remained stable since 2011 due to energy efficiency improvements—declined for the second year in a row in 2017, whereas it increased in Canada.[71]

In 2017, total energy consumption increased by 2.3% vs. 1.1% in 2016. Global energy consumption was spurred by the rebound in China—since 2009 the world's largest energy consumer—triggered by sustained economic growth. Chinese energy consumption rose twice as fast as in 2016, pulled-up by strong industrial demand, offsetting three years of low consumption, energy efficiency gains and policies to decarbonize the economy.

Energy consumption also grew in most Asian countries: India, Indonesia, Malaysia and South Korea. Japan's consumption increased for the first time since 2013 driven by economic growth. A strong economy also raised energy consumption in Europe—Germany, France, Italy and Turkey—whereas it decreased in the United Kingdom, Canada and Russia. Energy consumption remained stable in the U.S. for the second year in a row, due to lower electricity demand and energy efficiency improvements. Brazil increased energy consumption after two years of contraction; in Mexico and Argentina it declined.

Over the 17-year period: 2000 to 2017 total global energy consumed has increased 41% when renewable energy increased only 3% of energy consumed. Thus far, total energy consumed has increased almost 14 times as much as the increase in renewable energy. See Table 1 that follows:

The following global fuel consumption data is made available by British Petroleum where primary energy (all utility delivered energy) is measured in standard units: *millions of tons oil equivalent called—Mote*. This is simply a way to compare all energy sources to one system of measurement easily converted to: tons of coal; barrels of oil; kilowatt- hours; cubic feet of gas; etc. See the results in Table 1 and the calculations below.

Table 1 - Global Energy Consumption Analysis

Units: Mtoe	2000	2008	2017
Total Energy Consumed	9614	11,793	13,576
Total Renewable Energy	51.8	123.9	486.8
%Renewable Energy of Total	.53%	1.05%	3.58%
% Inc. in Energy Consumed	Base Year	22.6%	15%

Global Total Energy Consumption: 2000 = 9614 Mtoe; 2008 = 11,793; Mtoe 2017 = 13,576 Mtoe[72]
Global Renewable Energy Consumption: 2000 = 51.8 Mtoe; 2008 = 123.9 Mtoe; 2017 = 486.8 Mtoe[73]
Global trends 2000 to 2017 in renewable energy consumption compared to global power consumption:
2000: Renewable global energy consumed: 51.8 Mtoe /Total global energy consumed: 9614 Mtoe =.53%
2008: Renewable global energy consumed: 123.9 Mtoe /Total global energy consumed: 11793 Mtoe =1.05%
2017: Renewable global energy consumed: 486.8 Mtoe /Total global energy consumed: 13576 Mtoe =3.58%

Global consumption of utilities has steadily increased since the beginning of the 1st Industrial Revolution. Since then population, consumption and per-capita consumption have all increased together. Productivity improvements were fueled almost entirely by fossil fuels. At this juncture, the high rate at which we're burning fossil fuels is as crucial as the decreasing amount of it remaining in

Earth's core.

China is the world's largest energy consumer at 3105 Mtoe with 18.5% of global population: a 1.25 energy-per-capita factor. The U.S. is second largest energy consumer totaling 2201 Mtoe with just 4.28% of global population: an energy per capita factor of 3.8. India is next consuming 934 Mtoe with 17.7% of global population: energy per capita factor equals .40. Russia is fourth consuming 744 Mtoe with 1.89% of all people; a 2.91 energy per capita value. Brazil consumes 291 Mtoe with 2.76% of all people: an energy per capita number of .80. The 3.80 factor affiliated with the United States means that each American on average consumes nearly twice the energy as the average global citizen (3.80 vs. 1.78 in Table 2 below).[74]

Table 2 – Profile Countries: Energy/ % Population/Energy per Capita

Country	%Global Energy[75] Consumption	% Global Population	Energy Per Capita Factor
Brazil	2.2% (291 Mtoe)	2.76%	.80
China	23.2% (3105 Mtoe)	18.50%	1.25
India	7.0% (934 Mtoe)	17.70%	.40
Russia	5.5% (744 Mtoe)	1.89%	2.91
USA	16.3% (2201 Mtoe)	4.28%	3.80
5 Country Total	53.8% (7275 Mtoe)	45%	1.20
Global Total	100% = 13576 Mtoe	100% 7.6 Billion	1.78

Consumption per capita of freshwater for the year 2016 shows that America consumed more freshwater per person than the other five profiled countries and all global countries with the exception of New Zealand. Freshwater consumption per capita for the profile countries follows: U.S. = 1583 cubic meters/person; India = 585 cubic meters/person; China = 443 cubic meters/person; Russia = 438 cubic meters/person; Brazil = 415 cubic meters/person.[76]

Utilities of Consumption

From a global perspective, CO_2 emission levels of 414.8 ppm advocate for programs to address climate change; the tell-tale symptoms are being felt around the world. The increasing climate change effects will cause complications with the availability of nearly all the utilities of consumption discussed in this chapter. Of course, increasing population and human per capita consumption will also impact the availability of water, fossil fuels, timber and topsoil; pollution levels; the ability to produce all types of food.

You can see from the countries profiled that all have issues with freshwater, even countries like Brazil that possesses more freshwater than any other country. Freshwater issues in undeveloped countries are dire, and they worsen each year. While fracking has increased the amount of natural gas and oil being harvested annually, it's uncertain how long newly fracked wells will last, the level of environmental damage they pose, the ability of fossil fuel reserves to keep pace with a growing population consuming more energy.

The data shown in Table 1 clearly shows that the rate of installing renewable solar, wind and hydropower generation has not even kept pace with the increasing energy consumption overall. Minimizing CO_2 generation while energy demands continue rising along with population and higher socio-economic status, is unattainable.

All lifeforms on Earth require a stable climate, air, water and nourishment to survive. Yet, humans need more resources than other lifeforms to compensate for our inability to survive in the wild without tools and accessories. Intelligence, dexterity, the ability to adapt using knowledge and reason, reacting to change with differing tools and practices within our lifetime, have enabled Homo sapiens to advance further away from the world of nature.

Having exceeded many of humankind's natural limits we've increasingly used fossil fuels to take up the slack. While technology allows us to do more in less time with fewer people, governments around the globe have subsidized the hidden nature-costs of *economic efficiency*. The rate at which we're burning fossil fuels is altering the air, climate, water, soil and biodiversity.

Embracing Sufficiency

The treadmill of consumption, production and waste continues to accelerate, the United States of America leading the charge, burning an energy supply that's declining rapidly, eliminating the energy sources for all life that sustain us. *Nature and the utilities of consumption are the earthly providers for all that we consume — they must be conserved at all costs.*

12

Life-Consuming-Life

This chapter title might sound morbid, but it's the nature of things — what all lifeforms do to survive. Subsistence is an endless cycle of life-consuming-life that sometimes doesn't seem natural, right or fair; in the real world we live in — it's the most natural thing of all.

It seems to me that too many of us have no idea where our food comes from, the health content of the average human diet, the resources used to produce our food — the artificial waste and environmental damage we're leaving behind. Have you ever really thought about how much and which types of food we consume each day, the impact on our health, happiness and welfare; the influence excessive consumption has on us and the rest of the world?

In this chapter we'll explore how much of which food varieties humans consume; the quantities and types of resources used to produce them; how human per capita food consumption has changed over time; the issues regarding excess food consumption and how to address them. We'll also review a more viable diet that many of us can follow that's healthier, expends fewer nature-resources with minimal impact on biodiversity and the environment.

Over 2 million years ago the early hominids were evolving and adapting as hunter-gatherers within the world of nature. They roamed the landscape hunting game, scouting for plant food, relocating when the food supply ran out. Eventually, they learned to cook their food and store crops, consuming more plant-based foods year-round instead of meat. They set down roots instead of moving around. Eventually, hunter-cultivators had spread across Europe and Asia. They used selective breeding to develop new varieties of plants and domesticating animals, modifying them over the centuries—at the same time humans were domesticating themselves.

Fast forward to the 18th century, the Industrial Revolution brought about more dietary changes. Advanced machinery provided for the manufacture of margarine and vegetable oils while growing affluence created different classes of food consumption. Industrialization modified the composition of basic energy foods. Throughout Europe and England obesity was becoming common amongst the upper classes. Where before the Industrial Revolution 75% of calories for common folk came from high-fiber starchy foods, with modernization 60% of all calories were supplied by fiber-free fats and sugars.

In America between 1880 and 1976 consumption of cereal fiber decreased by 90%. During that same period the energy derived from protein increased from 12 to 15% of all calories; fat intake rose from 25 to 42%; starches fell from 53 to 22%. Carbohydrate totals decreased from 63 to 46% and sugar consumption increased from 10 to 24%. While some of these changes might seem quite small over a century, they were significant—just the beginning of a growing new trend. Across developed countries the average weight of men in 1863 ages 30 to 34 was 148 lbs., a century later this number had increased to 170 lbs. Most recently, the current obesity crises began after 1970 and it continues today.[1]

When considering the modern human diet—its relationship to status and culture, human health and the long-term survival of our species—the issues become complicated, more convoluted than for any other species. These days, little food is available in the wild to meet the needs of modern human lifestyles; most of the foods we consume are shipped long distances to customers around the world. Current day food providers include fisherman, farmers, and breeders; pesticide and herbicide manufacturers; seed and fertilizer companies; producers of farming and fishing equipment; a variety of food processing, transport, distribution and sales organizations. As shoppers we are the ultimate gatherers, wandering through bustling mega-sized grocery stores cramming our baskets full with a greater selection of goods that any true hunter-gatherer could ever have imagined.

Today, estimates across the globe measuring the percent of labor involved in all facets of food production and distribution range from the lowest: England-1.11%; Germany-1.28%; the U.S.-1.66%; Canada-1.95%; to the highest: Zambabwe-68% and Tanzania-73%. Many poorer countries are unable to provide any data on this. The countries with the lowest labor percentages represent those using the greatest amount of automation. Yet, automation alone cannot produce large amounts of food. A stable climate, ideal growing conditions, large tracts of fertile land with a steady and adequate water supply are the key natural resources required. It's no surprise that nations possessing the greatest amounts of the nature-resources, high technology and automation are the principal producers of many basic food crops today.[2]

By air, sea and land modern transport and refrigeration technologies have expanded global food exports year after year. On the global stage, one country might produce the most of certain food crops, yet another might be the largest exporter of it. While certain countries possess the unique ability to increase food production to meet growing global needs, it usually comes with the cost of further environmental degradation. Agricultural output is measured in dollars or tons; it's important to look at both—nature-costs are hardly ever considered. While dollars place a monetary value on a unit of product dependent on the markets where it's traded, tons measure its actual weight without any monetary assessment.

Food production requires good weather, ample freshwater, lots of fertile and tillable land. Four countries around the world excel at producing food: China, India, the United States and Brazil. It's no surprise that all of these countries rank amongst the top five for total geographical size. Russia while possessing the largest land area of all countries, lacks the population level, weather and fertile soil to be a top food producer.

China is the world's largest food producer, importer and consumer of food. While much of China's land is mountainous, the areas south and east are fertile and productive. China possesses the world's largest agricultural labor force—some 315 million farm workers—nearly the current population of the entire United States. India is rated as the second largest food producer followed by the U.S. and then Brazil. Yet, India's food productivity is much lower than China, Brazil and the U.S. The value of much of India's food produce is too expensive to be affordable for many native Indians.

The U.S.—with the smallest workforce and the most automated equipment—is the most cost-efficient food producer of all countries. Many states in the union are solid food producers of a variety of crops; California, Iowa, Texas, Nebraska and Illinois are the largest food producing American states.

Since colonial times, Brazil has been a strong agricultural producer of sugar cane. Today, nearly a third of Brazil's landscape is used for crop production: coffee, sugarcane, soybeans and corn, as well as fruits: oranges, pineapples, papaya, and coconuts that grow well in the warmer climate. Brazil also produces a large amount of beef, ranked second behind the U.S.[3]

In 2017, the United States was the top food exporter ($72.68 Billion) including maize, soybeans and milk, imported by Canada, Mexico, China, Japan and Germany. Germany was second ($34.62 Billion) with exports comprised of sugar beets, milk, wheat, and potatoes, imported by the U.S., France, U.K. and China. The United Kingdom is the next largest food exporter ($29.54 Billion) of milk, wheat, sugar beets, and barley, foods imported by the E.U., China, Germany and the United States. China ranked fourth in food exports ($25.15 Billion); its largest food exports include maize, rice, fresh vegetables, and wheat, imported mostly by the U.S., Hong Kong, Japan and South Korea.[4]

Over the years, food production and distribution networks around the globe have developed through a patchwork of climate, nature-environment, culture and religious issues that have met the challenge of feeding humanity—albeit disproportionately—through natural disasters, wars and famine. The current global trade of food products is a complex web of natural resources, production, trade and politics. Poorer countries are looking to rise in status; richer countries want to hold onto what they have. All the while, the global population continues to grow. Food is the true nature-connection, the bond between all life and the natural world. Agriculture is one of the largest and *the* most significant industry in the world—the future looks murky.

The rate of population growth presents a serious food issue. Over the 40-year period from 1959 to 1999 the global population doubled from 3 to 6 billion humans. The global population growth rate peaked in the late 1960s at 2%. Today at 1.09%, the growth rate is nearly half that value with a total human population level of 7.7 billion. The population growth rate is projected to continue declining, reaching 1% in 2023, .5% in 2052 and .25% by 2076. And though the rate of growth is declining, global population will continue to increase throughout the 21st century, just slower than before. Estimates project the human population will reach 9 billion in 2037, 10 billion by 2055 and then 11 billion in the year 2088.[5]

You may have heard of the term *ecological footprint*. I like to think of humanity's ecological footprint as an accounting of the relationship between humanity and nature: the resources required by humans to survive compared to those the natural world has to give. Humans have already altered the natural world via the overexploitation of the global landscape; the mass extinction of species and global climate change. A growing human population, rising affluence and per capita consumption are all pushing planet Earth toward a tipping point. With the population expected to reach 9 billion by 2037, how can Earth's natural resources possibly keep up with our growing demand for food? From my perspective, the short, simple answer is—they can't.

The human ecological footprint is largely dependent on the

foods that makeup the average human diet. The types and the amount of food we eat have a huge impact on the volume and varieties of resources needed to support the daily nourishment of the average human being. Just 3% of Americans follow a strict vegetarian diet; the majority of the rest of us consume a lot of meat. Meat consumption has been growing at a rate of 5% per year. In 2018, estimates for average Americans projected meat consumption to total 203 lbs. per capita: 58 lbs. of beef, 50 lbs. of pork and 95 lbs. of poultry.[6]

Three-fourths of Americans consume diets low in vegetables, fruits, dairy and oils; more than half meet or exceed total grain and protein recommendations. A majority exceed recommendations for added sugars, saturated fats and sodium; only 20% of adults meet physical and activity guidelines for aerobic and muscle strengthening activities. The eating patterns of too many Americans are too high in calories, in excess of 3750 calories per capita per day—second highest in the world. The high percentage of Americans overweight or obese suggests that many are consuming excessive calories and getting little physical exercise; more than two-thirds of all adults and nearly one-third of all children and youth in the U.S. are considered overweight or obese.[7]

Developing countries around the world are following America's lead, moving up the food chain and increasing food consumption per capita. As the economies of some of the most populous countries grow—China and India—their diets are changing to include more meat and dairy products.

In 2014 researchers from Bard College, the Weizmann Institute of Science and Yale University, published their research on the production inputs required for beef, pork, chickens and laying hens, dairy cows, potatoes, wheat and rice, in the U.S. food production system versus the calories they produced. Data for the study was collected over the period from 2000 to 2010. The results were published in the *Proceedings of the National Academy of Sciences*. The researchers first calculated the feed costs for each group. Data collected from the U.S. Departments of Agriculture, Interior and Energy were used to determine the land area, water and fertilizer needed to produce the animals and plants we consume, standardizing the outputs by conversion to calories.

The study concluded: beef requires roughly 28 times more land; 6 times more fertilizer; 11 times more water to produce the same number of calories when compared to the other food sources in the study. Furthermore, the study performed the same comparison for crops including potatoes, wheat and rice to determine they require 2 to 6 times fewer resources than pork, chicken, eggs or dairy to produce the same number of calories.

The study generally concluded that beef production consumes 10 times more resources when compared to poultry, dairy, eggs or pork. The study discusses the uniquely high resource demands of beef along with the many environmental benefits of making simple and easy-to-implement dietary changes. The elimination or reduction of beef and other meats from our diet can provide huge environmental benefits, while reducing the adverse effects of consuming too many calories from meat and dairy sources. The key message of this study is—we can reduce consumption and waste, and become healthier too.[8]

With the elimination of beef from one's diet, individually we can reduce the effective annual consumption of the resource inputs of land, water, topsoil, grain and energy by roughly one-half: 45,000 gallons of water; 200 lbs. of grain; 900 lbs. of topsoil and 25 gallons of energy equivalent gasoline, while consuming the average American diet of pork and chicken and replacing the beef portion with fruits, green vegetables, potatoes, oats, wheat and rice. The resulting beefless diet still provides enough protein for individuals and its ultimately healthier and less costly. See Appendix-10 for details of the calculations.

If one person can save annually: 45,000 gallons of water; 200 lbs. of grain; 900 lbs. of topsoil and 25 gallons of energy equivalent gasoline per year, then 1% of Americans—3.3 million of us—could change over to a beef-less diet or equivalent and the savings would exceed 149 billion gallons of water; 660 million lbs. of grain; 2,970 million lbs. of topsoil; 825,000 gallons of gasoline equivalent energy.[9]

And just imagine…if 30% of Americans (99 million people) or affluent people around the world followed a similar or equivalent diet—the people that could be fed, the people and resources that could be saved, the CO_2 emissions that could be eliminated…

Today almost a billion people on Earth don't have enough food to eat. Many of the poorest people around the world depend on fish for their survival. Aquaculture and fisheries are critical components for the mitigation of poverty, the development of robust food security. Millions of small to medium size fisheries depend on fish and aquaculture for a living. Fishing and fish farming increase food supplies and provide nutritious animal protein; they offer a range of important micronutrients to human diets while contributing to food security. Fish foods can help fill the void caused by hard times when other foods become scarce. Fishing and aquaculture provide jobs and income so people can buy other foods to supplement their diet. *However, it is important to isolate fish farming and other aquaculture activities from natural ecosystems to prevent pollution and species corruption.*

Over 100 million tons of fish are produced worldwide each year, providing some 2.5 billion people with at least 20% of their average animal protein per capita. This protein is extremely important in developing countries, especially in island and coastal regions where often as much as 50% of the necessary animal protein is obtained from fish. In areas where food is least secure—portions of Africa and Asia—protein from fish is essential to provide a large share of the low levels of animal protein consumed in these areas. In poor countries without social security or unemployment compensation, fishing is the last resort supplied by nature as it was eons ago. Yet, it too needs to be practiced sustainably; over-fishing can lead to the depletion of all oceanic food resources.

Substantial economic activity is associated with fisheries and aquaculture supporting some 200 million people. International trade in fish has created lots of jobs in related industries: packaging and processing. Roughly 38% of all fish species are traded internationally, totaling nearly $60 billion. While this is a significant revenue source for poor countries the increased income can reduce the seafood available for consumption within these countries. It makes one wonder, what's wrong with this picture when those producing a critical food product have limited access to it because it's more valuable to wealthier countries.[10]

In a study published in the November 3, 2006 issue of the journal *Science,* researchers in a study conducted by the National Center for Ecological Analysis and Synthesis (NCEAS) funded by the National Science Foundation concluded: the marked reduction in marine-life populations of all species globally is reducing the ocean's capacity to produce seafood, fight disease, filter pollutants and the ability to compensate for the results of climate change—rising ocean temperatures and acidity—and overfishing. Based on these trends the authors of the study further concluded that all species of wild harvested seafood will collapse—defined as 90% depletion of a species' baseline population—by the year 2050. Can you imagine if such a tragedy should occur, the devastation of the global food supply that would result?

The report was completed over a four-year period by a team of ecologists and economists from a dozen research centers, after a thorough review of records for fish harvests going back to 1950. The team was first to analyze all available data on marine fish and other ocean species and their ecosystems over that period. The study's conclusion was based upon data showing that the number of collapsed commercial fisheries had accelerated—the extinction of all global fish stocks could become a reality, as early as 2048.

The study included the historical records of 64 large marine regions—representing 80% of all global seafood production—concluding that: *biodiversity was the critical factor in the overall survival of an ecosystem; and the rate of species extinction from ocean ecosystems was accelerating.* Over the period studied, 29% of the world's fisheries had collapsed. The most vulnerable habitats were those where overfishing had already caused the extinction of some species within that ecosystem. These conclusions were based solely on available data, and readily understood without computer models.

In many cases the extinct species was identified as a *keystone species,* a species critical to the survival of a particular ecosystem. Examples of keystone species include: Sharks, Sea Otter, Snowshoe hare, the African elephant, Prairie dogs.

In addition to declining fish populations, the study also concluded that the seas were becoming more prone to outbreaks of algal growths and other diseases, less resistant to the effects of climate change and pollution. The study also called for establishing an international approach for protecting the oceans, similar to methods used along the coastal waters of north-west America and Canada, considered some of the best-preserved fisheries in the world.[11]

For millennia humankind has relied on the oceans, not only for seafood but also flood control and waste detoxification by recycling sewage into nutrients and scrubbing toxins out of the water—benefits that are disappearing. Perhaps the study's most vital conclusion is the need to: *fundamentally change the way ocean species are managed separately—to managing all species within a functioning ecosystem together.* Otherwise, this may be the last century wild seafood will be available for all of humanity to enjoy. Back in 2006 when the study was released the scientists emphasized that there was still time to turn this process around. It is now 13 years later and the global consortium of power brokers still have not yet been able to agree on steps to minimize the impact of climate change or other key environmental concerns—but that doesn't mean *we* should stop trying.

One organization, Greenpeace has launched a campaign targeting a list of twenty-two over-fished species currently sold by suppliers and ingested by consumers. Around the world: Atlantic Halibut, Monkfish, sharks and Blue Fin Tuna are just some of the species most threatened by overfishing. Other species not usually associated as seafood are also impacted as part of unintended bycatches: loggerhead turtles, sharks, dolphins and whales. Decreasing Alaskan Pollock populations have triggered declines in other populations including the endangered Northern Fur Seal.

Greenpeace determined the overall status of each species by

evaluating these critical factors: threatened or endangered; the use of detrimental fishing methods for harvesting (e.g. bottom trawling); the harvest of non-target species negatively through by-catch; species caught illegally by unregulated fishing operations; species critically in need by local communities for their livelihood.

Seafood consumers concerned with fish sustainability should reconsider the purchase of the following species at risk: Alaska Pollock; Atlantic Cod, Halibut, Salmon and Sea Scallop; Bluefin and Big Eye Tuna; Chilean Sea Bass; Greenland Halibut; Atlantic turbot; Grouper; Hoki; Monkfish; Ocean Quahog; Orange Roughy; Red Snapper; Redfish/Ocean Perch; Sharks, Skates and Rays; South Atlantic Albacore Tuna; Swordfish; Tropical Shrimp; Yellowfin Tuna.

In addition, Greenpeace is encouraging that roughly 40% — instead of the current 1% — of the oceans be considered as "no-take" zones so as to allow fish stocks to recover.[12]

———————————

Extensive food waste is predominant around the world in the production, distribution and sale of food products, from the farmer all the way to the dinner table. Farmers suffer through weather issues, pests and disease, poor prices at the time of harvest, labor shortages, high quality food standards and safety issues. Processing plants incur significant losses while trimming and weeding out products that won't meet the high standards of grocery store customers, many of which are discarded due only to cosmetic imperfections. Food products are often mishandled or transported without proper levels of refrigeration on their way from distributors to stores.

At stores, ready-made foods left over at end of day, discarded products, and those exceeding label dates are often thrown out. Food products delivered to restaurants and other food service companies offer menus with large inflexible portions, and a broad range of selections with cooked food time-limits, resulting in large amounts of wasted food. At home, normal spoilage, poor planning, confusion over date labels and over preparation all add to the amount of food garbage sent from homes to landfills.

Total food loss estimates from retail, food service and households for the major food items are: eggs-2%, fats & oils-7%, processed fruits and vegetables-8%, sweeteners-10%, grain products-14%, meat, poultry and fish-18%, dairy-19%, fresh fruits and vegetables-22%. Agricultural production in America accounts for roughly 80% of all U.S. water consumption and 10% of the energy expended.

Many shoppers are confused by the dates stamped on perishable and nonperishable goods: *Use by* and *Best by* dates. *These dates do not indicate food safety and they are not regulated*; they are simply the manufacturer's suggestion for enjoying peak quality. Many people interpret these dates as an indication of the product's health safety; when these dates are exceeded, they throw it away accordingly. *Sell by* dates indicate the last day an item should be for sale in the store, as determined by the store or the supplier. It can be sold after that date, but to be fair to the customer it should be offered at a reduced price. The exception to *Use by* and *Sell by* dates are federal government requirements and regulation of *Use by* dates on infant formula and other specific products regulated by certain states.

Food recovery is the name given to the process of collecting wholesome food for distribution to the needy. It includes recovering food from farm fields, the collection of perishable and nonperishable foods from distributors, food service establishments and grocery stores. Food recovery organizations have to deal with liability concerns, distribution and storage issues while raising the funds to provide for food collection, packaging and distribution. In 1996 the Food Donation Act was signed into law to protect donors from food safety liabilities; the law's existence is not well known and there is little confidence in the protection it offers.

Donor businesses need reliable organizations to receive food donations. Volunteer staffs at recovery operations are often unable to provide that level of consistency. Transportation is the main barrier for food recovery operations that often have to make large investments in transportation to handle increasing quantities of perishable food donations. On the other hand, businesses need to trust that food collections will be consistent and reliable in order to participate. Cooked food donations ready to eat, present another difficult situation because they're not always consistent with the timing and needs of food recovery organizations. In the U.S., estimates are that only 10% of the available and edible food is recovered each year.[13]

Feeding America is a success story for a non-profit organization that has been responding to the hunger crisis in America for more than 35 years, providing food to people in need through a network of food banks nationwide. In the late 1960s, John van Hengel created the concept of food banking in Phoenix, AZ. A retired businessman, van Hengel was a volunteer at a soup kitchen looking to find food to serve the hungry. One day he met a desperate mother who often rummaged through grocery store garbage bins to find food for her children. She suggested to him that there should be a place where—instead of food being thrown out—discarded food could be stored for people to pick up. With that idea an industry was born.

Van Hengel established the very first food bank in the U.S.: "St. Mary's Food Bank" in Phoenix, AZ. In its first year, van Hengel and his volunteers distributed 275,000 pounds of food to people in need. Word of the food bank's success quickly spread and states around the country began to take note. By 1977 food banks had been established in 18 cities across the country.

As the number of food banks increased, van Hengel created a national organization for food banks. In 1979 he established "Second Harvest" which was later called "America's Second Harvest the Nation's Food Bank Network". In 2008 the network changed its name to Feeding America to better reflect the mission of the organization.

Today, Feeding America is the nation's largest domestic hunger-relief organization—a powerful and efficient network of 200 food banks across the country. As food insecurity rates hold steady at the highest levels ever the Feeding America network of food banks has risen to meet the need, feeding some 46 million people at risk of hunger, including 12 million children and 7 million seniors. You can learn more about how to get food to people in need at www.feedingamerica.org.[14]

Embracing Sufficiency

John van Hengel, who had Parkinson's disease and had recently suffered several strokes, died on Wednesday, October 5, 2005 in a Phoenix hospice care facility, according to an announcement from America's Second Harvest, the national hunger-relief organization that grew out of his efforts.

Since the period known as the Enlightenment, humanity has been opposing nature with the belief that we are superior to nature's ways. Whenever we surpass an apparent nature-limitation we think we've won the battle—but we don't understand the objective of the game. Nature's objective is not the survival of the human species—it's the survival of *life on Earth*, and that has to be our goal as well. We need to learn how to live within nature. Only when we accept nature as our partner can we begin rebuilding the natural world we've decimated, and begin renewing the wounded sustenance of all earthly species.

The principles of relevance, respect and simplicity discussed extensively in my first nature book (*The Nature of Life and Humanity*) encourage living more relevant lives by applying only relevant technologies to support the survival of all life; learning how to respect each other by working towards the common goals we share; living closer to nature; reducing population growth; while consuming and wasting less.

The situation we've created seems so simple: there's too many people consuming and wasting too much stuff. The usual reaction of governments is to tweak the production side of the equation by clearing land to grow more food and producing more stuff, what we've been doing for centuries. Clearing the land causes the elimination of forests and vegetation that serve as carbon reservoirs. Increasing water, energy and fertilizer consumption boosts soil erosion while reducing natural fertility, resulting in the loss of critical species that perform vital functions for all ecosystems.

Other options for improving crop yields include the creation of better yielding plant varieties via genetic modification (GMOs); the development of new herbicides, pesticides and farming methods;

the utilization of drip irrigation systems to increase water efficiency.

While creating new GMO plant species may improve crop yields markedly, they might also alter a plant's ability to deter certain pests or to evolve positively to counteract environmental change. No-till farming reduces soil erosion as well as the labor and energy for plowing the fields in the spring, but requires additional herbicide applications to combat the excessive weeds. Monsanto's Roundup Ready GMO seeds have been modified to be resistant to both Roundup and 2,4-d herbicides allowing for increased herbicide use. Already this has resulted in varieties of super-weeds that evolved to improve their own resistance to these commonly used herbicides.

While it's possible that GMOs could provide a breakthrough to increase crop yields, there are just as many possible downsides that we're not yet aware of. As discussed in Chapter 9, some of the new GMO herbicide resistant seeds have been genetically modified to be sterile as well. This means farmers can no longer save seed from the previous year's crop for planting, eliminating a significant cost savings, preventing the seeds from evolving and being passed down to future generations. The only remedy farmers have to combat the developing super-weeds is to apply more herbicide.

On the consumption side of the equation we need to do everything possible to promote the reduction of population growth in the U.S. and around the world, through improved education, family planning, birth control and cultural changes regarding gender issues. And those of us contemplating having children should seriously consider the world they will inherit, doing all we can to train our youth to be better nature stewards than generations past, to cherish each youngster as nature's child by providing a shining example of what relevant, respectful and simpler lifestyles are all about.

The single most important dietary change we can make is to significantly reduce the amount of meat we consume, especially beef but also pork, chicken and dairy products. The excessive calories derived from meats can be partially replaced with increased amounts of fresh fruits and vegetables. When in season, try to choose more regionally grown organic produce to support local growers.

When you decrease meat consumption you also reduce the amount of protein in your diet. To calculate the amount of protein needed to maintain a healthy diet simply multiply your weight in pounds by .36 to determine the minimum number of grams of protein you should consume daily. For a more accurate accounting you need to consider your age, activity level, muscle mass, weight and overall general health. *For me the basic method calculates out to 180 lbs. x .36 = 64.8 rounded to 65 grams of protein per day or 455 grams per week.* One pound of beef contains on average 80-100 grams of protein, pork has 90 grams, turkey 130 grams and one chicken thigh 112 grams of protein. Lean (93%) ground turkey possesses 5.5 protein grams/ounce.

I am not a vegetarian but on an annual basis I consume almost no beef. The following is a rough estimate of how I obtain the amount of protein I need while consuming almost no beef and small amounts of chicken, turkey, pork and fish along with other protein sources including veggie burgers, turkey bacon, peanuts, almonds, broccoli, eggs, milk, cottage cheese, soup, orange juice, bananas and cheese on a weekly basis.

I usually have old fashioned rolled oats and orange juice or equivalent for breakfast (58 protein grams/week), a sandwich and soup for lunch (155 protein grams/week), for dinner a combination of the non-beef meats listed previously with a vegetable and baked potato, pasta or equivalent (154 protein grams/week), drinks: milk, apple cider or fruit juice (126 protein grams/week). The total amount protein supplied by these food totals 493 protein grams, exceeding the 455 grams per week calculated previously. This is not my entire diet; it includes just the foods that supply the amount of protein I need. Imagine that during World War II American families were rationed an average of 2.6 pounds of meat per week; in England the allowance was just one pound per week.

To reduce waste, refrain from overbuying perishable products at bargain prices without the ability to consume them before they spoil. Locate leftovers in clear view in the refrigerator so they can be rotated and consumed on a first-in, first-out basis. Date all canned goods and stock them by date and type, using oldest dates first. Refrain from purchasing unhealthy snacks and other desirable too-easy-to-munch foods and having them in the home. Maintain only minimum stocks of healthier snacks because consuming too much of a good thing, is also a bad thing. Replace disposable plastic water bottles with reusable bottles. Reduce the amount of fish consumed from those overfished species in danger of extinction.

There isn't a more relevant activity for humans to partake in than growing a portion of their own food. The physical exercise, getting outside, learning about plant life, pests, soil and weather conditions are all worth the effort, not to mention the financial and dietary attributes. If you have a partner, gardening can literally help you grow together. With children, watching plants take hold as a family is a great way to teach them about nature and involve them in the process.

Simplicity is an important consideration when starting a garden. You don't need an array of rototillers or other mechanized fuel consuming and polluting devices, or huge quantities of fertilizer and pesticides. All you need is good soil, water and the sun while utilizing organic growing methods and the compost made from household green waste, along with a shovel, rake and hoe to enjoy a bountiful harvest year after year. Digging, raking, hoeing, cultivating, weeding and harvesting are all good workouts performed at your own pace.

Start small and increase your plot gradually, applying the expertise you gain with each growing season. Try planting a few perennials: strawberries, asparagus or rhubarb, or biennials including swiss-chard or kale to start your harvest early each season without too much effort in the spring. For your annual plants if you select open pollinated annuals best suited to your growing season and conditions you can save seed from those plants that produce the best fruit, thereby selecting the best genetic offspring for planting in the upcoming season. In the process you'll be developing a strain of the plant variety best suited to your growing conditions. A significant portion of the water for garden consumption during dry periods can be met by collecting rainwater.

If you have little potential garden space, consider planting some edible plants and flavorful herbs in your front yard, or turn the strip between your yard and the street into a vegetable garden. When it comes to landscaping, consider fruit trees and berry bushes instead of ornamentals. In colder climates you can extend the growing season with a greenhouse, cold frames or row covers. Also consider container gardens or vertical gardening techniques. You can grow a surprising bounty of produce on a small balcony or deck. If you live in a city high-rise join a community garden. If growing your own food isn't possible, an alternative is to join a local pick your own or regional organic cooperative, or simply buying local organically produced produce.

Where you buy your food, its dietary components and the distance farm to market; the pesticides, antibiotics, genetic modification and artificial fertilizers used to produce it are all important considerations. You should also determine whether the establishment where you buy your food is a good corporate citizen, that they use resources efficiently, supply locally produced foods, treat their workers fairly, and support local initiatives.

Farmer's Markets are a great place to shop. Try to buy locally produced and organically grown food products as much as possible. Whether you grow your own food or purchase it from a co-op, during those times when fresh produce is in full bloom, make every effort to preserve it for the months after the growing season. Freezing, drying or canning are the most practical means of accomplishing this. If you have an unheated space in the cellar, consider turning it into a root cellar for squash and root plants (potatoes, carrots and onions).

Food, green waste and garbage disposal is another concern. The amount of green waste and recyclables stuffed into plastic bags and hauled out to the curb weekly for pickup to be dumped into local landfills is unconscionable. When disposing of household waste, identify and recycle each item identified as recyclable; look for the universal recycling symbol—a triangle with arrows rotating clockwise. Collect all green waste for composting. It can be used to enrich the soil for vegetable and flower gardens. Eventually, apartment complexes should also provide the compost option as well, either providing green waste to local community composting facilities or composting the green waste for use on the property. Most electronics and metal waste can and should be taken directly to local solid waste transfer stations. Smart purchasing in the first place will minimize the amount of garbage that later has to be hauled out to the curb.

With fresh air, clean water and a well-balanced diet of quality food, all living species are prepared to perform the functions of life they've evolved to pursue. Generally, that includes living life and providing for the continuation of the species in the form of generations to come. For humans that involves a complex combination of physical, mental, social and spiritual activities promoting our general good health in addition to the dietary changes already discussed. It's important to be active daily, using as many of the body's natural movements as possible. Depending on your age, having a set workout of simple exercises that won't over stress any one group of muscles is important. A combination of simple Yoga positions combined with basic strength and aerobic exercises, jogging or walking works well for me. If there's a sport you enjoy, actively pursue it for as long as you can. Hiking, jogging, bicycling or just walking around your neighborhood are other ways to be outside while getting some exercise and being closer to nature. The degree to which we are able to pursue these activities changes as our body ages, but it's important to keep at it to whatever degree you can.

Many people develop a habit of hiring out home maintenance tasks because they are physically demanding and time consuming. Others purchase expensive, energy consuming devices to accomplish these tasks quickly and easily. Many of these same individuals keep fit by joining fitness clubs with the cost of membership, travel costs and time spent commuting to and from the facility. The alternative is to keep fit by doing simple exercises at home, jogging, taking daily walks while performing home maintenance tasks with more manual equipment, saving energy, material and money in the process.

Our minds need a workout as well which usually isn't an issue while we're still working for a living. For those who are mentally unchallenged by their work, or retirees who are not working at all, keeping mentally active can be trying. Reading books of all types is a good way to relax, learn and extend one's horizons. Learn something new: an instrument, a foreign language or a new game. Get involved in your community, take a class, join a club or spend some time in nature. The key is to develop a few interests and hobbies over the course of a lifetime varying in the type of physical and mental skills required. Pursuing these hobbies or interests alongside a career and into retirement are the best ways to keep your mind and body fit and active for life.

———————

Humans are a complicated species. We don't reproduce, consume resources or interact with the environment predictably, making it difficult for ecologists to calculate Earth's carrying capacity for humanity—the largest number of people that our global environment can support comfortably for the long term. Computing this number requires the prediction of future demographic trends, available resources, new technology and economic development. By considering humanity's current impact on nature and projecting that into the future, ecologists can predict the ecological footprint of humankind: the number of planet Earth's needed support human resource requirements at current consumption and waste levels. There are limits—be it carrying capacity or ecological footprint—to the life-sustaining resources Earth can provide us. I think those limits are beyond our current understanding and ability to calculate accurately, yet I believe we've already surpassed them. In any case we can rest assured—if we're not already there, we're approaching the edge of the cliff, inching closer each day—*and there won't be a lot of warning or recourse when we get there.*

13

Too Many Choices—Too Few Options!

New Year's Day 2019, fireworks displays around the world have ushered in the New Year with the usual big-bang. The New Horizon Spacecraft has just completed a flyby of the mysterious space object named *Ultima Thule*. Located some 4 billion miles from Earth—it's the farthest object ever visited by human technology. I shake my head and shudder at all the muss and fuss, the wasted resources, the noise…to celebrate *what* I ask—that we've survived yet another year? I look forward thinking…wondering if its fate that I'm sitting down on New Year's Day to write the first draft of the last chapter of this book that I've been steadily researching, losing sleep over and typing away at for the last 18 months.

Outside the temperature has reached 52 degrees, unusual for January in central New York State. The wind is steady and strong, gusts are pounding pine cones onto the roof and siding of our home. We gaze out the back window and watch the half dozen lofty Norway spruce trees swaying, tipping their hats to absorb the force, taking turns, working together to form a defensive front on the goal-line protecting our home.

Its 6:05 AM, the power has just gone out. I sit in the dark under candlelight, struggling to write the first words of the New Year. The lights pop back on for ten minutes, then off again. I relight the candle and continue on where I left off; images of humanity gripped in the clutches of disharmony and discord flash through my mind.

My thoughts drift back to grocery shopping last week with my partner. We were standing in front of the soup isle, me standing by the cart, she scanning the shelves, "how about some creamy chicken noodle?" I nod, "sounds good to me". She replies, "And how about some black bean soup?" I smirk as I place it in the cart. She grins back at me—she knows I hate black bean soup. My mind drifts off as it does so often as I wander around today's supermarkets and supermalls, the variety of suppliers, the vast number of choices offered by each—for essentially the same thing. The words, *Too Many Choices...Too Few Options* pop into my head. I ask her to write it down so I won't forget it, as I do so quickly these days. "Sounds like a good title for the last chapter" I said. She thought about it for a moment...looked back at me grinning and nodding.

Within the hour the lights pop back on. I hear the refrigerator hum; the furnace and blower are running full speed. The trees are still, and all is well. My first thought—*was this just another nature-shot across the bow, or will this be the year—the year the lights go out and never come back on*?

Not yet, I still have hope that a majority of us can embrace more nature-relevant, respectful and simpler lifestyles, to work together with nature and sing in joyous harmony once again.

Many chapters ago we began a journey through time and space to arrive at a different place, me as the writer and I hope you as the reader. But is it a better place? From my perspective it is, only because of the deeper understanding I now possess regarding the issues we're all faced with. If you ever want to really learn about something, try writing a book about it—seriously. Fortunately, there are no limits as to how well one can understand any concept. Yet most of humanity seems unable or unwilling to perceive or understand the magnitude of the issues we face, which deeply perplexes me.

Back at the beginning, nomadic hunter-gatherers fashioned tools out of bones and stones; they used fire to cook their food and wore fur clothing for warmth. Life was good, people living off the land free to use by all. Destiny, or simply the increasing human population prompted a shift to hunter-cultivating: roving hunters who supplied the meat; cultivators who farmed the land. Human clothing transitioned from furs to fabrics. Woven baskets and clay pottery were created to handle crops and process food. The cultivators learned how to selectively breed plants and animals by pairing up those possessing the most desired traits. The domestication of plants and animals ultimately lead to the subjugation and domestication of all humanity, via our dependence on tools.

Over many centuries the human species was able to spread out across the planet, settling into their chosen landscape, forming new tribes, creating languages, cultures and religious beliefs that would stamp their mark on all future generations. Advancements in metalworking led to the design of successively superior tools made of copper, bronze and iron. Armed with an axe one person could fell and chop up a tree. Wood became the primary building material used for construction, shipbuilding, industry, home building and heating. Vast spans of timber began falling like dominoes across Europe and Asia; the improved metal weaponry increased the intensity, frequency and casualties of war.

The combination of new metals and tools led to the creation of complex machines—most notably the printing press—which brought about dramatic change, and then more change, occurring more rapidly with each passing generation. Those of us who've experienced first-hand the transformations brought about by the Internet, can hardly imagine the awe people must have felt back then.

Years later, most of the forests had been stripped away across Europe and parts of Asia; coal became the new fossil fuel of choice for industrial use and home heating. With coal came the steam engine, the Industrial Revolution and the widespread mechanization of labor. By the 20th century humans had achieved production capacities nearly meeting the basic needs of humanity across the developed world.

The invention of the internal combustion engine revved up the pace of human-time, clicking along with the increasing speed of technological change. One Great-War followed another, and suddenly the challenge for achieving continuous economic growth shifted from growing production to stimulating the demand to consume more goods—the incredible Golden Age of Consumption had begun.

After World War II the developing military-industrial complex, automated production capacity improvements, increasingly seductive and aggressive advertising all spurred the tendency for overconsumption. Brick and mortar sales outlets called shopping centers, and then shopping malls with stores all under one roof; readily available credit; technological advances in plastics, metals, electronics, computers and the Internet; all served to fuel the growth of consumption and waste in America and around the world for the next half-century. By the year 2000 global population had increased tenfold; human consumption per capita in developed countries had increased tenfold and more.

The period I've dubbed *the Golden Age of Consumption* became the roaring twenties on steroids. It wasn't long before deep problems began to emerge: the Gulf Oil Embargo in 1973 hinted there might be limits to the quantities of key natural resources. The publication of key environment books including: *Silent Spring, Limits to Growth, Small is Beautiful*, and *Entropy* to mention a few, each in their own way helped to define the environmental problem and the key issues with distinction. The terror attacks that came later on 9-11 will have us all soul-searching for the rest of our days—*why and how could they?*

The creation of plastics was instrumental in launching a host of new products capable of injection molding, cheap and ready to use. Most of these products had short life-times; they were quickly disposed of in open dumps. The fossil materials and energy needed to produce them, the lingering non-biodegradable waste they left behind created new and unique human waste issues.

Concerns about climate and environmental matters have been

mounting each year, with new dire reports regarding one or another issue popping up almost daily. It's been going on so long I think it falls on deaf ears. There are simple things we can all do to make a huge difference, beginning as individuals and spreading throughout society, prompting enough of us to work in harmony together to fight for the sustenance of life on Earth. I believe it's our sole option—the only chance our children and grandchildren have for the human species to be able to continue on.

-Too Many Choices-

While climate change reigns supreme at the top of environmental issues, many other serious nature-problems are in need of resolution: air pollution; biodiversity loss; the quality and quantity of freshwater; fertile topsoil; the availability of clean energy sources and other key natural resources are all critically important.

It's hard to believe that with so many critical issues to be resolved, there has been so little movement towards identifying which to focus on and how to proceed. While most of these issues are connected and caused by the same human activities, others require unique programs for their resolution. Discussions and research that focus only on climate change can obscure important issues in other critical areas. Most climate change solutions are often technology driven, requiring the consumption of more energy and resources, without consideration of simpler solutions like good old common sense. For example, if the major contributors to nature-problems result from too many people, consuming excessive resources too fast, it would seem that population reduction and control, reducing resource consumption and waste ought to be issues moved near the top of the list—yet no one ever mentions reducing human consumption as a possible part of the solution.

While I believe climate-change is a critical problem, I don't think we can address it exclusively. We've known for some time that the excessive burning of fossil fuels causes the accumulation of CO_2 and methane in the atmosphere that's trapping in heat and warming the planet. Basic climate change solutions require severe reductions in the burning of fossil fuels—most importantly coal and oil—supplanting them with cleaner energy sources: natural gas, wind, water and solar power.

The more challenging methods are classified as negative CO_2 solutions: capturing CO_2 and storing it deep in the ground (carbon sequestration); suctioning CO_2 out of the air, converting it into carbon blocks to be burned as fuel (A2F-Air to Fuel); cloud seeding to create massive clouds to block out the sun and cool the earth, offsetting the heat entrapped by the CO_2 (Geo-engineering). The other well-known solution is the nuclear option: building more nuclear power plants to replace some of the fledgling coal burners.

With the rapid accumulation of CO_2 gases and the degradation of other key environmental factors, I believe we have a limited number of options: *The Do-Nothing Approach* is what a majority of humankind has been doing thus far—*a lot of talk and almost no action.* Selecting this approach is like putting on the goggles and head-phones to watch the virtual-reality show offered by modern media, presenting just how great life is with the tag line—*keep the good times rolling.*

The-Technology-Can-Solve-Everything solution addresses climate-change by using carbon sequestration or air-to-fuel-system technology to capture the CO_2 after it's generated, storing it deep underground or turning it into carbon-blocks for fuel. With this option humankind can sit back, relax and continue on as we have been: growing the economy; burning fossil fuels like there's no tomorrow; consuming the way we have been—*and everything will be okay…maybe.*

The Nature-Conscious Consumer is a middle of the road option favoring nature-conscious technologies using the concepts of nature-relevance, respect and simplicity as its theme. This approach favors the application of well-tested and evaluated technologies, along with targeted consumption and waste reductions, addressing critical environmental issues: climate stability, air and water quality; topsoil and biodiversity loss; energy and natural resource limitations. It requires the human species to drastically change the way we live. The human population and the global economy will have to stop growing—*already it may be too late.*

It's important to realize that most environmental issues are connected. Changes impacting climate-change affect biodiversity on land and in the seas; each environmental matter in some way influences all of the others. While most high-tech options may target just one environmental issue, many other ecological concerns can individually or combined bring humanity down. The habits that have caused our predicament have occurred over centuries of spiritual, cultural, governmental and technology change. The foundation for modern human society is cracking. We must figure out how to change our ways, repair the cracks and start anew. To do otherwise would allow us to simply follow the same path again and again—an exercise in futility that humanity and nature cannot afford.

-Too Few Options-

I favor *The Nature-Conscious Consumer* as our only potential solution. We obviously need to burn a lot less coal, supplanting the lost power by increasing the capacity needed to serve the growing population anticipated with PV-solar technology, wind turbine generation and more efficient natural-gas generating plants. In addition, richer countries—where per capita energy and resource consumption is by far the highest in the world—will need to decrease consumption by quantity and type considerably (energy, water, food and resource consumption and a wide range of consumer goods). *Developed countries have created more of the problem—they will need to provide the guidance and example, taking the lead, embracing more of the solution.*

Globally, solar power is expanding faster than any other energy source. In 2015 over 500,000 solar panels were installed each day totaling 153 Giga-Watts of capacity to become the fastest-growing global source of electricity. For the first time generating capacities for renewable electricity has overtaken coal to become the world's leader in installed power sources. The main reason was the sudden expansion of solar and onshore wind systems in China, where two wind turbines were installed every hour, an increase significant enough for China to become the new global leader in renewable energy. In America, the average household requires 28 to 34 panels to generate enough energy to supply household needs.

How sustainable are solar panels? First of all, I think it's important to be careful when we use the term *sustainable energy source*. In my view, the sun is the only true sustainable energy source in our solar system, yet even it has a finite lifetime, albeit a very long one. A photovoltaic solar panel is often considered a sustainable energy source because they convert the sun's energy into electricity, but I disagree. Photovoltaic solar panels are made up of a variety of man-made materials requiring the consumption of natural resources and energy for their manufacture. The panels themselves and the materials they're made of have a limited useful life. While many of the various components may be completely recyclable, others might not be. A significant amount of energy is required to manufacture the semiconductor materials alone, requiring each collector to convert nearly two years-worth of solar power to replace the energy required for its manufacture. Photovoltaic solar collectors have a nominal life of twenty to thirty years. Since they represent the overwhelming majority of solar panels in use today, I will drop using the term *photovoltaic* and call them simply solar panels or PV solar panels.

To protect owners from less than nominal performance, most solar panel manufacturers guarantee their solar panels will generate at least a specified amount of power under normal weather conditions. Solar panels lose their power generation efficiency over time; manufacturers typically guarantee 90% power conversion after 10 years, 85% after 25 years.

Currently, most countries lack any procedures or infrastructure specifying the recycling of solar panels. The majority of panels being disposed of today are either damaged or defective; the annual current decommission rate remains very low. With more solar panels being installed each day, we will soon experience the need to replace and recycle some of the earlier panels installed over twenty years ago. These are the kinds of issues we often run into when applying technology solutions—plastics and the plastic waste we are dealing with now are prime examples. We need to start planning now for how to recycle those solar panels coming off-line, making design changes to new panels, ensuring that recycling and reuse issues in the future will be seamless and sustainable for the new solar panels being installed today.

The International Renewable Energy Agency (IRENA) provides a vast amount of information and data regarding all types of renewable energy. By 2050 they estimate that 60 and 78 million tons of material from solar panels worldwide will be coming out of service. It is critical that panels coming offline be recycled. Solar panels are difficult to recycle because they include such a wide variety of material types: lead, copper, gallium, cadmium and aluminum; silicon solar cells and a variety of other synthetic materials. Much like plastics, the differing material types must be separated and reprocessed separately; some of the materials may be reusable as is.

In 2016 IRENA published a study indicating that recyclable materials from scrap solar panels could be worth $15 billion by the year 2050. If you happen to be a young entrepreneur you might want to consider recycling solar panels as an endeavor, among many of the new types of business opportunities that are likely to evolve.

PV Cycle is a European solar panel recycling association that has developed a mechanical and thermal treatment process with a 96% recovery rate for silicon-based photovoltaic panels; the remaining 4% is used to generate some of the energy consumed by using a waste-to-energy technology in the recovery process. The recovery rate for silicon-based panels was previously 90%; non-silicon-based solar panels can have a recovery rate as high as 98%.

In the EU the disposal process guide for disposing and recycling all electrical and electronic equipment waste is the European Union's (WEEE) directive covering solar panels. No such guidelines exist in the U.S. except for the state of California. For now, the EU and California guidelines can provide a starting point for what recycling should consist of. As solar panel production efficiencies increase costs will decline; the installed base of solar panels will continue to grow. To achieve the concept of a *sustainable energy source*, the recycling process globally should attain nearly a 98% recovery rate for materials.

Solar panels have long been touted as *the* solution for many environmental issues caused by excessive resource consumption. On the surface, it might seem that generating clean energy using solar panels would generate no environmental concerns. Even though generating electricity with solar panels is better than burning fossil fuels—especially considering solar panel efficiencies and the energy payback discussed previously—there are significant PV environmental production issues that still need to be addressed.

The majority of PV solar panels are manufactured using quartz, the most common form of silica (silicon dioxide) that's refined down to elemental silicon. Quartz is extracted from mines where miners are exposed to the lung disease silicosis. The first level of refinement converts the quartz into metallurgical-grade silicon, using huge furnaces that consume lots of energy while emitting carbon dioxide and sulfur dioxide. These compounds are not considered to be too harmful to workers in silicon refineries, or the immediate environment.

Next, metallurgical-grade silicon is refined further into polysilicon which gives off silicon tetrachloride—a very toxic compound. During the refinement process hydrochloric acid is combined with metallurgical-grade silicon, creating a colorless inorganic compound and volatile liquid—the principal precursor to the ultrapure silicon used in the semiconductor industry—that reacts with the added hydrogen to produce polysilicon and liquid silicon tetrachloride. Three to four tons of silicon tetrachloride are produced for each ton of polysilicon.

Most manufacturers recycle the silicon tetrachloride since it requires less energy than obtaining it from raw silica to make more polysilicon. However, the reprocessing equipment can cost tens of millions of dollars. Consequently, some operations just throw away this valuable and toxic by-product. When exposed to water, silicon tetrachloride releases hydrochloric acid that acidifies the soil and emits harmful fumes.

In the early days of PV panel manufacturing when production volumes were low, solar cell producers could purchase enough silicon from silicon wafer rejects of the IC chip manufacturers who required more stringent silicon purity levels. When PV production levels grew, solar panel-makers required much higher volumes of silicon, exceeding those available from semiconductor chip manufacturer rejects. China responded by subsidizing the construction of many new polysilicon refineries there. At the time, most countries including China had not yet addressed the requirements needed to establish a process for the proper disposal of silicon tetrachloride waste.

Since 2008, PV panel manufacturing has been relocating from Europe, Japan and the U.S. to China, Malaysia, the Philippines and Taiwan. Today, nearly half of the world's photovoltaics are manufactured in China. As a result, the overall environmental safety record for the industry has been generally good, however, the countries producing the most photovoltaics usually do the worst job of protecting the environment and their workers.

Recently, it has been reported that researchers from Rohm and Haas Electronic Materials, a Dow Chemical subsidiary, have identified ways to substitute for the hydrofluoric acid used to produce PV solar cells. Sodium hydroxide (NaOH) is the current best substitute. Though still a caustic material, wastewater containing sodium hydroxide is more readily treated, disposed of and safer for workers when compared to hydrofluoric acid. Another variation is a newer approach that uses thin-film solar cell technology to replace the majority of PV-panels currently manufactured, using polysilicon as the starting point. As the market share for thin-film PV panels grows, they can become just as power efficient as a silicon-based PV cell; they will become cheaper to manufacture because they consume less energy and material to build.[2]

In a report filed by the National Renewable Energy Laboratory (NREL) entitled *2017 State of Wind Development in the United States by Region*, the executive summary reports that by the end of 2016, the installed base of wind capacity in America was estimated at 6.4% of total electricity demand, and further that wind energy has the potential to meet more of the nation's energy needs. In 2016, the industry took a step forward by commissioning the nation's first offshore project—the 30 Mega-Watt Block Island project in Rhode Island.

Wind energy is becoming one of the largest renewable electricity generating capacities in the United States, and fourth largest overall.[3] Corporate and other non-utility purchases of wind energy continue to influence wind farm expansions across the country. The continued advancement of wind energy is needed to achieve the U.S. Department of Energy (DOE) plan for wind-power to provide 20% of the capacity needed by 2030, and 35% by the year 2050.

At the DOE National Laboratories researchers have determined that wind technology innovation may provide a critical component for the broader power network, lowering electricity costs and the expansion of the American wind-power labor force. But there are many challenges, including the reduction of turbine costs as well as increasing wind energy production and reliability.

Hub heights—the distance from the turbine platform to the rotor—and rotor diameters have increased significantly, boosting wind turbine power capacities. Turbines originally designed for sites with lower wind-speeds have been increasing in market share; pending and proposed projects are continuing for even-taller turbines. Turbine size scaling up and down the range has boosted wind project performance, contributing to lower costs. Wind-power unit sale prices are near all-time lows, making them competitive with natural gas units. Financial analysts project that increases in wind-power capacities will continue for the next several years before peaking.

Demand for wind-power is being driven by corporate wind energy purchases and state-level renewable energy portfolio standards (RPS). Yet, from the market perspective natural gas prices are expected to remain low; projections for increasing total electric power demand are modest. The inefficient American power grid as well as competition with solar energy, are critical limiting factors to increasing wind-power generation in the U.S. Given the number of dissimilar issues facing the prospects for wind energy development, meeting the planned for wind energy capacities—especially after the year 2020—are uncertain.

Beyond difficult market issues there are many challenging human land-use issues that conflict with wind energy generation, largely dependent on the proximity of wind-farms to local populations. According to the American Wind Energy Association, by year end 2017 some 29,000 Mega-Watts of wind capacity were under construction or in advanced development. In 2017, the U.S. experienced a number of wind energy successes. Yet, many challenges remain requiring more development in order for wind-power to become a viable energy resource that can be responsibly harnessed around the country.[4]

Wind is plentiful, everlasting and economical. For centuries humans have utilized the power of wind to propel our ships and grind our grain. Today wind-power remains one of the most environmentally compliant and sustainable methods for converting one of nature's forces to do the work of humankind. Wind turbines while on the job give off no toxic pollution or global warming emissions, qualifying it as a viable and large-scale alternative to burning fossil fuels. However, a certain amount of energy is consumed during the manufacture of the components that make up a wind turbine; the energy consumed during their manufacture has to be replaced before the wind turbine can be considered an energy producer. Let's call that the payback energy; we will discuss that later while addressing wind turbine recycling. Despite wind-power's considerable potential, there are a number of environmental issues resulting from large-scale wind turbine operation that need to be acknowledged and alleviated.

The land needed for wind-power operations is largely dependent on the site topography: wind turbines located on hill tops use less space; those mounted on level ground take up more of the landscape. Because wind turbines have a much smaller footprint than their overall size, they don't actually occupy that much of the land. When installed on level ground the turbines are typically spaced from 5 to 10 rotor diameters apart (the diameter of the wind turbine blade). Since wind turbines are mounted high off the ground, the needed access roads and transmission lines encompass a relatively small portion of the land allotted for the wind facility. A survey conducted by NREL concluded that between 30 to 141 acres were allotted for each megawatt of power generated, yet less than one acre of the allotted territory was compromised permanently, and less than 3.5 acres per megawatt was temporarily unusable during construction.[5] A large majority of the land is available for use as highways, agriculture and hiking trails.[6] Wind facilities can be located on abandoned or underused industrial areas or other acceptable commercial locations.[7] The industry utilizes the established best practices for planning and siting offshore and land-based wind generation projects.[8]

The larger environmental issue is the impact of wind-farms on wildlife—primarily birds and bats—that has been well researched and documented. The latest studies conducted by the National Wind Coordinating Committee's (NWCC) review of peer-reviewed research concluded that the evidence of bird and bat deaths from wind turbine collisions were caused by changes in air pressure resulting from the rotating turbines and the general habitat disruption of the wind farm. The NWCC concluded that the number of impacts were relatively small and not a threat to species populations.[9]

Other research regarding wildlife behavior—that bats are most active when wind speeds are low—combined with technology advancements have reduced bat deaths more than half by keeping the wind turbines motionless during low wind-speed periods without significant reductions in power production. The U.S. Fish and Wildlife Services has coordinated efforts to include the concerns of industry, state and tribal governments and nonprofit organizations, by convening an advisory group that has made comprehensive recommendations on wind farm siting and best management practices.[10] Offshore wind turbines have a similar effect on marine birds; they also influence fish and other marine wildlife. Some studies have suggested that wind turbines are acting as artificial reefs that may actually increase fish populations. The impact varies with each site underlining the need for proper research and monitoring systems to properly address the unique issues posed by each new offshore wind facility.[11]

The human issues regarding public health and quality of life are the sights and sounds produced by wind turbines revolving across the landscape. The sounds generated by wind turbines are caused by the turbine blades moving through the air, and the mechanical noise generated by the turbine itself. All turbine sound levels are largely dependent on wind speed and turbine design.

Some people living close to wind facilities complain about noise and vibration issues; while the studies—Canada and Australia government-sponsored studies—indicate that neither have a direct impact on human health. That's easy to say if you don't live near a wind turbine—why its most important to take community concerns seriously by following *good neighbor* practices for siting turbines by initiating an open dialogue with community members.[12] Researchers have concluded that it may be possible to use technology advances, including the minimization of blade surface imperfections and the utilization of sound-absorbent materials to reduce wind turbine noise.[13] Also, there are certain lighting conditions where wind turbines can create an effect known as *shadow-flicker*. This can be minimized with careful siting, planting trees or installing window awnings or curtailing wind turbine operations when certain lighting conditions exist.[14]

Other issues include the Federal Aviation Administration (FAA) requirements that any structures over 200 feet high be installed with white or red lights to ensure aviation safety. However, in a multi-turbine wind project it's not necessary to light up each tower if no lighting gaps exist greater than a half-mile, and the turbines are painted white.[15]

When considering aesthetics, wind turbines can elicit a variety of responses: stoic energy gathering giants, harmlessly capturing wind energy, replacing harmful fossil-fuel combustion; to huge, noisy, eyesores on the landscape, killing more birds than generating sustainable amounts of power. These days it seems that so many issues involving human consumption compete with nature resources and are becoming increasingly confrontational. Unfortunately, nature's only apparent recourse is catastrophic failure, or the evolutionary compromise of the species impacted; only time will tell which will come first. The decision to accept the altered skyline in trade for cleaner power generation should be decided in an open public dialogue.[16]

While minimal global warming emissions occur during a wind turbine's life, emissions are generated during the manufacture of the materials, their transport to the installation, construction on-site, assembly, operation and maintenance, decommissioning and disassembly.[17]

Most estimates of wind turbine life-cycle global warming emissions are between 0.02 to 0.04 pounds of CO_2 equivalent per kilowatt-hour generated. For comparison, estimates of life-cycle global warming emissions for natural gas generated power, range from 0.6 to 2 pounds of CO_2 equivalent per kilowatt-hour. Estimates for coal-generated power are 1.4 to 3.6 pounds of CO_2 equivalent per kilowatt-hour.[18] Compared to wind-power: natural gas generates 43 times the CO_2 per kilowatt hour; coal generates 83 times the CO_2 per kilowatt hour. Wind turbines don't consume any fossil or nuclear fuels, they're just churning with the wind while approximately 1 lb. of coal and 1,000 cubic feet of natural gas are consumed to generate 1,000 kilowatt-hrs. of electricity.

Water use issues regarding wind-power include the water consumed to implement wind-power operations which is minimal, the water used to manufacture all of the components: primarily steel and cement. There are no significant amounts of water consumed as part of turbine operation. Recycling wind turbines is the remaining issue that's very important in order to guarantee the long-term sustainability of the technology.

According to the Global Wind Energy Council by year end 2016 some 341,320 wind turbines were in operation around the world, bringing the total installed global capacity to 597 Giga-Watts; there were 64,200 wind turbines generating electricity in the U.S. As time goes on wind turbine diameters are getting larger and mounted higher with increasing generation capacities. Some of the larger turbines have 260 ft. blades mounted 720 ft. off the ground that produce 8 megawatts of electricity capable of powering 3,000 homes.[19]

With an estimated life ranging from 20-25 years many of the earliest turbines installed in California, Germany and Denmark will begin decommissioning soon. These will be the first systems to come off the line to be dismantled and recycled. The process and methods for decommissioning and recycling as much of the materials as possible, will be an important part of promoting wind turbine sustainability for the future. There are an estimated 8,000 parts—most of them made of steel or copper—that make up the average wind turbine. A majority of these items will only require cleaning, melting down and reforming. The primary components are the turbine, the foundation and tower, the generator and gearbox.

Most new turbines have cylindrical steel towers in preassembled segments for ease of manufacture and transport. The towers have a conical shape that's wider at the base and consume less steel. The gearbox is subject to a lot of wear and tear; they make a lot of noise and require more regular maintenance and repair. Most gearbox components are recyclable; located between the turbine blades and the generator the function of the gearbox is to transfer the power from the slowly rotating blades to the requirements of the higher frequency electrical generator. Gearboxes can be the weak-link in wind turbine reliability since they're noisy and prone to failure. Rare-earth elements are critical components in any efficient electrical generator; the requirements for proper recycling them have not been extensively studied or researched.

While the latest turbine blades are lighter, more aerodynamic and power efficient, they're less durable and not designed for recycling. Some of the newer blades are made with reinforced composite-glass or carbon with little scrap value; they usually end up in landfills. These recycling issues are important; they need to be addressed soon to allow the continued application of wind-power into the future.[20]

In Cameron County, Texas the San Roman Wind Farm owned by AC-CIONA Energy was completed and started up on December 2016, with a capacity of 93 Mega-Watts. The tower is made of steel with an 87.5-meter hub-height; a wind-power rating of AW 125/3000 (3,000 kW, cut-in wind speed: 3.5 meters/second; rated wind speed: 12.0 meters/second; Cut-out wind speed: 25.0 meters/second). The San Roman Wind Farm includes 31 of these wind turbines capable of powering 30,000 homes. The project design was completed according to studies regarding wildlife and habitat concerns to minimize the environmental impact. The turbine foundation is designed to secure the overall structure including the turbine and blades to the ground. The site required excavation to a depth of 10 feet with a reinforcing cage made of 68.5 tons of steel, filled with 18,000 cubic feet of cement and backfilling the base.[21]

Do you ever feel like you're just going through the motions, that life is pulling you along with no plan or direction in sight? So many rules, obligations, opinions and concerns weigh on us each day, sometimes prompting our conscious minds to give up and turn off. All too often we end up following along with the flow of this crazy mixed-up world. How can we ignore the glitzy world of Hollywood, politics, sports, high-tech Google-land, on-line chatter, global crises and despair, mass shootings, the nagging cellphone, emails, tweets and popups to find a moment to relax, let alone resolving any real world problems—like rescuing planet Earth from the jaws of humanity and the cosmos.

Which goals and strategies we should pursue; what are the details of our plan? What can be done to undo the mistakes made by the human species over the ages against the natural world we call our home? While searching for a better word to explain the new method of consumption many are promoting, I've come up with the term: *nature-conscious-consuming* as a better description of the concept.

In the future a world that advocates nature-conscious-consuming, governments within a renewed and balanced United Nations will develop international agreements and policies, laws and regulations; provide fiscal structures, incentives, infrastructure and service support; offer guidance for businesses and consumers; while monitoring and enforcing regulations.

Businesses will choose to support ethical practices including sustainable sourcing, production and distribution; eco-efficiency and waste reduction; honest product promotion, recycling innovation and example-setting. Consumers will choose to support those businesses that use innovation to create new and improved products and services with minimal nature costs and maximum social value; withdrawing those products and services least sustainable from the marketplace. Marketing programs will be designed to enable and encourage consumers to choose and utilize products that are efficient and sustainable.

The role of civil societies will include a broad range of programs including independent product assessment; product critique and endorsement; public safety and good practice campaigns; creative entrepreneurial leadership and best-choice recommendations. Consumers should reconsider their lifestyle choices and purchasing decisions; establish their political positions; support, discuss and share their ideas and experiences with friends and family.

The main drivers of human consumption and waste are global population growth; global affluence and an expanding culture of consumerism. Global middle-class consumers are projected to triple by 2030; many of them will be hoping to evolve toward increasing per-capita consumption levels as occurred previously in developed countries.

Nature-conscious-consuming will help consumers make decisions regarding expending resources so as to improve the environment, personal health and quality of all life, or otherwise. By recognizing that our actions to buy or not to buy impact the economy, environment, social relations and ourselves, we take a huge step towards global sustainability and the realization of consumer power. Nature-conscious consuming promotes selecting a necessary sustainable item—where to buy it, how to use and dispose of it.

Fifty years of excess resource consumption has led to the degradation of 60% of all Earth's ecosystems. By 2040, the energy and material resources necessary to support industrial growth will increase consumption to 170% of Earth's bio-capacity. Yet, human well-being and sociality are not necessarily reliant on high consumption levels. Consumer attitudes are increasingly concerned with environmental, economic and social issues, and more consumers are inclined to act on these concerns. These interests can be blunted by product availability, price, ease-of-use, performance, differing priorities and force of habit.

The changes and challenges needed to lead us down the path to sustainable lifestyles require more informed purchasing decisions and behavioral changes. Consumers need the backing of governments, businesses and civil society. Businesses will need to develop a dialogue between consumers, retailers, marketers, policymakers and other businesses, to define sustainable products and lifestyles and formulate actionable policies and goals.[22]

Nature-conscious consumers function on three distinct levels of decision making: personal product decisions; commercial decisions regarding which businesses to deal with; political actions—locally, statewide, nationwide and globally—to be supported or rejected. I believe the following goals represent aggressive first step objectives for all global citizens—especially those of us fortunate enough to afford a sustainable standard of living.

Some beginning goals for consideration by individuals and family members to reduce consumption:

1. *Reduce red-meat consumption by 50% and other meats by 25%.*
2. *Reduce sugar and salt consumption by 25%.*
3. *Reduce household solid waste (garbage) by 50%.*
4. *Achieve recycling levels for paper, glass and metal at 95%.*
5. *Recycle 95% of all plastic categories 1-5.*
6. *Eliminate using plastic shopping bags, fast-food Styrofoam containers.*
7. *Reduce electrical power consumption by 20% of average kilowatt consumption.*

8. Reduce consumption of fossil fuels by 20% by volume.
9. Reduce water and paper consumption by 20% by volume.
10. Reduce consumption of frivolous items by 20% in dollars.

These goals are similar to those I set for myself when I began taking steps to minimize personal consumption and waste levels. I would call these goals the *low hanging fruit* of personal consumption and waste reduction programs. In my case I used the *one-half-again* method to set the next round of goals: having reduced my intake of red-meat by 50% in the first round, my new goal was another 50% reduction down to 25%, and so on. Eventually, you get to where you feel comfortable. Currently, I consume almost zero red-meat during the year. It feels right and I'm content with it. At this point, whenever I do partake in eating beef, I can only withstand small amounts of it.

See Appendices 1-10 to review more specific methods for accomplishing these reductions. Each section of the Appendix is designed to provide more explicit instructions to achieve the personal goals listed above as follows:

Appendix 1 – Reducing Garbage/Increasing Recycling
Appendix 2 – Reducing Consumption of Utilities
Appendix 3 – Efficient Home Appliances
Appendix 4 – Electronic Device Power Efficiency
Appendix 5 – Home Efficiency & Maintenance
Appendix 6 – Mind, Body & Spirit
Appendix 7 – Measuring Your Progress
Appendix 8 – Supporting Good Business Practices
Appendix 9 – Supporting Environmental Government Policies
Appendix 10 – Beefless Diet Example Calculations

Today we live in a world bursting at the seams with too many people suffering to survive. The developed world struggles with how to handle the mass human migration from famine ridden and war-torn regions to wealthier countries around the globe; some nations have simply decided to close their doors, disallowing immigration altogether. Refugees from the misery of war, disease and lack of food have no choice for themselves or their children but to try to find a better place where they might have an inkling of a chance. Those midway in the spectrum—the shrinking middle class of the developed world—are strangling themselves by working long hours at mediocre pay rates, commuting long distances by car or mass transit just to make ends meet, relying on credit cards to make up for growing income shortfalls. Nonetheless, over-consumption and excessive waste endures.

For a species that's supposed to be so damn smart I have difficulty with how humanity can hack away at our planet scavenging for every bit of oil, coal and natural gas etc., fulling realizing that there's a limit to what remains of these energy stockpiles, that replacing them is unlikely anytime soon. While we're very creative about finding new ways to squeeze more energy out of the ground—fracking for natural gas and deep sea oil well drilling— we do so at the peril of the potential costs: oil well blowouts; polluting underground water aquifers; increased earthquake activity; vast quantities of water mixed with toxic fracking chemicals; added CO_2 emissions.

How can we continue pursuing these activities with zero regard for the future? The growing U.S. national debt is just a drop in the bucket compared to the nature-debt humanity is accruing. What are the nature-costs of economic growth on a planet that's essentially a closed system with limited resources? How much is the continuation of our *over-consumptive lifestyles* really worth?

As far as we know there's only one true energy source: electromagnetic energy visible or otherwise—the light we can see and the wavelengths we can't. The remaining energy is stored in the atoms that comprise all matter. Dark-matter is simply matter that's so dense, the gravity it possesses captures all the electromagnetic energy (light) that strikes it. The gravitational force possessed by dark-matter is so strong that light is not fast enough to escape its grip—*dark matter is invisible because it captures all visible light and invisible electromagnetic waveforms.*

Fossil fuels are the most readily used energy sources; they store solar energy and are readily combustible with oxygen. Another possible power source is the incredible potential of nuclear fusion — the generating source of the solar energy projected from the sun. I remain a pessimist that we'll ever find a way to harness fusion power without the unintended outputs being more than nature or humanity can handle. In any event, should we all sit by and place all our bets on fusion or some other hi-tech fix in hopes that *they* will figure out a way to utilize it, so that *we* can continue our excessive, consumptive ways? Are we willing to gamble the fate of humanity on that possibility? Does it really matter which solution we select — if we don't learn from the lessons of our past and change human lifestyles to consider nature-relevance, respect and simplicity as the three foundational pillars of a more viable human society.

Modern human lifestyles pose a direct affront to the natural world; they are artificial, unsustainable and ultimately unhealthy for the human mind, body and spirit. All we have to do is look back at history and pay attention to what's happening today. What have been the costs of so-called progress? What will we have left at the end of the day? Let's take a look at some historical examples of human technological progress.

Hunter-cultivators were the first to create a system of agriculture to grow food and methods for breeding plants and animals. This was a major step forward for humankind, providing better control of future food supplies. The ability for humans to raise animals and produce their own food increased human population growth. As domesticated animal populations increased; wild animal populations declined.

Fast forward many centuries: animals are raised and fed in a congested mass of animal and food waste. Their feed contains antibiotics to fight bacteria, increase growth rates and their eventual size. These poor animals spend their lives squeezed into small pens with little or no chance of breathing outside air, or feeling the light of day. These raising pens provide inhumane treatment and unhealthy food for their miserable, albeit short lives. The stockpiling and disposal of animal waste in these feedlots is creating a substantial air and water pollution problem.

The extensive use of antibiotics in animal feed provides another opportunity for bacteria to develop immunity to many of the existing antibiotics. This has led to the evolution of strains of bacteria that are immune to all available antibiotics; physicians are unable to treat patients infected by these bacteria. The relatively low prices for foods produced in many high-volume feed-lots and meat processing plants allow too many of us to consume excessive amounts of these foods, in lieu of more wholesome choices that are by far much healthier.

The automobile is another key human technological achievement. Let's consider the pros and cons of its development, its overall impact on society. In 1908, Henry Ford culminated the development of the assembly line just in time for the release of the Model-T. The automobile was initially used by the rich to replace horse drawn wagons for traveling around town and between cities. The more efficient assembly line process lowered its selling price, making it affordable for the middle class. The Model-T was the perfect car for the burgeoning auto market; the automobile would become the average man's passion. Within ten years of its release the Model-T represented one-half of all cars on the road in America. When the Ford Company ceased its manufacture more than 15 million had been produced. The automobile was unique, providing a degree of mobility and independence that humans had never experienced.

From the search for oil to the layout of our cities, the construction of massive highway systems and bridges to the manner in which modern society functions and prospers, the automobile has been one of the chief catalysts of change affecting all aspects of human life. The automobile and the infrastructure supporting it may have consumed more energy and resources, produced more pollutants than any other device created by humankind. From so many perspectives the automobile is the invention that has negatively impacted Earth's biosphere the most, yet most of us can hardly imagine our lives without one.

During the Second World War a shortage of natural resources forced nations from both sides to search out alternatives for certain raw materials. *Bakelight* was one of the first plastics used as insulation for wire and many other electrical devices. Nylon was another polymer used as a substitute for silk to make rope, parachutes and similar items. After the war, plastics were created for all kinds of new applications. It weighed less, and injection molding made it cheaper to manufacture items made of plastic than other materials. Polymers were applied to most everything: shopping bags, soda bottles, pipe, fencing material to product enclosures.

At the time there was little consideration for the disposition of plastics at the end of their functional life, except to toss it into the garbage. During the last half of the 20th century, plastic litter has collected throughout the countryside and cities, floating in streams, rivers, lakes and oceans across planet Earth. Development programs are underway to develop new methods for gathering up the plastic pollution in our waterways and oceans, to keep it from killing marine wildlife. Meanwhile the plastic buried in landfills will take centuries to decay, while leaking an assortment of hazardous chemicals into the air and soil.

The impact of the Internet on humanity has been perhaps greater than any technological development, transcending more broadly and quickly across humanity than any other human creation. The storage, transmission and display of data; search engines capable of acquiring topical and personal information, available to billions of people, is without precedence.

The Internet is the premier Information Age technology ever developed. People, companies and institutions around the world have all experienced the gravity of this technological development. The breadth and speed of the transformation has triggered lifestyle changes for most all of humankind. Having grown up with the Internet, our youth take it for granted. Those of us who understand its capabilities as well as its drawbacks with an older mindset have lingering doubts about its impact on our future.

Before the Internet, there was no need to create passwords for umpteen Internet accounts, changing them often to more complex versions; the constant need to back up data offline or on *the Cloud*, to keep it from being stolen by computer hackers who are glad to hold onto it and return it for a fee. The constant need to purchase up-to-date security firewall protection against spyware, viruses and corrupt websites is a constant concern.

Most of all, I think it's the imposing quantity of data out there with conflicting information, creating confusion about the content of all knowledge, and the accuracy of whatever is being conveyed. What is the value or the cost of so much false or misleading information? Incalculable! I guess it depends on one's perspective, those creating the false information and placing it out there, or those who search it out, accept it as being true and pass it on down the line.

The nuclear power used to generate electricity is another example of technology gone awry. The Three Mile Island disaster was one of the first nuclear accidents, occurring on March 28, 1979 in reactor number 2 of Three Mile Island Nuclear Generating Station (TMI-2) near Harrisburg, Pennsylvania. It's the largest U.S. commercial nuclear power accident ever. The accident was caused by failures in the non-nuclear secondary system, combined with a faulty pilot-operated relief valve in the main system. This allowed large amounts of reactor coolant to escape. The Three-Mile Island nuclear disaster rallied anti-nuclear safety concerns among activists and the public, resulting in new regulations for the nuclear industry. The partial meltdown caused the release of radioactive gases and radioactive iodine into the environment.[23]

Chernobyl—*the World's Worst Nuclear Disaster*—occurred on April 25-26 in 1986 when the light water graphite moderated reactor #4 at the Chernobyl Nuclear Power Plant—65 mi north of Kiev in the USSR—exploded, producing a plume of radioactive debris that drifted over parts of western USSR, Eastern Europe and Scandinavia. The event occurred during a late-night safety test which simulated a station blackout power-failure, during which the safety systems had been intentionally turned off. A combination of inherent reactor design flaws and operator error resulted in the reactor losing control.

Water flashed into steam creating an explosion; the fire that followed produced considerable updrafts for nine days, pushing plumes of mixed fission products into the atmosphere. Radioactive material was precipitated onto parts of the western USSR and Europe. It was just this past year—thirty-three years after the meltdown—that workers still laboring at the site completed a movable roof cover to keep radioactivity from escaping, allowing robots to be used to begin recovering the reactor components. The current extensive, movable roof structure is designed to last for another 100 years—*when it will have to be replaced once again.*[24]

In Japan in 2011, the Fukushima Power plant meltdown occurred after a major earthquake caused a tsunami that disabled the power supply and cooling system of three Fukushima Daiichi reactors, causing a major nuclear accident on March 11. All three of the cores melted during the first three days of the event, with high radioactive releases over days 4 through 6. Two weeks later the three reactors (units 1-3) were stabilized. An official *cold shutdown condition* was announced in mid-December. Currently, an effort is being made to design robotic devices that can enter the facility and begin dismantling the reactors; radioactivity levels are still too high for humans to endeavor there.[25]

I've previously expressed my belief that technology alone won't be able to resolve all of the current and forthcoming environmental issues we might face. My background is in engineering. I have spent my entire professional career designing, developing, managing, and eventually teaching and writing across broad areas of engineering and technology. I am not a complete technology pessimist, but I have experienced directly the many benefits and problems related to many technological advances that are implemented to aggressively without careful evaluation.

My primary concerns are how quickly we embrace seemingly brilliant new ideas, evaluating them as no-brainers and applying them quickly and broadly with little insight, deep evaluation and consideration for the possible negative outcomes. The automobile, plastics, nuclear power and the Internet are just a few examples of technology achievements that might have evolved differently if they had been considered more thoroughly and introduced more slowly.

However, we will need every *practical and thoroughly evaluated* technical innovation to resolve environmental problems within the scope of acceptability by the natural world, today and for the long term. Technology isn't a bad thing; it's how quickly and poorly we apply it that's often the problem. It's like finding a new toy that were not quite sure how to play with—until we break it!

Another issue regarding our reliance on technology is the added material and energy consumed for the purpose of saving human energy and time to complete a task. We have created a vast portfolio of tools, devices and gadgets that consume vast amounts of natural resources to save human time and effort around the home and the workplace. If you are able, it isn't a bad thing to perform simple tasks around the home with manual tools. Instead of dragging out the vacuum cleaner all the time, try using a regular broom and dust pan to perform simple daily cleanups.

Get rid of the riding mower, use a push mower instead or better yet get rid of the lawn altogether and plant wildflowers. Use a hand rake to gather up the leaves instead of one of those godforsaken motorized blowers. Free up a lot of the clutter in your kitchen cabinets and your garage, those items you thought you had to have but never use. Take them to a local *Habitat for Humanity ReStores*, the *Salvation Army* or equivalent in your area to be resold, or recycle them or send them out with the trash.

When you step back and look at all the things you've acquired over time that once seemed so necessary, how many are items you haven't used in a long time, that you simply don't need and never really did? At the core of our consumption problem is our need and willingness to exchange the human-time to accomplish a task for a device that can perform it with little effort and time, while consuming more materials and energy to produce and operate the device than performing the task manually. This type of consumption is accumulative for as long as we continue using the device or its replacement.

This morning I happened to watch a report on the Consumer Electronic Show 2019 displaying some novel new home appliances for consumers: a $105 tooth brush that can brush your teeth—tops and bottoms in 10 seconds; a secure drop-off box costing $300 for all your next day shipments of unnecessary items; a robotic clothes folding machine for a mere $995; a device called a Love-Bot that can be your robotic fuzzy teddy-bear friend for just $3,000 each. Do these products sound like candidates for your *gotta-have list*? Time is precious to all of us—but so is the material and energy we need to save in reserve for our progenies.

I find it interesting that whenever a news-story is published or broadcast about the environment, climate change is the issue most often discussed; other key environmental issues are seldom mentioned. I understand that climate change was brought to the forefront of the environmental agenda by all the coverage of Al Gore, his book and movie entitled *An Inconvenient Truth* and the eventual Global Climate Change Conference and Treaty and so on.

I also realize that it's easier for reporters and politicians to talk about one well known sound-bite than a number of other more complicated issues that are less infamous and not well understood. However, it seems that certain politicians and businessmen are able to readily sweep aside concerns regarding climate change, ignoring all the other critical environmental issues with an argument of double-talk that is simply ridiculous, to an audience that may not want to hear the gory details of this serious issue.

It's important to realize that any one of a number of critical nature-resources: air, water, climate, energy, topsoil, biodiversity and other key natural resources can shut down humanity in a flash— together the threat they pose is undeniable. *All of these nature-resources are interdependent on one another; they are critical for the survival of life on Earth—we need to preserve them all!*

The modern-day world that humanity lives in was built on the backs of slaves, human creativity and technology, religion, culture and the fruits of nature, to increase human production and wealth that would eventually dominate the masses. While nature has provided us seemingly endless amounts of energy and materials to produce food and commodities, exceeding those needed to support a growing humanity—the advertisers and marketers stepped in with a slew of advertising, sales pitches and easy credit that have increased resource consumption and waste, much to the demise of the natural world.

So, what is the purpose of life? The primary goal of all lifeforms is to survive and reproduce sufficiently to continue the survival of the species. Sitting atop the food chain, I believe the broader goals for humanity extend far beyond that. Human livelihood is more important than just the human species; in essence—humanity represents the survival of all life on Earth. If you have or plan on having children are you confident there will be a reasonable opportunity for them to pursue a happy and productive life, enjoying the same nature-resources that you and I have experienced?

I don't believe that all of the technology, information and material wealth advances we enjoy have made us a happier society. We don't need to have the best of everything. What we need to focus on is the restoration of the nature-world that we must leave behind for future generations. How can we bring children into this world if we aren't willing to provide them the same level of nature-resources that were available to us?

Practically speaking, the only choices we have are to continue on as we have been, allowing the human population to rise, doing little to curb environmental issues, promoting increasing consumption to keep the economy growing while applying every bit of technological wizardry we can muster to help resolve any and all critical issues that might arise. The only other option is for Americans to set an example for the world: showing how people can work together behind a common cause—to embrace nature-relevant, respectful and simpler lifestyles. We can accomplish this by reducing our personal consumption and waste while purchasing essential goods and services from quality and conscientious suppliers who treat nature and their workers, with the same respect afforded their customers and stockholders.

New technologies and products should be promoted, developed and applied only if they are sustainable and relevant with regard to: energy and material consumption; emissions and recyclability; biodegradability and zero waste, with negligible health hazards.

The fight to save nature's treasures from the grips of excessive technology, consumption and waste will not be waged on the sea-lanes, battlefields, in outer or cyberspace, but in the homes, stores, shopping malls and websites where we buy all our stuff. *Consumers-United* across the globe will be the soldiers leading the fight, armed with the simplest of weapons—*wallets zippered closed*. Consumers-United possesses all the necessary economic power in our wallets—no assault rifles or extended ammunition cartridges necessary—just a large group of stingy *Consumers-United*, peacefully buying basic necessities from suppliers with proven track records for supporting environmental sustenance. With enough support and connectivity…we can do it—*we are the ones who ultimately control our consumption and our future. As individuals all we can do is something—together we can do everything.*

Sometime after the point we became human, we began working together in groups to hunt and survive. While hunter-gatherers got along for the most part, they did have their skirmishes which usually ended with one of the groups deciding to move onto new territory. Since then human history has recorded the number of times humans have fought with each other in efforts to dominate one another. Examples of humans working together have always been as a team—fighting together as one, to save the homeland from invaders or to win a game—that's why sports are so engaging to us.

Well folks, there's little territory remaining and a declining number of practical technology rabbits to pull out of our magical hats. We can't win this game of survival by fighting nature, we—all of humanity must work together—not to fight nature or anything else but our own stubbornness and stupidity, regarding the need to change our wasteful customs and ways of life. We need to become more practical, reasonable and respectful about what's really important and create a human lifestyle that coexists with the natural world, embracing sufficiency to provide for future generations for as long our life-friendly planet will have us.

If the reign of humanity does come to a premature end, the

gravesite for Homo sapiens will sit alongside all the other premier species come and gone, driven into oblivion. Those with the largest environmental footprints, will surely have the largest headstones. The epitaph for dinosaurs might read something like—*They grew too large…they broke the evolutionary branch—they never had a chance!* Humanity's demise might be summarized as—*Incredibly smart, yet lacking patience and wisdom, capable of adapting quickly…but chose not to—so sad!*

Humans have proven their ability to wage war with each other, seldom for the cause of nature, and life on earth. Our clash with nature is a war we can't win. The natural world isn't our enemy— nature won't ever concede or negotiate. Nature sustains us and all with equal regard; each species is a cog in the domain of life. This isn't the end of the story, it's just the beginning—*life on earth is for us to keep.*

Epilogue

Fifty years ago, today July 16, 2019—the 50th anniversary of the first mission to land a human on the moon—I had completed my freshman year in a five-year Electronics Engineering program. That summer I worked as a general laborer, trudging along pipeline right-of-ways painting line markers, terminal buildings and oil tanks at pipeline terminals. I liked the tough, tangible work, the contrast with my studies. I worked outside most of the time, without a book in my face or a slide-rule in my hands.

Back then, the pipeline company I worked for pumped gasoline, fuel-oil and jet-fuel through a network of pipelines from refineries located in Linden, NJ to Rome and Utica, NY. The jet-fuel was used to top off three strategic storage tanks in the event of a nuclear war, providing enough fuel to supply the strategic bomber force stationed at Rome's Griffiss Air Force base for the duration of any nuclear conflict. Four more larger storage tanks were located about 10 miles from the base in Verona, NY, used specifically to top off the three tanks near the base on a daily basis in the event of a longer engagement.

In 1989—under the strain of severe economic woes—the USSR dissolved from within into a conglomerate of separate states. The Cold War came to a swift, screeching halt. Soon afterwards, Griffiss Air Base closed; the functions the base had provided were stripped down and moved to other places, draining a huge part of the local economy here to locations spread out across the country.

A few years later Oneida Ltd.—one of the largest manufacturers in the county, and the last remaining silverware producer in the U.S.—moved manufacturing to China. At the end of the day, the Oneida Indian Nation's new Turning Stone Casino became the largest employer in Oneida county. Where before, companies including General Electric, Sperry Univac, Mohawk Data Science, Cogar, ICL, Savage Arms and many others had reigned supreme, Remington Arms, Revere Copper & Brass and Camden Wire Co., along with a number of other offshoot wire companies and a number of startups, make up much of the manufacturing base that remains. It's a story similar to many experienced across America, along with the transformations occurring across land and sea throughout the ecosystem we call Earth.

Later, when the Air Force Base had closed, the three jet-fuel storage tanks located in Rome were torn down and replaced with a composting facility. The Cold War between the U.S. and the USSR, the day-to-day threat of nuclear annihilation, began fading away with hopes of better days lying ahead.

Fifty years later we are again facing a new cold war with Russia and other countries as we ponder further space exploration and a number of serious environmental challenges. All of humanity needs to start reconsidering the value of building up our weaponry or pursuing further space exploration, compared to applying simpler and more appropriate technologies to salvage the possibilities for life to survive on Earth.

Many of the current environmental issues covered in this book have developed further during the two-year period it has taken to complete it. Let's review the status of some of these stories where new information has become available.

In chapter 10, *Mt. Waste-more to Recovery & Salvation*, the latest development is China's strict enforcement of its new *National Sword Policy* that began back in January of 2018, banning the import of plastics and other recyclables that had previously been processed by China's recycling centers. At the time China was processing 50% of all global recyclables, going back twenty-five years.

The policy change came about after many global recycling programs had transitioned from requiring consumers to separate paper, plastics, cans and bottles to allowing *single-stream* pick-up in one blue-bin. This brought about a significant increase in food and material contamination of otherwise recyclable materials, rendering them unusable. Another factor prompting the ban is that plastic packaging and components have become increasingly complex over the years: multilayered, with mixed compositions, colors and additives that preclude the possibility of recycling.

Embracing Sufficiency

Prior to China's ban, 95% of plastics collected for recycling in the EU and 70% of those in the U.S., were sold and shipped to Chinese processors. From there they were turned into useable plastic material, usually at a lower level of function. Favorable shipping rates on cargo vessels carrying Chinese consumer goods abroad that otherwise would have returned empty, combined with China's low labor costs and high demand for recycled materials, made the practice profitable.

Currently, China disallows imports of all but the cleanest, high-grade materials, requiring all imported materials to be 99.5 % pure, a requirement most exporters cannot meet. While the policy change was announced as an attempt to eliminate the piles of unsorted, filthy and unsanitary materials engulfing Chinese recycling facilities, it's hard to believe that the current trade disagreement between the U.S. and China had nothing to do with it.

There are countries that have attempted to fill the recycling void left by the China ban, primarily in Southeast Asia—India, Vietnam, Thailand, Indonesia and Malaysia—that lack the infrastructure to handle recyclables efficiently; many of them were overwhelmed by the sheer volume and have since cut back their recyclable material imports appreciably as well.

One year later, China's imports of plastic waste had fallen to a trickle, shifting supply chains in regard to why, how and where recycled items could be processed. The major problem area occurred with plastic waste; China's mixed paper imports have only dropped by a third, aluminum and glass have been impacted only slightly.

Consequently, vast amounts of plastics are being dumped in landfills, incinerated or being littered around the world. Already across America many areas have minimized their collection of recyclables or stopped collecting them altogether. Overall, across America disposal costs are increasing, recycling plants are closing and a lot more plastics are ending up in landfills.

Perhaps, more importantly we've learned that previous to the ban only 9% of the discarded plastics sent to China were being recycled; 12% were being burned. The rest was dumped in landfills or left to be washed away by streams and rivers and into the oceans. While China had previously accepted a broad range of waste materials, for the most part they were not handling plastics properly. Nonetheless, the sudden loss of China and other willing countries to act as global garbage dumps will bring about the transfer of humanity's massive global waste problem—created over the last sixty years—back to the wealthier countries that generate a majority of the garbage—including an estimated 8 billion tons of nearly indestructible plastics.[1]

———————

The next story is a follow-up on a second Roundup glyphosate case filed against Monsanto and Bayer AG, its corporate parent, claiming damages for diseases experienced by the plaintiffs caused by the use of glyphosate-based products, similar to the Dewayne Johnson case discussed at the end of Chapter 9. In November of 2018, Dewayne Johnson accepted the $78 million award offered by the court's decision.

Since then a second case has been filed by Edwin Haldeman from *Wine Country* in Sonomo County, California. Mr. Haldeman used Roundup herbicide to kill weeds and overgrowth on his 56-acre property, beginning in the 1980s and continuing through 2012. Three years later Haldeman was diagnosed with non-Hodgkins lymphoma.

On March 19, the first phase of the trial concluded after a review of the scientific data that Monsanto's RoundUp was a substantial factor in causing Mr. Haldeman's cancer. The second phase, which established accountability, concluded that Monsanto and their corporate parent were both liable because they failed to include a label warning of the weed-killer's risk of causing cancer during its application. Evidence was produced from the company's own internal studies that questioned the product's overall safety, in addition to proof of the company's efforts to influence various government studies regarding the product's safety—which lead to the conclusion *that Monsanto knew about the risk and did nothing to advise them of the danger.*

On March 27, 2019 in San Francisco, California the jury in the Hardeman vs. Monsanto case awarded Edwin Hardeman more than $80 million. This was another groundbreaking decision in the ongoing public debate regarding the safety and health effects of using glyphosate as a weed-killer to those who handle the product, but also those people around the world who are ingesting certain levels of glyphosates in their food.[2]

Pilliod v. Monsanto Co. is the third case to come to trial, regarding Monsanto's Roundup Weed-killer that concluded with a decision in favor of the plaintiffs. Unlike the other lawsuits, this case is unique and ultimately more damaging. As a married couple in their 70s both had developed non-Hodgkins lymphoma, an extremely rare form of cancer, within four years of one-another after both had used Roundup to kill weeds on their properties for decades. They never used protective gear because they believed Roundup to be safe.

The basis for their claim was that Monsanto lied about the risks, that the Pilliods surely would have taken any protective steps if they had been offered. The disease has taken a heavy toll on them and most likely has shortened their lives. This is the third case decided against Monsanto where the plaintiffs had developed non-Hodgkin lymphoma. The chance that both Alva and Alberta Pilliod would be diagnosed with the disease has been calculated at roughly 20,000 to 1.

The Pilliods were awarded $55 Million in compensatory damages and $1 billion each in punitive damages for their Roundup-linked non-Hodgkin lymphoma cancers. This has been reported as the largest personal injury award this year, eighth largest in U.S. history. If you search around your local hardware or garden supply store you will likely see Roundup for sale in easy-carry bottles without disclaimers, a description of what's in it or a warning label about how to properly use it. Some 13,400 lawsuits filed against Monsanto/ Bayer-AG await their day in court, sometime in the near future.[3]

Epilogue

Amid all the talk about successful lawsuits filed against Monsanto regarding the toxicity of glyphosate, is it any surprise that the stuff is showing up in our food. Monsanto first introduced Roundup—their glyphosate-based herbicide—in 1974. From the court deliberations previously reviewed, it appears that Monsanto has long been aware of the potential danger of using glyphosate; yet they have pursued all methods of convincing the public and regulating authorities otherwise. Furthermore, investigations that previously studied the human impact of physical contact with glyphosate-based herbicides may have been biased toward Monsanto, creating a conflict of interest in an attempt to influence the EPA to continue permitting glyphosate use in the U.S.

In Germany, a February 2016 study states that traces of glyphosate herbicide were showing up in many places, even foods grown organically, possibly due to wind drift or contaminated soil. From 2001 to 2015, urine samples taken from individuals up to 29-years of age living in Greifswald—a northeastern German city—found nearly a third of the samples collected contained glyphosate concentrations at or above the limit of 0.1 parts per billion. Another German study in March 2016 showed that glyphosate enters the body through food and drinking water; 75% of the study group showed glyphosate levels five times higher than the legal limit for drinking water.

Despite these reports, Monsanto was purchased by Germany's Bayer Company in 2018. Consequently, Bayer's board of directors has recently received a vote of no-confidence in response to recent court decisions against Monsanto. Germany is still pondering whether to prohibit the use of glyphosate-based herbicides there, however: Belgium, Bermuda, Colombia, the Netherlands, Sri Lanka, Kuwait, Qatar and the United Arab Emirates already have.[4]

The Environmental Working Group (EWG) is another environmental group that sponsors toxicological testing. In October 2018, Alexis Temkin PhD. working for a group commissioned by EWG detected glyphosate in each sample of popular oat-based cereals and other oat-based foods marketed to children. Roughly three-fourths of the samples exceeded the 160 parts-per-billion (ppb)—EWG's glyphosate level acceptable for foods.

Data from the study disclosed: Quaker Old-Fashioned Oats contain 390 ppb; Quaker Steel Cuts Oats-530 ppb; Back to Natural Organic Honey Almond Granola-620 ppb; Quaker Dinosaur Eggs Brown Sugar Instant Oatmeal-620 ppb; and Cheerios Toasted Whole Grain Oat Cereal-490 ppb.

The data of most interest may be those brands where no trace of glyphosate was found, they include: *Nature's Path Organic Honey Almond Granola; Simple Truth Organic Instant Oatmeal; Original Kashi Heart to Heart Organic Honey Toasted Cereal; Cascadian Farm Organic Harvest Berry Granola Bar; KIND Oats and Honey with Toasted Coconut; 365 Organic Old-Fashioned Rolled Oats; Bob's Red Mill Organic Old-Fashioned Rolled Oats.*

Quaker Oats responded to the study with the following points: *Quaker does not add glyphosate during any part of the milling process; Glyphosate is used by many farmers as a pre-harvest herbicide; the oats upon their arrival in our facility are thoroughly dehulled, cleaned, roasted and flaked. The levels of glyphosate that remain are well below limits and well within compliance of the safety standards set by the Environmental Protection Agency (EPA) and the European Commission as safe for human consumption.*

The European Union has established one level of acceptability for glyphosate in food consumed within the EU; the EPA and EWG and perhaps many other organizations have developed others. As consumers we want to know how much glyphosate in our food and water is acceptable. Most experts I've heard discuss this topic generally agree—we truly don't know.

Monsanto's Roundup has been a popular herbicide applied to many food crops as a weed-killer ever since 1974. At the time it was well accepted as another herbicide in the farmer's toolbox of weed eradicators, considered safer than the two other most-popular herbicides: 2-4,d and dicamba.

It was the development and release of genetically modified (GM)-seeds making the most popular food crops resistant to

Monsanto's Roundup and other herbicides, that promoted its meteoric rise in the marketplace, becoming number one in the field of
applied pesticides. The data showing the increased glyphosate
herbicide applications in America over the period from 2000 to 2014
is as follows: 2000-78,750 lbs.; 2005-157,500 lbs.; 2010-235,814 lbs.;
2012-236,318 lbs.; 2014-249,906 lbs.[5]

In order to understand the broader GM-plant and glyphosate
problem it's important to realize that Roundup weedkiller—which
is made up of the herbicide glyphosate—is not a genetically modified substance. Roundup resistant seeds developed for the most
popular grain and other food crops that are genetically modified to
be resistant to glyphosate—are genetically modified(GM)-plants.

The use of glyphosate resistant GM-plants has allowed the application of increasing amounts of glyphosate and other herbicides
to combat the so-called super-weeds that have developed their own
immunity to glyphosate-based herbicides. To further embattle the
evolving weeds, Monsanto has genetically added another herbicide
named dicamba to their repertoire of GM-plants resistant to herbicides. Continuing the cultivation of more herbicide resistant seeds
of both glyphosate and dicamba will lead to increasing amounts of
both herbicides in our food supply. Herbicides are like antibiotics—
there are a limited number of them.

There is no happy ending for this game of humanity repeatedly
bidding to stay one step ahead of nature—time is on nature's side.
What happens when farmers are unable to use herbicides as a
weedkiller for the majority of their food crops? I believe that day
will come in one form or another, either we'll either run out of herbicides to embattle the weeds and rendered unable to feed ourselves,
or herbicide levels in our food will become so extensive that our
food will become deadly for increasing numbers of people and in-
nocent species as well.

The bottom line is—we probably won't have enough data collected, over a long enough time to determine glyphosate's toxicity
for another 15 years. In the meantime, we must seriously consider
weaning ourselves from consuming foods where herbicides and
other pesticides are applied, causing the people who consume them

to be sick. Also, steps must be taken to make sure those who work in close proximity to herbicides are warned about their toxicity along with the specific measures to protect themselves.

Finally, we must wean ourselves from using herbicides and other pesticides over a period of time. This can be accomplished by requiring staged limits for herbicide and pesticide applications that are increasingly stringent, much like the increasing gasoline mileage per gallon goals that had been required of automobile manufacturers, mandated by the Obama administration until the current administration rescinded them.

We must make broad changes in the way human societies are structured, modifying our lifestyles so that our children and grandchildren can have a chance to successfully support themselves, and the continuation of all species on Earth.

———————

Please Review

As an author I rely on readers like you to pass on your opinion of the content, quality and most importantly the message provided by this book. Did the content and style of the writing deliver the information in an understandable and meaningful way? Can you remember any *ah-hah* moments delivered in the book that you felt were significant to the point of providing deeper insight into one or another environmental or human-nature issue? If you believe humanity is truly facing a significant environmental tragedy, do you care enough to share your thoughts about *Embracing Sufficiency* by completing a review so that potential readers can consider this book and potentially learn more about the history and the problems facing humanity, and the lifestyle changes we will all have to make?

Check out my author website to view my biography and the other books I have published:
https://www.amazon.com/D.-Joseph-Stadtmiller/e/B001HMYV82/ref=ntt_dp_epwbk_0

You can contact me directly at my writer's email address:
josephstadtmiller@gmail.com

Thanks for reading! Joseph Stadtmiller

Appendix 1- Reducing Garbage/Increasing Recycling

Reduce solid waste (garbage) by 50% by composting green waste and recycling 95% of all pertinent paper, glass, metals and plastics waste products.

Around the world some one trillion plastic bags are used each year with less than 5% of all plastics being recycled. In the U.S. we use over 380 billion plastic bags and wraps yearly that consume roughly 12 million barrels of oil to produce. There are three basic categories of plastics: single-use convenience items (e.g. shopping bags); packaging for most of the foods or liquids or were purchase in the grocery store; plastics used to make components not readily replaceable that comprise many of the more durable items we purchase (e.g. custom plastic components for computers, printers etc.).[1]

The plastic shopping bags that end up scattered across the landscape, rotting away in landfills or floating around our waterways are problematic around the world. They can be readily replaced with reusable shopping bags you carry with you when you're shopping. Keep your reusable bags in your vehicle so they're always available when you decide to shop. Plastic shopping bags are not usually accepted for pickup at municipal recycling facilities because they jam up most sorting machines. Dependent on your state or locality, they're usually recyclable at supermarkets and other stores where they're given out.

The next step is to eliminate or minimize the use of polystyrene (better known as Styrofoam, recycling category #6) used to make cups, fast food trays and packing materials. Many larger fast food companies have stopped using Styrofoam, replacing it with types of cardboard. Yet it remains predominant in use at local levels. Styrofoam is mostly air, when it's melted down there's not much material that can be reclaimed; it is seldom accepted for recycling. Styrofoam is a nuisance toxic pollutant that takes up space and is hard to coral in landfills. When you receive it as packaging material for goods you purchase, your only option is to file a complaint with your supplier with the threat to purchase elsewhere in the future. The main alternative for manufacturers is to go back to using cardboard for packing material; most will resist this due to higher costs. Eco-friendly companies will be the first to make the switch, so try to locate them and support them.

Polyethylene terephthalate (PET#1) soda and single use water bottles are the most commonly recycled plastic bottles. Single use water bottles are readily replaced with refillable plastic water bottles; make sure they are BPA safe. There are few options currently available to replace plastic soda bottles and similar purchases, except to consume less of them, or to buy fewer of them in larger containers; in either case, be sure to recycle them. Some states have so-called bottle bills where a mandatory deposit is paid by customers and repaid when the bottle is returned (5 cents in N.Y.). In most other states in the U.S. recycling is the only other option. It's important to make the effort to recycle all #1 through #5 recyclable plastic types, unless instructed otherwise by your local recycling facility. More importantly, recycle all glass, clean paper and metal items; all these materials can be efficiently recycled and they don't belong in landfills.

For all those things we purchased that didn't work out so well—some of the garbage trash we haul out to the curb each week—we want to be sure it doesn't include any recyclables or food waste. Food waste takes up an increasing amount of space in landfills. I toss all my food waste—except for meat— into the compost pile along with leaves, grass clippings and any other plant remains. As long as you have some lawn space and perhaps a flower garden, you can make a small compost pile of your own. Otherwise, there are a growing number of municipalities that pick-up food waste at the curb and process it in huge food processors to make compost and natural gas. The energy produced is used to operate the landfill and the recycling center. In some areas, private operators will pick up food waste and sell it to food waste processing facilities.

You will be surprised at how little there is to haul out to the curb after removing food waste and recyclables: glass, plastic, paper and metal. In my case there's so little garbage compiled weekly that I usually haul it out to the curb just once a month. The recycle bin is full every week...and the vegetable garden just keeps growing.

Appendix 2 - Reduce Consumption of Utilities

Decrease household water consumption by 20%

Reducing water consumption is critical now and for the future. Americans use about 80 to 100 gallons of water per capita per day. In average households toilets are the largest water consumer, largely dependent on whether it's an older model drawing 3-4 gallons per flush or 1.6 gallons with newer models. Filling a bath tub can consume as much as 36 gallons of water. Showers use a lot less water, especially when low-flow 2 gpm (gallons per minute) shower heads are used instead of older 5 gpm models. Municipalities around the country that already face water shortages are specifying maximum flow rates for water faucets and shower heads and gallons per flush for toilets.

Installing aerators on faucets is another way to reduce water flow rates dependent on the application; aerators come in different flow rates. For example, a kitchen sink that's often used to fill containers fitted with an aerator that slows the process too much, might not be appropriate; perhaps a medium sized aerator rated at 1 gpm will work. Washing face and hands, brushing teeth and shaving are common bathroom tasks that are good applications for a .5 gpm aerator. In any case, turn the faucet off while brushing teeth, drying off or shaving at times when you don't need to have the water running. Wash your face and hands in brisk water instead of wasting water waiting for it to warm up—using less hot water saves energy too!

Old dishwashers consuming 16 gallons of water per cycle can waste a lot of hot water. New ENERGY STAR models consume as little as 6 gallons per cycle. In our home when we remodeled our small kitchen with just the two of us, we decided against buying a dishwasher. After meals we clean off all food residues before stacking the dishes. After a couple of days when we're ready to wash, we fill up the sink with soapy water and let them soak. Using two basins; we rinse in the second basin. Without a dishwasher we have saved a lot of money and space; there's no maintenance and we consume less energy and water.

Water consumption can also be reduced when your older model clothes washer—using 40 gallons/load—is nearing replacement by considering the latest clothes washers that consume 25 gallons/load. Reduce your lawn area will also minimize the amount of water used to water your lawn; use rain barrels to store water for watering flower and vegetable gardens.[2]

Appendix 2 - Reduce Consumption of Utilities

Decrease fossil fuel consumption (Coal, Fuel Oil and Natural Gas) and Electricity—by 20% for home heating and cooling

Coal, natural gas, gasoline and heating oil are the fossil fuels that we use to heat and cool our homes and buildings, power our vehicles and provide electricity. Most of the coal burned in the U.S. annually—54% of it—is used to generate electricity. It takes about one pound of coal to generate one kilowatt hour (kwh) of electricity. Natural gas heats our homes and manufacturing processes; it's a key component in fertilizer production and is replacing coal to generate cleaner electricity. Nuclear, hydropower, solar and wind are non-fossil fuels used to produce electric power.[3]

Living space is a prime concern when projecting home energy expenditures. The bigger the living space, the more energy and materials are consumed to build, maintain and live in the home. New home sizes—their layout and physical orientation regarding the sun—are critical issues, especially as existing neighborhoods are resurrected and plans for new communities are developed. We have to start thinking small while working towards maximum energy efficiency, creating new ways to use available space more efficiently while orienting new homes to take full advantage of solar power.

Home heating and cooling consumes more energy than all other home energy needs, accounting for over half of all energy costs. Living space, wall thickness, insulation levels (R-rating), air flow, heating/cooling efficiencies and the energy sources used, are all central matters. Solar, biogas and geothermal energy are the only renewable sources practically available for homes; solar is the least expensive and more readily installed.

Most homes older than 25 years have standard 2x4 thicknesses (these actually measure 1.5"x3.5") providing for 3.5 inches of wall insulation. Dense packed insulation can be blown into most of these homes that have no insulation. It's important to make any planned changes to wiring or plumbing affecting the outside walls to be insulated *before* having it blown in. Most new homes built today have 2x6 (1.5"x5.5") wall studs that support 5.5 inches of wall insulation. In the future double-2x6 inch walls will be utilized providing 11 inches of insulation thickness.

Insulation provides a thermal barrier between the home's living space and the outside world. The priorities for insulation are foremost in the highest ceiling; the outside walls and then the first floor, respectively. Insulation values are measured by thermal resistance or R-value, a recognized standard for resistance to heat flow. The higher the R-value the greater insulating capacity provided. Differing insulating materials have varying heat resistance properties. The total R-value of your home's insulation—walls, ceiling and floors—is determined by the thickness and type of insulation, where and how it's installed. R-values are cumulative: the total R-value is the sum of all R-values for the insulation in a particular section of the home. The Department of Energy (DOE) recommends minimum values for homes depending on their location: mild climates: R-11 in walls and floors, R-19 in ceilings; moderate climates: R-19 in walls and floors, with R-30 in ceilings; cold climates: a minimum of R-19 in walls and floors, between R-38 to R-49 in the ceilings.[4]

For example: an older home with 3.5-inch wall spaces located in a cold climate like where I live in central New York State (Zone 6 on the regional chart), the desired R-value is R-13; this is attainable by having insulation cellulose insulation blown into an empty 3.5-inch wall space. Increasing the wall thickness to 2x6 inch boards (actually 1.5"x5.5") an R-20 value can be attained.

Windows and doors are the next most important items for limiting the transfer of heat. ENERGY STAR rated windows and doors are tested and rated to keep out heat and cold. All windows, doors and skylights sold in the U.S. receive an ENERGY STAR rating based on testing by the National Fenestration Rating Council (NFRC). The NFRC does not distinguish between *good* and *bad* windows; it sets minimum efficiency performance standards that meet mandated performance levels. The ENERGY STAR rating enables consumers to identify those products with superior energy performance. The ENERGY STAR label qualifies windows, doors and skylights providing performance ratings in five categories: U-Factor, Solar Heat Gain Coefficient, Visible Transmittance, Air Leakage and Condensation Resistance.

U-Factor measures the rate of heat transfer for windows/skylights with values ranging from 0.25 to 1.25; the lower the U-factor the better the insulation capacity. The Solar Heat Gain Coefficient (SHGC) measures the fraction of solar energy transmitted, telling how well the window blocks heat caused by sunlight. SHGC is measured on a scale of 0-to-1; typical values range from 0.25 to 0.80. The lower the SHGC number, the less solar heat is transmitted through the window.

Visible Transmittance (VT) measures the amount of light the window lets through, measured on a scale of 0 to 1; values generally range from 0.20 to 0.80. The higher the VT, the more light passes through the window.

Air Leakage (AL) measures the rate at which air passes through joints in the window. A lower AL value means less air leakage. Most building codes require an AL value of equal or less than 0.3 cf·m/ft². Condensation Resistance (CR) measures how well the window resists water build-up. Condensation Resistance is scored on a scale from 0 to 100. The higher the condensation resistance factor, the less build-up the window allows.

Generally speaking, the best performing windows, doors and skylights will be those which have a low AL, CR and U-Factor value with a higher number for VT. The preferable SHGC number depends on whether the climate is predominately hot or cool: a lower SHGC keeps out solar heat better in hotter climates; a higher value allows more solar heat in, more desirable in cooler climates. The ENERGY STAR qualification for windows, doors and skylights is based on having a U-factor equal or less than .35, and an SHGC rating of .32.[5]

Residential Heating, Ventilating and Air Conditioning (HVAC) systems in the U.S. account for roughly 50% of home energy costs. While heating systems can utilize many energy sources, for the most part cooling systems are powered by electricity.

Natural Gas, propane and fuel oil furnaces have experienced rapid development improving their energy efficiencies. Residential furnace efficiencies are rated according to their *annual fuel utilization efficiency* (AFUE). AFUE ratings of the best performing systems range from 90 to 98.5% efficient. Condensing furnaces/boilers have been leading the way in efficiency improvements. Condensing furnaces condense the water vapor produced during combustion in a second heat exchanger that captures the heat from the water vapor. The AFUE rating for a condensing furnace can be 10% higher than a non-condensing unit. A condensing furnace is more expensive; it can save money over its operating life.

Other design innovations include: electronic ignition to replace pilot lights in older gas furnaces; sealed combustion systems that draw in outside air to the burner, pushing exhaust gases directly outside. High efficiency condensing furnaces have special venting and condensate drainage requirements. The heat exchanger used by a condensing furnace extracts heat from the combustion process until the exhaust gases have cooled and condensed. The lower temperature flue gases escape from special plastic pipe instead of a chimney.

The latest furnace control technologies include various types of proportional control of the heat output. Previously, temperature control was accomplished with simple On-Off control: the furnace puts out maximum heat until reaching the desired temperature and turns the system off. This results in overshooting the desired temperature and wasting energy in the process. Newer furnace controllers use various types of proportioning control to reduce the heat output in stages as the temperature approaches the setting, providing slower, smoother and more efficient temperature control. Also, many newer systems provide some level of proportional or staged control of the fan speed circulating the air, slowing down the fan speed as it nears the desired temperature setting. The combination of proportional control of both heat output and fan speed have provided tighter and smoother temperature control and incremental improvements in energy efficiency.

According to the U.S. Energy Information Administration, roughly 88% of American households are equipped with some type of air-conditioning. In the U.S. approximately 185 billion kilowatt hours of energy is consumed annually for residential cooling, roughly 60% of total U.S. electrical consumption. The energy consumption of air conditioners and their release of refrigerant gases into the atmosphere have been long time concerns.

Air conditioners have two basic parts: an evaporator inside and a condensing unit outside. Refrigerant is circulated between the evaporator and condenser, capturing heat from the inside and transferring it to the condenser outside. There are essentially two types of air conditioners: central and window type units. A central air system's energy efficiency is measured in two ways: the basic energy efficiency rating (*EER*) and the seasonal energy efficiency ratio (*SEER*). Window units have an EER rating only and are typically rated lower than central A/C units, due to their lack of space to accommodate more advanced features. It's important to realize that air conditioners lower air temperature while removing moisture. The amount of moisture removed depends on how much air passes through the air conditioner. An air conditioner operating at high fan speed can drop room temperature quickly by cooling a smaller volume of air; an air conditioner with variable speed settings can attain the same result by processing a larger volume of air, cooling each unit volume by a smaller amount resulting in more dehumidification, since a higher volume of air runs through the device. An air conditioner capable of variable speeds can operate at a higher temperature setting while providing the same comfort level because the air is less humid. On the other hand, window units do not have duct losses which can decrease an air conditioner's energy efficiency by up to 30%. Window units also offer separate room-by-room control.

When purchasing a central air unit look for a SEER rating of at least 13 with R410A refrigerant and a low decibel noise rating. The unit should possess a diagnostics port and a two-stage compressor operational at full power, only on the hottest days. For maximum comfort and efficiency, air conditioners should be sized correctly for the room area being cooled. When buying a room air conditioner select one with an EER rating of at least 11.

Hot Water Heaters comprise nearly 18% of American household energy consumption, the second largest after space heating and cooling. Roughly 8 million water heaters are sold in the U.S. annually, 96% are tank storage units the rest are tankless: on-demand hot water heaters. Storage-tank water heaters are replaced on average every 13 years. For decades hot water has been provided by storage tank water heaters that heat water to the desired temperature and maintain it continuously. Newer, tankless water heaters—gas or electrically heated models—heat water only as it is drawn from any hot water outlet. By heating water only when needed tankless water heaters save energy on the order of 20 to 30% when compared to storage tank water heaters. Without a tank that will eventually leak, a quality tankless water heater will outlast a storage type nearly two to one and require much less space. However, tankless water heaters may require a higher capacity electrical circuit for electrically powered units, a larger gas inlet pipe for gas fueled units to heat the water quickly, increasing installation costs—make sure you determine this before ordering a new unit. Gas fueled units usually require a vent pipe different from those used by conventional gas water heaters, increasing installation costs further. Because they heat water more slowly, tankless water heaters have limitations as to how many hot water faucets can be in operation at once. Summing up, tankless water heaters last longer, save energy and space, cost more—initial cost-plus installation—require more professional service and usually don't perform as well as older traditional storage type units when the demand for hot water at any given time exceeds the system's ability to heat the water quickly enough.

Appendix 2 - Reduce Consumption of Utilities

Traditional storage tank water heaters are usually powered by natural gas or electricity. While both electrical and natural gas storage-tank water heaters are efficient at heating the water, their inefficiencies result from the heat loss through the tank walls over time and then the piping as hot water is transported to the various water outlets.

Newer, storage type heat pump water heaters are about twice as efficient as electric-resistance tank water heaters. A heatpump water heater uses a compressor like those found in air conditioners to take heat out of the room air and transfer it to the water in the tank. A heatpump water heater transfers heat from the room where it's located to the water in the storage tank, cooling the room as it heats the water. Since heatpump water heaters don't make heat in the same way as electrical resistance heaters — they're more efficient; it simply transfers heat from the air in the room to the water in the tank instead of creating all of the heat from electricity.

While a heatpump water heater is capable of better efficiency, it can't heat water as quickly as electric resistance elements. Electric resistance type elements can heat 20 gallons of hot water per hour. Heat pumps can supply only about 8 gallons per hour, with even lower rates if the ambient air temperature where the heat pump is located is below 68°F. To counteract this deficiency, heatpump water heaters are also equipped with electric resistance elements that are utilized whenever the heatpump can't keep up with the hot water demand. While this feature increases the heating rate, it also reduces energy efficiency. Most heatpump water heaters have control selections that provide three modes of operation: heatpump-only mode (an energy-efficient mode without long showers), hybrid mode (heatpump operation plus electric resistance as backup) and electric resistance-only mode (a mode for cold weather when it might not be desirable to cool the space where the hot water heater is located). Generally speaking, heat pump water heaters provide higher efficiencies when used in hotter climates and where the consumption of hot water is spread out over time instead of all at once.

When used in heatpump only mode, heatpump water heaters are roughly twice as efficient as electrical resistance types, but there are limits to the amount of hot water available at any given time. Otherwise, heatpump water heaters are typically taller, noisier and more mechanically complicated. They absorb space heat from the house during the winter, require a condensate drain and are more expensive. Their life expectancies are unproven but projected to be similar to electrical resistance types.

Appendix 2 - Reduce Consumption of Utilities

The usual tactic employed to conserve the energy consumed by any appliance is to purchase one with higher efficiency, but that logic doesn't always apply to hot water heating systems. If you're dissatisfied with the performance of traditional storage type water heaters, you could spend thousands of dollars on a newer high-tech water heater that might reduce your energy consumption by 15%, but if your home is wasting 25% of the hot water produced by the newer hi-tech equipment it clearly won't solve the energy waste problem.

The most effective ways to improve hot water heating efficiency is to insulate the hot water tank and all the hot water pipes. Repair any leaking faucets and showerheads and install low-flow fixtures and aerators. Purchase efficient hot water consuming appliances—dishwashers and clothes washers—and wash your clothes in cold water. The temperature settings of storage type water heaters should be reduced to a maximum of 120 °F.

In many states government programs are currently available—dependent on income level—subsidizing the improvement of home energy efficiencies by the purchase and installation of insulation, windows, doors, and HVAC systems. The ability to provide further energy efficiency enhancements, the implementation of multiple renewable energy sources is paramount to meeting future energy challenges.

Utilizing photo-voltaic solar power is probably the best way to employ solar energy in a residence. These systems require the installation of PV solar panels—usually on the roof—facing due south and tilted at the optimum number of degrees dependent on the latitude of the site. The number of collectors required: depends on the surface area available; the power to be generated; and system cost limitations. The collectors themselves produce DC electricity which an inverter converts to AC, synchronizing the resulting AC power waveform with incoming utility power. If the power needed by the household is less than what's being generated by the solar panels, the inverter pumps that extra power back into the utility grid—effectively selling the power back to the utility. If the household requires more power than what's available from the solar collectors, the inverter draws the extra power needed from the utility. Whenever solar panels produce power, they're saving the energy that otherwise would have been drawn from the utility.

Since there's no need to store solar energy in batteries; synchronous inverter type solar systems are the simplest and most efficient types of solar power systems. The efficiency and investment payback period for these systems is highly dependent on the orientation of the solar collectors: regarding facing due south; the average amount of sunshine available annually; the amount of shading impeding efficient collector placement. If you desire protection from long term power outages, you can add battery backup units to the system to provide the energy reserve to cover those situations.

If you expect to live in your home for 15 years or longer the installation of a solar photo-voltaic system should be considered, especially if you're consuming large amounts of energy after having already made the efficiency improvements described earlier. A site study should be completed to determine the viability of any renewable energy source. With solar the key considerations are: latitude, shading factor of trees or structures; the direction the sloped roof line of the house is facing (ideally due south in higher latitudes); the high and low average annual temperatures of the location as well as the available sunlight.

There are two primary types of solar energy generation: solar thermal collectors which heat a liquid which can be used only for heating or photo-voltaic (PV) collectors which generate electricity useable for powering any electrical device.

Appendix 3 - Efficient Home Appliances

Decrease appliance power consumption by 20%

Stoves, ranges and ovens consume roughly 10% of the energy consumed by average American households. The basic kitchen stove includes an oven along with two large and two smaller burners. In the U.S., stoves are powered by gas or electricity which is not normally the case around the world. This is especially true in developing countries where biomass, dung, wood and coal are the cooking fuels of choice. The types of stoves sold in the U.S. are gas, electric resistance, electric inductive and microwave ovens. Stoves powered by electricity are usually less expensive; gas powered stoves generally cost less to operate. A modern gas stove with electronic ignition reduces the gas consumed by about 30% when compared to older gas stoves with a pilot light; otherwise the energy efficiency of gas-burning cooktops generally doesn't vary.

Electric cooktops offer several energy efficient options. The more efficient units are more expensive initially; they won't be cost-effective unless you cook often. In addition to standard electric coil elements there are a number of new types of electric burners: solid disk elements, radiant elements under glass, halogen and induction elements. Solid disk elements and radiant elements are mounted under glass, easy to clean but not as energy efficient, taking longer to heat up and more difficult to replace than electric coil units.

Halogen cooktops use bulbs filled with a halogen gas to create radiant heat under a ceramic glass surface to heat the food. The food is cooked by the radiation from the bulb as well as heat conduction between the ceramic cooktop and the pot. This approach uses less electricity than a standard coil element, but only with a very flat pan which maintains good contact with the burner.

Induction elements are the most energy efficient of all burner technologies, providing 90% of the energy for cooking, whereas gas burners typically deliver only 55% and standard electric ranges supply 65%. Induction elements use electromagnetic waves to turn the bottom of the pot into an active heating surface, providing accurate temperature control while keeping the cooktop surface cool. An induction element is capable of boiling water up to 50% faster than a regular stove. With induction technology the pots and pans must be made of steel or cast-iron, metals that react to a magnetic field—aluminum, copper, glass and Pyrex cookware will not work.

Convection ovens are more efficient because they continually use a fan to circulate heated air around the food being cooked. Because they distribute heat more evenly convection ovens can reduce cooking time and temperatures cutting energy consumption as much as 30% while cooking food more evenly. Covering oven racks with aluminum foil to prevent spills reduces this efficiency by blocking the flow of hot air. Convection ovens allow either traditional or convection baking and roasting.

Cooking multiple dishes in the same oven is also more efficient. Preheating your oven wastes energy and is unnecessary unless you're baking breads or pastries. Preheat only when needed and keep the preheat time to a minimum. Use the broiler whenever possible; it requires no preheating. Occasionally, check the seal on the oven door for cracks or tears. Keep the oven clean and use the proper cookware. Pots should have flat bottoms, straight sides and tight-fitting lids. In the oven use glass or ceramic pans instead of metal to reduce temperature settings by 25°F while cooking foods just as quickly. Make sure your stovetop electric coils work properly on electric ranges. The entire burner portion of the element should change color when turned on high; a worn-out element wastes a lot of energy. Keep stovetop burners and reflectors clean to reflect the heat. With gas ranges use a moderate flame setting to conserve gas.

Stoves and ovens last for many years representing energy efficiency decisions that will be paid for over a long time. Whether choosing electricity or gas, self-cleaning ovens have more insulation than standard ovens; they use less energy. Whichever type of stove is being used, the energy consumed can be reduced by employing simple practices: use the burner closest to matching the pot size; use lids on pots and pans to allow cooking at lower settings; keep drip pans under conventional coil burners clean. If possible, install your range away from the refrigerator. Heat from the range will make the refrigerator work harder. If you have to place hot and cold appliances next to each other, place a sheet of foam insulation between them.

When using the oven, check the oven temperature with a separate oven thermometer to ensure your oven control is accurate. Make sure the oven door seal is tight; while baking avoid opening the oven door—roughly 20% of the heat is lost each time the door is opened. Turn the oven off a few minutes before cooking is complete and let oven heat finish the job. The burner flame on gas stoves should be blue. A yellowish flame indicates the gas ports should be cleaned or adjusted; the gas ports can be cleaned with pipe cleaners. When buying a new stove consider your basic needs; look beyond the initial price to consider energy efficiency. A high-end expensive induction cooktop won't be cost-effective if you seldom cook; money spent on an oven too large will be wasted.

Microwave ovens have become one of the most widely used household appliances. Since microwave ovens heat only the food and not the utensils, they use electricity more efficiently; they consume only 30% to 50% as much energy as conventional ovens. A microwave oven uses electromagnetic radio waves called microwaves to heat food. These waves are absorbed by the water, fats and sugars in the food that produce atomic motion that's transformed into heat. Most plastics, glass and ceramics won't absorb microwaves; they let the energy pass right through. Electromagnetic waves are incapable of traveling inside metal conductors; when metal objects are placed inside a microwave oven—they reflect the waves and create sparks inside the oven. In conventional ovens, heat migrates via conduction from the outside of the food to the middle. The radio waves in a microwave oven penetrate the food to excite the water and fat molecules deep in the food, cooking it more evenly.

Since all microwave ovens are equally energy efficient, choosing which one to purchase depends more on price, size, reliability and features. It makes sense to purchase the microwave oven that best fits your situation and lifestyle.

Dishwashers are a fixture in most American homes but that's not the case worldwide. In America and much of Western Europe roughly 75% of all households have dishwashers; around the world the percent of average families that own a dishwasher is much lower.

Dishwashers manufactured before 1994 consume more water and energy when compared to today's ENERGY STAR certified models. On average ENERGY STAR rated models are about 5% more energy efficient and 15% more water efficient than standard models. Design innovations have made dramatic differences. Soil sensors determine just how dirty the dishes are throughout the wash, adjusting the cycle to achieve optimum cleaning with minimum water and energy use. Improved water filtration removes food particles from the wash water, providing more efficient use of detergent and water throughout the cycle. More efficient jets use less energy to spray detergent and water over the dishes when cleaning. Innovative dish rack designs maximize cleaning by strategically situating the dishes. Better temperature control boosts water temperatures to 140°F allowing for improved disinfection; the final clean-water rinse assures that dishes come out sparkling.

Dishwashers consume water and electricity in addition to the energy used to heat the water it consumes. A case can be made that dishwashers consume about the same amount of water and energy as hand washing and drying, but this is true only if you disregard the energy and materials needed to manufacture the dishwasher; the space and materials required to install and maintain one in the home. In spite of the technical innovations that have improved dishwasher performance, in a smaller and energy efficient future home, the practicality of having a dishwasher may be marginal. All the dishwashing and drying in my home is done by hand, the old-fashioned way.

Clothes washers are available in top and front-loading types. Top-loading washers are available in traditional and high-efficiency models. Many have earned an ENERGY STAR rating. Front-loading washers have become more popular due to their larger capacity. Front loading washers spin more water out of fabrics, reducing energy and water consumption. More sophisticated washer technologies provide efficient use of energy, detergent and water, across various sizes and types of loads, consuming as much as 75% less energy and 40% less water than older models.

Because they're more popular, front-loading washers offer most of the newest washing technologies. While earlier clothes washers were limited to large-small and hot-cold settings these features have been expanded with special cycle settings for most types of clothing: fabrics including heavy-duty, normal, delicate and permanent press with other options like prewash, second rinse, bulky-bedding, cotton, hand-wash/wool and steam. Newer clothes washers have a broader selection of temperature settings; they allow washing and rinsing clothes to occur at different temperatures. Older washers have settings for load size; newer washers have sensors measuring the size of the load and adjusting water usage accordingly. Many washers come standard with steam-cleaning which gently penetrates fabrics to remove, dirt, oil, odors and wrinkles without damaging the clothing.

Many new washers come with touch-screens. Antibacterial wash cycles use more advanced internal heating mechanisms to heat water to temperatures that kill bacteria, maintaining that temperature throughout the wash cycle. A large majority of the newer high-tech washers have earned an ENERGY STAR rating; they are comparatively energy and water efficient. The yellow Energy-Guide label indicates just how much energy an appliance will use over the course of one year.

Clothes Dryers can consume as much energy as newer energy efficient refrigerators, clothes washers and dishwashers combined. A strong

Appendix 3 - Efficient Home Appliances

federal energy efficiency standard for clothes dryers is badly needed for long-term energy savings. Consumers, utilities, manufacturers and the federal government are working together to demonstrate the cost-effectiveness and user acceptance of advanced dryer technologies. While other major appliances have undergone significant energy efficiency improvements over the past 20 years, energy efficiency standards for clothes dryers have remained essentially unchanged. With some 89 million residential clothes dryers in use across the United States, clothes dryer performance standards and technology are long overdue for improvement. Electric dryers dominate the U.S. market in spite of the fact that natural gas dryers typically cost less to operate. If all of America's electric dryers were updated to the most efficient models sold around the world, U.S. consumers could save $4 billion worth of energy per year, preventing roughly 16 million tons of carbon dioxide emissions annually, equivalent to the pollution from three coal-fired power plants. Policies for clothes dryers in the U.S. should include: updated methods for measuring dryer energy use; improved dryer technologies; the use of labeling programs to help consumers identify the most efficient models; offering utility rebates for the most energy efficient models.

Beyond these improvements—the ways in which dryers are used is important. Selecting a lower operating temperature will slow the drying process while reducing energy use significantly. Stopping the dryer before all the clothes are completely dry saves energy while reducing wrinkles and wear on the fabric.

Perhaps the best solution is the method we use in my home: hanging clothes outside on a clothesline to dry in the warm weather or on drying racks or clotheslines inside in our cellar during inclement weather. During the winter, drying clothes inside helps to add moisture to the dry indoor air which also helps to hold in the heat better.

New refrigerator/freezer technologies illustrate how energy efficiency standards can be used to improve both appliance function and efficiency. In 1976 the California Energy Commission established the first refrigerator/freezer efficiency standards eventually adopted by the U.S. Department of Energy in 1987. Since then the energy efficiency of residential refrigerators in the U.S. has improved to the point where an average refrigerator sold today consumes only 25% of the energy required by a 1975 model, even though the size of refrigerators has increased by 20% with added features such as icemakers and water dispensers. Nonetheless, refrigerator/freezers must keep food cool or frozen 24 hours a day, requiring almost 14% of the average home's energy consumption. Refrigerators and freezers come in a wide array of styles and sizes. The simplest have a large access door with a freezer compartment and refrigerated space located behind it. Top-mount versions have separate doors for the refrigerator with a smaller freezer area above it, saving energy while freezer temperatures are kept more constant behind a separate door. Bottom-mount refrigerators have the freezer section under the refrigerator with separate doors for each.

Side-by-side refrigerators include a freezer on the left alongside a refrigerated compartment. This design is more expensive and less efficient than traditional top-mount designs, usually available only in refrigerators larger than 22 cubic feet. The French-door refrigerator is a newer concept combining the best of the bottom mount and side-by-side designs offering two side-by-side doors opening on a refrigerator section placed above a single pullout freezer drawer. This provides a full-width refrigerator with the convenience of swing doors, if only one narrow refrigerator door is opened less cold air escapes.

You can buy a refrigerator without a freezer, usually the simplest and most economical refrigerator to purchase, providing the largest capacity but without a freezer compartment. Stand-alone freezers come in two styles: chest or upright. Chest freezers that open from the top are the most economical because nearly all the interior space provides storage; their insulation provides high energy efficiency.

Upright freezers cost more and provide roughly 15% less usable storage capacity than chest models, but have a smaller footprint and adjustable shelves. Refrigerators must meet federal standards for minimum operating efficiency. Refrigerators exceeding these standards run more efficiently, providing greater long-term energy savings. Manufacturers and retailers can voluntarily place ENERGY STAR labels on appliances that meet or exceed standards set by the EPA and the U.S. Department of Energy. ENERGY STAR qualified refrigerators are required to use 20% less energy than other models. Look for the Energy-Guide label that indicates the kilowatt-hours (kWh) consumption of electricity a particular refrigerator/freezer uses in a year. The smaller that number, the less energy the refrigerator uses and the less it will cost to operate.

While energy labels help consumers make wise choices, they can be confusing. The ENERGY STAR program indicates more than the most efficient refrigerator, it divides them into categories awarding ENERGY STAR labels to the best performing refrigerators in each category.

Appendix 3 - Efficient Home Appliances

Refrigerators in some categories use more energy than refrigerators in other categories. The most efficient ENERGY STAR side-by-side unit with ice dispenser may use more energy than a similar top-mount model that doesn't qualify for ENERGY STAR status. Likewise, the yellow Energy-Guide label details the energy use (kWh/year) range of all similar models. The yellow sticker compares electricity consumption only with models in the same category; side-by-side refrigerator/freezers are only compared to other side-by-side refrigerator-freezers and not with other models.

The best way to use the Energy-Guide label is to look at the listing detailing the expected energy use in kilowatt/hours per year and compare that figure with the expected energy use of all other models to make the best energy choice. When the yellow label estimates an appliance's yearly operating cost that figure is based on the average cost of electricity.

Explore the ENERGY STAR product database. Compare the actual energy use numbers on Energy-Guide labels to determine the most efficient. Consider your needs and purchase the right size refrigerator. The most energy-efficient models are typically 16-20 cubic feet. Consider skipping the ice-maker and dispenser. Through-the-door icemakers and water dispensers are convenient but they increase a refrigerator's energy use by 14 to 20% and they can cause more problems than they solve (e.g. plumbing leaks). A manual defrost refrigerator uses half the energy of models with automatic defrost. Refrigerators with anti-sweat heaters consume 5 to 10% more energy. Chest freezers are usually more efficient than upright models; they are better insulated and cold air doesn't readily escape when the door is opened. Automatic defrost freezers can consume 40% more electricity than similar manual-defrost models.

In order to minimize refrigerator/freezer energy consumption locate it away from heat sources such as an oven, dishwasher or even direct sunlight from a window, if possible. If the kitchen layout requires installing a dishwasher or stove next to the refrigerator, place a sheet of foam insulation between them. Leave at least a one-inch space between any appliance and the wall or cabinets to make sure air can circulate around the condenser coils. Check door seals to make sure they are airtight. Close the door on a dollar bill and try to pull it out. Or place a bright flashlight inside the refrigerator, direct the light toward a section of the door seal, with the door closed and the room dark, look for light through the door seal.

Check the temperature setting, a fridge that is 10°F colder than necessary can use 25% more energy. Refrigerators should be kept between 35 and 38°F and freezers at 0°F. A full refrigerator retains cold better than an empty one. If your refrigerator is nearly empty, store water-filled containers inside. The mass of cold items will enable the refrigerator to recover more quickly after the door has been opened. On the other hand, don't overfill it because that will interfere with the circulation of cold air inside. Open the door as little as possible. Regularly defrost manual defrost models, frost buildup increases the amount of energy needed to keep the motor running. Once you develop a habit of these practices you won't have to think about doing them.

Many refrigerators have small heaters built into the walls to prevent moisture from condensing on the outer surface. In some units this feature can be turned off with an energy-saver or power-saver switch. Unless you have noticeable condensation, keep this switch set on the energy-saving setting.[6]

Appendix 4 - Electronic Device Power Efficiency

Decrease electronic device power consumption by 20%.
Roughly 39.5 million televisions were shipped in 2017 to customers in the U.S. As TVs increase in screen size they consume more energy. Energy efficiency has become a key factor that consumers consider when selecting a new TV.[7]

Televisions are getting larger, sharper and thinner as their energy efficiencies improve. Yet, total energy consumption is increasing with screen sizes. The latest flat-screen technologies are more efficient per screen size but the ever-larger screens can consume more power. The newer flat-screen technologies include: Plasma TVs, Liquid-Crystal Display (LCD) TVs, LED & LCD TVs and Organic Light-Emitting Diode Televisions (OLED TVs).

Nearly all homes in the United States own at least one television; TVs accounted for approximately 25% of annual consumer electronics electricity consumption in 2017. With televisions getting bigger and using more energy, it's no wonder that most consumers say that energy efficiency will be a factor in their next television choice. Look for the ENERGY STAR label to save energy, save money, and help protect the climate.

ENERGY STAR certified televisions are on average 25 % more energy efficient than conventional models; they save energy in all modes: Sleep, Idle and On. The ENERGY STAR label can be found on standard to large screen TVs with the latest features like Ultra High-Definition (UHD) and internet connectivity. Some ENERGY STAR models incorporate organic light emitting diodes (OLEDs)—the latest in screen lighting technology.

Saving energy with ENERGY STAR certified home entertainment products helps to protect the climate. A home equipped with TVs, set-top boxes, a Blu-Ray player and sound-bar with an ENERGY STAR rating can save nearly $140 over the life of the products. If each TV, DVD player and sound-bar purchased in the U.S. this year was ENERGY STAR certified: annually more than $250 million would have been saved; 2.9 billion pounds of greenhouse gas emissions would have been prevented— roughly equal to the emissions of nearly 290,000 cars.

Currently, the flat screen televisions sold in the U.S. are mostly Liquid Crystal Displays (LCDs) with some OLED TVs, and then plasma TVs. Liquid Crystal Displays or LCDs are known as trans-missive displays because the light isn't generated by the liquid crystals but by a light source located behind the panel shining light through the display panel, modifying its color and brightness to create an image. LCDs are the most popular kind of TV technology today; most are backlit with light-emitting diodes

(LEDs): either an array of LEDs in the back of the panel or along the edge.

Organic Light-Emitting Diode or OLED TVs are another emitting type display. Unlike LCD TVs, where LEDs only provide the backlighting, an OLED TV possesses LEDs, miniaturized by their organic, carbon-based material, that provide lighting and control of color and brightness directly: each pixel is a tiny light-emitting diode.

Plasma TVs are known as *emissive* displays because the display panel provides the colored light necessary to create the image. The panel is composed of miniature gas-filled cells, similar in operation to fluorescent lamps, which glow when gas is energized to become plasma.

Digital Televisions: come in two subgroups differentiated by picture sharpness, usually described as the number of lines of resolution.
Standard Digital TVs (SDTV) – display an image composed of 480 horizontal and 640 vertical lines.

High-Definition TVs (HDTV) – display an image composed of either 720 or 1080 horizontal, and 1280 or 1920 vertical lines respectively.

UHDTVs were introduced in late 2012; however limited content is currently available for viewing in the UHD format. Some television manufacturers feature UHDTVs that up-convert content to UHD.

Ultra-High-Definition TVs (UHDTV) – have an aspect ratio of at least 16:9 and at least one digital input capable of carrying and presenting native video at a minimum resolution of 3,840 – 2,160 pixels.

4K UHDTV (2160p) has a resolution of 3840 – 2160 (8.3 megapixels), 4 times the pixels of a current 1080 HD TV.

8K UHDTV (4320p) has a resolution of 7680 – 4320 (33.2 megapixels), 16 times the pixels of a current 1080 HDTV.

When comparing TV pictures:
Contrast ratios are a measure of color representation: how the color information appears against a dark background—the higher the number, the better the color representation.

What is progressive scan? There are two ways a TV picture can be updated to display moving images. One way is to use an interlaced signal; the second is the utilization of a progressive scan signal. An interlaced signal—the method used by the standard analog screen—updates half of the scan lines (i.e. every other scan line) at a time (typically every 1/60th of a second, though some panels can update faster). A progressive scan signal updates all of the scan lines every 60th of a second; a progressive scan technology creates a sharper picture with less flicker.

What's a pixel? The term pixel is shorthand for picture element. A pixel is the smallest piece of information displayed on a digital screen—the tiniest dot that a picture is made of; one mega-pixel equals one million pixels.

Other Television Features:
Automatic Brightness Control (ABC) - The ABC feature is a self-acting mechanism that controls the brightness of the TV relative to the brightness of the room in which it is located. The ABC feature is intended to enhance the viewing experience and also save energy.

Local Dimming is different than ABC; it's typically used with LED-backlit LCD TVs when sections of LED backlighting are turned off or dimmed to produce deeper blacks and to save energy.

Network-Connected or Smart TVs can be connected to the Internet over Ethernet or Wi-Fi. Network-connected TVs allow viewers to download or stream content from the Internet to their TVs. These Smart TVs can have varying levels of ability to run apps, display interactive on-demand content, and provide access to other Internet-based programs in addition to providing traditional broadcasted television.

Pre-set Picture Settings - Many TVs are shipped with pre-set picture settings that viewers can select; such as vivid, sports or cinema. These settings reflect changes in brightness and contrast ratio to enhance the content in a particular way. The default picture setting is the setting used to earn the ENERGY STAR. To ensure the rated energy savings be sure to use the ENERGY STAR setting as much as possible.[8]

In addition to the power consumed while operating, many large-screen TVs don't shut off completely. Manufacturers have decided that most people don't want to wait for their sets to warm up—so most TVs go into a standby mode where they continue to consume a small but significant amount of power over time. Some require pressing a separate button, changing default power settings or unplugging the unit entirely—to power down the TV completely.
Consumers are becoming more energy conscious and TV

manufacturers are responding with innovative, energy saving designs. One option is a power saver mode with a trio of sensors to optimize the intensity of the LCD's backlight. The brighter the room the more backlighting is needed. A TV with a power saver mode can detect the relative darkness and brightness of the room and adjust the light needed to illuminate the picture. Other more efficient TV technologies include a sensor that constantly adjusts the brightness of scenes being presented on the TV. If the scene takes place at night the backlight dims slightly to save energy for the daytime scenes.

Whichever TV technology you choose, you can optimize its energy efficiency by powering down the TV completely when not in use. Read the operators manual to determine if it has a power saver mode. Disable *Quick Start* options that place the TV in a standby mode as a default setting. Manually dim the intensity of the contrast and brightness controls. Watch the TV in a dark room which improves picture clarity while requiring less backlight. You can use a power strip to completely turn off the TV to prevent it from consuming power. More importantly, we should all be asking ourselves—just how big and how many televisions do we really need?

Appendix 5 - Home Efficiency & Maintenance

Increase home power consumption efficiencies by 10% by performing system and routine maintenance while changing temperature setting practices.

In a more balanced and viable world, the living space for a family of four should be no larger than 1500 square feet, almost half the average size (2700 square feet) of most new homes being constructed in America today. If you were born into the *baby boom generation* post WWII like I was, 1000 square feet was the average home size for a middle-class family.[9]

The topic of home insulation was discussed previously in *Appendix 2-Reducing Utilities of Consumption*. Home heating and cooling requirements also depend greatly on the weather and geographical location: ranging from northerly zones with minimal air conditioning, where the heating fuel is likely to be natural gas or fuel oil—combined with solar or geothermal sources—or to the south where cooling and heating loads are more balanced allowing the use of high efficiency electric heat pumps or natural gas, combined with solar or geothermal energy sources for heating and cooling.

Consider the efficiency of all heating and cooling appliances: furnaces, air conditioners, water heaters, stoves and refrigerator/freezers. Consider replacing those where the efficiency is much lower than newer models. When buying necessary new appliances for your home, always look for the ENERGY STAR label to help make the most energy-efficient decisions. The simplest way to choose any appliance is to select the smallest, simplest and most reliable piece of equipment that consumes the least amount of energy.

You can estimate the annual or monthly energy consumption of any appliance by taking the power rating off the label, usually in listed watts (W) or kilowatts (kW), and multiplying that number times the average number of hours the appliance is on per day to compute the Watt-hrs. or kWatt-hrs per day. Multiply that value by the number of days the appliance will be used in a month or a year to determine the total energy consumption of the appliance over that period.

To estimate the hours a refrigerator operates at maximum wattage, divide the total time the refrigerator is plugged in by three. Even though refrigerators are continually powered—they cycle the compressor on average 8 hours per day.

Maintaining HVAC systems is another way to save energy and maintain system performance and efficiency. Change air filters regularly and learn how to properly use a programmable thermostat if you have one. Have your heating and cooling equipment maintained annually by a licensed contractor. Reduce air leaks and stop drafts by using caulk, weather stripping and insulation to seal your home's envelope; add insulation to your attic. A knowledgeable homeowner or skilled contractor can save up to 20% on heating and cooling costs and significantly enhance home comfort with comprehensive sealing and insulating measures. Utilize blinds and drapes on the appropriate windows to block the sun during warm weather, or to reduce heat loss in cold weather.

Air infiltration occurs when outside air moves in or out of your home, causing heating and cooling systems to work harder to maintain a comfortable temperature in the home. Many infiltrations can be reduced with inexpensive and simple solutions. If you see light coming in under the bottom of a door you should replace or adjust the threshold weather-stripping. Adjusting the door shoe threshold or installing a new one is the best way to eliminate this source of air leaks. The goal is to have a snug fit that minimizes the gap between the door and the floor while allowing the opening and closing of the door.

Weather stripping is also needed around door frames. Use a soft, flexible seal that won't harden over time. Look for elongated mounting holes that will allow for adjustments of the weather stripping. A wood door may change its shape and dimensions slightly in response to varying moisture conditions; it's important to maintain a tight seal without making the door too difficult to close.

Light switches and outlets on exterior walls are other common locations for air leaks. Foam inserts are available in most hardware stores with the appropriate cutouts to seal switch and receptacle outlet boxes. These inserts cover the space between the outlets and the electrical box and fit under the faceplate. For outlets with the worst air leaks, install receptacle faceplates with spring-loaded covers for the holes that the mating plugs connect to.

Attic access hatches with no weather stripping are another source of leaks. The foam gaskets available at most hardware stores are an easy and inexpensive solution to minimize these leaks; install a self-adhesive foam gasket at the edge of the attic opening. When you close the attic hatch, the gasket will prevent air leakage from your home into the attic

Anywhere pipes pass through walls are areas where air can leak in and out of your home. Use spray foam sealant to seal between the drywall and the pipe. The spray foam will expand and harden. Once hardened, cut the excess foam off with a utility knife and push the escutcheon ring back into place. If you feel a draft near windows, the original caulking and weather-stripping need replacing. Remove the old caulking and apply new caulking at interior and exterior locations where the window meets the house. You can use most types of door weather stripping to create a good seal at the top and bottom of older double hung wood-framed windows. Foam or felt weather-stripping may also be used to seal gaps where the two sashes overlap. The sides of the sash are more difficult; they must slide along the material you select to seal them with.

Many homes built between the 1960s and 1980s have aluminum-framed sliding windows with a fibrous seal built into the edges. This seals the window frame and the area between the two slider panels. You may be able to find the same material for replacement. A crack in a wall or ceiling allows heated air to escape from your home. Patch or plaster over any cracks as necessary.

Make sure your fireplace damper is in good working condition and closes securely when not in use; a tightly sealed glass screen can help reduce heat loss from a leaky damper. Remove window air conditioners during the winter when they're not in use. Otherwise, air conditioners should be tightly covered on the outside; sealed on the inside for the winter.

Caulking is necessary wherever two different building materials or parts of the house meet. These include areas around: outside door frames; windows; foundation sills; and electrical boxes. Penetrations, cracks and other infiltration points can also be sealed using inexpensive and easy-to-apply caulking. Silicon caulk is recommended for exterior areas because of its high durability and flexibility; it's more expensive than latex-based caulk but it maintains a tighter seal for longer. Acrylic latex caulk is a good general-purpose caulk for plugging gaps in wood, plaster and drywall. It will last for ten years or longer. If you plan to paint over the caulking once it's installed, check the label for paint compatibility.

When you're at home keep thermostats set for energy economy. A few degrees difference in temperature settings can significantly affect the amount of energy used. In summer set your thermostat between 76 and 78°F; winter between 66 and 68°F. Make changes gradually so your body can easily adjust to the change in temperature and dress appropriately for the season. The key to hot weather comfort is to keep the air moving; use a fan as much as possible instead of air conditioning. While you sleep, set thermostats for low energy use, during summer between 78 and 80°F; in winter between 55 and 60°F. Use a fan in the bedroom in the summer and plenty of blankets in the winter. The key is keeping the body warm or cool without warming or cooling the whole bedroom. Set your thermostats for low energy use when you leave the house for a short time. When the home will be vacant longer term adjust the thermostat accordingly.

Common sense says that more energy is consumed heating up or cooling a home than maintaining it at a certain temperature; this is not necessarily true. It takes about as much energy to reheat your home to the previous set temperature as the amount of energy saved while the temperature was dropping; the total energy saved is the difference between the energy required to maintain the lower setting compared to that needed to maintain the higher setting. Consequently, the longer the temperature remains at the lower setting, the more energy is saved. The other key factor to consider is the amount of time needed to reheat the house to the higher setting, which may be undesirable. The general rule I use is: if the time period where no one is at home is relatively long — over three hours — I set the thermostat set-point lower for heating applications; otherwise I leave it set at the normal setting.

In the summer set your thermostat between five and ten degrees higher when you leave the house for a longer period; in winter set it five to ten degrees lower. If a room is not in use, don't heat or cool it more than necessary. Close the doors to rooms not in use; keep the windows closed and shades down; close off heating or cooling vents in these rooms almost completely.

Adjust your heating and cooling systems to work more efficiently. You can waste energy dollars by overworking your air conditioning or heating system. If you have a central air system, check the ducts to make sure they aren't leaking. Seal any leaks at the joints. Instead of using duct tape, the latest research recommends sealing ducts with mastics (rubbery sealants) that are painted on and allowed to harden. Metal ducts should be held together with sheet metal screws; flexible duct connections should be secured with metal or plastic bands. Make sure the system is balanced. Balancing the system involves adjusting the air volume control dampers (if your system has them) and adjusting the air supply registers in each room. Use ceiling fans to achieve an even temperature from floor to ceiling.

Try making adjustments so each area of your home gets just the right amount of cool or warm air. The registers farthest away from the central heating/cooling unit should be wide open while those nearer should be partially closed. In each room try to adjust the registers so air is directed to the most often used part of the room. You can make these adjustments yourself; the best way to balance the entire system is to have an expert with the necessary instruments make all the adjustments needed. Most of the air supply registers on air-conditioning and heating systems should remain at least partially open to avoid damage to your unit. Heating or cooling unit filters may be blocked by accumulated dust and dirt causing the system to run longer, consuming more energy. Some filters can be washed; others need to be replaced every one or two months.

On an outdoor heat pump or air conditioning unit, cleaning the coil is important to ensure efficient operation. An air conditioner that's always drawing in fresh, warm outside air uses more electricity than one that merely re-cools the air already in your home. Especially in the hottest weather, try closing the fresh air intake at least part of the time and see if the air in your home remains fresh enough for your comfort.

Move any furniture, draperies or other obstructions that may be blocking the flow of heated or cooled air from registers or from an individual heating or air-conditioning unit. In summer open up your house to cool it at night and close it up during the day. Determine which windows and doors provide the best airflow. During the day keep the sun's heat out by adjusting shades, blinds, draperies and awnings. Let out the hot air through vents in your attic or in two-story homes by opening the upper part of double hung windows in the upstairs windows. Cut shrubs or tree foliage which interferes with cooling breezes through windows, being careful not to affect any shade they might offer. Electric window fans can provide cooling more economically than an air conditioner. An exhaust window fan can push out warm interior air and pull in cool air. Exhaust fans in the attic will push hot air out one end of the attic and pull cooler air in the other end; a cooler attic benefits the living area right beneath it. A whole-house fan mounted in the attic is better yet.

Let the sun help heat your home in cold weather. Even in the coldest winters the sun shines brightly at times. Remember to pull up the shades, open the draperies and blinds on the house's sunny side to let in those warm rays. Utilize the rooms with the most sun during the colder months. In winter close your curtains and draperies at night or on overcast days for extra insulation.

Fireplaces are warm and nostalgic but they're not particularly efficient at generating heat in your home. As the hot air rises the fireplace chimney draws warm air from the room and the rest of the house, pulling much of the heat up and out the chimney. If you have leaks in your house, cracks or gaps in your windows, doors or walls, the chilly outside air will be sucked in.

Dress for the weather to keep your body warm or cool. It's easier to maintain your body at a comfortable temperature than your whole house. During the summer wear loose fitting clothes, open collars and open-weave materials. Choose natural fibers rather than synthetics; keep the air moving to help evaporate perspiration from your skin. Consider using a dehumidifier; dry air more readily accepts the moisture cooling your skin when you perspire. In the winter dress warm, avoid drafts and keep the air moist. In cold weather a humidifier can help keep the air in the 40% humidity range. Use less hot water in the bathroom, kitchen and laundry. Take short showers instead of baths and use a low-flow showerhead. Don't run the hot water tap unnecessarily while you wash up or shave in the sink. If you use a dishwasher do fewer larger loads. It takes almost as much energy to wash a partial load in a dishwasher as a full load. The same is true for washing clothes. Try to wait for full loads and use cool water with the appropriate detergents to wash your clothes.

The best way to reduce energy consumption at home is to supplant the use of energy consuming appliances with manual tools. A good quality broom functions well in many everyday situations. Otherwise, every effort should be made to select the most energy efficient and practical appliances for necessary tasks when needed. Drying clothes on racks or on a clothesline—inside or outside—can save a lot of energy. It is sad that many modern building communities and developments outlaw the use of outside clotheslines because they're considered unsightly. It's another example of how prim and proper society has become, that we're willing to waste energy to avoid the unappealing sight of our clothes hanging on a clothesline. And what's worse—we're teaching our children to have the same values.

Replace the most frequently used light fixtures or light bulbs with ENERGY STAR rated products to reduce lighting costs. ENERGY STAR lighting provides bright, warm light with less heat, consuming less energy than standard lighting and lasting many times longer. Choose fluorescent or LED lighting over incandescent. They may be more expensive, but they'll last many times longer and are much cheaper to operate. Use your lights, TV and other appliances more wisely. It's just common sense to turn off the lights and the TV when you're not in the room.

These days most homes have multiple TVs and computers, all

connected to DVD players, tablets, smart phones, game consoles, external monitors and printers. While these devices are all packed with features, the energy they consume can add up to nearly 10% of a household's monthly energy consumption. The problem is that people forget to turn these devices off when not using them and many continue drawing power even after they've been turned off. You can completely remove power from these devices by unplugging or using a power strip to completely disconnect them. Another solution is to replace conventional power strips with advanced power strips (APS) which can help reduce the electricity wasted when these devices are idle. APS strips are designed primarily for home entertainment centers and home office areas where many electronic devices are plugged into a power strip. They function by preventing the electronics from drawing any power when they're in standby mode or off.

Reducing, reusing and recycling in your home helps conserve energy while decreasing pollution and greenhouse gas emissions resulting from resource extraction, manufacturing and disposal. If there is a recycling program in your community, recycle newspapers, beverage containers, paper, and other goods. Composting food and yard waste at home reduces the amount of garbage sent to landfills, reducing greenhouse gas emissions while improving garden soil. Not only does recycling provide additional resource life, it reduces the volume of garbage to be picked up and buried in landfills.

Besides its consumption, water requires lots of energy to pump, treat and sanitize it; saving water also reduces energy consumption as well as greenhouse gas emissions. Three percent of the nation's energy is used to pump and treat water. Saving water around the home is easy to do. Pursue simple water-saving actions such as not letting the water run while shaving or brushing your teeth. Save money while conserving water by using products with a *Water-Sense* label. Water-Sense is a partnership program by the EPA seeking to protect the future of our nation's water supply by offering simple ways to use less water with water-efficient products. This program helps consumers make smart water choices that save money and maintain high environmental standards without compromising performance. Products and services that have earned the Water-Sense label have been certified to be at least 20% more water efficient without sacrificing performance.

A leaky toilet can waste many gallons of water per day, so repair all toilet and faucet leaks quickly. Many water leaks can be repaired simply by cleaning toilet flapper valves in toilets or changing gaskets in most faucets. Run your dishwasher only with a full load; better yet don't invest in a dishwasher at all, save the space and energy by washing and drying dishes as a family project by hand. Collect rain in barrels; be smart when irrigating your landscape by watering during the coolest part of the day and only when truly needed. Drip irrigation is a very effective means of irrigating all kinds of gardens.

If generating your own solar power is not an option you can purchase environmentally friendly electricity generated from renewable energy sources directly from your utility company, or buy solar panels that have been installed in regional solar farms. Buying renewable solar power offers a number of environmental and economic benefits over conventional electricity, including lower greenhouse gas emissions while helping to increase clean energy supplies.

Decrease purchasing of miscellaneous unnecessary goods by 20%.

When purchasing necessary consumer items, tools, appliances and furniture, purchase only those products which are inherently simple and rugged in their design and function, energy efficient and repairable over the long term. Favor manual tools as much as possible, hand grass clippers instead of gasoline powered weed-wickers or better yet, utilize lawn borders which can be mulched. Take good care of all your necessary possessions; your hard-earned money was spent to purchase them. It just makes good sense to use them properly, maintain them, protect them from the weather and store them appropriately.

Recycle all batteries that are not rechargeable and buy a battery charger for the rechargeable batteries you use most often. Using rechargeable batteries can save money while allowing better utilization of natural resources and they can also be recycled.

In general, it's important to be frugal, making sure to buy only the items needed to accomplish necessary tasks, resolving issues in a way that will bring peace and harmony into the lives of you and your loved ones. How many times have you bought some frivolous item in haste and later wondered why you wasted your money? It's often better to do without and decide later on than to buy on impulse.

To minimize your daily travel, encourage employers to offer commuter benefits which address limited or expensive parking; reduce traffic congestion; improve employee recruiting and retention while minimizing environmental impacts associated with single-driver commuting. When you drive, determine the fuel efficiency of your vehicle and make environmentally informed choices when purchasing your next vehicle. Learn more about the fuel economy and environmental labels shown on all new vehicles, including advanced technology vehicles like electric cars or plug-in hybrids.

Drive smart to improve your fuel economy and reduce greenhouse gas emissions. Go easy on the brakes and gas pedal, avoid hard accelerations, reduce your time spent idling and unload unneeded items in your trunk to reduce weight. Use cruise control if you have it. For vehicles with selectable four-wheel drive, utilize two-wheel drive when it's safe to do so.

Perform maintenance and get regular tune-ups following the manufacturer's maintenance schedule while using the recommended grade of motor oil. A well-maintained car is more fuel efficient, reliable and safer while producing fewer greenhouse gas emissions. Check your tire pressure regularly. Under inflation increases tire wear, reduces your fuel economy and leads to higher greenhouse gas and other air pollutant emissions. Give your car a break by using public transportation, carpooling, walking or biking whenever possible. Leaving your car home just two days a week can reduce your greenhouse gas emissions by an average of two tons per year not to mention the savings on gasoline. Minimize the amount of driving for vacation and leisure travel and try to combine errands and leisure activities into one trip.

Make dietary changes to reduce beef consumption by 50% and other meats by 25%, making sure to maintain proper iron and protein dietary content.

If possible, consider growing some of the food you eat—there isn't a more relevant activity for humans to partake in. The physical exercise, getting outside, learning about plant life, pests, soil and weather conditions are all worth the effort, not to mention the financial and dietary attributes. If you have a partner, gardening can literally help you grow together. With children watching plants take hold as a family is a great way to teach them about nature and involve them in the process.

Simplicity is an important consideration when starting a garden. You don't need an array of rototillers or other mechanized fuel consuming and polluting devices or huge quantities of fertilizer and pesticides. All you need is good soil, water and the sun while utilizing organic growing methods and the compost made from household green waste, along with a shovel, rake and hoe to enjoy a bountiful harvest year after year. Digging, raking, hoeing, cultivating, weeding and harvesting are all good workouts performed at your own pace. Start small and increase your plot gradually applying the expertise you gain with each growing season. Planting a few perennials such as strawberries, asparagus and rhubarb or biennials such as swiss-chard and kale will start your harvest early each season and without too much effort in the spring. If you select open pollinated annuals best suited to your growing season and conditions, you can save the seed from the plants that produce the best fruit thereby selecting the best genetic offspring for planting in the upcoming season. In the process you'll be developing a strain of the plant variety best suited to your garden's growing conditions. A significant portion of the water for garden consumption during dry periods can be met by collecting rainwater.

If you have little potential garden space, consider planting some edible plants and flavorful herbs in your front yard or turn the strip between your yard and the street into a vegetable garden. With landscaping, consider fruit trees and berry bushes instead of ornamentals. In colder climates you can extend the growing season with a greenhouse, cold frames or row covers. Also consider container gardens and vertical gardening techniques. You can grow a surprising bounty of produce on a small balcony or deck. If you live in a city high-rise, join a community garden. If growing your own food isn't possible, one alternative is to join a local pick your own or regional organic cooperative or simply buying local organically produced produce.

Where you buy your food, its dietary components, distance from farm to market, the pesticides, antibiotics, genetic modification and artificial fertilizers used to produce it are all important considerations. You can also determine whether the establishment where you buy your food is a good corporate citizen: uses resources efficiently; supplies locally produced foods; treats their workers fairly while supporting local initiatives.

Farmer's Markets are a great place to shop. Try to buy locally produced and organically grown food products as much as possible. Whether you grow your own food or purchase it from a co-op, during those times when fresh produce is in full bloom try to preserve it for the months after the growing season. Freezing, drying or canning are the most practical ways to accomplish this. If you have an unheated space in the cellar, consider turning it into a root cellar for winter squash and root plants (potatoes, carrots and onions).

Food, green waste and garbage disposal is another concern. The amount of green waste and recyclables stuffed into plastic bags and hauled out to the curb weekly as for garbage pickup to be dumped into local landfills is unconscionable. When disposing of household waste identify and recycle each item identified as recyclable: most all metals; clean paper; with plastics look for the universal recycling symbol—a triangle with arrows rotating clockwise—and recycle all category 1-4 recyclables if recycling is offered where you live. Some areas around the U.S. also accept category 5, 6 and some 7 plastics, but check with your local recycling facility for sure.

Collect all green waste for composting. It can be used to enrich the soil for vegetable and flower gardens. Eventually, apartment complexes should provide the compost option as well, either providing green waste to local community composting facilities or composting the green waste for use on the property. Most electronics and metal waste can and should be taken directly to local solid waste transfer stations. Smart purchasing in the first place will minimize the amount of garbage later hauled out to the curb.

With fresh air, clean water and a well-balanced diet of quality food, all living species are prepared to perform the functions of life they have evolved to pursue. Generally, that includes living life and providing for the continuation of the species in the form of generations to come. For humans that involves a complex combination of physical, mental, social and spiritual activities promoting our general good health in addition to the dietary changes already discussed. It's important to be active daily, using as many of the body's natural movements as possible. Depending on your age it's important to have a set workout of simple exercises that won't over stress any one group of muscles. A combination of simple Yoga positions combined with basic strength and aerobic exercises, jogging or walking works well. If there's a sport you enjoy actively pursue it for as long as you can. Hiking, jogging, bicycling or just walking around your neighborhood are other ways to be outside while getting some exercise and being closer to nature. The degree to which we're able to pursue these activities changes as our body ages but it's important to keep at it to whatever degree we can.

Many people develop a habit of hiring out home maintenance tasks because they are physically demanding and time consuming; others purchase expensive, energy consuming devices to accomplish these tasks quickly and easily. Many of these same individuals try to keep fit by joining fitness clubs with the cost of membership, travel costs and time spent commuting to and from the facility. The alternative is to keep fit by doing simple exercises at home, taking daily walks while performing home maintenance tasks with more manual equipment while saving energy, material and money in the process.

Our minds need a workout which usually isn't an issue while we're still working for a living. But those who are unchallenged mentally by their work or retirees who are not working at all, staying mentally active and fit can be trying. Reading books of all types is a good way to relax, learn and extend one's horizons. Learn something new: an instrument, a foreign language or a new game. Get involved in your community, take a class, join a club or spend some time in nature. The key is to develop a few interests and hobbies over the course of a lifetime varying in the type of physical and mental skills required. Pursuing these hobbies or interests alongside a career and into retirement are the best ways to keep your mind and body fit and active for life.

Appendix 6 - Mind, Body & Spirit

Goals listed in Chapter 13:

1. Reduce red-meat consumption by 50% and other meats by 25%.
2. Reduce sugar and salt consumption by 25%.
3. Reduce household solid waste (garbage) by 50%.
4. Achieve recycling levels for paper, glass and metal at 95%.
5. Recycle 90% of all plastic categories 1-5.
6. Eliminate using plastic shopping bags, fast-food Styrofoam containers.
7. Reduce electrical power consumption by 20% of average kilowatt consumption.
8. Reduce consumption of fossil fuels by 10% of volume.
9. Reduce water and paper consumption by 20% by volume.
10. Reduce consumption of frivolous items by 20% in dollars.

Appendix 7 - Measuring Your Progress

Sometimes it helps if you measure your progress towards achieving reductions in consumption and waste by using a simple means for measuring and recording your progress. Consumption levels are best tracked monetarily—except for utilities such as electricity, gasoline, fuel oil and natural gas—where significant price variations favor recording their actual usage in gallons, kilowatt-hours, therms etc. Utilization expenses include the money expended to purchase an appliance or tool and consuming it over time (i.e. any appliance, tool, furniture or accessory). Utilization expenses should include just the total initial price of an item excluding monthly payments for items bought on time. The most significant consumption expenditures are typically groceries, gasoline, telecommunications, electricity, water, fuel oil and natural gas. Utilization expenses comprise the initial purchase price of all tools, appliances, vehicles, furniture or other items consumed over a long period of time.

To make the tracking process simple it's best to record the consumption and utilization of the following items on a monthly basis: the quantity consumed and the total cost of each utility source consumed in the household (electricity, gasoline, natural gas, fuel oil and water), groceries; meat consumption; appliances; tools; accessory items; maintenance and travel expenses.

In order to eliminate the impact of seasonal climate variations on heating, cooling and electrical consumption, it is best to record the degree-day total for each month. Degree-days—heating or cooling—are simply a way to measure and compare how relatively hot or cold it was during any month for comparison with prior years. Degree-days are usually determined based upon a desired temperature of 65°F. Let's say that in November the average daily temperature for the entire thirty-day month was 42°F. This indicates that on average the home heating system needed to raise the house temperature from 42 to 65°F, a total of 23°F for each of the days in November. The total heating degree-days for that November period is equal to 690 (23 degrees x 30 days). Tracking degree-days is important to allow for changes in consumption to be attributed either to varying weather patterns or to the actual changes in consumption that have occurred. For example, if the previous year's November degree-day total was only 590, indicating that it was 100 degree-days warmer (15%) than the current year, without any other changes in consumption practices the current year should have consumed roughly 15% less heating energy.

To minimize garbage waste, make sure you know the rules regarding recycling in your area. Recycle all items deemed recyclable and dispose of all hazardous items: medical waste, pesticides, batteries etc. properly. Compost all food, excluding meats, and green waste in compost bins or boxes for use in flower or vegetable gardens. The actual garbage put out to the curb each week represents the true measurable household waste. You can manually compress your garbage and record how much total garbage you dispose of each month: the number of bags, garbage cans etc., and challenge yourself with goals for reducing that number.

Each year plan a budget for the consumption, utilization and waste-items you choose to monitor and reduce based upon any historical data you have along with annual targets you'd like to meet. The units for electricity are typically *kilowatt hours*, a number shown on most electric power bills, *therms* representing the volume of natural gas consumed on most gas energy bills, *gallons* of water and *bags* of garbage. All other items are measured in dollars. Compile the data and monitor the results of your efforts changing your habits accordingly to achieve the results you desire. These steps may seem minimal but they can really add up to have an impact on the environment if enough people start applying them.

To better understand your energy consumption and carbon emissions you can periodically calculate your household's carbon footprint: an estimate of the household greenhouse gas emissions resulting from the energy use, transportation and waste disposal in your household. There are numerous carbon footprint calculators available on the Internet; some are more complex and accurate than others. It's best to start out simple and progress through the more complex calculations as you gain experience. Spread the word by discussing with family and friends how consumption and utilization efficiency is good for their homes and good for the environment, because it lowers energy and natural resource consumption, greenhouse gas emissions and air pollution.

It's not really necessary to keep track of consumption reductions or your carbon footprint, as long as you're happy with the progress you're making. It is important to realize that simply reviewing the dollar amount of an energy bill month after month may be misleading; it may continue increasing even while reductions in consumption are actually decreasing due solely to price increases. Also, it's difficult to compare HVAC energy consumption for any given month from year to year when the degree of cold or hot weather differs significantly as shown by the degree-day calculation.

In order to reduce consumption, utilization and waste, we can all take the steps discussed in this section: sustaining our livelihood in dwellings reflecting the technical and viable creativity of our values; developing and maintaining efficient households; pursuing simple healthy diets and life-styles; utilizing only the most needed and efficient, tools and appliances; practicing recycling and supporting those businesses and governmental actions that support a future for all life.

See Appendices 8 and 9 for information on Supporting Good Business Practices and Environmental Government Policies respectively.

Appendix 8 - Supporting Good Business Practices

Goal #9: Increase the percentage of good business partners you patronize.

Sufficiency based businesses should support ethical practices including sustainable sourcing, production and distribution; eco-efficiency and waste reduction; honest product promotion; recycling innovation and example-setting. Businesses should focus on innovation to create new and improved products and services with minimal nature costs; maximum social value while withdrawing those products and services least sustainable from the marketplace. Marketing programs should be designed to enable and encourage consumers to choose and utilize products that are efficient, sustainable and meet their basic needs. The key aspects of sufficiency-based businesses should minimize consumption and eliminate planned obsolescence; reduce the materials and other resources consumed in all aspects of the product's manufacture, sale, use and disposal.

Types of businesses to focus on:
- Organic and Non-GMO food producers
- Non-herbicide food producers
- Certified free-range meat producers
- Photovoltaic Energy Installation and Service Providers
- Electronic Device Manufacturers
- Appliance Manufacturers

Automobile manufacturers focusing on: fuel efficiency; small size and safety; the most relevant features for fuel performance and safety; a focus on transportation not entertainment; ease of serviceability; cost reductions by using similar parts year after year, unless mandated by safety, efficiency performance or cost improvements.

Clean Energy Producers: environmentally certified solar, wind, geothermal and hydropower energy suppliers.

The following is a sufficiency-oriented company profile that was presented in paper entitled *Towards a sufficiency-driven business model: Experiences and opportunities* by Bocken and Short, August 7, 2015[10].

Vats is a British furniture company that manufactures and retails furniture designed by Dieter Rams. Vitsœ's furniture is known as a German design classic.

Vitsoe trains their sales people to under-sell customer needs with no sales commissions paid or discounts offered to customers; installation and support services are provided at cost. This practice helps ensure that unnecessary sales, consumption and waste are minimized. Their sales strategy is focused on creating loyal customers viewed as ambassadors for their product line; a focus on developing longer term business growth based upon the trust and reputation developed through the customer relationship created by positive word-of-mouth recommendations to drive future sales to new customers and ensures the ongoing profitability of the company.

Sufficiency-related elements in Vitsoe's business model exemplify sufficiency by striving to eliminate built-in obsolescence through its design and production systems; consciously avoiding short-lived fashion cycles or trends. Vitsoe avoids the cycle of replacement and repurchasing by going against the industry norm of designing and manufacturing products intended to have a limited useful life. They consciously under-sell products by training sales staff to offer customers the minimum they need, measuring performance on customer satisfaction rather than sales numbers. Various services are offered at a nominal cost to encourage customers to reuse rather than discard products. Most importantly, Vitsoe does not trade shares publicly because the owner feels demands of external shareholders could compromise the company's vision.

Vitsoe trains their sales people to under-sell customer needs with no sales commissions paid or discounts offered to customers; installation and support services are provided at cost. This business helps ensure that unnecessary sales, consumption and waste are minimized. Their sales strategy is focused on creating loyal customers viewed as ambassadors for their product line. This sales strategy implies focusing developing longer term business growth based upon the trust and reputation developed through the customer relationship created by positive word-of-mouth recommendations to drive future sales to new customers and ensures the ongoing profitability of the company.

Sufficiency-related elements in Vitsoe's business model exemplify sufficiency by striving to eliminate built-in obsolescence through its design and production systems; consciously avoiding short-lived fashion cycles or trends. Vitsoe avoids the cycle of replacement and repurchasing by going against the industry norm of designing and manufacturing products intended to have a limited useful life. They consciously under-sell products by training sales staff to offer customers the minimum they need, measuring performance on customer satisfaction rather than sales numbers. Various services are offered at a nominal cost to encourage customers to reuse rather than discard products. Most importantly, Vitsoe does not trade shares publicly because the owner feels demands of external shareholders could compromise the company's vision.

Sufficiency-based business model innovations

Strategies of successful sufficiency-based businesses: sharing without ownership; multiple customers share a product; customers never own the product but a service is sold. The business is paid for the service rather than ownership. This creates create convenience and transparency for the customer.

Energy and resource reduction: solutions minimizing energy and resource consumption by individuals and businesses; providing add-on services to assist consumers in reducing consumption; public subsidies and or preferential tax treatment to improve acceptance of the business concept.

Moderating sales and promotion by a conscious moderation of sales activities: eliminating manipulative consumer marketing campaigns without sales incentives. The business model is built on customer long-term relationships and trust; with the payback of a strong reputation and customer loyalty.

Extending product life by providing products designed to last a lifetime: repairable, upgradable and impervious to fashion trends. A premium price or service charges can justify slower sales; customers benefit in through savings over the long product life.

Direct reuse: creation of second-hand markets for used goods to reduce waste to landfills. Consumers are encouraged to pay premium price because a strong used market creates re-sale value offsetting initial higher purchase costs.

Full life cycle sufficiency: design and product use are focused on minimizing resources, the most important example is to make only the most prudent innovations. Unfortunately, thus far most of these solutions have been focused on lower income countries.[11]

Appendix 9 - Supporting Environmental Government Policies

Warning from the United Nation's Intergovernmental Science-Policy Platform on Biodiversity and Ecosystem Services (IPBES)

The latest warning from the UN regarding the impending environmental crisis was issued on May 6, 2019. The Guardian's reporter, *Calla Wahlquist* issued the following report which I have summarized entitled, *UN environment warning: 10 key points and what Australia must do* - from native species to Indigenous land management and water efficiency: Australia's role in the extinction crisis.

PARIS, 6 May 2019 – Nature is declining globally at rates unprecedented in human history—and the rate of species extinctions is accelerating, with grave impacts on people around the world now likely, warns a landmark new report from the Intergovernmental Science-Policy Platform on Biodiversity and Ecosystem Services (IPBES), the summary of which was approved at the 7th session of the IPBES Plenary, meeting last week (29 April – 4 May) in Paris.[12]

The UN's Intergovernmental Science-Policy Platform on Biodiversity and Ecosystem Services said in the report: "Global warming must stay below 2°C to save coral reefs." A sobering new UN report indicates that the planet is in serious danger due to the accelerating decline of the Earth's natural life-support systems. The ten key points of the report follow:

1. Human life will be severely impacted if we do not protect biodiversity. More than one million plant and animal species are now threatened with extinction, including 40% of all amphibian species, 33% of reef-forming corals and a third of all marine animals. Terrestrial native species have declined in abundance by 20% since 1990; 690 vertebrate species have gone extinct since the 16th century. Human society is under an urgent threat from loss of Earth's natural life.

Australia alone has lost 27 species of mammals in just over 200 years of colonization. If unchecked, loss of biodiversity could lead to the collapse of entire ecosystems. "We are eroding the very foundation of our economies, livelihoods, food security, health, and quality of life worldwide," the Intergovernmental Science-Policy Platform on Biodiversity and Ecosystem Services chair, Sir Robert Watson, said.

2. Species are dying at the cost of food security. Modern agricultural practices have seen the diversity of species grown for human consumption narrowed to the most productive varieties. Those varieties are used in place of local species that were farmed previously. As of 2016, 559 of the 6,190 domesticated breeds of mammals used for agriculture were extinct and a further 1,000 are threatened. Wild relatives of domestic crop species are also under threat. The report indicated that biodiversity loss has become a serious risk to global food security, by undermining the resilience of many agricultural systems to threats such as pests, pathogens and climate change.

3. We should support Indigenous knowledge and land management. Nature is declining less rapidly in land that is owned or managed by Indigenous peoples, but it is still declining due to competing interests including mining and unsustainable agriculture and fishing. About 25% of all land globally is traditionally owned, managed, used or occupied by Indigenous peoples, including 35% of all formally protected areas and 5% of all remaining terrestrial areas with very low human intervention. The report found that despite Indigenous peoples proactively confronting problems of both climate change and habitat loss, regional and global plans to combat biodiversity loss and climate change are not making use of Indigenous knowledge. It recommends promoting Indigenous knowledge and land management systems in drafting the global and regional response to looming environmental threats.

4. About 40% of Australia's land mass is formally recognized either under native title or land rights laws. According to the UN, we need to bump that number up. Promoting Indigenous governance and self-determination through the recognition of land tenure is a global recommendation from the report. Doing so will promote positive contributions of Indigenous peoples and local communities to sustainability.

5. Reforestation for carbon sequestration could harm biodiversity. Restoring native ecosystems is an indispensable part of both staving off mass extinction and mitigating the effects of climate change; what is good for mitigating one issue can harm another. Australia's political parties are urged to act as the UN panel issues a grim extinction warning. The report warns that reforestation of cleared or previously un-forested areas, as well as large-scale bioenergy plantations, risks establishing monocultures. That is bad for biodiversity and could threaten food and water security; undermine local jobs and intensify social conflict. Scientists have already warned of a version of this occurring in Victoria's central highlands where

Appendix 9 - Supporting Environmental Government Policies

Mountain Ash forests continue to be logged at what experts warn is an unsustainable rate. If logging continues that ecosystem is projected to collapse by 2067; to be potentially replaced by an open acacia woodland with dire consequences for several threatened species and the security of Melbourne's water supply.

6. We have to protect green spaces in cities. Urban areas have doubled globally since 1992. In Australia, one of the fastest growing areas is in western Melbourne where 55% of the 1,200 native plant species in the remaining grasslands are under threat of extinction in the next 100 years. The report recommends maintaining green spaces or green wedges in the city as wildlife corridors and cleaning up metropolitan waterways is a key measure to protect biodiversity in urban areas. It also recommends promoting rooftop gardens, urban agriculture movements and expanding native vegetation cover in both existing urban and peri-urban areas and in new developments.

7. We are losing a lot of water to agriculture. More than one-third of the world's land surface and nearly three-quarters of all available freshwater resources are devoted to crop or livestock production. Crop production occurs on about 12% of all ice-free land world-wide and grazing on 25% of total ice-free land and 70% of drylands — which includes all of Australia. The report recommends measures including protecting wetland biodiversity areas, limiting the expansion of unsustainable agriculture and mining, reversing the de-vegetation of catchment areas, reducing fertilizer use that causes polluted run-off, and minimizing the negative impact of dams. It also recommends investing in water efficiency measures in Australia that would include converting open irrigation channels to closed pipelines, as well as encouraging the use of household rainwater collections.

8. We need to ditch subsidies that encourage environmentally harmful practices.
Economic incentives traditionally reward business practices that deliver strong economic returns — often at the price of environmental harm — over those that promote conservation or restoration.

Biodiversity: what the UN has found and what it means for humanity. By getting rid of environmentally harmful subsidies and promoting economic incentives that measure value in environmental and social terms as

359

well as economic terms, we would increase sustainable land and sea management. That move will be opposed by vested interests, the report says, but will promote better outcomes.

9. We will lose all the coral if we can't keep climate change below 2°C. Half of the live coral cover in the world has been lost since the 1870s; the rate of that loss has accelerated in recent decades, notably in the Great Barrier Reef. If global temperatures increase +1.5°C coral reef cover is expected to decline again, to 10-30% of former levels. In a +2°C future coral reef cover will be just 1% of what it was before the industrial revolution. Losing the reefs will increase the risk of floods and hurricanes impacting between 100 million and 300 million people who live in 100-year coastal flood zones. The only way to stave off this damage is to keep climate change below 2°C.

10. We need to take an ecosystem-based approach to managing fisheries. That includes setting quotas, protecting key marine biodiversity areas, and reducing pollution from run-off. About 33% of global fish stocks are overfished while only 7% are under-fished. The companies and profits behind industrial fishing are concentrated in a few countries but cover 55% of the oceans, mainly in the northern hemisphere. We need to develop legally binding global agreements for responsible fisheries and urgently work towards eliminating illegal, unreported or unregulated fishing.[13]

Appendix 10 - Chapter 12 Beefless Diet Calculations

Chapter 12: Example 12.1 - Beefless Dietary Example Calculations
Note: Sources listed here are shown in chapter 12 listing

Let's consider one example: In 2014 U.S. consumption of meat per person totaled 153.3 lbs.: 51.5 lbs. beef; 43.1 lbs. pork; 58.7 lbs. poultry.[9] What are the savings in water, grain, topsoil and energy if one American refrains from eating beef for one year but continues consuming the average amounts of pork and chicken replacing the beef with a healthier diet including fruits, green vegetables, potatoes, rice, oats and rice.

In 2014 the Bard College study concluded that beef requires roughly 28 times more land; 6 times more fertilizer; 11 times more water to produce the same number of calories when compared to the other food sources in the study. Furthermore, the study performed the same comparison for crops including potatoes, wheat and rice to determine they require 2 to 6 times fewer resources than pork, chicken, eggs or dairy to produce the same number of calories. The study generally concluded that beef production consumes 10 times more resources when compared to poultry, dairy, eggs or pork.

Calculation:
In 2014 U.S. consumption of 51.5 lbs. of beef per person, 43.1 lbs. of pork per person and chicken 58.7 lbs. per person.[1] Totaling 153.3 lbs. of meat per person. The water required for beef is 15,400 liters/kg; pigs 6,000 liters/kg, poultry 4,300 liters/kg.[2]

Converting from liters to gallons and kilograms to pounds: 1 liter = 0.26417 gallons and 1 kg. = 2.20462 lbs.
For Beef: 15,400 liters/kg. x .26417 gallons/liter = 4068 gallons/kg. x 1kg. / 2.20 lbs. =1845 gallons/lb.
For Pork: 6,000 liters/kg. x .26417 gal/liter = 1585 gallons/kg. x 1kg. /2.20462 lbs. = 719 gallons/lb.
For Chicken: 4,300 liters/kg. x .26417 gallons/liter = 1136 gallons/kg. X 1kg. /2.20462 lbs.
= 515 gallons/lb.
Therefore: the water in gallons/lb. required for beef 1845 gallons/lb.; pigs 719 gallons/lb.; chickens 515 gallons/lb.

There are many numbers being thrown around for the amount of grain needed to produce 1 lb. of beef dependent on grazing and feedlot amounts ranging from 2 to 20 lbs. of grain to produce 1 lb. of beef. I've decided to use 8 lb. of grain to produce 1 lb. of beef as a fair estimate taking into account both grazing and feedlots. Therefore, for this example 2 lbs. of grain produce 1 lb. of chicken; 4 lbs. of grain produce 1lb. of pork and 8 lbs. of grain produces 1 lb. of beef.[3]

Appendix 10 Chapter 12 Beefless Diet Calculations

Also, 35 lbs. of topsoil are consumed to produce 1 lb. of beef and 1 gallon of gasoline energy equivalent; for pork the estimates are 17 lbs. of topsoil and .5 gallons of gasoline per lb. of pork; 9 lbs. of topsoil and .25 gallons of gasoline are consumed for each lb. of chicken.[4]

Producing 51.5 lbs. of beef requires:
Water = 51.5 lbs. beef x 1845 gal./lb. beef = 95,018 gallons
Grain = 51.5 lbs. beef x 8 lb. grain/.lb beef = 412 lbs.
Topsoil = 51.5 lbs. beef x 35 lb. topsoil/ lb. beef = 1803 lbs.
Energy equiv. gasoline = 51.5 lbs. beef x 1-gallon gasoline = 51.5 gallons

Producing 43.1 lbs. of pork requires:
Water = 43.1 lbs. pork x 719 gal./lb. = 30,989 gallons
Grain = 43.1 lbs. pork x 4 grain/lb. pork = 172 lbs.
Topsoil = 43.1 lbs. pork x 17 lb. topsoil/ lb. pork = 733 lbs.
Energy equiv. gasoline = 43.1 lbs. pork x .5 gallons gasoline = 22 gallons gas
45,000 gallons of water; 200 lbs. of grain; 900 lbs. of topsoil and 25 gallons of energy equivalent gasoline.

For 58.7 lbs. of poultry requires:
Water = 58.7 lbs. poultry x 550 gal./lb. = 32,285 gallons
Grain = 58.7 lbs. poultry x 2 lb. grain/lb. = 117 lbs.
Topsoil = 58.7 lbs. poultry x 9 lb. topsoil/ lb. = 528 lbs.
Energy equiv. gasoline = 58.7 lbs. x .25 gallons gasoline = 15 gallons gas

The average American meat diet per person currently requires:
Water: 95,018 (beef) + 30,989 (pork) + 32,285 (poultry) = 158,292 gallons
Grain: 412 lbs. (beef) + 172 lbs. (pork) + 117 lbs. (poultry) = 701 lbs.
Topsoil: 1803 lbs. (beef) + 733 lbs. (pork) + 528 lbs. (poultry) = 3064 lbs.
Energy: 51.5 gal.(beef) + 22 gallons (pork) + 15 gallons (poultry) = 88.5 gallons gas

Subtract beef and average American meat consumption requires:

Water: 30,989 (pork) + 32,285 (chicken) = 63,274 gallons of water
Grain: 172 lbs. (pork) + 117 lbs. (chicken) = 289 lbs. of grain
Topsoil: 733 lbs. (pork) + 528 lbs. (chicken) = 1261 lbs. of topsoil
Energy: 22 gallons (pork) + 15 gallons (chicken) = 37 gallons gas

Total savings of resources for one-year beefless diet:
Savings: water = 158,292 - 63,274 = 95018 gallons
Savings grain = 701 lbs. - 289 lbs. = 412 lbs.

Appendix 10 - Chapter 12 Beefless Diet Calculations

Savings topsoil = 3064 lbs. – 1261 lbs. = 1803 lbs.
Savings = 88.5 gallons gas – 37 gallons gas = 51.5 gallons gas

The significance here is that the elimination of beef reduces the amount of each consumption type (water, grain, topsoil, energy) by more than one half the value that included beef. Consider this—the elimination of beef from the scenario in this example allows just one individual to reduce their effective consumption of water, grain, topsoil and energy by more than half—the water, grain, topsoil and energy consumed with beef as part of the diet, meaning one could continue this diet for 2 years and 4 months years before consuming the total sum of water, grain, topsoil and energy needed to support equivalent energy—just imagine if just 1% of Americans could change over to this diet or the equivalent…the savings would exceed: 300 billion gallons of water; 1.331 million lbs. of grain; 5.826 million lbs. of topsoil; 166,000 gallons of gasoline equivalent energy.

Chapter 1 - The Essence of Life: Sources

[1]*The Water Cycle*, The USGS Water Science School, U.S. Department of the Interior, U.S. Geological Survey, https://water.usgs.gov/edu/watercyclesummary.html

[2]Yong, Ed, *The World's Oldest Fossils Are 3.7 Billion Years Old*, The Atlantic, Aug 31, 2016, retrieved 1.14.2019, https://www.theatlantic.com/science/archive/2016/08/the-worlds-oldest-fossils-are-37-billion-years-old/498056/

[3]*Stromatolites: The Oldest Fossils*, fossilmuseum.com, retrieved 1.17.2019, http://www.fossilmuseum.net/Tree_of_Life/Stromatolites.htm

[4]*Plants Don't Convert CO2 into O2*, howplantswork.com, 2009, Retrieved 1.15.2019, https://www.howplantswork.com/2009/02/16/plants-dont-convert-co2-into-o2/

[5]Sarmiento, Esteban, G.J. Sawyer, Richard Milner, *The Last Human*, A Guide to Twenty-Two Species of Extinct Humans, 2007, Yale University Press, 2007, chapter: *The Earliest Hominids*.

[6]*How and When Did Humans Discover Fire?* American Conference on Science and Health, https://www.acsh.org/news/2016/07/23/how-and-when-did-humans-discover-fire

[7]Sarmiento, Esteban, G.J. Sawyer, Richard Milner, *The Last Human*, A Guide to Twenty-Two Species of Extinct Humans, 2007, chapter: "Then There Was One", Yale University Press, 2007.

[8]Hogenboom, Melissa, *We Did Not Invent Clothes Just to Stay Warm*, BBC Earth, September 19, 2016, Retrieved 1.15.2019, http://www.bbc.com/earth/story/20160919-the-real-origin-of-clothes

[9]Harvard University, *Archaeologists Discover Oldest-known Fiber Materials Used By Early Humans*. ScienceDaily, 11 September 2009. http://www.sciencedaily.com/releases/2009/09/090910142352.htm

[10]Balfet, Helene J., *Basketry*, Encyclopedia Britannica, 2019, Retrieved 1.15.2019, https://www.britannica.com/art/basketry

[11]Pain, Stephanie, *Arrow points to foul play in ancient iceman's death*, New Scientist, Daily news, 26 July 26, 2001, Retrieved 1.15.2019, https://www.newscientist.com/article/dn1080-arrow-points-to-foul-play-in-ancient-icemans-death/

[12]Belluckjune, Pam, *This Shoe Had Prada Beat by 5,500 Years*, June 9, 2010, Retrieved 1.16.2019, https://www.nytimes.com/2010/06/10/science/10shoe.html

[13]*Ancient Greece Shoes and Footwear*, Ancient Greece Facts.com

History & Facts about Ancient Greece, 2019, Retrieved 1.16.2019,
http://www.ancientgreecefacts.com/greek-shoes/
[14]Gascoigne, Bamber, History World, from 2001, ongoing, retrieved
1.16.2019. *Hunter-gatherers to Farmers, Doing what comes naturally.*
http://www.historyworld.net/wrldhis/PlainTextHistories.asp?Para-
graphID=ayh
[15]Stadtmiller, Joseph, *The Nature of Life & Humanity*, Chapter 1, pages 16-
23, Kindle Direct Publishing, 2016.

Chapter 2 - Domestication & Subjugation: Sources

[1]Kline, Katie, *The story of the fig and its wasp*, ESA Ecological Society of
America, May 20, 2011, retrieved 1.22.2019,
https://www.esa.org/esablog/research/the-story-of-the-fig-and-its-wasp/
[2]Hirst, K. Kris, *Wheat Domestication, The History and Origins of Bread and
Durum Wheat*, ThoughtCo. , April 17, 2018, retrieved 1.22.2019,
https://www.thoughtco.com/wheat-domestication-the-history-170669
[3]Hirst, K. Kris, *The Domestication and History of Modern Horses*,
ThoughtCo. , Sept. 1, 2018, retrieved 1.22.2019,
https://www.thoughtco.com/horse-history-domestication-170662
[4]Hecht, Jeff, *Donkey domestication began in Africa*, New Scientist, The Daily
Newsletter, June 17, 2004, retrieved 1.22.2019,
https://www.newscientist.com/article/dn6032-donkey-domestication-be-
gan-in-africa/
[5]Meyer, Amelia, *Domestication and Use of Elephants*, Elephants Forever
2015, retrieved 1.23.2019,
https://www.elephantsforever.co.za/elephant-domestication.html
[6]Vann Jones, Kerstin. *What secrets lie within the camel's hump?* Sweden:
Lund University. Archived from the original May, 23 2009, retrieved 7
January 2008, *www.djur.cob.lu.se/Djurartiklar/Kamel.html*
[7]Wheeler, Jane C., Journal of Camelid Science 2012, *South American came-
lids past, present and future*, 2012, retrieved 1.23.2019,
http://www.isocard.net/images/journal//FILE486198178b052d8.pdf
[8]Red junglefowl (Gallus Gallus), Archive.org, retrieved 1.23.2019,
https://www.thoughtco.com/the-domestication-history-of-chickens-
170653
[9]Barber, E.J.W., *Prehistoric Textiles: The Development of Cloth in the Neolithic
and Bronze Ages*, Princeton Univ. Press 1991, pages 30-32.
[10]Micu, Alexandru, "How the Copper Age changed humanity", March

21, 2017, https://www.zmescience.com/science/copper-age-23234234/

[11]*Bronze Age,* History.com, retrieved 1.23.2019,
https://www.history.com/topics/pre-history/bronze-age

[12]*Iron Age,* History.com, retrieved 1.23.2019,
https://www.history.com/topics/pre-history/iron-age

[13]*Medieval Warfare,* retrieved 1.23.2019,
http://www.medievalwarfare.info/

[14]Castelow, Ellen, *The Longbow,* retrieved 1.23.2019,
 https://www.historic-uk.com/HistoryUK/HistoryofEngland/The-Long-bow/

[15]*The Crossbow — A Medieval Doomsday Device?* Editor, Military History Now, May 23, 2012, retrieved 1.23.2019,
https://militaryhistorynow.com/2012/05/23/the-crossbow-a-medieval-wmd/

[16]*Pike Weapons, Medieval Chronicles,* retrieved 1.23.2019,
http://www.medievalchronicles.com/medieval-weapons/pike-weapons/

[17]*Warfare in the Middle Ages,* Global Security.org, retrieved 1.23.2019,
https://www.globalsecurity.org/military/world/war/warfare-medie-val.htm

[18]Bellis, Mary, *Abraham Darby and the Iron Revolution.* ThoughtCo., Feb. 19,2019.
https://www.thoughtco.com/abraham-darby-1991324 retrieved 1.23.2019

[19]*The Iron Bridge* (1779) Shropshire, England, Bridges of Dublin 2019, retrieved 1.23.2019,
http://www.bridgesofdublin.ie/bridge-building/famous-bridges/the-iron-bridge-1779

[20]*Henry Cort, English manufacturer,* Encyclopedia Britannica updated: Jan 1, 2019, retrieved 1.23.2019,
https://www.britannica.com/biography/Henry-Cort

[21]Cartwright, Mark, *Siege Warfare in Medieval Europe,* Ancient History Encyclopedia, May 24, 2018, retrieved 1.23.2019,
https://www.ancient.eu/article/1230/siege-warfare-in-medieval-europe/

Chapter 3 - Painted Words: Sources

[1]Howard, Brian Clark, *Iran's Centuries-Old Windmills May Soon Stop Turning*, January 13, 2017, retrieved 1.24.2019, https://news.nationalgeographic.com/2017/01/nashtifan-iran-windmills/

[2]Vance, James E., *History of ships*, Encyclopedia Britannica, retrieved 1.24.2019, https://www.britannica.com/technology/ship/History-of-ships

[3]*History of U.S. Wind Energy*, Office of Energy Efficiency & Renewable Energy, retrieved 1.24.2019, https://www.energy.gov/eere/wind/history-us-wind-energy

[4]Andrade, Tonio, 2016,*The Gunpowder Age: China, Military Innovation, and the Rise of the West in World History*, Princeton University Press, ISBN 978-0-691-13597-7, page 15.

[5]Ibid, p. 40.

[6]*Alexander John Forsyth*, Undiscovered Scotland, retrieved 1.24.2019, https://www.undiscoveredscotland.co.uk/usbiography/f/alexanderjohn-forsyth.html

[7]Bellis, Mary, *Johannes Gutenberg and His Revolutionary Printing Press*, 1.21.2019, retrieved 1.25.2019, https://www.thoughtco.com/johannes-gutenberg-and-the-printing-press-1991865

[8]Roe, Joseph Wickham, *English and American Tool Builders*, New Haven: Yale University Press, 1916, Chapter 1.

[9]A. Jones, A. and E. N. Simons, *Story of the Saw*, Spear & Jackson Limited, retrieved 1.25.2019, pages 12-19, http://toolemera.com/bkpdf/Story%20of%20the%20Saw(2).pdf

[10]Ibid, pages 23-27.

[11]King, Adam, Univ. of South Carolina, Columbia, *Mississippian Period: Overview*, 10/03/2002, last edited by New Georgian Encyclopedia Staff on 06/08/2017, retrieved 1.26.2019, https://www.georgiaencyclopedia.org/articles/history-archaeology/mississippian-period-overview

[12]Hudson, Charles M. (1997), *Knights of Spain, Warriors of the Sun: Hernando de Soto and the South's Ancient Chiefdoms*, University of Georgia Press, ISBN 978-0-8203-5290-9.

[13]Decker, Kris De, *Hand powered drilling tools and machines*, Low-Tech Magazine: Doubts on progress and technology, December 15, 2010, retrieved 1.25.2019 https://www.lowtechmagazine.com/2010/12/hand-powered-drilling-

tools-and-machines.html

[14] Heffernan, Tim, *This Is America's Last Steam Powered Sawmill*, Mechanics Illustrated, Feb. 20, 2013, Retrieved 4.10.2019, https://www.popular-mechanics.com/home/g1093/this-is-americas-last-steam-powered-sawmill/

Chapter 4 - Wooden Ships: Sources

[1]*Examples of Fossil Fuels: History and Applications*, greenandgrowing.org, 2018, Retrieved 4.16.2019,
https://www.greenandgrowing.org/examples-fossil-fuels/
[2]*Pliny the Elder, Pliny's Natural History*, 77-79.
[3]*A Brief History of the Age of Exploration*, ThoughtCo.com, 2019, Retrieved 4.18.2019, https://www.thoughtco.com/age-of-exploration-1435006
[4]*Szczepanski, Kallie, Zheng He, Ming China's Great Admiral, History and Culture*, ThoughtCo.com, July 16, 2017, retrieved 1.30.2019,
https://www.thoughtco.com/zheng-he-ming-chinas-great-admiral-195236
[5]Hocker, Fred & McManamon, John M., *Mediaeval Shipbuilding in the Mediterranean and Written Culture at Venice*, Mediterranean Historical Review, 21: 1-37, 10.1080/09518960600682174.
[6]History World, *World trade: from the 1st to 15th century AD*, Retrieved 10.6.2019,
http://www.historyworld.net/wrldhis/PlainTextHistories.asp?ParagraphID=gpy
[7]Wilde, Robert, *Coal in the Industrial Revolution*, January 18, 2018, retrieved 1.31.2019,
https://www.thoughtco.com/coal-in-the-industrial-revolution-1221634
[8]Freese, Barbara, *Coal: A Human History*, Penguin Books 2004, Chapter 3, ISBN 9780142000984.
[9]*The Darby Family, Quakers in the World*,
http://www.quakersintheworld.org/quakers-in-action/271
[10]Smil, Vaclav, *Energy and Civilization, A History*, MIT Press, Chapter 5: pages 228-235, ISBN: 9780262035774.
[11]Horn, Jeff; Rosenband, Leonard; Smith, Merritt (2010), *Reconceptualizing the Industrial Revolution*, Cambridge MA, USA, London: MIT Press, pages 65-87.
[12]*Primary energy statistics*, The Shift Project Data Portal, 2019, Retrieved 4.18.2019,

http://www.tsp-data-portal.org/Breakdown-of-Electricity-Generation-by-Energy-Source#tspQvChart

[13]Lucas, Robert E., Jr. (2002), *Lectures on Economic Growth*, Cambridge: Harvard University Press. pp. 109–10.

[14]Roderick Floud and Paul Johnson, January15, 2004, *Review of The Cambridge Economic History of Modern Britain*, Times Higher Education Supplement, http://deirdremccloskey.org/articles/floud.php

[15]Belford, Paul, *Hot Blast Iron Smelting in the Early 19th Century*, Historical Metallurgy 2012, Historical Metallurgy Society, 46 (1): pg. 32–44.

[16]Roe, Joseph Wickam (1916), *English and American Tool Builders*, New Haven: Yale University Press, London: Humphrey Milford, Oxford University Press, MDCCCCXVI, Chapters IX and X.

[17]Hopley, Claire, *A History Of The British Cotton Industry*, July 29, 2006, Retrieved 4.19.2019, https://britishheritage.com/british-textiles-clothe-the-world/

[18]Gupta, Bishnupriya, Cotton Textiles and the Great Divergence: Lancanshire, India and Shifting Competitive Advantage, 1600-1850 (PDF), *International Institute of Social History*, Department of Economics, University of Warwick.

[19]Smil, Vaclav, *Energy and Civilization, A History*. MIT Press (2017), Chapter 5, pages 237-240.

[20]*The Industrial Revolution (1750–1900) Chemicals*, Encyclopaedia Britannica, 2019, Retrieved 4.19.2019, https://www.britannica.com/technology/history-of-technology/The-Industrial-Revolution-1750-1900

[21]Bellis, Mary, *The History of Concrete and Cement*, March 06, 2019, Retrieved 4.19.2019, https://www.thoughtco.com/history-of-concrete-and-cement-1991653

[22]Kennedy, Maev (2015-12-25) *Light brigade: carrying the torch for London's last gas street lamps*, The Guardian, Archived from the original on December 25, 2015, Retrieved 4.19.2019, https://www.theguardian.com/culture/2015/dec/25/londons-last-gas-street-lamps

[23]Chance Brothers & Company, *Grace's Guide to British Industrial History*, 2019, Retrieved 4.18.2019, https://www.gracesguide.co.uk/Chance_Brothers_and_Co

[24]Nicholas-Louis Robert (1761–1828): *Papermaking machine*, Retrieved 4.19.2019, https://multimediaman.wordpress.com/2016/04/24/nicholas-louis-robert-

1761-1828-papermaking-machine/
[25]Jones, Alan, *A Brief History of The Plough*, Retrieved 4.19.2019,
http://www.ploughmen.co.uk/about-us/history-of-the-plough
[26]*Andrew Meikle Scottish inventor*, The Editors of Encyclopaedia Britannica, Jan. 1, 2019, Retrieved 4.18.2019,
https://www.britannica.com/biography/Andrew-Meikle
[27]*British workers strike for better wages and political reform (The Plug Plot Riots)*, 1842, Global Nonviolent Action Database, Retrieved 2.2.2019,
https://nvdatabase.swarthmore.edu/content/british-workers-strike-better-wages-and-political-reform-plug-plot-riots-1842
[28]Wilde, Robert, *Coal Mining in the UK during the Industrial Revolution*, Updated Dec. 27, 2018, retrieved 2.2.2019,
https://www.thoughtco.com/coal-mining-conditions-in-industrial-revolution-1221633
[29]Johnson, Ben, *The Manchester Ship Canal*, Retrieved 4.20.2019,
https://www.historic-uk.com/HistoryMagazine/DestinationsUK/The-Manchester-Ship-Canal/
[30]Wilde, Robert, Updated February 19, 2018, Retrieved 4.20.2019,
Population Growth and Movement in the Industrial Revolution,
ThoughtCo.com,
https://www.thoughtco.com/population-growth-and-movement-industrial-revolution-1221640
[31]History of Air Pollution, Retrieved 4.20.2019,
http://www.enviropedia.org.uk/Air_Quality/History.php
[32]Air Pollution in Victorian-era Britain, November 14, 2017, Retrieved 4.20.2019,
http://theconversation.com/air-pollution-in-victorian-erabritain-its-effects-on-health-now-revealed-87208

Chapter 5 – Eternal Combustion: Sources
[1]Stadtmiller, Joseph. *The Nature of Life and Humanity*, Second Edition, 2017, 107-109.
[2]*Territorial Expansion of the United States: 1783-1853*. Mapping History University of Oregon,
http://mappinghistory.uoregon.edu/english/US/US09-01.html
[3]Engelman, Ryan, *The Second Industrial Revolution, 1870-1914.*
http://ushistoryscene.com/article/second-industrial-revolution/
[4]Finch, Roy G. State Engineer and Surveyor. *The Story of the New York State Canals*, http://www.canals.ny.gov/history/finch_history.pdf

[5]*River Towns, River Networks*. On the Water, Smithsonian National Museum of American History.
http://americanhistory.si.edu/onthewater/exhibition/4_4.html

[6]Blakemore, Erin. *Native Americans Have General Sherman to Thank for Their Exile to Reservations*. Nov. 13, 2017.
https://www.history.com/news/shermans-war-on-native-americans

[7]Mokyr, Joel and Robert H. Strotz. *The Second Industrial Revolution 1870-1914*. Professor of Arts and Sciences and Professor of Economics and History, Northwestern University 2003.

[8]*History of Oil Lamps*. History of Lamps 2019.
http://www.historyoflamps.com/lamp-history/history-of-oil-lamps/

[9]*A Brief History of Lubrication*, 2019 Isel: Technology.
https://iselinc.com/technology/brief-history-lubrication/

[10]McKithan, Cecil. (March 1978). *Drake Oil Well* (PDF). National Register of Historic Places Inventory—Nomination Form, Pennsylvania Historical and Museum Commission.
http://www.dot7.state.pa.us/CRGIS_Attachments/SiteResource/H001206_01H.pdf

[11]Wise, David Burgess. *Lenoir: The Motoring Pioneer*. The World of Automobiles, p.1181-2. London: Orbis Publishing, 1974.

[12]Scientific American: page 193, 1860-09-22

[13]*Jean-Joseph Étienne Lenoir*, The Motor Museum in Miniature, MMIM Hall of Fame, Retrieved 2.6.2019,
http://www.themotormuseuminminiature.co.uk/inv-jeanjoseph-etienne-lenoir.php

[14] Ayers, Robert. *Technological Transformations and Long Waves*. PDF, Chapter 4.5 pages 30-32,
http://pure.iiasa.ac.at/id/eprint/3225/1/RR-89-001.pdf

[15]*The Development of the Pennsylvania Oil Industry*. American Chemical Society: August 26-27, 2009.
https://www.acs.org/content/dam/acsorg/education/whatischemistry/landmarks/pennsylvaniaoilindustry/pennsylvania-oil-industry-historical-resource.pdf

[16]*The Three Stages of Refining"*, Planete-Energies, Jan. 6, 2015.
https://www.planete-energies.com/en/medias/close/three-stages-refining

[17]*11 World's Largest Oil Refineries by Processing Capacity*. ListNBest 2019,
https://www.listnbest.com/11-worlds-largest-oil-refineries-processing-capacity/2/

[18]Crouch, Tom D. *The Bishop's Boys: A Life of Wilbur and Orville Wright*,

New York: W. W. Norton & Company, 2003, page 228.

[19]Jakab, Peter L. *Visions of a Flying Machine: The Wright Brothers and the Process of Invention.* page 156. Smithsonian History of Aviation and Spaceflight Series, Washington, D.C.: Smithsonian, 1997.

[20]*Inventing a Flying Machine –The Breakthrough Concept, The Wright Brothers and the Invention of the Aerial Age.* Smithsonian Institution, Archived from the original January 17, 2015, Retrieved March 5, 2013.

[21]*Wright Brothers History Wing-The Wright Story-Inventing the Airplane,* wright-brothers.org, Archived from the original on October 21, 2014. http://www.wright-brothers.org/History_Wing/History_Intro/History_Intro.htm

[22] Ayers, Robert, *Technological Transformations and Long Waves*, PDF, Chapter 4.6-4.11. http://pure.iiasa.ac.at/id/eprint/3225/1/RR-89-001.pdf

[23]Bellis, Mary. *Biography of Henry Ford*. August 15, 2018. https://www.thoughtco.com/henry-ford-biography-1991814

[24]Keegan, John *(1998)*. *The First World War. Hutchinson, Page 8.*

[25]Willmott, H.P. (2003). *World War I*, New York: Dorling Kindersley, Pages 10-11,307.

[26]Billings, Molly, *The Influenza Pandemic of 1918*, June, 1997 modified RDS February, 2005. https://virus.stanford.edu/uda/

[27]*Stock Market Crashes, This Day in History 1929*, History.com Staff. https://www.history.com/this-day-in-history/stock-market-crashes

[28]Clemens, Peter, *Prosperity, Depression and the New Deal: The USA 1890– 1954*, Hodder Education, 4. Auflage, 2008, ISBN 978-0-340-965887, p. 114.

[29]Morris, Charles R, *A Rabble of Dead Money: The Great Crash and the Global Depression*: 1929–1939 (Public Affairs, 2017).

[30]*Smoot-Hawley Tariff Act*. the Editors of Encyclopaedia Britannica, United States 1930. https://www.britannica.com/topic/Smoot-Hawley-Tariff-Act

[31]*Dust Bowl*, HISTORY, History.com editors. October 27, 2009, Updated Jan. 29, 2019. https://www.history.com/topics/great-depression/dust-bowl

[32]Alchin, Linda, *Social Effects of the Great Depression*, Part 2. American Historama 2017 Siteseen Limited Updated 2018-01-09. http://www.american-historama.org/1929-1945-depression-ww2-era/social-effects-of-great%20depression-part-two.htm

[33]*The Great Depression and World War II*. The Smithsonian, The National Museum of American History.

http://americanhistory.si.edu/treasures/depression-wwii

Chapter 6 - The Golden Age of Advertising: Sources

[1]*American Advertising A Brief Story*, History Matters, http://historymatters.gmu.edu/mse/ads/amadv.html

[2]Goodman, Matthew. The Sun and the Moon: The Remarkable True Account of Hoaxers, Showmen, Dueling Journalists, and Lunar Man-Bats in Nineteenth-Century. Basic Books: A member of Perseus Books Group New York, 2008. Part 2, Chapter 9.

[3]Hower, Ralph. The History of an Advertising Agency: N. W. Ayer & Son 1869-1949. 1949 page 185.

[4]Pope, Daniel. The Making of Modern Advertising. Basic Books, First Edition April 20, 1983) pages 42-46.

[5]Tolliday, Steven & Jonathan Zeitlin. The Automobile Industry and its Workers: Between Fordism and Flexibility. St. Martin's Press (New York: 1987) pages 1–2.

[6]Henry Ford and Innovation, From the Curators. Chapter 2, The Model-T and the Assembly Line, pages 4-7. https://www.thehenryford.org/docs/default-source/default-document-library/default-document-library/henryfordandinnovation.pdf?sfvrsn=0

[7]Ibid. pages 8-10

[8]Ford's Assembly Line Turns 100: How It Changed Manufacturing and Society. New York Daily News, October 7, 2013. Archived from the original on November 30, 2013. Retrieved August 27, 2017. https://www.nydailynews.com/autos/ford-assembly-line-turns-100-changed-society-article-1.1478331

[9]Marx, Karl. Comment on James Mill, Economic and Philosophical Manuscripts of 1844: 1844.

[10]Hopkins, Claude C. My Life in Advertising. Harper & Brothers Publishers. New York and London 1927, page 38-46.

[11]Hopkins, Claude C. Scientific Advertising. Carl Galletti, Phoenix, AZ.

[12]Monroe, Harry and Rich Kleinfledt. Narrators of U.S. History, American History: Life in the U.S. After World War Two. December 28, 2006 http://www.manythings.org/voa/history/197.html

[13]The Postwar Economy: 1945-1960, U.S. Department of State. https://www.exploros.com/summary/The-Post-War-Economy-1945-1960

[14]Young, William H. The 1950s - American Popular Culture Through History. 2004, Greenwood Press, ISBN13: 978-0313323935, pages 39-60.

[15]Oakley, J. Ronald. God's Country: America in the Fifties, New York: W.W. Norton, 1986, page 239.

[16] Scott, Kaitlin, History of Advertising, 1950s. https://mascola.com/insights/history-of-advertising-1950s/

[17]The Ethical Nag. https://ethicalnag.org/2013/11/03/vintage-ads-cigarettes/

[18]Blinder, Alan S. The Anatomy of Double-Digit Inflation in the 1970s. Chapter 12 Pages 261-282.

[19]Scott, Kaitlin, *History of Advertising*, 1970s. http://adage.com/article/adage-encyclopedia/history-1970s

[20]Ibid

[21]Scott, Kaitlin, *History of Advertising*, 1980s. http://adage.com/article/adage-encyclopedia/history-1980s

[22]Technology Has Changed Advertising Forever. Huffington Post. https://www.huffpost.com/entry/technology-has-changed-advertising-forever_b_599c64d4e4b09dbe86ea3764

Chapter 7 – Rise of Consumerism: Sources

[1]Engelman, Ryan. *The Second Industrial Revolution, 1870-1914.* http://ushistoryscene.com/article/second-industrial-revolution/

[2]Zimbalist, Sherman and Brown, Andrew, Howard J. and Stuart. *Comparing Economic Systems: A Political-Economic Approach*. October 1988, Harcourt College Pub., pages 6–7, ISBN 978-0-15-512403-5.

[3]Adams, James Truslow. *The American Dream, 1931, The Epic of America*, page 404.

[4]Bradford, William. *Bradford's History of the Plymouth Settlement, 1608-1650*. Rendered into modern English by Harold Paget, E.P. Dutton & Company, 1920, page 21.

[5]Boorstin, Daniel, historian. *Credit History: The Evolution of Consumer Credit in America*. PDF, pages 1-7.

[6]Calder, Lendol. *Financing the American Dream*. Princeton University Press 1999. Chapter 1.

[7]MacDonald, Jay and Taylor Tompkins. *The History of Credit Cards*. July 11, 2017. Creditcards.com. https://www.creditcards.com/credit-card-news/history-of-credit-cards.php

[8]Anami, Haruya. *Thirteen Days' Thirty Years After: Robert Kennedy and the Cuban Missile Crisis Revisited*. Journal of American & Canadian Studies

(1994) Issue 12, pages 69-88.

[9]Harrington, Michael, *The Other America,* Simon and Schuster, 1997.

[10]*Lyndon Johnson.* History.com.
https://www.history.com/topics/us-presidents/lyndon-b-johnson

[11]Merikle, Phillip. *Subliminal Advertising.* Department of Psychology, University of Waterloo.
https://www.psychologistworld.com/influence-personality/subliminal-advertising.

[12]Joseph, Chris. *Types of Stereotyping in Advertising.*
http://smallbusiness.chron.com/types-stereotyping-advertising-11937.html

[13]Stadtmiller, Joseph. *The Nature of Life and Humanity,* 2017. Chapter 8, pages 167-175.

[14]Our World in Data. *World Population Growth,* 1750-2015 and projections until 2100.
https://ourworldindata.org/wp-content/uploads/2013/05/updated-World-Population-Growth-1750-2100.png

[15]Shah, Anup. *Stress on the environment, society and resources?* 2001.
http://www.globalissues.org/article/214/stress-on-the-environment-society-and-resources

[16]Jackson, Tim. *Prosperity without Growth: Economics for a Finite Planet,* Earthscan Dunstan House, Copyright 2009, ISBN: 978-1-84407-894-3 eISBN: 978-1-84977-000-2.

Chapter 8 - The Promise of Polymers: Sources

[1]Freudenrich, Craig Ph.D. *How Plastics Work.*
https://science.howstuffworks.com/plastic.htm

[2]*The History of Plastics,* PPC Polymer Plastics Company.
https://polymerplastics.com/history_plastics.shtml

[3]*The Difference Between Thermoplastic and Thermosetting Plastic.* Osborne Industries, May 15, 2017.
https://www.osborneindustries.com/news/difference-between-thermoplastic-thermosetting-plastic//

[4]*Resin Identification Code.* Wikipedia.
https://en.wikipedia.org/wiki/Resin_identification_code

[5]Beaudry, Frederic. *Recycling Different Plastics. Updated January 16, 2019.*
https://www.thoughtco.com/recycling-different-types-of-plastic-1203667

[6]The Association of Plastic Recyclers, PVC (Polyvinyl Chloride, Resin Identification Code #3). *Plastics Recycling.*

https://www.plasticsrecycling.org/pvc

[7]*San Jose Recycles*, Plastic #4 (LDPE).
https://sanjoserecycles.org/guide/4-plastic-ldpe/

[8]LeBlanc, Rick. *An Overview of Polypropylene Recycling*. The Balance Small Business. Updated July 31, 2017.
https://www.thebalancesmb.com/an-overview-of-polypropylene-recycling-2877863

[9]McTigue-Pierce, Lisa. *Sustainable Packaging P&G's PureCycle cleans recycled PP to 'near virgin' quality*. Sustainable Packaging April 18, 2018, Packaging Digest.
http://www.packagingdigest.com/sustainable-packaging/pgs-purecycle-cleans-recycled-polypropylene-to-near-virgin-quality-2018-04-18

[10]*Green Styrene: Recycling, Energy Recovery & Disposal*. 2019. YouKnowStyrene.org.
https://youknowstyrene.org/green-styrene/recycling/

[11]*AZoM, AS Resin/Styrene Acrylonitrile /SAN (C8H8)n-(C3H3N)m Plastic Recycling*. AZO Materials. Dec. 10, 2012. https://www.azom.com/article.aspx?ArticleID=7959

[12]Rogers, Tony, *Everything You Need to Know About ABS Plastic*, Creative Mechanisms. July 13, 2015.
https://www.creativemechanisms.com/blog/everything-you-need-to-know-about-abs-plastic

[13]*Everything You Need to Know About Bioplastics*. Creative Mechanisms Staff. Dec. 21, 2016.
https://www.creativemechanisms.com/blog/everything-you-need-to-know-about-bioplastics

[14]*Compostable Plastics*. worldcentric.org. 2019.
http://www.worldcentric.org/biocompostables/bioplastics

[15]Biello, David. *Plastic (Not) Fantastic: Food Containers Leach a Potentially Harmful Chemical*. Scientific American, February 18, 2008.
https://www.scientificamerican.com/article/plastic-not-fantastic-with-bisphenol-a/

[16]Hamilton, Jon. *Most Plastics Leach Hormone-Like Chemicals*. March 2, 2011. NPR All Things Considered.
https://www.npr.org/2011/03/02/134196209/study-most-plastics-leach-hormone-like-chemicals

[17]Adams, Mike. *Six Baby Bottle Manufacturers Quietly Agree to Remove Bisphenol-A (BPA) from Baby Bottles*. March 9, 2009. Nature News.
https://www.naturalnews.com/025804_BPA_Baby_Bottles.html

[18]*Bisphenol A: EU ban on baby bottles to enter into force tomorrow.* European Commission Press Release, Brussels. May 31, 2011.

[19]*The European Union Proposes Further Restrictions on BPA Use,* PackagingLaw.com. September 18, 2017.
www.packaginglaw.com/news/european-union-proposes-further-restrictions-bpa-use

[20]*The U.S. Food and Drug Administration States Its Position on BPA.* Fit Pregnancy. Com, July 31, 2007.

[21]*Bisphenol A (BPA): Use in Food Contact Application.* U.S. FDA updated November 2014.
https://www.fda.gov/NewsEvents/PublicHealth-
Focus/ucm064437.htm#summary/

[22]Bodamer, David. *14 Charts from the EPA's Latest MSW Estimates.* Waste360.com, Nov 16, 2016.
https://www.waste360.com/waste-reduction/14-charts-epa-s-latest-msw-
estimates

[23]Dell, Jan, Independent Engineer. *U.S. Plastic Recycling Rate Projected to Drop to 4.4% in 2018.* October 4, 2018. Plastic Pollution Coalition.
https://www.plasticpollutioncoalition.org/pft/2018/10/4/us-plastic-recy-
cling-rate-projected-to-drop-to-44-in-2018

Chapter 9 - Synthetic Sustenance: Sources

[1]Schouten, Henk J., Frans A. Krens, Evert Jacobsen. Cisgenic plants are similar to traditionally bred plants: International regulations for genetically modified organisms should be altered to exempt cisgenesis. EMBO Reports.
https://www.ncbi.nlm.nih.gov/pmc/articles/PMC1525145/

[2]FDA Approves 1st Genetically Engineered Product for Food, The Washington Post, March 24, 1990.
https://www.latimes.com/archives/la-xpm-1990-03-24-mn-681-story.html

[3]Ashswathi, P. Recombinant DNA Technology: Definition and History. Biology Discussion.com.
http://www.biologydiscussion.com/dna/recombinant-dna-technology-
definition-and-history-genetics/65418

[4]Bevan, M. W.; Flavell, R. B.; Chilton, M. D. (1983). A chimeric antibiotic resistance gene as a selectable marker for plant cell transformation. Nature volume 304, pages 184–187.
https://www.nature.com/articles/304184a0 5Rachna, C. Difference Between Phenotype and Genotype

[5]Rachna, C. Difference Between Phenotype and Genotype. May 26, 2018 https://biodifferences.com/difference-between-phenotype-and-genotype.html

[6]Herbert Boyer (1936-) and Stanley N. Cohen (1935-) Develop recombinant DNA technology, showing that genetically engineered DNA molecules may be cloned in foreign cells. Genetic News Network, Genetics and Genomics Timeline 1973. http://www.genomenewsnetwork.org/resources/timeline/1973_Boyer.php

[7]Bevan, M. W.; Flavell, R. B.; Chilton, M. D. (1983). A chimeric antibiotic resistance gene as a selectable marker for plant cell transformation. Nature. 304 (5922): 184–87. Bib code:1983Natur.304.184B. doi:10.1038/304184a0. https://www.nature.com/articles/304184a0?error=cookies_not_supported&code=7c58794b-2d64-46ef-ac05-c3e4b6c9f957

[8]Tripathi, Savarni (2007). Development of Genetically Engineered Resistant Papaya for papaya ringspot virus in a Timely Manner. Methods in Molecular Biology. 354: 197–240. doi:10.1385/1-59259-966-4:197. ISBN 1-59259-966-4. PMID 17172756. https://link.springer.com/protocol/10.1385/1-59259-966-4:197

[9]Hanahan, Douglas, Erwin F. Wagner, Richard D. Palmiter. The origins of oncomice: a history of the first transgenic mice genetically engineered to develop cancer. CSH Press, Genes and Development. http://genesdev.cshlp.org/content/21/18/2258.full

[10]Ganzel, Bill. The Herbicide 2, 4-D, the Ganzel Group. 2009. https://livinghistoryfarm.org/farminginthe70s/pests_04.html

[11]A historical perspective on dicamba. Iowa State University, December 19, 2017. Extension and Outreach. https://crops.extension.iastate.edu/blog/bob-hartzler/historical-perspective-dicamba

[12]o-Anisic Acid, Chemicalland21.com, Retrieved 2.23.2019,-ANISIC ACD http://chemicalland21.com/specialtychem/finechem/o-ANISIC%20ACID.htm

[13]Butler, Ph.D. David A. Connections: The Early History of Scientific and Medical Research on "Agent Orange". 13 J.L.&Pol'y(2005). http://brooklynworks.brooklaw.edu/jlp/vol13/iss2/3

[14]Tu, Mandy, Hurd, Callie and Randall, John M., "Weed Control Methods Handbook: Tools and Techniques for Use in Natural Areas", The Nature Conservancy, Chapter 6 - General Properties of Herbicides.

https://www.invasive.org/gist/products/handbook/methods-hand-book.pdf

[15]Jhala, Amit, - Extension Weed Management Specialist, Pre-emergence Residual Herbicides are the Foundation of Soybean Weed Control, University of Nebraska–Lincoln, 3.29.2018,
https://cropwatch.unl.edu/2018/pre-emergence-residual-herbicides-are-foundation-soybean-weed-control

[16]Charles, Daniel, Lords of the Harvest: Biotech, Big Money, and the Future of Food, Pages 60 & 61.

[17]Ibid, Pages 67- 69.

[18] Colbert, Treacy. GMOs Pros and Cons. October 5, 2016.
https://www.healthline.com/health/gmos-pros-and-cons

[19]Ibid.

[20]Which genetically engineered crops and animals are approved in the US?
Genetic Literary Project.
https://gmo.geneticliteracyproject.org/FAQ/which-genetically-engineered-crops-are-approved-in-the-us/

[21]Pros and Cons of Genetically Modified Foods. Health Research Funding HRF.
https://healthresearchfunding.org/pros-cons-genetically-modified-foods/

[22]The Rise of Superweeds—and What to Do About It. The Union of Concerned Scientists. December 2013.
https://www.ucsusa.org/food_and_agriculture/our-failing-food-system/industrial-agriculture/the-rise-of-superweeds.html#, W366DvZFyP9.

[23]Bradley, Kevin. Dicamba Injury Reports 2018: Drift Issues Becoming More Evident. University of Missouri, Division of Plant Sciences. 2018.
https://agfaxweedsolutions.com/2018/06/21/dicamba-injury-reports-2018-drift-issues-becoming-more-evident/

[24]Gaud, William S. The Green Revolution: Accomplishments and Apprehensions. retrieved August 2018.
http://www.agbioworld.org/biotech-info/topics/borlaug/borlaug-green.html

[25]Charles, Daniel. In A Grain of Golden Rice, A World of Controversy Over GMO Foods. March 7, 2013.
https://www.npr.org/sections/thesalt/2013/03/07/173611461/in-a-grain-of-golden-rice-a-world-of-controversy-over-gmo-foods

[26]Ye X, Al-Babili S, Klöti A, Zhang J, Lucca P, Beyer P, Potrykus I (2000). Engineering the provitamin A (β-carotene) biosynthetic pathway into

(carotenoid-free) rice endosperm. Science 287:303-305. January 14, 2000.
http://www.goldenrice.org/PDFs/Ye_et_al_Science_2000.pdf

[27]Everding, Gerry. Genetically modified golden rice falls short on lifesaving promises. June 2, 2016. Washington University in St. Louis, June 2, 2016.
https://www.sciencedaily.com/releases/2016/06/160602220711.htm

[28]Lynas, Mark. The True Story About Who Destroyed a Genetically Modified Rice Crop. Slate Group, August 26, 2013.
https://slate.com/technology/2013/08/golden-rice-attack-in-philippines-anti-gmo-activists-lie-about-protest-and-safety.html

[29]Golden Rice, the Status. PhilRice, Philippine Department of Agriculture. International Rice Research Institute.
http://www.philrice.gov.ph/golden-rice/about-gr/#squelch-taas-accordion-shortcode-content-2

[30]13Vital Pros and Cons of GMOs. Vitana.org.
 8.23.2018, https://vittana.org/13-vital-pros-and-cons-of-gmos

[31]Big 6 Pesticide and GMO Corporations.
https://www.sourcewatch.org/index.php/%22Big_6%22_Pesticide_and_GMO_Corporations.

[32]Percentage of genetically modified crops in the U.S. in 1997 and 2018, by type (as percent of total acreage). Statistica.com 2018.
https://www.statista.com/statistics/217108/level-of-genetically-modified-crops-in-the-us/

[33]Trends in glyphosate herbicide use in the United States and globally. Environmental Sciences Europe. 2016.
https://www.ncbi.nlm.nih.gov/pmc/articles/PMC5044953/

[34]Summary, Global Status of Commercialized Biotech/GM Crops: 2013, Dedicated to the late Nobel Peace Laureate, Norman Borlaug, founding patron of ISAAA, on the centenary of his birth. March 25, 2014.
www.isaaa.org/resources/publications/briefs/46/executivesummary/

[35]Where are GMOs grown and banned? Genetic Literacy Project - Science not Ideology 2016.
https://gmo.geneticliteracyproject.org/FAQ/where-are-gmos-grown-and-banned/

[36]Freedman, David H. The Truth about Genetically Modified Food: Proponents of genetically modified crops say the technology is the only way to feed a warm-in, increasingly populous world, Critics say we tamper with nature at our peril. Who is right? September 1, 2013, Scientific American.

https://www.scientificamerican.com/article/the-truth-about-genetically-modified-food/

[37]Man Dying of Cancer Blames Monsanto's Roundup as Trial Opens. Editor Liberty Headlines. July 9, 2018.
https://www.libertyheadlines.com/man-dying-of-cancer-blames-monsantos-roundup-as-trial-opens/

[38]Gillam, Carey. One man's suffering exposed Monsanto's secrets to the world. August 11, 2018.
https://www.theguardian.com/business/2018/aug/11/one-mans-suffering-exposed-monsantos-secrets-to-the-world

[39]Papantonio, Mike. Monsanto's Big Horror Show: Roundup. August 28, 2018.
https://trofire.com/2018/08/28/monsantos-big-horror-show-roundup/

[40]Kirkpatrick, Noel. California man accepts $78 million award in Roundup law-suit. MNN.com. November 2, 2018.
https://www.mnn.com/family/protection-safety/stories/dying-man-monsanto-trial-roundup-cancer-risk

Chapter 10 - Mount Waste-More to Recovery & Salvation: Sources

[1]*Tons of waste dumped globally this year*. Theworldcounts.com.
http://www.theworldcounts.com/counters/shocking_environmental_facts_and_statistics/world_waste_facts

[2]*Black Death pandemic, medieval Europe*. Encyclopedia Britannica, Jan 17, 2019. https://www.britannica.com/event/Black-Death

[3]Cohen, Steven, Hayley Martinez and Alix Schroder, *Waste Management Practices in New York, Hong Kong and Beijing*. Dec. 2015 page 3.
http://www.columbia.edu/~sc32/documents/ALEP%20Waste%20Managent%20FINAL.pdf

[4]*A Complete Guide To Recycling History*. DTM-SKIPS & Concrete.
1.10.2017. https://www.dtmskips.co.uk/recycling-history/

[5]*History of the Garbage Man*. Garbage Man Day.org, 2018.
http://www.garbagemanday.org/history-of-the-garbage-man/

[6] Hickman Jr., H. Lanier and Richard W. Eldredge. *A Brief History of Solid Waste Management in the US during the Last 50 Years, Part 1*. April 15, 2016.
https://www.mswmanagement.com/landfills/article/13023338/a-brief-history-of-solid-waste-management-in-the-us-during-the-last-50-years-part-1

[7]Hickman Jr., H. Lanier. *A Brief History of Solid Waste Management in the US During the Last 50 Years, Part 2*. September 7, 2016.
https://www.mswmanagement.com/landfills/article/13025970/a-brief-history-of-solid-waste-mangement-in-the-us-during-the-last-50-years-part-2

[8]Ibid. Part 3. March 1, 2000.

[9]*The War Episode 2: Rationing and Recycling*. Public Broadcasting System (2007). https://www.pbs.org/video/war-rationing-and-recycling/

[10]*Why Not Recycle?!* The County of Santa Barbara, Resource Recovery & Waste Management Division. 2019.
http://lessismore.org/materials/28-why-recycle/

[11]*Advancing Sustainable Materials Management: 2015 Fact Sheet*. Environmental Protection Agency. Table 1. Generation, Recycling, Composting, Combustion with Energy Recovery and Landfilling of Materials in MSW, 2015.
https://www.epa.gov/sites/production/files/2018-07/documents/2015_smm_msw_factsheet_07242018_fnl_508_002.pdf

[12]*The Recycling Symbol and You*. Onondaga County Resource Recovery Agency (OCRRA).
http://sustainability.syr.edu/wp-content/uploads/2017/04/The-Recycling-Symbol-and-You-Feb-2009.pdf

[13]*A Brief History of Recycling*. 2018. AmericanDisposalServices.com. 2019.
https://www.americandisposal.com/blog/a-brief-history-of-recycling

[14]Miller, Chaz. *The Garbage Barge*. Waste 360. Feb 01, 2007
https://www.waste360.com/mag/waste_garbage_barge_recycling

[15]Granger, Trey. *What's Banned in Landfills: A State-by-State Guide*. Earth 911. November 27, 2017.
https://earth911.com/business-policy/landfill-bans/

[16]*Bottle Bill Resource Guide*. Container Recycling Institute, BottleBill.org. 2019.
http://www.bottlebill.org/index.php/current-and-proposed-laws/usa/additional-links

[17]*U.S. municipal solid waste generation from 1960 to 2015*. Statistica the Statistics Portal, 2018.
https://www.statista.com/statistics/186256/us-municipal-solid-waste-generation-since-1960/

[18]*Recovery of U.S. municipal solid waste for recycling from 1960 to 2015*. Statistica the Statistics Portal. 2018.
https://www.statista.com/statistics/193923/recycling-of-us-municipal-solid-waste-since-1960/

[19]*Gross recycling rate of bottles in the U.S. from 2000 to 2016*. Statistica, the Statistics Portal. 2018.
https://www.statista.com/statistics/207614/total-us-bottles-collected-since-2000/

[20]*U.S. municipal solid waste generation and discards from 1960 to 2015*. Statistica the Statistics Portal. 2018.
https://www.statista.com/statistics/219791/us-municipal-solid-waste-generation-and-discards/

[21]*Tons of waste dumped globally this year*. The World Counts-World Waste Facts.
http://www.theworldcounts.com/counters/shocking_environmental_facts_and_statistics/world_waste_facts

[22]*Which Countries are Recycling Leaders?* Planet Aid.org. March 13, 2016.
http://www.planetaid.org/blog/global-recycling-rates

[23]Hoornweg, Daniel and Perinaz Bhada-Tata, *What a Waste*. A Global Review of Solid Waste Management, Chapter 3 Table 4, World Bank, Urban Development Series – Knowledge Papers , March 2012, No. 15.

[24]*Toxicity of Plastics*, Blastic EU, 11.14.2018,
https://www.blastic.eu/knowledge-bank/impacts/toxicity-plastics/

[25]"State Plastic and Paper Bag Legislation", NCSL-National Conference of State Legislatures, 2/27/2019, Retrieved 3.4.2019,
http://www.ncsl.org/research/environment-and-natural-resources/plastic-bag-legislation.aspx#Bans

[26]Mason, Jessica, "Barring Plastic Bag Bans, another ALEC Law Takes Aim at Local Democracy", March 16, 2016, Retrieved 11.16.2018,
https://www.prwatch.org/news/2016/03/13060/barring-plastic-bag-bans-another-alec-bill-takes-aim-local-democracy

[27]"What Is Used to Make Styrofoam?", Reference.com 2019, Retrieved 3.3.2019,
https://www.reference.com/science/used-make-styrofoam-65f6ebc9703ddbd1

[28]"Mayor de Blasio Announces Ban On Single-use Styrofoam Products In New York City Will Be In Effect Beginning 2019", NYC-The Official Website of the City of New York, June 13, 2018, Retrieved 11.16.2018,
https://www1.nyc.gov/office-of-the-mayor/news/295-18/mayor-de-

blasio-ban-single-use-styrofoam-products-new-york-city-will-be-effect
[29]"Managing and Transforming Waste Streams – A Tool for Communities", How Communities Have Defined Zero Waste, Environmental Protection Agency (EPA), November 24. 2017, Retrieved 11.18.2018, https://www.epa.gov/transforming-waste-tool/how-communities-have-defined-zero-waste
[30]"Road To Zero Waste Plan" Zero Waste Associates, December 2013, Retrieved 11.18.2018,
Prepared by: Zero Waste Associates
https://www.fcgov.com/recycling/pdf/RoadtoZeroWasteReport_FINAL.pdf
[31]Videos for Oneida Herkimer Solid Waste Authority, 2019.
https://www.ohswa.org/recycle/our-facilities/recycling-center
[32] Oneida Herkimer Solid Waste Facility Reaches One Million Tons Recycled. July 2019.
https://www.ohswa.org/news/oneida-herkimer-solid-waste-authority-reaches-1-million-tons-recycled/

Chapter 11 Utilities of Consumption: Sources

[1]*The Water Cycle*. The USGS Water Science School, U.S. Department of the Interior, U.S. Geological Survey. https://water.usgs.gov/edu/watercyclesummary.html
[2]*Water consumption statistics*. Worldometers, 2019.
www.worldometers.info/water/
[3]Surie, Mandakini Devasher. *South Asia's Water Crisis: A Problem of Scarcity Amid Abundance*. Asia Foundation.org. March 25, 2015.
https://asiafoundation.org/2015/03/25/south-asias-water-crisis-a-problem-of-scarcity-amid-abundance/
[4]Frankel, Jeremy. *Crisis on the High Plains: The Loss of America's Largest Aquifer – the Ogallala*. University of Denver Water Law Review. May 17, 2018.
http://duwaterlawreview.com/crisis-on-the-high-plains-the-loss-of-americas-largest-aquifer-the-ogallala/
[5]*Groundwater depletion*. U.S. Geological Survey. The USGS Water Science School Dec. 9, 2016.
https://water.usgs.gov/edu/gwdepletion.html
[6]Hoekstra1, Arjen Y. Mesfin M. Mekonnen. *The Water Footprint of Humanity*. Department of Water Engineering and Management, University of Twente. Edited by PeterH. Gleick. Pacific Institute for Studies in

Development, Environment, & Security, Oakland, CA. December 21, 2011.
https://waterfootprint.org/media/downloads/Hoekstra-Mekonnen-2012-WaterFootprint-of-Humanity.pdf

[7]The United Nations World Water Development Report 2015: *Water for a Sustainable World*. UNESCO. WWAP (United Nations World Water Assessment Programme). 2015.
http://www.unesco.org/new/en/natural-sciences/environment/water/wwap/wwdr/2015-water-for-a-sustainable-world/

[8]Stadtmiller, Joseph, *The Nature of Life and Humanity* 2nd edition, 2016, Chapter 11.

[9]Tam, Laura, *Learning from Australia's Millennium Drought*. Urbanist Article July 7, 2016.
https://www.spur.org/publications/urbanist-article/2016-07-07/learning-australia-s-millennium-drought

[10]Turner, Andrea, Stuart White, Joanne Chong, Mary Ann Dickinson, Heather Cooley, and Kristina Donnelly. *Managing Drought: Learning from Australia*. The Pacific Institute. February 2016.
http://pacinst.org/publication/managing-drought-learning-from-australia/

[11]*Seawater Desalination Costs*. Wateruse Assoc. Desalination Committee. January 2012.
https://watereuse.org/wp-content/uploads/2015/10/WateReuse_Desal_Cost_White_Paper.pdf

[12]*Project: Forests and Climate*. Environmental Paper Network. Environmen-tal.com. 2018.
https://environmentalpaper.org/project/forests-climate-biomass/

[13]Gibbs, David, Nancy Harris, Frances Seymour. *By the Numbers: The Value of Tropical Forests in the Climate Change Equation*. World Resources Institute. October 4, 2018.
https://www.wri.org/blog/2018/10/numbers-value-tropical-forests-climate-change-equation

[14]*Global oil consumption from 1970 to 2017* (in million metric tons). Statista, The Statistics Portal.
https://www.statista.com/statistics/265261/global-oil-consumption-in-million-metric-tons/

[15]*World coal consumption, top 10 countries*. 2017. ENI, School Energy & Environment.
www.eniscuola.net/en/mediateca/world-coal-consumption-top-10-

countries-2017/

[16]*Natural gas consumption worldwide from 1998 to 2017* (in billion cubic metars). Statista, The Statistics Portal. https://www.statista.com/statistics/282717/global-natural-gas-consumption/

[17]Stadtmiller, Joseph, *The Nature of Life and Humanity*, 2nd Edition 2016. Ch. 13 pages 242-244.

[18]*The Cosmic Origins of Uranium*. World Nuclear Association. November, 2016.
http://www.world-nuclear.org/information-library/nuclear-fuel-cycle/uranium-resources/the-cosmic-origins-of-uranium.aspx

[19]Wikipedia, Brazil (2009), October 7, 2018.
http://en.wikipedia.org/wiki/Brazil

[20]*Total petroleum consumption*. Knoema Corporation, World Data Atlas Topics Energy Oil. February 2019.
https://knoema.com/atlas/topics/Energy/Oil/Petroleum-consumption?baseRegion=BR

[21]*Production of crude oil including lease condensate*. Knoema Corporation, World Data Atlas Topics Energy Oil. February 2019.
https://knoema.com/atlas/topics/Energy/Oil/Production-of-crude-oil?baseRegion=BR

[22]*Crude Oil including Lease Condensate Reserves*. Knoema Corporation, World Data Atlas Topics Energy Oil. December 2018.
https://knoema.com/atlas/topics/Energy/Oil/Crude-oil-reserves?baseRegion=BR

[23]Martinez, Jose D. *Brazil on the Road to Fossil Fuel Independence*.
EzineArticles. August 13, 2008.
http://EzineArticles.com/1407703

[24]Avins, Jenni. *Brazil has more freshwater than any other country, but its biggest city is running dry*. Quartz, February 26, 2015.
https://qz.com/351145/brazil-has-more-freshwater-than-any-other-country-but-its-biggest-city-is-running-dry/

[25]Meyer, Amelia. *Brazil Environmental Issues*. Brazil.org. 2010.
https://www.brazil.org.za/environmental-issues.html

[26]Novais, Andrea. *Recycling of Waste in Brazil*. The Brazil Business.
May 15, 2015.
http://thebrazilbusiness.com/article/recycling-of-waste-in-brazil

[27]*East&Southeast Asia: China, World Factbook*. Central Intelligence Agency.
https://www.cia.gov/library/publications/the-world-factbook/geos/ch.html

[28]China Population, Worldometers.
www.worldometers.info/world-population/china-population.

[29]*Population of China* (2018), China Population (1950 – 2018).
https://www.livepopulation.com/country/china.html.

[30]Roser, Max and Esteban Ortiz-Ospina, 2018.*World Population Growth*.
OurWorldInData.org.
https://ourworldindata.org/world-population-growth.

[31]*Preparing for China's Urban Billion*. McKinsey Global Institute, February
2009. pages 6, 52.
https://www.mckinsey.com/featured-insights/urbanization/preparing-
for-chinas-urban-billion

[32]*Largest producers of CO2 emissions worldwide in 2016*, Statistica. 2018. The
Statics Portal.
https://www.statista.com/statistics/271748/the-largest-emitters-of-co2-in-
the-world/

[33]Albert, Eleanor & Xu,Beina. *China's Environmental Crisis*. Council on
Foreign Relations, Backgrounder. January 18, 2016.
https://www.cfr.org/backgrounder/chinas-environmental-crisis

[34]*Nuclear Electricity Production, People's Republic of China*. International
Atomic Energy Agency, Power Reactor Information System 2018.
https://pris.iaea.org/PRIS/CountryStatistics/CountryDetails.aspx?cur-
rent=CN

[35]Hill, Joshua S., *China Installed 18.6 GW Of Solar PV In 2015, But Was All
Of It Connected?* Clean Technica. July 7th, 2016.
https://cleantechnica.com/2016/07/07/china-installs-18-6-gw-solar-pv-
2015-connected/

[36]Walker, Beth and Liu Qin. *The Hidden Costs of China's Shift to Hydropower*. July 29, 2015.
https://thediplomat.com/2015/07/the-hidden-costs-of-chinas-shift-to-hy-
dropower/

[37]Lannes, Bruno, Richard Hatherall, Jason Ding, Weiwen Han and Mike
Booker. *Consumption in China: Ten Trends for the next 10 Years. June 13,
2018.* Bain & Company.
https://www.bain.com/insights/consumption-in-china-ten-trends-for-the-
next-ten-years/

[38]*India Country Profile*. BBC News. 2.18.2019.
https://www.bbc.com/news/world-south-asia-12557384

[39]*India's Population*. Worldometers. 10 2.2080.
http://www.worldometers.info/world-population/india-population/

[40]Overpopulation in India, India Celebrating.com
https://www.indiacelebrating.com/social-issues/overpopulation-in-india-causes-effects-and-solutions/
[41]Hays, Jeffrey. *Environmental Issues in India*. Facts and Details. June 2015.
http://factsanddetails.com/india/Nature_Science_Animals/sub7_9c/entry-4267.html
[42]*BP Statistical Review of World Energy*. 67th Edition. June 2018.
https://www.bp.com/content/dam/bp/en/corporate/pdf/energy-economics/statistical-review/bp-stats-review-2018-full-report.pdf
[43]*Global Wind Statistics 2017*. Global Wind Energy Council. 2017.
http://gwec.net/wp-content/uploads/vip/GWEC_PRstats2017_EN-003_FINAL.pdf
[44]Snyder, Shannyn. *Water in Crisis – India*. The Water Project.
https://thewaterproject.org/water-crisis/water-in-crisis-india
[45]Russia. Countries and Their Culture. September, 2018.
https://www.everyculture.com/No-Sa/Russia.html
[46]*World Population: Past, Present, and Future*. September 19, 2018.
https://www.worldometers.info/world-population/russia-population/
[47]*BP Statistical Review of World Energy*. 67th Edition. June 2018.
https://www.bp.com/content/dam/bp/business-sites/en/global/corporate/pdfs/energy-economics/statistical-review/bp-stats-review-2018-full-report.pdf
[48]Duddu, Praveen. *The world's biggest natural gas reserves*. Hydrocarbon Technologies. November 2013.
https://www.hydrocarbons-technology.com/features/feature-the-worlds-biggest-natural-gas-reserves/
[49]*The World's Largest Oil Reserves By Country*. World Atlas.com.
October 23, 2018.
https://www.worldatlas.com/articles/the-world-s-largest-oil-reserves-by-country.html
[50]Smith, Brett, *Russia: Environmental Issues, Policies and Clean Technology*.
AZoCleantech. July 24, 2018.
https://www.azocleantech.com/article.aspx?ArticleID=542
[51]Hays, Jeffrey, *Environmental Issues in Russia*. Facts and Details.com. May 2016.
http://factsanddetails.com/russia/Nature_Science_Animals/sub9_8c/entry-5062.html
[52]America the Beautiful: *17 Amazing Landscapes in the USA*. Pics Art February 6, 2015.

https://picsart.com/blog/post/america-beautiful-17-amazing-landscapes-usa/

[53]Scheb, John M.; Scheb, John M. II (2002). *An Introduction to the American Legal System*. Florence, KY: Delmar, p. 6. ISBN 0-7668-2759-3.

[54]Selko, Adrienne. *Top 10 Manufacturing Countries in 2020*. Industry Week. The Economy Competitiveness. Dec 09, 2015.
https://www.industryweek.com/competitiveness/top-10-manufacturing-countries-2020/gallery?slide=10

[55]*Leading 20 import countries worldwide in 2017* (in billion U.S. dollars)
https://www.statista.com/statistics/268184/leading-import-countries-worldwide/

[56]*Top 20 export countries worldwide in 2017* (in billion U.S. dollars)
Statistica.com. 2017.
https://www.statista.com/statistics/264623/leading-export-countries-worldwide/

[57]Radu, Sintia, U.S. News and World Report. *These Are the World's Happiest Countries-The U.S. falls again in the annual quality-of-life assessment produced for the United Nations*. March 20, 2019.
https://www.usnews.com/news/best-countries/articles/2019-03-20/these-are-the-worlds-happiest-countries

[58]*Trends in world military expenditure 2013*. Stockholm International Peace Research Institute. 1988-2018.
https://www.sipri.org/research/armament-and-disarmament/arms-transfers-and-military-spending/military-expenditure

[59]*Most Influential Countries*. U.S. News. 2019.
https://www.usnews.com/news/best-countries/best-international-influence

[60]Dobush, Grace. *The U.S. Is the Unhappiest It's Ever Been*. Fortune Media. March 20, 2019.
http://fortune.com/2019/03/20/u-s-unhappiest-its-ever-been/

[61]*Primary energy consumption in the U.S. from 1998 to 2017* (in million metric tons of oil equivalent) Statista-The Statistics Portal 2018.
https://www.statista.com/statistics/265571/primary-energy-consumption-in-the-united-states/

[62]*Short Term Energy Outlook*. EIA U.S. Energy Information Administration, October 10, 2018.
https://www.eia.gov/outlooks/steo/report/coal.php.

[63]*Natural gas consumption in the United States from 1995 to 2018* in trillion cubic feet. Statista-The Statistics Portal 2018.

https://www.statista.com/statistics/184329/energy-consumption-from-natural-gas-in-the-us-from-1995/

[64]*Oil consumption in the United States from 1990 to 2018* (in million metric tons). Statista-The Statistics Portal 2018.

https://www.statista.com/statistics/264825/oil-consumption-in-the-united-states/

[65]*Total electricity end use in the U.S. from 1975 to 2017* (in billion kilowatt hours). Statista-The Statistics Portal 2018.

https://www.statista.com/statistics/201794/us-electricity-consumption-since-1975/

[66]*Water Use in the United States, Total Water Use*. U.S.G.S-U.S. Government Survey, 2015.

https://water.usgs.gov/watuse/wuto.html

[67]Peeples, Lynne. *10 U.S. Cities With the Worst Air Pollution*. Health.com. Sept. 26,2016.

https://www.health.com/health/gallery/0,,20490855,00.html?#

[68]-Grandoni, Dino, The Energy 202: EPA loses a tenth of its criminal in-vestigate-tors since Trump's election. Washington Post, June 21, 2018.

https://www.sfgate.com/news/article/Energy-202-EPA-loses-a-tenth-of-its-criminal-13013633.php

[69]Spangler, Todd and Nathan Bomey. *Trump administration wants to freeze gas-mileage standards, reversing Obama*. Detroit Free Press and USA TO-DAY. August 2, 2018.

https://www.usatoday.com/story/money/cars/2018/08/02/trump-epa-fuel-economy-standards/887683002/

[70]Devine, Jon. *Trump's Attack on Clean Water: What You Need to Know*. June 27, 2017, NRDC.

https://www.nrdc.org/experts/trumps-attack-clean-water-what-you-need-know

[71]*Electricity domestic consumption, breakdown by country (TWh)*. Enerdata Global Statistical Yearbook 2018.

https://yearbook.enerdata.net/electricity/electricity-domestic-consump-tion-data.html

[72]-Statistical Review of World Energy. June 2018.

https://www.bp.com/content/dam/bp/en/corporate/pdf/energy-econom-ics/statistical-review/bp-stats-review-2018-full-report.pdf

[73]*World Renewable Energy Consumption from 1998 to 2017* in millions metric tons of oil equivalent. Statistica.com.

https://www.statista.com/statistics/274101/world-renewable-energy-consumption/

[74]*Countries in the world by population (2018)*. Worldometers, 2018.
http://www.worldometers.info/world-population/population-by-country/

[75]*Total Energy Consumption by Country*. Enerdata Global Energy Statistical Yearbook 2018.
https://yearbook.enerdata.net/total-energy/world-consumption-statistics.html

[76]*Annual water consumption per capita worldwide in 2016, by select country*. Statista. The Statistics Portal, 2016.
https://www.statista.com/statistics/263156/water-consumption-in-selected-countries/

Chapter 12 - Life-Consuming-Life: Sources

[1]*How Did the Agricultural and Industrial Revolutions Change Human Diets?* Paleodiabetic.com. January 1, 2015.
https://paleodiabetic.com/2015/01/01/how-did-the-agricultural-and-industrial-revolutions-change-human-diets/

[2]Roser, Max. *Share of the labor force employed in agriculture, 2017*. Our World in Data. Share employed in agriculture.
https://ourworldindata.org/employment-in-agriculture

[3]Dillinger, Jessica. *Which Countries Export the Most Food?* World At-las. April 25, 2017.
https://www.worldatlas.com/articles/the-american-food-giant-the-largest-exporter-of-food-in-the-world.html

[4]Ross, Sean. *4 Countries That Produce the Most Food*. Investopedia. Updated May 4, 2019.
https://www.investopedia.com/articles/investing/100615/4-countries-produce-most-food.asp

[5]*Current World Population*. Worlometers.info.
https://www.worldometers.info/world-population/

[6]Hill, Caty. *This chart proves Americans love their meat*. Dec 1, 2016.
https://www.marketwatch.com/story/this-chart-proves-americans-love-their-meat-2016-08-15

[7]*Current Eating Patterns in the United States*. Dietary Guidelines. Health.gov. Nov. 25, 2015.
https://health.gov/dietaryguidelines/2015/guidelines/chapter-2/current-eating-patterns-in-the-united-states/#figure-2-1

[8]Eshela, Gidon, Alon Sheponb, Tamar Makovc & Ron Milob. *Land, irrigation water, greenhouse gas, and reactive nitrogen burdens of meat, eggs, and dairy production in the United States*. Physics Department-Bard College, Weizmann Institute of Science and Yale School of Forestry and Environmental Studies, Proceedings of the National Academy of Sciences (PNAS), August 19, 2014.
www.pnas.org/cgi/doi/10.1073/pnas.1402183111

[9]*U.S. Per Capita Availability of Red Meat, Poultry and Fish Lowest Since 1983*. USDA, United States Department of Agriculture- Economic Research Service, February 06, 2017.
https://www.ers.usda.gov/amber-waves/2017/januaryfebruary/us-per-capita-availability-of-red-meat-poultry-and-fish-lowest-since-1983/

[10]Kourous, George. *Many of the world's poorest people depend on fish*. FAO Newsroom. Food and Agriculture Organization of the United Nations, June 7, 2005.
http://www.fao.org/newsroom/en/news/2005/102911/index.html

[11]*Science study predicts collapse of all seafood fisheries by 2050*. Stanford Report, Stanford University. November 2, 2006.
https://news.stanford.edu/news/2006/november8/ocean-110806.html
Lead author of the Science study is Boris Worm of Dalhousie Uni-varsity and co-authors are; Nicola Beaumont of the Plymouth Marine Laboratory; J. Emmett Duffy of the Virginia Institute of Marine Sciences; Carl Folke of Stockholm University and the Royal Swedish Academy of Sciences; Benjamin S. Halpern of the National Center of Ecological Analysis and Synthesis (NCEAS); Jeremy B. C. Jackson of the Scripps Institution of Oceanography and the Smithsonian Tropical Research Institute; Steven Palombi and Fiorenza Micheli of Stanford's Hopkins Marine Station; Enric Sala of Scripps; Kimberly A. Selkoe of NCEAS; John Stachowicz of the University of California-Davis; and Reg Watson of the University of British Columbia. The study was conducted at the National Center for Ecological Analysis and Synthesis (NCEAS), and funded by the National Science Foundation, the University of California and the University of Southern California.

[12]Mok, Kimberley. *So Much for Fish & Chips: Greenpeace List of Most Overfished Species*. March 11, 2008.
https://www.treehugger.com/natural-sciences/so-much-for-fish-chips-greenpeace-list-of-most-over-fished-species.html

[13]Gunders, Dana. *Wasted: How America Is Losing Up to 40 Percent of Its Food from Farm to Fork to Landfill*. Natural Resources Defense Council,

August 2012.
https://www.nrdc.org/sites/default/files/wasted-food-IP.pdf
[14]*Our History*. Feeding America. 2018.
https://www.feedingamerica.org/about-us/our-history

Chapter 13 Too Many Choices—Too Few Options: Sources

[1]Godsen, Emily. *Global renewable power capacity overtakes coal as 500,000 solar panels installed every day*. The Telegraph October 26, 2016.
https://www.telegraph.co.uk/business/2016/10/25/global-renewable-power-capacity-overtakes-coal-as-500000-solar-p/

[2]Lozanova, Sarah, *Are Solar Panels Recyclable?* September 21, 2018.
https://earth911.com/eco-tech/recycle-solar-panels/

[3]*What is U.S. electricity generation by energy source?* EIA, U.S. Energy Information Administration. 2018.
https://www.eia.gov/tools/faqs/faq.php?id=427&t=3

[4]Oteri, Frank, Ruth Baranowski, Ian Baring-Gould, and Suzanne Tegen. *State of Wind Development in the United States by Region*. 2018.Golden, CO: National Renewable Energy Laboratory. NREL/ TP-5000-70738.
https://www.nrel.gov/docs/fy18osti/70738.pdf

[5]Denholm, P., M. Hand, M. Jackson, and S. Ong. 2009. *Land-use requirements of modern wind9-power plants in the United States*. Golden, CO: National Renewable Energy Laboratory.
https://www.nrel.gov/docs/fy09osti/45834.pdf

[6]Hand, M.M.; Baldwin, S.; DeMeo, E.; Reilly, J.M.; Mai, T.; Arent, D.; Porro, G.; Meshek, M.; Sandor, D. *Renewable Electricity Futures Study*. National Renewable Energy Laboratory (NREL). 2012.
eds. 4 vols. NREL/TP-6A20-52409. Golden, CO: National Renewable Energy Laboratory.
https://www.nrel.gov/docs/fy13osti/52409-ES.pdf

[7]*Brownfields' Bright Spot: Solar and Wind Energy*. National Renewable Energy Laboratory (NREL), June 14, 2010.
https://www.solarpowerworldonline.com/2010/06/brownfields-bright-spot-solar-and-wind-energy/

[8]Michel, J.; Dunagan, H.; Boring, C.; Healy, E.; Evans, W.; Dean, J.; McGillis, A.; Hain, J. 2007. *Worldwide Synthesis and Analysis of Existing Information Regarding Environmental Effects of Alternative Energy Uses on the Outer Continental Shelf*. MMS 2007-038. Prepared by Research Planning and ICF International. Herndon, VA: U.S. Department of the Interior,

Minerals Management Service.
https://hmsc.oregonstate.edu/sites/hmsc.oregon-
state.edu/files/main/mmsaefinalsynthesisreport.pdf
[9]National Wind Coordinating Committee (NWCC). 2010. *Wind turbine interactions with birds, bats, and their habitats: A summary of research results and priority questions.*
https://www1.eere.energy.gov/wind/pdfs/birds_and_bats_fact_sheet.pdf
[10]Arnett, E.B., M.M.P. Huso, J.P. Hayes, & M. Schirmacher. 2010. *Effectiveness of changing wind turbine cut-in speed to reduce bat fatalities at wind facilities.* A final report submitted to the Bats and Wind Energy Cooperative. Austin, TX: Bat Conservation International.
[11]Fish and Wildlife Service (FSW). *Recommendations of the wind turbine guidelines advisory committee.* March 4, 2010.
https://www.fws.gov/habitatconservation/windpower/Wind_Turbine_Guidelines_Advisory_Committee_Recommendations_Secretary.pdf
[12]Michel, et al. 2007Chief Medical Officer of Heath of Ontario. 2010. *The potential health impact of wind turbines.* Toronto, Ontario: Ontario Ministry of Health and Long-Term Care. American Wind Energy Association (AWEA) and the Canadian Wind Energy Association (CanWEA). 2009. *Wind turbine sound and health effects: An expert panel review.*
https://www.fws.gov/habitatconservation/windpower/Wind_Turbine_Guidelines_Advisory_Committee_Recommendations_Secretary.pdf
[13]Bastasch, M.; van Dam, J.; Syndergaard, B.; Rogers, A. 2006. *Wind Turbine Noise – An Overview.* Canadian Acoustics (34:2), 7–15.
https://tethys.pnnl.gov/publications/wind-turbine-noise-overview
[14]*Renewable Electricity Futures Study.* National Renewable Energy Laboratory. 3.31.2019.
https://www.nrel.gov/analysis/re-futures.html
[15]*Environmental Impacts of Wind Power.* Union of Concerned Scientists: Energy, Renewable Energy. March 5, 2013.
https://www.ucsusa.org/clean-energy/renewable-energy/environmental-impacts-wind-power
[16]*Tapping into Wind.* Union of Concerned Scientists. April 2011.
https://www.ucsusa.org/clean_energy/our-energy-choices/renewable-energy/renewables-tapping-into-wind.html
[17]*Electricity from Renewable Resources: Status, Prospects, and Impediments.* National Academy of Sciences. Chapter 1. 2010.

http://ebook4scaricare.com/gratis/electricity-from-renewable-resources-status-prospects-and-impediments-americas-energy-future/
[18]IPCC, 2011: IPCC Special Report on Renewable Energy Sources and Climate Change Mitigation, Prepared by Working Group III of the Intergovernmental Panel on Climate Change, Cambridge University Press, Cambridge, United Kingdom and New York, NY, USA, 1075 pp. (Chapter 7 & 9).
https://www.researchgate.net/publication/263353791_Renewable_Energy_and_Climate_Change
[19]51.3 GW of global wind capacity installed in 2018. Global Wind Energy Council (GWEC).
https://gwec.net/51-3-gw-of-global-wind-capacity-installed-in-2018/
[20]Lozanova, Sarah, Can Wind Turbines Be Recycled? Earth 911. August 7, 2017.
https://earth911.com/business-policy/wind-turbines-recycle/
[21]Renewable energy for more than 30,000 homes in Texas. San Roman Wind Farm.   https://sanromanwind.us/
[22]Sustainable Consumption Facts and Trends. 2008. Executive Summary, World Business Council for Sustainable Development, Executive Summary, pages 6-36.
https://www.wbcsd.org/Programs/People/Sustainable-Lifestyles/Resources/Sustainable-consumption-facts-trends
[23]40 years ago: Three Mile Island nuclear accident. CBS News. March 24, 2019.
https://www.cbsnews.com/news/three-mile-island-nuclear-accident-40-years-ago/
[24]Chernobyl at 25th anniversary: Frequently Asked Questions. April 2011, World Health Organization, April, 23 2011.
https://www.who.int/ionizing_radiation/chernobyl/20110423_FAQs_Chernobyl.pdf
[25]Fukushima Daiichi Accident. World Nuclear Organization, October 2018.
http://www.world-nuclear.org/information-library/safety-and-security/safety-of-plants/fukushima-accident.aspx

Epilogue: Sources

[1]Easen, Nick. Plastic Recycling: how to cope after China's ban. Raconteur- Sustainability/Future of Packaging 2018, July 18, 2018.
https://www.raconteur.net/sustainability/plastic-recycling-china-ban
[2]Wallace, Anne. Jury Awards Edwin Hardeman $80.2 Million in

Roundup Cancer Lawsuit. Lawyers and settlements.com. April 15, 2019. https://www.lawyersandsettlements.com/legal-news/monsanto-facing-lawsuits-over-alleged-roundup-cancer/jury-awards-edward-hardeman-80-2-million-in-roundup-cancer-lawsu-23071.html

[3]Wallace, Anne. *Jury Awards Alberta and Alva Pilliod more than $2 Billion in Roundup Cancer Case* May 20, 2019. https://www.lawyersandsettlements.com/legal-news/monsanto-facing-lawsuits-over-alleged-roundup-cancer/jury-awards-alberta-alva-pilliod-more-than-2-billion-in-roundup--23087.html

[4]Wilson, Audrey. *Let's Talk Food: Is glyphosate in our foods?* Hawaii Tribune-Herald, January 22, 2019. https://www.hawaiitribune-herald.com/2019/01/22/features/lets-talk-food-is-glyphosate-in-our-foods/ https://www.mnn.com/food/healthy-eating/blogs/glyphosate-food-consumer-information

[5]Benbrook,CM. *Trends in glyphosate herbicide use in the United States and globally*. Environ Sci Eur. 2016;281):3. Epub 2016 Feb 2. https://www.ncbi.nlm.nih.gov/pubmed/?term=Benbrook%20CM%5BAuthor%5D&cauthor=true&cauthor_uid=27752438
2000-78,750 lbs.; 2005-157,500 lbs.; 2010-235,814 lbs.; 2012-236,318 lbs.; 2014-249,906 lbs.

Appendices: Sources

[1]Anderson, Marcia. *Confronting Plastic Pollution One Bag at a Time*. The EPA Blog. Nov. 1,2016. https://blog.epa.gov/2016/11/01/confronting-plastic-pollution-one-bag-at-a-time/

[2]*How much water does the average person use at home per day?* USGS. Water Questions & Answers. https://water.usgs.gov/edu/qa-home-percapita.html

[3]*How many pounds of coal is burned to produce one KWH?* Boiler heating. https://unic.co.in/how-much-coal-is-required-to-generate-1-mwh-of-electricity-/

[4]*Insulation R Value Chart*. Great Day Improvements LLC. 2019. https://www.greatdayimprovements.com/insulation-r-value-chart.aspx

[5]Independently Tested and Certified Energy Performance. Energy Star.gov

https://www.energystar.gov/products/building_products/residential_windows_doors_and_skylights/independently_tested_certified_energy_performance

[6]*Energy-Efficient Appliances. How to choose long-lasting home appliances that will save you energy and expense.* Earth Easy.com
https://learn.eartheasy.com/guides/energy-efficient-appliances/#energyefficientappliances

[7]*Digital Television Shipments in the U.S. 2017.*Statistica.com. 2017.
https://www.statista.com/statistics/220739/forecast-of-dvd-player-shipments-in-the-us/

[8]*Certified Products, Electronics: Television, Energy Star Ratings.* 2019.
https://www.energystar.gov/products/electronics/televisions

[9]Mason, Moya K. *Housing: Then, Now, and Future.* 2019.
http://www.moyak.com/papers/house-sizes.html

[10]*Towards a sufficiency-driven business model: Experiences and opportunities.* Bocken, N.M.P.[ab], Short, S.W.[b] Industrial Design Engineering, [a]Delft University Technology, Landbergstraat 15, 2628 CE Deft, [b]The Netherlands Institute for Manufacturing, Department of Engineering, University of Cambridge, Cambridge CB3 0FS, United Kingdom. August 7, 2015.
https://www.repository.cam.ac.uk/bitstream/handle/1810/249112/Bocken_et_al-2015-Environmental_Innovation_and_Societal_Transitions-VoR.pdf;sequence=4

[11]Ibid.

[12]*UN Report: Nature's Dangerous Decline 'Unprecedented'; Species Extinction Rates 'Accelerating'.* The Intergovernmental Science-Policy Platform on Biodiversity and Ecosystem Services (IPBES). Approved at the 7th session of the IPBES Plenary, meeting (29 April- 4 May 2019) in Paris.
https://www.un.org/sustainabledevelopment/blog/2019/05/nature-decline-unprecedented-report/

[13]Walquist, Calla. *UN environment warning: 10 key points and what Australia must do.* The Guardian.com. May 27,2019.
https://www.theguardian.com/environment/2019/may/07/un-environment-warning-10-key-points-and-what-australia-must-do: